Exploring *The Orville*

Exploring *The Orville*
Essays on Seth MacFarlane's Space Adventure

Edited by DAVID KYLE JOHNSON
and MICHAEL R. BERRY

Foreword by André Bormanis

McFarland & Company, Inc., Publishers
Jefferson, North Carolina

Library of Congress Cataloguing-in-Publication Data

Names: Johnson, David Kyle, editor. | Berry, Michael R., 1961– editor. | Bormanis, André, writer of foreword.
Title: Exploring The Orville : essays on Seth MacFarlane's space adventure / edited by David Kyle Johnson and Michael R. Berry ; foreword by André Bormanis.
Description: Jefferson, North Carolina : McFarland and Company, Inc., Publishers, 2021 | Includes bibliographical references and index.
Identifiers: LCCN 2021007024 | ISBN 9781476681924 (paperback : acid free paper) ∞
 ISBN 9781476642529 (ebook)
Subjects: LCSH: Orville (Television program)
Classification: LCC PN1992.77.O76 E97 2021 | DDC 791.45/72—dc23
LC record available at https://lccn.loc.gov/2021007024

British Library cataloguing data are available
ISBN (print) 978-1-4766-8192-4
ISBN (ebook) 978-1-4766-4252-9

© 2021 David Kyle Johnson and Michael R. Berry. All rights reserved

No part of this book may be reproduced or transmitted in any form or by any means, electronic or mechanical, including photocopying or recording, or by any information storage and retrieval system, without permission in writing from the publisher.

Front cover image © 2021 Vadim Sadovski/Shutterstock

Printed in the United States of America

McFarland & Company, Inc., Publishers
Box 611, Jefferson, North Carolina 28640
www.mcfarlandpub.com

Acknowledgments

The editors would like to thank:

Seth MacFarlane for conceiving of *The Orville*
and writing our little book a blurb,

André Bormanis for his contributions to
the production of this book, including writing the foreword,

Tom Costantino for his dedication to *The Orville*
and bringing this modest project of ours to certain people's attention,

Patrick Welsh for his encyclopedic knowledge of *The Orville*
which helped improve many essays,

all the contributors for their hard work and patience with us
(we know it wasn't easy),

and Sabrina Travers for her tireless citation and formatting efforts
(you had the most thankless task).

Table of Contents

Acknowledgments v
Foreword by ANDRÉ BORMANIS 1

The Teaser and Theme: What Is *The Orville*?

Is *The Orville* … *Star Trek*?
    L. BROOKE RUDOW 6

Introduction: How *The Orville* Does Philosophy
    DAVID KYLE JOHNSON 23

Act I: Gender, Sex and Feminism

Finding the Female: Gender in Moclan Society
    CATHERINE NOLAN 34

Darulioian Assault: *The Orville* and Sexual Consent
    MICHAEL R. BERRY 48

Toward a Queer Utopia: Alien Alterity and Sexuality in
The Orville
    LIZ FAIRCHILD 62

The Orville: A Meta-Pop Culture Phenomenon for Feminism
    FRANCESCA PUTIGNANO 75

Act II: Religion and Reason

Avis Vult! Krill and the Dangers of Religion
    DARREN M. SLADE 98

Resisting Dogma and Damnation with *The Orville*
    L. BROOKE RUDOW 122

Act III: Science and Politics

"If the Stars Should Appear" and Climate Change Denial
    DAVID KYLE JOHNSON   140

"Majority Rule" and a Critique of Pure Democracy
    PATRICK WELSH   165

Act IV: Love, Care and Nepotism

Loving Isaac
    MIMI MARINUCCI   180

The Space Between and Beyond: Timeless Depictions of Care
    SHAUN RESPESS   196

Nepotism on *The Orville*
    JOE SLATER   209

Act V: The Funny and the Final Flyout

The Ethics of "Sophomoric" Sci-Fi: *The Orville,* Pop Culture, and Lacan
    LEIGH E. RICH   226

Thinking About Bad Taste in a Funny Way
    CHRISTOPHER M. INNES   245

Making Sense of Time Travel in *The Orville*
    DAVID KYLE JOHNSON   261

The Credits: About the Contributors   273
Index   277

Foreword

André Bormanis

Many years ago, I had the good fortune to work on a couple of projects with the legendary Ray Bradbury, who was my favorite writer when I was growing up. Asked about the "prophetic" qualities often ascribed to science fiction writers who seemed to predict, decades in advance, some novel feature of modern society, Ray once said, "I'm not trying to predict the future, I'm trying to prevent it." In his seminal novel *Fahrenheit 451*, Bradbury presciently described the insidious influence of mass media on society, the constant thirst for distraction, and the growth of illiteracy to the point that owning books became a crime. As he said, he wasn't trying to predict the future—he was sounding an alarm about the present and its *implications* for the future. Alas, not enough people paid attention.

For over twenty-five years I've been a television writer and consultant, living and working in Los Angeles. I'm currently a writer and co-executive producer on the Fox/Hulu series *The Orville*, which follows the adventures of the crew of a starship four hundred years in the future. I began my career in television as the science consultant for the *Star Trek* television and film franchises. My job then was to ensure that the scientific concepts and technical language in our scripts was scientifically credible. This did not mean sticking purely to the facts of astronomy, physics, biology and so on as we knew them at the time—*Star Trek* takes place hundreds of years in the future and imagines technologies (warp drives and transporters) that are impossible given the current state of science. But *Star Trek* needed the audience to believe that such things could, someday, be possible, and this of course would require new inventions and understanding beyond our present knowledge. And if starships do someday become a reality, our galactic explorations are sure to reveal phenomena that defy present-day science. Indeed, the credibility of the *Star Trek* universe would be undermined if this were *not* the case. In addition to developing stories and writing scripts, I also advise the writers on *The Orville* in this capacity today.

Foreword

The popularity of *Star Trek* specifically, and science fiction generally, has been recognized as a useful tool for teaching science to young students and the general public. Important concepts in physics, chemistry, biology, psychology, and social science have all been featured, directly or indirectly, in many *Trek* stories. So it should come as no surprise that science fiction, like *The Orville*, can also be an effective vehicle for exploring and teaching philosophy—the inquiry into the fundamental nature of existence, mind, reason, values, ethics, gender ... of knowledge and meaning itself.

Seth MacFarlane created *The Orville* in part to carry on the tradition of allegorical storytelling that *Star Trek, The Twilight Zone*, and other science fiction series have pioneered on television over the decades. As those shows demonstrated, exploring the human condition in the present moment through the lens of an imagined, almost Utopian future, or through the eyes of strange alien beings, is a powerful engine for generating stories that engage the mind as well as the heart.

So much has changed in the world over the past several decades, but much has also remained the same. One major change, for example, is that advances in the science of genetics have led to a situation, almost certainly unprecedented in the history of this planet, where a species (ours, of course) is in a position to take control of its evolution at the molecular level. At the same time, we are running an uncontrolled experiment on our planet's biosphere that could have disastrous consequences for future generations. Racial inequality and economic injustice persist in the so-called "advanced" nations. The sudden proliferation of social networks is connecting our seven and half billion (and growing) fellow humans in ways that both bring us closer and threaten to tear us apart, and raise profound questions about privacy and the ownership of information. It's certainly an interesting time to be a science fiction writer.

Another astonishing change I've witnessed in my lifetime is the growing acceptance of openly gay people in democratic societies. When I was growing up (not all that long ago!) homosexuality was considered a form of mental illness, something that could and should be treated by practitioners of psychiatry and psychotherapy. But by the end of the 1970s, the American Psychological Association and the American Psychiatric Association had taken "homosexuality" off the list of psychological disorders, and today, gay marriage is a right in the United States and a growing number of other countries. Teachers, doctors, plumbers, scientists, and even astronauts can now be open about their sexual orientation, which would have seemed all but unthinkable when I was young. But, in a way, things have also stayed the same. There has been such a substantial backlash on this topic, especially among religious fundamentalists of various faiths, that the discourse on sexual orientation and gender identity continues to be very fertile territory for speculative fiction. In other words, it's not like we've "moved past" this issue so that any commentary on it would amount to little more than preaching to the choir. LGBTQ rights are in need of commentary, just as much as they ever were. Among the crew of the *Orville*, Lieutenant Commander Bortus, an officer from an ostensibly all-male race known as the Moclans, gives us an opportunity to explore the anxieties aroused by nontraditional sexuality and gender roles in society, a subject that philosophers have been investigating and illuminating for many years.

None of us who are privileged to work on the writing staff of *The Orville* have any academic credentials in the various disciplines of philosophy, but as writers and human beings we sometimes find ourselves pondering deep philosophical questions. We frequently talk and argue about pressing social issues, and challenge each other to find interesting fodder for stories in the fractious social dynamics of the world we live in today. But much of the writing process is intuitive, guided by the needs of dramatic criteria, the drives of the characters, the arc of the story, and so forth. It is a process of both creation and discovery, and when we begin to outline a story, we don't always know where it will take us. But if we conceive an episode that starts a conversation about the dangers of direct democracy, the fight for gender equality, or the tension between religious certainty and intellectual freedom, then we've accomplished something beyond providing an hour's worth of enjoyable entertainment (a goal most of us find laudable in and of itself).

I think I can speak for the rest of the writers when I say we feel a certain sense of pride when thinkers and scholars of the caliber represented in this volume apply some of their energy and analytical skills to uncover deeper meaning in our humble efforts. There are so many fascinating ideas and discussions here that I hesitate to pick out specific examples. The range of essays reflects the range of modern philosophy—from environmental ethics to social justice to queer studies.

We will never build the better future we all believe in if we're not willing to take a critical look at the present. The work of philosophers is essential for clarifying the deficiencies of our current society, and to help point the way to strengthening the ethical and moral foundations necessary to create an inclusive and visionary future that leaves no sentient being behind. For me, the egalitarian, humanistic, and broadly prosperous world depicted on *The Orville* cannot arrive soon enough.

André Bormanis is a television writer and producer. He holds a BS in physics from the University of Arizona, and an MA in science, technology, and public policy from George Washington University. He is a writer and co-executive producer of The Orville.

The Teaser and Theme
What Is The Orville*?*

Is *The Orville* ... *Star Trek*?

L. Brooke Rudow

The Orville is a genetic chimera. It's not *Star Trek*, but it is. It's not fanfiction, but it is. It's not a parody, but it is. It's not original, but it is. Many are claiming that *The Orville* is more *Star Trek* than *Star Trek* (*Discovery*, that is). Others are arguing that it's an unethical rip-off. But regardless of which side of these debates you might fall on, *The Orville* undoubtedly stands as this disruptive, confusing, and totally uncanny stranger to the modern TV model. Resisting easy categorization, it calls up questions about what counts as canon, what defines a genre, and just how much overzealous (and influential) superfans can get away with. And the central question for me, and for this essay, is how does *The Orville* do it? How can it both *be* and *not be* all these things at once?

In multiple interviews leading up to the airing of the first season, writers and production staff described *The Orville* as an homage to *Star Trek*. In the first section, I consider the claims that *The Orville* is but an homage. I argue that MacFarlane takes the show far beyond homage and treads into the wonky world of fanfiction. In the second and third sections, I spell out more clearly what fanfiction is, arguing that it constitutes a particular and peculiar genre—one that is a genre-disrupting genre. As an artistic style, it both meets and resists the conditions that define it as its own genre. And as a genre, it troubles and undermines existing genres. I argue that this is precisely what makes *The Orville* so uneasy in the minds of audiences. Going far beyond homage, it flies in the face of generic classification (in both senses) and is, thus, best understood as a type of fanfiction. However, even this classification is uneasy, as I show. Ultimately, *The Orville* defies all complete characterization in a way that makes *people* uneasy—in a really good way.

In the final section, I consider the value of *The Orville* as fanfiction. Already at the margins of accepted artistic form, fanfiction is not only disruptive to genre; it is disruptive to the status quo. Fanfiction opens a space where artists can go beyond what's given, a space where limits are respected but transgressed. *The Orville* does this masterfully. By engaging yet resisting generic classification, *The Orville* uses the familiarity and comfort of the *Star Trek* canon to bring to the fore issues and questions that may be uncomfortable, questions that are largely ignored, silenced, or resisted in the *Star Trek* canon's continuing saga. Though there are important questions to be found in the episodes themselves, I think we can see the show as questioning the canon itself, or perhaps the sci-fi genre as a whole. *The Orville* reasserts a system of values lost in much of today's television. Though *Star Trek: Discovery* retains the names, the places, and the copyrights, of course, it misses something essential to the canon it claims to extend: the spirit.

Mad Idolatry: Homage or Rip-Off?

Even before *The Orville* premiered, critics were uneasy. They'd seen the trailers, heard the buzz; they had their doubts. They asked, "Isn't this just another *Star Trek*?" So doubtful they were, in fact, that one critic asked Dana Walden, the CEO of Fox Television Group, if she was worried about being sued. She laughed it off saying:

> We're not really concerned. We obviously have a big legal team. We vet things, so it's not like we're just flying by the seat of our pants out here. Seth's intention is to do something that *clearly pays homage* to *Star Trek*, that clearly was inspired a lot by *Star Trek* … but I can't imagine, especially when you see the direction that the *Star Trek* franchise is moving, that anyone involved would consider it anything other than a compliment.[1]

It's just an homage! It's a compliment! *Star Trek* proper need not fear. And besides, homages like these are nothing new, right? She went on:

> Most shows have some DNA of previous shows. There are very few shows that I've worked on that weren't *slight reinventions* of something that's come before it. It is a certain format of storytelling, it's a certain act structure, there are certain limitations to what we all do in this storytelling form, so I find it to be flattering and I know Seth holds the *Star Trek* franchise in the highest regard.[2]

MacFarlane himself made a similar point in a *Mindscape* interview with Sean Carroll.

> The idea of … a naval ship in space rather than on the waters is something that's been around since probably before the 1930s, but obviously in film that seems to be where it emerged in the most memorable way from the serialized films that come from that era.… *Star Trek* was the first franchise to solidify it, to kind of work out the kinks.… *Star Wars* or *Buck Rogers* or subsequent shows, they all are taking cues from the original *Star Trek*. *Star Wars* uses the term "cloaking device," that's something they got from *Star Trek*. They wrote the book for all of us.[3]

But in that same interview, MacFarlane went on to undercut the point by basically admitting that, when it comes to *Star Trek* specifically, *The Orville* is a particularly close match:

> And I think, for us, if the Star Trek franchise was doing that particular thing at this point in time, then there might not be a place for *The Orville*. But because they're not, they've gone more of the streaming serialized direction. It's left this big wide opening that we've been able to step into with our show and we've been having a blast.[4]

Indeed, *Orville* writer, director, and executive producer David A. Goodman made the connections more explicit:

> There's no getting around that there's some Star Trek inspiration in this show. There's no getting around that Seth wanted an uplifting show that presented a positive view of the future, which is what Roddenberry said about his original show. So they share that philosophy. The difference for us is Seth is very much aware—and this makes it more like *Star Trek* in a certain way than anything else—he's making a show for everybody.[5]

And while Brannon Braga, who also writes, directs, and executively produces *The Orville*, crassly dismissed the severity of the similarities… "There can be no doubt we are paying tribute to the *Star Trek* ethos—and others such as *The Twilight Zone* ethos—but we don't just want to rip shit off"[6] … *Orville* director Jonathan Frakes (who also stared on *Star Trek: The Next Generation* and has directed for *Star Trek: Discovery*) seems to have calmly admitted them:

> [Seth MacFarlane] clearly wanted [*The Orville*] to look like [*The Next Generation*]. So, he hired the cinematographer [Marvin Rush] and the camera operator, and Brannon Braga, who wrote "[Star Trek:] First Contact" among other things that are fabulous. Robbie Duncan McNeill, one of our wonderful directors from [Star Trek:] *Voyager*, James Conway, who directed a bunch of great *Next Gen* episodes; he hired me. He filled the room with *Next Gen* people so that the show would look and feel like it. I think he did it.[7]

These sentiments of homage and the show's "DNA" are echoed again and again, by the cast, by writers and directors, and on the surface, the shared DNA is pretty obvious. After all, like Frakes, *The Orville*'s aforementioned David A. Goodman also worked on *Star Trek*. He was a writer and producer of *Star Trek: Enterprise*. And *The Orville*'s Brannon Braga not only wrote *Star Trek: First Contact* (as Frakes mentioned), but also helped write *Star Trek Generations* and was executive producer of *The Next Generation*, *Voyager*, and *Enterprise*. Penny Johnson Jerald, who plays Dr. Claire Finn, played Kasidy Yates Sisko in *Star Trek: Deep Space Nine*. And even Marina Sirtis, who starred as Councilor Troi on *Next Generation*, made a guest appearance as a school teacher in *The Orville* episode "Sanctuary." The list goes on and on. As this book's introduction makes clear, Seth would probably say the shared DNA lies more in its allegorical narratives, long character memory, and liberal politics. But that the show just shares "some" DNA seems a bit of an understatement. As far as straightforward *Star Trek* family goes, *The Orville* undoubtedly deserves a seat at the grown-up table.

While MacFarlane, Braga, Goodman, Frakes, and Walden, among others, insist that the show merely pays homage and takes inspiration from the *Star Trek* canon, these claims seem disingenuous. Ira Madison III at *Daily Beast* calls it "a blatant, thieving rip-off."[8] In a tweet, Vox critic Emily VanDerWerff accuses MacFarlane of "filing the serial numbers off *Star Trek*."[9] But life-long *Trek* fan Liz Shannon Miller at *IndieWire* makes the rip-off case in detail. She points out that the music sounds like vintage *Star Trek*, that each act break fades to black just like, well, vintage *Star Trek*, and she details the thinly veiled name imitations, "The crew of the ~~Enterprise~~ Orville, who work for the ~~Federation~~ Union, use ~~replicators~~ synthesizers and transporters (they actually use the word "transporting") in their daily lives. Oh, but watch out for those pesky ~~Klingons~~ Krill! They're always causing trouble."[10] Seeing through the homage mirage she proclaims, "After watching the actual show, its intentions became clear: Seth wanted to cosplay being captain of the U.S.S. Enterprise. And Fox let him do it."[11] Finally, Miller condemns the show saying that it is creatively, morally, and ethically bankrupt:

> The lack of creativity is clear, given how it takes the basic framework of a "Trek" series and files off the serial numbers. But morally, it's hard to imagine how anyone involved with this project could be comfortable with walking onto that set, watching those episodes, and seeing how blatant the imitation is. And ethically, it's frustrating to see that the systems put into place to keep creators from ripping others off in such a blatant manner failed here.[12]

Yet, in spite of her obvious and seething hatred for the show, and likely for MacFarlane himself, Miller makes some important points. The show really *is* a bit too close for comfort. An homage, it's true, is a work of art done in the style of a (usually) well-known predecessor. For example, *Black Mirror* did a riveting, yet totally disturbing homage to *Star Trek* with its episode "USS Callister." The uniforms, the set, the crew, the captain's speaking style all gesture back to the original *Star Trek*.[13] And this is how homages normally work. They are limited artistic tributes within a larger work. Yet, if the work in its entirety is co-opted, homage can quickly sour to rip-off.

Nonetheless, dismissing the show as nothing but an uncreative, immoral, and unethical rip-off is too hasty. As I'll argue, there's a lot more going on with *The Orville* than many of these critics care to notice, something that fans can see and appreciate, something that drives many viewers away from *Discovery* and into the arms of another fan. Namely, *The Orville* isn't a rip-off; it's really good fanfiction.

Identity (Part 1): Fanfiction, Canon, and the Generic Class

In order to make the case that *The Orville* is fanfiction, I've got to say something about what fanfiction is by discussing its features, those that mark fanfiction as a distinct generic class. This requires an excursion into genre theory.

Adena Rosmarin details traditional theories of genre, which come in two basic types: historical and theoretical.[14] Historical views take it that genres are discovered, after the fact, within a body of art based on preexisting artistic facts. On theoretical views, however, a genre is deduced by identifying essential qualities. Theoretical genre is pure form, intrinsic, and something with a distinct substance or reality.[15] Aristotle, for example, advocates pure form.[16] Opening the *Poetics*, he says, "I propose to treat of poetry in itself and of its various kinds, noting the essential quality of each."[17]

Rosmarin points out that the historical model has pretty obvious problems; it rests on a paradox.[18] She quotes René Wellek, "How can we arrive at a genre description from history without knowing beforehand what the genre is like, and how can we know a genre without its history, without a knowledge of its particular instances?"[19] But ultimately, both theories are deceptive. While the art critic claims to discover genre, she is actually in the process of *constructing* the genre:

> Whereas in either case the critic presents himself as describing or representing what antecedes his text—the historical genre being derived from observation of preexisting literary facts, the theoretical genre being deduced from a preexisting theory of literature—in both cases the genre is actually conceptualized, textualized, and justified by the critic's present tense act, by his writing of the genre's definition.[20]

While the critic may believe she is only describing, she creates, she defines. Thus, she cannot "find" the genre in the text, nor are there any essential qualities. The critic builds a genre, identifying similarity in difference. But the similarities identified are pragmatic, and they contribute to a particular end. Rejecting traditional genre theory, Rosmarin offers her own pragmatic, or critical, genre theory.

Pragmatic genre theory recognizes its constitutive power and defines genre as a tool of critical explanation. "The genre is the critic's heuristic tool, his chosen or defined way of persuading his audience to see the literary text in all its previously inexplicable and 'literary' fullness and then to relate this text to those that are similar or, more precisely, to those that may be similarly explained."[21] The advantage of a pragmatic genre theory, a constructive rather than discovered theory, is that it can be *used* rather than simply described. Rosmarin points out that then we have as many genres as we need as well as genres that are defined by our needs, "They ... serve the explanatory purpose of critical thought, not the other way around."[22] This pragmatic genre theory is essential especially for understanding fanfiction as a genre distinct from the genres on which it is parasitic.

It will be helpful, at this point, to distinguish genre from canon. My use of the word "canon" is borrowed from Sheenagh Pugh.[23] Pugh defines canon as "the source property used as material by fanfic writers."[24] For example, the *Star Trek* canon consists of all *officially* released—that is, legally sanctioned by Paramount and the CBS television network—*Star Trek* items, be they films, television series, episodes, books, soundtracks, missing scenes, cut scenes, video games, etc. We can think of canon as within a genre—*Star Trek* canon is a part of the sci-fi genre—but I want to propose that we consider, for the purposes of this essay, canon as a kind of sub-genre, and what I'll go on to argue in regard to genre membership applies equally to canon membership.

The *Star Trek* canon is what Pugh would call an open canon.[25] Because the series and films are ongoing, *Star Trek* makes for tricky fanfiction territory. Closed canons make for good fanfic fodder given that a story will not become irrelevant or false based on the release of a new episode or film. For example, if I write a story about Captain Ed Mercer eventually remarrying Kelly before the canon is closed, an episode might come along wherein Kelly dies before the marriage could have taken place. Now my story is rendered implausible or impossible and will be rejected by the fanfic community. By and large, fanfiction must stay within the bounds of the canon. Fanfiction takes up the characters, places, and events as given, as the limiting material through which a new story can be told. The truer one stays to the canon, the better the fanfiction can be. But how close must fanfiction follow and, if it's too close, what distinguishes fanfic from the canon?

An example will help work through the issues. Around 1987 or 1988, MacFarlane and his friends created their own *Star Trek* fan film.[26] MacFarlane stars as Captain Kirk, and the mini episode is complete with cringy special effects (though impressive for teens in the 1980s), homemade costumes, and a homemade Bridge. Moreover, at least in the fan film available on YouTube.com, all the characters exist in the original canon and nothing occurs that would violate that world. Here we can ask how MacFarlane's fan film and script differs from canon scripts. For the sake of highlighting how a pragmatic view of fanfiction is so useful, let us adopt the framework of theoretical genre and see where it gets us. On this view, there should be an essential, formal quality that distinguishes young MacFarlane's film from the canon. How might we identify this quality? While some fanfic authors write "Alternative Universe" fanfiction that deviates significantly from what is "allowed" by the canon, MacFarlane's film stays strictly within the limitations set by the *Star Trek* universe.[27] That is, provided he does a good job writing the script, MacFarlane's episode is, or at least could be, indistinguishable in form and content from a bona fide episode of *Star Trek*. Would it *be* canon? One might argue that the *Star Trek* canon is written by particular authors, and episodes written by someone else don't count. Authorship defines canon. Yet, as most people know, television series are written by many authors, authors who come and go. Over the lifespan of *Star Trek*, the show has had hundreds of writers. *The Next Generation* alone had over 50, many of whom worked on but one or two episodes.[28] There is no reason why MacFarlane could not simply be added to this list as another sanctioned author. Okay, perhaps it's the cast that makes canon "canon." William Shatner is Captain Kirk, not MacFarlane. But wait, so is Jimmy Bennett and Chris Pine and maybe even Vic Mignogna.[29] Here again, there's nothing essential about actors remaining the same. In fact, there does not seem to be an essential quality at all, but rather a superficial one. This is highlighted by the fact that though the fan film is not canon, it could *become* canon.

If the executives at CBS happened upon MacFarlane's work and decided to produce his episode, this would effectively pull his fanfiction into the canon, rendering it no longer fanfiction.[30] The difference between fanfiction episode and canon episode is that one has been admitted to the legally sanctioned collection of *Star Trek* television episode screenplays. If CBS buys it and owns it, if MacFarlane gets paid, then while it may not become immediately part of the canon, it has ceased to be fanfiction. It can no longer claim *that* generic status. However, that the work is now legally sanctioned is *not* an essential quality. Nothing in the script or film lets us know this. The way a work is accepted by a community of individuals is not tied to the work's form, it is not intrinsic, nor is it a distinct substance or reality. It is nothing but a practical consideration, a pragmatic quality. Given that the *only* feature separating MacFarlane's script from, say, Kemp Powers' (*Star Trek: Discovery*)—and this is the accepted defining feature separating the two[31]—is its monetary/legal status, the pragmatic genre theory, at least for fanfiction, is far more effective at explaining the generic class than is an Aristotelian theoretical approach. That is, good fanfiction is that which would be canon should it be legally recognized as such.

But hold on! The fanfiction we are worried about here is not some decades old fan film. I claimed that *The Orville* is fanfiction. Yet, *The Orville* seems to violate *every* feature, essential or not, of the fanfiction genre. The characters are not the same, the place names are different, the events of *Star Trek* do not constitute or limit the world of *The Orville*. Even weirder, the show *is* legally sanctioned, but as its *own canon*. And, as a canon in its own right, in what sense could I even possibly claim that *The Orville* is fanfiction? Well, it's complicated, and when things get complicated, who better to overcomplicate but (hopefully) illuminate them but Jacques Derrida?

Identity (Part 2): Disrupting the Purity of Genre

Derrida also rejects the theoretical approach.[32] Reflecting on his opening statements, "Genres are not to be mixed. I will not mix genres," he considers the various mundane ways it can be interpreted: as a neutral statement saying little more than a fact of the matter, as a statement insisting on the purity of genre, or as an imperative instructing how one may or may not use genre.[33] But he proposes a further interpretation that cuts through these; he takes the statement as a challenge. "I will not mix genres" indicates the impossibility of purity, that genre is essentially impure, contaminated. This impurity, he says, is engendered by the repetition inherent to a generic class.[34]

In order to identify a work as belonging to a genre, there should be an identifiable trait, a code by which to recognize that trait as "proving" membership. But in any such repetition the sameness must also reflects its difference. That is, in order to recognize a new episode of *The Orville*, I must identify both the sameness and difference in repetition. If only sameness, it's not a new episode. If only difference, it's not *The Orville*. Thus, the very traits that indicate its participation is the trait which forms an "invaginated" loop that defines the limits of its participation, showing that the work can never *be The Orville*, only participate in *Orville*-ness.[35] Derrida says:

> [This is] what I shall call the law of the law of genre. It is precisely a principle of contamination, a law of impurity, a parasitical economy. In the code of set theories, if I may use it at least figuratively, I would speak of a sort of participation without belonging—a taking part in without being part of, without having membership in a set.[36]

This trait of belonging Derrida calls the "remark" (and sometimes "re-mark") and his concern is that the remark, which is part of the work of art and points to genre through the work of art, somehow does not belong to the genre it designates. "The re-mark of belonging does not belong."[37] He explains that although a work must belong to a genre, its participation is never belonging in virtue of the remark, the trait of participation. The remark can come in many forms and be applied to many types:

> It need not be a designation or "mention" of the type found beneath the title of certain books (novel, *récit*, drama). The remark of belonging need not pass through the consciousness of the author or the reader, although it often does so. It can also refute this consciousness or render the explicit "mention" mendacious, false, inadequate, or ironic

14   The Teaser and Theme: What Is *The Orville*?

according to all sorts of overdetermined figures. Finally, this remarking-trait need be neither a theme nor a thematic component of the work—although of course this instance of belonging to one or several genes, not to mention all the traits that mark this belonging, often have been treated as theme, even before the advent of what we call "modernism."[38]

Derrida uses the novel: the trait designating "this is a novel" is not novelistic. It points to the genre, within the genre, yet is not a part of the genre.[39] Traits designating *The Orville* canon are not anything *Orvillean*. If they were, of course, then fanfiction *would be* canon. The remark makes something what it is without itself being that thing.

So, seemingly, to discover just what a work of art is, we must seek its remark. For fanfiction, what might make the remark apparent? For one thing, some fanfic writers, in an effort to pay respects (though not royalties) to the canon, clarify using, what Derrida calls, a "mention" at the outset that the characters, places, events, histories, the universe as a whole in which they operate is not their own. This makes identifying the remark quite easy; we are told, "This is fanfiction." But normally this is not the case, and Derrida points out that any mention might be a lie.[40] The mention cannot always be trusted.

I suggest that perhaps a viewer or reader's knowledge of the canon will indicate that the piece in question is not part of the canon. An unpaid, uncommissioned story based on the canon without being a part of the canon is a defining feature of fanfiction. However, once again, this "trait" relies upon the reader's knowledge and not something within the text. One might just as well be reading an episode not yet aired, or a reader might simply be unfamiliar with the canon. If you have not seen *The Orville* or much of it, or didn't pay close attention, you might assume the fanfiction you've been handed is a legitimate episode. Nothing in the text indicates its generic status as fanfiction. In fact, just the opposite, it indicates its belonging to another genre, the genre it disrupts.

Derrida's trouble with the remark is that it belongs without belonging. But the trouble with fanfiction is that the remark indicates *falsely*; it points to what it is not. It is misleading and is an extreme case of belonging without belonging. But what is so intriguing here is that this is not a weakness or problem with fanfiction; it is an artist's *goal*. The point is to approximate the canon, extend or deepen the canon, to seem to be a part without being a part. Fanfiction participates without belonging but in terms of its remark, is twice removed. In this, we find the law of the law of genre executed perfectly. Impurity and contamination are essential qualities. The fanfiction genre is contaminated by the canon. It bears the remark of the canon, claiming itself as belonging yet, by its very nature, cannot belong, should not belong. On the other side, the canon is contaminated. It cannot assert its limits as fanfiction continually intrudes, parasitic on the universe it holds. Fan fiction as genre is disruptive and corrupting. Without explicit mentioning, even canonical works cannot prove their authenticity and become vulnerable to the charge, or at least vulnerable to the doubt, "is this fan fiction, or the *real thing*?"

But we don't have to worry about this with *The Orville*, right? We know, it's not "the real thing," and presumably it's not trying to be the real thing. But what is the real thing? Frakes, when being interviewed about working on both *The Orville* and *Discovery*, commented, "There's room, obviously, in the fans' hearts for both types of '*Star Trek*.'"[41] For Frakes and for many fans, it is a type of *Star Trek*. But as a type of *Star Trek*, that is, belonging to this canon, what is the remark? What makes *The Orville* belong?

I suggest, here, that the "mention" of homage is a lie and not an unconscious one. I think that MacFarlane quite consciously sees *The Orville* as belonging with the canon, though what keeps *The Orville* tied to the *Star Trek* canon is less its set, costume design, closely related naming conventions, music, staff and writers, its stories, and film work—though each of these certainly contributes to it. What makes *The Orville* fanfiction in my view is its *spirit*. *The Orville* fixes itself in a canonical ethos that once ruled *Star Trek*, a spirit that has now been lost. *Discovery* takes up the broader contemporary move to overly hyped action sequences, bloody violence, and dark themes, themes which now dominate popular science fiction as well as superhero films. Sharing little more than superficial continuity, *Star Trek Discovery* is a strange new world, indeed. Yet, since *The Orville* is not and cannot be canon, it has to stand outside, gesturing in. It has to do what fanfiction does, even when it scarcely belongs there. It has to belong without belonging, in both places at once. And it is precisely through its not-belonging, its opposition to *Discovery*, that it belongs among the, or at least a, *Star Trek* universe.

New Dimensions: Ethos and The Orville

MacFarlane makes it no secret that he wants *The Orville* to stand in contrast to *Discovery* and other contemporary science fiction. He said before the show premiered:

> I kind of miss the forward thinking, aspirational, optimistic place in science fiction that *Star Trek* used to occupy. I think they've chosen to go in a different direction, which has worked very well for them in recent years, but what has happened is that it's left open a space that has been relatively unoccupied for a while in the genre.... So for me, it's a space that's waiting to be filled in this day and age when we're getting a lot of dystopian science fiction, a lot of which is great and very entertaining, but it can't all be *The Hunger Games*. It can't all be the nightmare scenario. I think there's some space for the

aspirational blueprint of what we could do if we get our shit together, and that's something that's been missing for me for a while.[42]

Though he doesn't overtly disparage the "nightmare scenario," MacFarlane clearly thinks we need something different from what our contemporary media has to offer. He sees *The Orville* as fulfilling a certain need and conceiving the show as fanfiction helps us understand what MacFarlane is doing with it. Pugh makes a distinction between two primary types of fanfiction stories: more-of and more-from.[43] More-of stories continue the canon. Dissatisfied with or distressed about the ending of the canon, simply missing the characters, or, if the canon is not closed, an interest in filling in gaps, fanfic writers will continue the story. This is what we saw with MacFarlane's fan film. He is working within *explicit* givens. He creates a new story, perhaps, but does not change anything about the content of the canon.

More-from stories have a different character; they question the canon and follow hinted at or vaguely alluded to possibilities. They tell the same story from a different perspective; they add depth, rather than just width, to the canon. It is a subtle difference between more-of and more-from because more-from stories might also continue the canon or (more often) stay within the bounds of the given canon. But they are critical and refuse to accept some of the givens of a canon. I think this is what is going on in *The Orville*; MacFarlane, and the fans, want more from *Star Trek*.

Though critics were especially harsh to the show in its first season, fans were immediately taken in.[44] They had found in *The Orville* what had been missing in *Discovery* and *Into Darkness*. Some say that it's the parable-like storytelling combined with a modern, though uplifting, perspective: "*The Orville* uses its adventure of the week format to explore modern-day social issues and tackle current moral dilemmas in a sci-fi venue…. The show is refreshingly progressive in its politics, and optimistic to its core."[45] Others say that it's the openness of the world—a world where more, anything, can happen, "It's a mystery box that the same ragtag group of space adventurers opens each week. Before we had five times more channels and streaming options than just episodes of [*The Original Series*], old-school television wasn't boxed into niche genres and a show like *Star Trek* could be about everything. *The Orville* just wants to emulate that."[46] Still others say that it's the characters, the way you know them, like them, and can understand their motivations:

> [On] The Orville, a gelatinous life-form (Yaphit) who was used for a quick gag in the first episode is fleshed out more and more throughout the season. Dann, another side-character, is both recognisable and hilarious, and our prior knowledge of his character gives us an interesting dynamic when he is sent on a blind date with Alara, the security officer of the ship. Last night, I was emotionally moved by an episode about

a character's pornography addiction—a concept so ridiculous that only some likeable characters and impeccable writing can pull off. I felt slightly guilty for regarding a story about alien pornography as more valuable than *Discovery*'s more serious and epic narrative, but when you are not given enough time getting to know your characters, it is really difficult to care.[47]

But I think MacFarlane puts it best when he says that *The Orville* gives us a future that we can see ourselves in, a future we want to imagine for ourselves:

> For me, there was this thing that Star Trek used to do, this space in science fiction that was very hopeful, very aspirational; it created a world you want to live in.... There's really been nothing like that in 20 years where a casual sci-fi show that's just about people spending their day-to-day lives on a spaceship. That's the inspiration that comes from [*Star Trek*] more than anything.[48]

Wanting something more from the canon, fanfiction creators use their art to bring the changes they long for into being. They refuse to accept the world as it is given and propose ways to move beyond it. In this sense, the value of fanfiction takes on a social or political character. Proposing that genre is best understood as a form of social action, Carolyn Miller argues that genre theory should not focus on substance or form, leading to detailed taxonomies, but should emphasize the action it is used to accomplish.[49] This is especially useful to thinking about more-from fanfiction and, especially, the value of what MacFarlane is doing with *The Orville*.

When genre is related to a cultural need, Miller says that it becomes "pragmatic, fully rhetorical, a point of connection between intention and effect, an aspect of social action."[50] Her theory of genre is based in rhetorical practice, in the conventions of discourse a society establishes as a way of acting together. Miller wants to build an essential connection between genre and "rhetorical situations," where a rhetorical situation is, "'a complex of persons, events, objects, and relations' presenting an 'exigence' that can be allayed through the mediation of discourse."[51] Exigence, for Miller, is a set of social expectations and social patterns that can provide a "socially objectified motive for addressing danger, ignorance, separateness. It is an understanding of social need...."[52]

And though genre is bound up with motive, it is not just a method of achieving our own ends. Rather, we learn through genre what ends we may have and learn to better understand the situations in which we find ourselves. She says that genre embodies some aspects of cultural rationality, useful for the critic by serving as an index of cultural patterns and for the student as keys to understanding how to participate in community action. Thus, genre is a rhetorical means for mediating private intentions and social exigence—it connects the private with the public, "the singular with the recurrent."[53]

18   The Teaser and Theme: What Is *The Orville*?

Critics have blasted MacFarlane for intending merely "to cosplay being captain of the U.S.S. Enterprise," but these critics miss something essential. Yes, he probably did want to play captain, but MacFarlane also tapped into a cultural need. By critically engaging the social exigence behind what the canon once was and what it has become, he instituted a fork in the canonical road. MacFarlane is not just giving us more-of *Star Trek*, instituting a return to bygone days. He's demanding more from the canon, more from the genre, more from television, and kind of, more from us.

More-from fanfiction raises questions and doubts in their audiences. It provokes thinking that goes beyond the givens and asks us to imagine the world—both the fictive and the real—from a different perspective. More-from fanfiction mediates private intentions and social exigence, connects the private with the public, and constitutes a genuine form of social action in Miller's sense. Fanfiction is disruptive *as* genre because it will not leave the status quo alone. It is critical and confrontational. Working within a canon it exploits relationships, ideas, and events that are controlled, ignored, or, perhaps, taboo. Indeed, as one viewer aptly noted, "The Orville is thrusting in the opposite direction to what is generally accepted in modern television, and I for one, am enjoying the rebellion."[54]

The point here is, *The Orville* is not just fanfiction, it's the best kind. Though all fanfiction is disruptive and subversive in some sense, more-from fanfiction, like *The Orville*, that questions the social order by way of the accepted cultural givens constitutes a powerful genre-disrupting genre, perhaps not new, but with a new agenda. It illuminates a cultural shift in attitude and an insistence on change. It highlights a social exigency, taking the form of that which it asks of us; that is, we must transgress the world we have and create the world we need. The dystopian "nightmare scenario" that dominates the present tells us that we are flawed, too flawed to overcome the conditions we face here and now. It says that it's too late, and all there is left to do is to keep—just barely and not without a lot of gory bloodshed—cleaning up messes. It says what we are now is all we will ever be.

The Orville demands more from us. It pokes fun at us, but in a genuine way. With quips like how funny and weird it is that humans used to give money to people to "give you stuff or do stuff" (S1E7) and astonishment that we were so complacent about environmental destruction, "God, they were on the verge of a major climate disaster and there's a whole page about teeth whitening" (S2E11), it takes the future as a time when we will have, quite obviously, moved beyond many of the social and political ills that plague us now. There are new challenges, sure, and even some old ones, but this optimistic future allows a setting in which our current problems can take focus and be examined, with a set of people who genuinely want to do right by each other. They, like us, are just figuring out how.

Returning to Derrida, the law of the law of genre is contamination, a rejection of the claims to pure canon. Belonging by not belonging, *The Orville* returns yet uniquely recreates an ethos of exploration and optimism that has been buried for too long. Any canon, any genre, is set by communities of interested individuals deciding how a set of discourses meets their needs, and the creation, maintenance, or disappearance of participants in any canon is ultimately up to them. Dr. Finn puts the question to us all saying, "Real is relative. Goals change. Things become more beautifully complicated. So, we have to stop every so often and reassess. What is it you really want?" (S2E13).

And audiences have answered pretty clearly. We want more *Orville*.

Notes

1. James Hibberd, "FOX: We're Not Worried *Star Trek* Will Sue Us," *Entertainment Weekly*, August 8, 2017, https://ew.com/tv/2017/08/08/star-trek-orville/.
2. Ibid.
3. Sean Carroll, hosts, "Seth MacFarlane on Using Science Fiction to Explore Humanity," *Mindscape* (podcast), August 5, 2019, https://www.preposterousuniverse.com/podcast/2019/08/05/58-seth-macfarlane-on-using-science-fiction-to-explore-humanity/.
4. Ibid.
5. WithAnAccentTV, "NYCC 2017: Brannon Braga & David A. Goodman—The Orville," *YouTube* Video, 11:11, October 13, 2017, https://www.youtube.com/watch?v=avyq9Be5GJE.
6. Brannon Braga, "Interview: Brannon Braga on How 'The Orville' Pays Tribute to Star Trek While Setting a New Course," interview by Anthony Pascale, *Trekmovie*, September 17, 2017, https://trekmovie.com/2017/09/14/interview-brannon-braga-on-how-the-orville-pays-tribute-to-star-trek-while-setting-a-new-course/.
7. Jonathan Frakes, "Jonathan Frakes on How 'Star Trek: Discovery' & 'The Orville' Fill Different Voids," interview by Jenna Anderson, *Comicbook*, March 28, 2018, https://comicbook.com/startrek/news/star-trek-discovery-the-orville-jonathan-frakes/.
8. Ira Madison III, "Seth MacFarlane's 'The Orville' Is a Shameless Humorless 'Star Trek' Rip-Off," *The Daily Beast*, September 10, 2017, https://www.thedailybeast.com/seth-macfarlanes-the-orville-is-a-shameless-humorless-star-trek-rip-off.
9. Emily VanDerWerff, Twitter post, August 8, 2017, 7:35 p.m., https://twitter.com/tvoti.
10. Liz Shannon Miller, "'The Orville' Review: Seth MacFarlane's 'Star Trek' Rip-Off Is Creatively, Morally, and Ethically Bankrupt." *IndieWire*, September 8, 2017, https://www.indiewire.com/2017/09/the-orville-review-seth-macfarlane-star-trek-rip-off-1201874080/.
11. Ibid.
12. I find it interesting, given the spirit of the critique, that Miller here seems to lift VerDerWerff's "serial number" phrase without due credit. *Ibid.*
13. For a great article that details all of the *Star Trek* references in "USS Callister," see Dany Roth's article "Black Mirror's 'USS Callister' Is a Bigger Homage to Star Trek Than You Thought" over at syfy.com
14. Adena Rosmarin, *The Power of Genre* (Minneapolis: University of Minnesota Press, 1985).
15. Rosmarin, *The Power of Genre*, 27–28.
16. Aristotle, *Poetics*, ed. and trans. S.H. Butcher (New York: The Macmillan Company, 1902).
17. Aristotle, *Poetics*, 7.
18. Rosmarin, *The Power of Genre*.

19. Rosmarin, *The Power of Genre*, 29.
20. Rosmarin, *The Power of Genre*, 28.
21. Rosmarin, *The Power of Genre*, 27.
22. Ibid.
23. Sheenagh Pugh, *The Democratic Genre: Fan Fiction in a Literary Context* (Glasgow: Seren Books, 2005).
24. Pugh, *The Democratic Genre*, 242.
25. Pugh, *The Democratic Genre*, 26.
26. The exact date is unknown, but MacFarlane was purportedly around 14 years old at the time. And though there are possibly more, I say "film" because as far as I can find, only one is available and verified.
27. Many fanfic writers/readers reject AU fan fiction as illegitimate, given that characters are merely coopted and then placed in situations that do not belong to their histories. Pugh, *The Democratic* Genre, 63–67.
28. "List of Star Trek: The Next Generation Writers," *Ranker*, September 25, 2019, https://www.ranker.com/list/list-of-star-trek-the-next-generation-writers/reference.
29. Mignogna plays Captain Kirk in a fan produced *Star Trek* web series called *Star Trek Continues*.
30. They did, in fact, happen upon MacFarlane's own episode (at his behest) and they did not, in fact, decide to produce it—hence, *The Orville* was born.
31. This is the distinction made by fanfic writers/readers themselves, though Pugh does not find this distinction satisfactory. However, the reason she does not find it satisfactory is seemingly because she is attempting to separate the fanfic genre by way of an essential quality—the theoretical method we are here rejecting. Pugh, *The Democratic Genre*, 55.
32. Jacques Derrida and Avital Ronell, "The Law of Genre," *Critical Inquiry* 7, no. 1 (Autumn 1980): 55–81, https://doi.org/10.1086/448088.
33. Derrida and Ronnel, "The Law of Genre," 55.
34. Derrida and Ronnel, "The Law of Genre," 57–58.
35. Derrida and Ronnel, "The Law of Genre," 59.
36. Derrida and Ronnel, "The Law of Genre," 59.
37. Derrida and Ronnel, "The Law of Genre," 65.
38. Derrida and Ronnel, "The Law of Genre," 64.
39. Derrida and Ronnel, "The Law of Genre," 65.
40. Derrida makes this point by considering Maurice Blanchot's *Madness of the Day*. Derrida explores the complexities of the remark in the work where the remark is explicitly indicated by a mention, yet the form of the work confuses and confounds such designation. Derrida and Ronnel, "The Law of Genre," 66–81.
41. Liz Shannon Miller, "From 'The Orville' to 'Star Trek: Discovery,' 'Librarians' Director Jonathan Frakes Has Found Massive Range Within the Realm of Sci-Fi," *IndieWire*, December 21, 2017, http://www.indiewire.com/2017/12/jonathan-frakes-director-interview-star-trek-orville-librarians-1201910085.
42. Tara Bennett, "Seth MacFarlane Wants to Reclaim Sci-Fi with The Orville," *SyFy Wire*, September 8, 2017, https://www.syfy.com/syfywire/seth-macfarlane-wants-to-reclaim-sci-fi-with-the-orville.
43. Pugh, *The Democratic Genre*, 10.
44. Critics rated the first season at 30%, whereas the fans gave it a 94%. Contrast this with *Star Trek: Discovery*, which received an 83% from critics, while audiences gave it a dismal 54% "Rotten Tomatoes Ranking, *The Orville*, Season 1," *Rotten Tomatoes*, 2017, https://www.rottentomatoes.com/tv/orville/s01. It's also interesting to note that one of the show's harshest critics, Liz Miller from above, did begin to come around and realized that her original assessments were hasty and unwarranted. She even detailed all the good things about *The Orville*, while maintaining that it still has many problems. Liz Shannon Miller, "'The Orville' Season 1: What's Improved, What Hasn't, and What May Be the Show's Fatal Flaw," *IndieWire*, December 11, 2017, https://www.indiewire.com/2017/12/orville-season-1-review-seth-macfarlane-1201905867/.
45. Scott Mendelson, "Seth MacFarlane's 'The Orville' Is the 'Star Trek' Show Fans Have Been Waiting For," *Forbes*, September 9, 2017, https://www.forbes.com/sites/scottmendelson/

2017/09/29/seth-macfarlanes-the-orville-is-the-star-trek-show-fans-have-been-waiting-for/#7f2b3fe76da8.
   46. Tim Surette, "The Curious Case of The Orville: Why Critics Hate It but Fans Love It," *TV Guide*, January 1, 2019, https://www.tvguide.com/news/the-orville-critics-fans-reviews/.
   47. Ciaran Kerr, "Editorial: How the Orville Ruined Star Trek Discovery for Me," *FilmBunker*, January 24, 2019, https://film-bunker.com/2019/01/24/editorial-how-the-orville-ruined-star-trek-discovery-for-me/.
   48. "Seth MacFarlane and Adrianne Palicki Talk Influence Behind *The Orville*," *CineMovie*, July 25, 2017, https://cinemovie.tv/Interviews/seth-macfarlane-adrianne-palicki-the-orville-comic-con-interview.
   49. Carolyn Miller, "Genre as Social Action," *Quarterly Journal of Speech* 70, no. 2 (1984): 151–167, doi:10.1080/00335638409383686.
   50. Miller, "Genre as Social Action," 152.
   51. Miller, "Genre as Social Action," 151.
   52. Miller, "Genre as Social Action," 158.
   53. Miller, "Genre as Social Action," 163.
   54. Ciaran Kerr, "Editorial: Critics vs. The Orville—What's Going On?" *FilmBunker*, October 1, 2018, https://film-bunker.com/2018/10/01/editorial-critics-vs-the-orville-whats-going-on/.

Bibliography

Aristotle. *Poetics*. Edited and Translated by S.H. Butcher. New York: The Macmillan Company. 1902.
Bennett, Tara. "Seth MacFarlane Wants to Reclaim Sci-Fi with The Orville." *SyFy Wire*, September 8, 2017. https://www.syfy.com/syfywire/seth-macfarlane-wants-to-reclaim-sci-fi-with-the-orville.
Carroll, Sean, host. "Seth MacFarlane on Using Science Fiction to Explore Humanity," *Mindscape* (podcast), August 5, 2019, https://www.preposterousuniverse.com/podcast/2019/08/05/58-seth-macfarlane-on-using-science-fiction-to-explore-humanity/.
de Moraes, Lisa. "Seth MacFarlane: 'The Orville' Occupies Sci-Fi Space 'Star Trek' Left Behind En Route to Dystopia." *Deadline*, August 8, 2017. https://deadline.com/2017/08/seth-macfarlane-orville-star-trek-cbs-television-studios-tca-1202144717/
Derrida, Jacques, and Avital Ronell. "The Law of Genre." *Critical Inquiry* 7, no. 1 (Autumn 1980): 55–81. https://doi.org/10.1086/448088.
Hibberd, James. "FOX: We're Not Worried *Star Trek* Will Sue Us." *Entertainment Weekly*, August 8, 2017. https://ew.com/tv/2017/08/08/star-trek-orville/.
Kerr, Ciaran. "Editorial: Critics Vs. The Orville—What's Going On?" *FilmBunker*, October 1, 2018. https://film-bunker.com/2018/10/01/editorial-critics-vs-the-orville-whats-going-on/.
Kerr, Ciaran. "Editorial: How The Orville Ruined Star Trek Discovery for Me." *FilmBunker*, January 24, 2019. https://film-bunker.com/2019/01/24/editorial-how-the-orville-ruined-star-trek-discovery-for-me/.
"List of Star Trek: The Next Generation Writers." *Ranker*, September 25, 2019. https://www.ranker.com/list/list-of-star-trek-the-next-generation-writers/reference.
Madison, Ira III. "Seth MacFarlane's 'The Orville' Is a Shameless Humorless 'Star Trek' Rip-off." *The Daily Beast*, September 10, 2017. https://www.thedailybeast.com/seth-macfarlanes-the-orville-is-a-shameless-humorless-star-trek-rip-off.
Mendelson, Scott. "Seth MacFarlane's 'The Orville' Is the 'Star Trek' Show Fans Have Been Waiting For." *Forbes*, September 9, 2017. https://www.forbes.com/sites/scottmendelson/2017/09/29/seth-macfarlanes-the-orville-is-the-star-trek-show-fans-have-been-waiting-for/#7f2b3fe76da8.
Miller, Carolyn. "Genre as Social Action." *Quarterly Journal of Speech* 70, no. 2 (1984): 151-167. doi:10.1080/00335638409383686.
Miller, Liz Shannon. "From 'The Orville' to 'Star Trek: Discovery,' 'Librarians' Director Jonathan

Frakes Has Found Massive Range Within the Realm of Sci-Fi." *IndieWire*, December 21, 2017. http://www.indiewire.com/2017/12/jonathan-frakes-director-interview-star-trek-orville-librarians-1201910085.

Miller, Liz Shannon. "'The Orville' Review: Seth MacFarlane's 'Star Trek' Rip-Off Is Creatively, Morally, and Ethically Bankrupt." *IndieWire*, September 8, 2017. https://www.indiewire.com/2017/09/the-orville-review-seth-macfarlane-star-trek-rip-off-1201874080/.

Orf, Darren. "'Star Trek: Discovery' Is Losing Itself in Darkness." *Popular Mechanics*, January 22, 2018. https://www.popularmechanics.com/culture/tv/a15839553/star-trek-discovery-episode-12-vaulting-ambition/.

Pugh, Sheenagh. *The Democratic Genre: Fan Fiction in a Literary Context*. Glasgow: Seren Books, 2005.

Rosmarin, Adena. *The Power of Genre*. Minneapolis: University of Minnesota Press, 1985.

"Rotten Tomatoes Ranking, *The Orville*, Season 1." *Rotten Tomatoes*. 2017. https://www.rottentomatoes.com/tv/orville/s01.

"Seth MacFarlane as Teenager in Star Trek Fan Film with His Friends." *YouTube* Video, 2:49. November 30, 2017. https://www.youtube.com/watch?v=sn_Sgcxg5PQ.

Surette, Tim. "The Curious Case of The Orville: Why Critics Hate It but Fans Love It." *TV Guide*, January 1, 2019. https://www.tvguide.com/news/the-orville-critics-fans-reviews/.

VanDerWerff, Emily (@tvoti). "Everybody is talking about how 'original' The Orville is, but it's just Seth MacFarlane filing the serial numbers off Star Trek. #tca17." *Twitter*, August 8, 2017. https://twitter.com/tvoti/status/895065884787523584.

Introduction

How The Orville *Does Philosophy*

DAVID KYLE JOHNSON

Every episode of *The Orville* starts with a "cold open" teaser; you just jump right into the show. Only once it has set the stage for the story do you get the introduction; the theme song plays over inspiring images of the USS *Orville* that sets the tone for the show's sense of exploration and adventure. With that in mind, and L. Brooke Rudow so skillfully setting the stage in her first essay, I hope to now give you a sense of the philosophical exploration and adventure that lies ahead.

When *The Orville* was first advertised, many thought it was just going to be "Spaceballs for *Star Trek*." This was partly because of creator Seth MacFarlane's comedic reputation; he is responsible for *Family Guy*, after all. But it was also because the show's first trailer made it seem as such. Set to a version of "Space Truckin'," and made by commercial editors at Fox who were not involved in the making of the show, the first trailer really concentrated on the show's comedic elements.

In reality, however, *The Orville* turned out to be much more like a combination of *Star Trek* (especially *The Next Generation*) and *M*A*S*H*. Like *Star Trek*, it tells the story of a starship and her crew. Like *M*A*S*H*, it involves comedy and characters you come to know and love. And, like both, it offers blunt, relevant, social, political, and philosophic commentary. Indeed, it seems that the kind of balance between comedy and drama, found in *M*A*S*H*, is explicitly what the creators were looking for.[1] MacFarlane had been talking, off and on, with Brannon Braga (who wrote for *Star Trek: The Next Generation*) and David A. Goodman (who wrote for *Star Trek: Enterprise*) about creating a show like *Star Trek*, with powerful storytelling, compelling character arcs, and forward-thinking politics, since 2000.[2] And Braga in particular had missed his days of writing for *The Next Generation* and wanted to capture a show that balanced comedy with serious drama like *M*A*S*H*.³ It's no coincidence that both Braga and Goodman became executive producers of *The Orville*.

To be clear, when MacFarlane began work on what would eventually become *The Orville* in March 2016, it was written as a comedic, science-fiction feature—one presumes much more along the line of *Spaceballs*. But those plans didn't last long.

> When I look back at it, I realize that wasn't really the show I wanted to do. We've taken that pressure off ourselves and veered more towards traditional science fiction without the pressure of having that comedy frosting on it to such a degree. I've been having a lot more fun. I've realized that, even more so than writing *Family Guy*, that it just comes flowing out, it just comes easier; so maybe I should've never been a comedy writer in the first place [laughs].⁴

It seems that, while his (admitted) comedic influence from *Jackass* was at play early on (and clearly rules in *Family Guy*), when it came to *The Orville*, MacFarlane let his (admitted) comedic influence from Albert Brooks take over.⁵ Indeed, he has acknowledged the "profound influence" Albert Brooks' *Defending Your Life* had on the making of *The Orville*, and if one watches the series' episodes in order, it seems that the more mature Brooks-esque influence becomes more pronounced over time.⁶ According to MacFarlane *The Orville* mixes drama and comedy, the sweet and the bitter, because "life is that way. You have one day where it's your birthday and you fall into the swimming pool by accident, and another day where you lose a family member. Those days have very different tones and it's all the same life."⁷

Something else *The Orville* has in common with *M*A*S*H* is that, even though there is character development through the seasons, each episode (except for the occasional two-parter) is a self-contained stand-alone episode. Indeed, in a way, this episodic approach is a counter-reaction to what has happened to science fiction (and *Star Trek* in particular) since 2000, which moved primarily to season-long story arcs—like those that took over *Star Trek: Enterprise* (particularly Season 3), and that can be found more recently in *Star Trek: Discovery* and *Star Trek: Picard*.⁸ As MacFarlane put it:

> I grew up with episodic sci-fi. I grew up with *The Twilight Zone*, obviously *Star Trek*; I miss that style of storytelling, which I see as a self-contained show that was based around an idea as opposed to a twist.… In the age of streaming shows where you're dealing with a story arc that lasts throughout the season, the diversity of stories becomes less in that format and it starts to become "How can I surprise the audience with a crazy twist?" rather than what used to be the case, which is "What new idea can I present to the audience this week?" You can really only do that with self-contained stories.⁹

The "new ideas" *The Orville* presents are often very philosophical in nature. Unfortunately, however, science fiction's ability to do things like philosophy has very often been doubted. It is, instead, perceived as juvenile escapism.

That's not to say that people don't recognize that science fiction can be used to teach philosophy. What philosopher, in their introduction to philosophy class, hasn't used *The Matrix* to teach about Cartesian skepticism (René Descartes' worry that we can't prove we aren't dreaming). What philosopher hasn't used *Star Trek*'s transporters to talk about personal identity? (Is the person who appears, reconstructed, on the planet the same person as the one who stepped into the transporter?) Indeed, William Irwin edits an entire series of books (*The Wiley/Blackwell Philosophy and Popular Culture Series*) that uses pop culture, including science fiction, to teach philosophy. But the idea that science fiction can *do philosophy* is often mocked.

But those who decry science fiction in this way ignore crucial elements of both the history of science fiction and of philosophy. Consider the fact that Plato used the Ring of Gyges story to motivate *The Republic*, that both René Descartes and Pierre-Simon Laplace imagined demons to make philosophic points, and that Robert Nozick used "The Experience Machine" thought experiment to refute consequentialist theories of ethics, like hedonism. Of course, most of these examples are more akin to fantasy than science fiction, but they do demonstrate how outlandish fictional stories can be used to make philosophical arguments.

Or take the second century Syrian philosopher Lucian of Samosata's work *A True History*, which involved an ocean-faring ship being whisked away by a whirlwind to the moon. It clearly has many things in common with science fiction but was also used by Lucian to satirize the sophists and the religion of his time. Indeed, what made *A True History* "true," wasn't that it was true—but that it was the only history around that admitted it was false. (Other equally ridiculous mythologies claimed to be true.) In the 1200s, Islamic philosopher Ibn al-Nafis used his work, *The Theologus Autodidactus*, about a spontaneously created man, to argue that Islam was compatible with empirical observation and that what Islam revealed could be reached by reason. In 1515, Thomas More used *Utopia* to criticize British society, and about a century later Francis Bacon used *The New Atlantis* to argue for a more scientific one. In 1705, Daniel Defoe used *The Consolidator* to poke fun at the politics and religion of his day—and this was all before Mary Shelley's *Frankenstein*, which is often considered to be the first work of science fiction. In other words, philosophers have been using science fiction to do philosophy for centuries, even long before "science fiction" was a recognized genre of literature.[10]

But science fiction writers are also doing philosophy. Like Mary Shelley, who seemed to be warning about the danger of scientists playing god, science fiction writers often intend their stories to have philosophical points, and even be philosophical arguments. As Kevin Kelly, founding editor of *Wired* magazine, once put it,

26   The Teaser and Theme: What is *The Orville*?

> [T]he science fiction authors ... of today ... [are] the people who are really wrestling with the great what-if questions [and] grappling ... not just with the political possibilities, but [questions like] "What does it mean to be human?" [and] "Where do we fit in the cosmos?" I think they are doing all the heavy lifting of the philosophical questions even as they're doing chase scenes....[11]

Now, this goes a bit too far. Philosophers themselves are doing a lot of the heavy lifting too. But the general sentiment is right. *Inception* is an argument that it's okay to abandon one's quest for reality to believe what you want, whereas *The Matrix* argues that the truth about reality must be sought at all costs. Carl Sagan's *Contact* argues that a scientific worldview is compatible with religious belief and *Transcendence* is an argument against fearing technology. *Westworld* is an argument that androids will be conscious, *Metropolis* an argument for labor unions, and *Gattaca* an argument against designer babies. *Starship Troopers* is an (extremely prescient) argument against fascism, and you could spend an entire book talking about philosophical arguments made by each and every episode of *Black Mirror*.[12]

And that brings us back to the purpose of this introduction (and the motivation for this book): to point out that *The Orville* is also doing philosophy. As Goodman puts it, "The show can't just be fun space action. Commenting on current society and social mores—we almost consider that our responsibility."[13] And it does so in a very specific way—with what we might call "episodic allegory." Now André Bormanis has called the show "parables" in the vein of "social commentary shows as was done in the original *Star Trek*,"[14] and that is perfectly accurate. But MacFarlane has used the word "allegory" specifically.[15] "[The Orville is] a classic style, episodic sci-fi adventure series that adheres to the traditional sci-fi method of storytelling which is to take elements of our society, whether it be social or political or scientific, and find ways to tell stories about those things in an allegorical fashion through the lens of sci-fi."[16]

What's perhaps most interesting, however, is that the show's approach seems to accomplish its goal—particularly its goal to affect its viewers—in a very specific way: it *cloaks our bias to creative cognitive dissonance* with something writer Darko Suvin called "cognitive estrangement."[17] To understand what that means, begin by reminding yourself that we all have biases that color how we see particular parts of the world. Depending on our political party, for example, we are apt to respond to a quote attributed to a president in a certain way. But if the origin of the quote is obscured, we are more likely to evaluate the quote without bias and judge it based on its own merit. We might draw the same conclusion we would have, but it will be free from the baggage of our prejudices or an uncharitable interpretation. Cognitively estranging us from the origin of the quote *cloaks our bias*. But if we discover that our unbiased opinion of the quote is different than the one we would have drawn otherwise—perhaps we initially agreed with the quote but then learned that it was from a president opposite our own political party—this is likely to create *cognitive dissonance*. Perhaps my positive or negative evaluation of that particular president was due to my own political bias, rather than an honest assessment. If so, I may have to reevaluate my position on a number of topics.

Lucasfilm's Chief Creative Officer John Knoll argues that science fiction can do exactly this.

> One of the big misconceptions about science fiction is that it's ... escapist entertainment for kids that [doesn't] tackle any serious themes. [But] the best science fiction gives you an opportunity to explore philosophical and moral themes. There are often societal problems that are very emotionally loaded ... [but] if you ... recast them in a science fiction setting, [and are thus] looking at a more novel situation, then you can leave some of those preconceived notions behind and ... reevaluat[e] it anew. [This] may cause you to rethink your position on the terrestrial version of that problem.[18]

As an example, consider a life-long Republican fan of George W. Bush watching *Star Wars Episode III: The Revenge of the Sith*, in 2005. Suppose this fan generally agrees with how Bush responded to the 9/11 attacks. "He did what was necessary to keep us safe and secure," this fan of Bush says. Now, while watching *Episode III*, he is likely to recognize that Emperor Palpatine is clearly the bad guy—an evil tyrant even. The strangeness of the science fiction setting estranges him cognitively and makes him evaluate Palpatine without bias. But upon reflection, he might come to realize that what Palpatine did in the movie is not that dissimilar to what Bush did. Just as Palpatine lied to draw the Republic into the clone wars, the Bush administration lied about Saddam Hussein having weapons of mass destruction to draw the U.S. into the Iraq war. Just like Palpatine used fears about the Republic's security to grant himself special emergency powers, Bush used fears about America's security to pass the USA Patriot Act. "It's a wonder" this Republican might say to himself in a moment of cognitive dissonance, "that Bush didn't, like Palpatine, reorganize our republic into an empire for the sake of a 'safe and secure society.' I didn't like Palpatine when he did those things. Why did I agree with Bush when he did?" You can see how this realization might cause one to reexamine their beliefs.

It is this kind of approach that *The Orville* often uses to make its arguments. Consider the first season episode "If the Stars Should Appear." The crew discovers a giant ship adrift with a population of millions living in an artificial bio-dome that will be destroyed by a star in six months. The inhabitants refuse to heed the crew's warnings because the idea that anything exists outside the dome is considered heresy by the society's religion, and the leader of the "dictatorial theocracy" that controls it is unwilling to "destabilize a system that has kept order for thousands of years." Their scientific ignorance, fueled by religious dogma, is infuriating; it's almost incomprehensible that a population could ignore such a threat. But then one realizes that this is exactly what we are doing with climate change caused by global warming. If one reacts as one should to the scientific ignorance in the episode, but thinks climate change is a hoax perpetrated by the Chinese, this realization could create serious cognitive dissonance. (This is why I devote an entire essay in this book to that episode.)

Or take "Majority Rule," the tale of a society ruled by a pure democracy where everything is decided by a popular vote on "the master feed." Lt. Cmdr. John LaMarr must go on an apology tour after the public is outraged by him grinding on a statue of Sargus frontier hero Mella Giffendon. We wonder how a technologically advanced society could try and convict people without due process. But then we realize that this kind of trial happens on Twitter all the time. Indeed, for this episode, Seth MacFarlane was inspired by the book *So You've Been Publicly Shamed* (by Jon Ronson), which catalogues how people's lives have been ruined, by minor missteps, via "trial by Twitter." Those who have participated in such events could be forced to rethink their role in them by this episode. (For more on this, see Patrick Welsh's essay on this episode.)

One's bias is barely cloaked in "Mad Idolatry," where a religion that worships first officer Commander Kelly Grayson is accidentally created on a planet with a multiphasic orbit. The crew watches, over the years, as the religion develops and people are tortured and killed in its name. By the planet's equivalent of the 21st century, megachurches of Kelly are bilking people out of money, worship of Kelly is corrupting public education, and holy wars are being waged in her name. In the end, however, the planet's society advances past that of *The Orville*—but does so explicitly *despite* Kelly's interference and the hurdle of religion itself. As the two members of the society that visit the USS *Orville,* Fadolin and Baleth, put it:

Fadolin:	….our world advanced just as it would have….
Baleth:	…We wouldn't have gotten to where we are without growing pains.
Fadolin:	Our planet worshiped you as a deity for many centuries. But had it not been you, the mythology would have found another face. It's a part of every culture's evolution. It's one of the stages of learning…
Baleth:	So you see commander, you didn't poison our culture with false faith. We flourish. You must have faith, in reason, in discovery, and in the endurance of the logical mind.

The dangers of religion are all obvious, of course, when it's a religion that worships Kelly; but cognitive dissonance sets in for those that realize their religion is not all that different.

Speaking of which: take the Krill and their religion. Unlike other species who, as their technological development increases their religiosity declines, the Krill have become more and more religious over time. According to their "Bible," the Anhkana, all the universe's resources are solely for their use and "that which is not of Krill is without soul." The union fears any conflict with them, as it could easily slip into an endless holy war. All of the worst horrors of Earth's religions are brought to mind: the crusades, manifest destiny, environmental exploitation, the justification of slavery and racism. If one is religious, one is forced to wrestle with their complicity in such crimes. (For more on what *The Orville* has to say about religion, see Darren M. Slade's essay.)

The cloak is thick in "Cupid's Dagger," where Darulio emits a pheromone that makes people fall in love with him. At first, the story seems like a kind of fun rom-com romp, where everyone is sleeping with everyone else. But then one realizes that Darulio's pheromone is very much like a date rape drug. Yet the episode seems to be largely uncritical of Darulio's actions. Is the moral of the episode confused, or just flat out wrong? Or is there an important difference between Darulio's pheromone and a date rape drug? These are difficult questions (which Michael R. Berry addresses in his essay).

Perhaps the most obvious example of cloaking bias to create cognitive dissonance comes from the all-male society of Moclans. Moclans have a scathing hatred of heterosexuality that is easy to abhor—but then, of course, one realizes that its directly analogous to biases people have against gays and lesbians in the real world. When Bortus inexplicably hatches a female child, we are angered when his husband Klyden legally forces the child to have a gender reassignment surgery—but then we realize that this likely makes us hypocrites about our attitudes towards transgender and intersex persons. (For more on such topics, see Liz Fairchild's essay.)

In fact, "About a Girl" even has a show, within the show, that cloaks bias to create cognitive dissonance to change Bortus's view of the gender reassignment surgery. After watching the Claymation *Rudolph the Red-Nosed Reindeer* with Lt. LaMarr and Lt. Malloy, he realizes that the "defect" he thinks his female child has might actually turn out to be an advantage.

Bortus:	Without Rudolph's nose, Santa would not have been able to complete his voyage.
LaMarr:	Looks like Santa got pretty lucky, huh?
Bortus:	Christmas would have been ruined if Rudolph had been euthanized at birth, as his father wished.
Malloy:	Yeah, I don't I don't know if that was ever on the table.
Bortus:	What was clearly a deformity became a supreme advantage. One can never know.
…[later]…	
Bortus:	Klyden I believe we should leave our baby unaltered….
Klyden:	Why would you suggest such a thing?

Bortus: Because I have witnessed events that have opened my eyes ... you must hear the tale of Rudolph. You will rethink your conviction, I promise you.

It's almost as if *The Orville* is acknowledging the approach it is taking by showing how other shows (or pieces of popular culture) have successfully pulled it off. (And, as Francesca Putignano's essay points out, this is not the only time it has done so.)

And then, when "Sanctuary" reveals that the Moclans are not an all-male species after all—that females are simply so reviled in their society that nearly every female born is secretly surgically forced to be male (you can apparently identify such Moclans by finding spots on their forehead)—we realize that a whole host of our biases were cloaked that now must be examined (many of which are examined by Catherine Nolan in her essay). One that is important to me is cultural relativism, the idea that what a culture thinks is moral rightly defines what is morally right in that culture. Many embrace this idea, but the Moclans invoke it to protect rampant sexism and the oppression of an entire gender. "I'm the first person to question the balance between cultural tolerance and ethical negligence," Captain Mercer insists in "Sanctuary," "but Admiral, this is over the limit." Or as Kelly puts it in "About a Girl," "you have to balance [cultural tolerance] against some universal code of ethics. I mean, suppose it was their custom to kill all newborn females. Should we respect their culture then?" This raises a plethora of issues to ponder. Should we be tolerant of all religions—even those that oppress and degrade women, or discriminate against sexual minorities? Or what about political views? Where is the balance between political tolerance and ethical negligence in our current political climate?

Some may think that addressing such issues by *cloaking bias to create cognitive dissonance* with "episodic allegory" is lazy. "The parallels are too obvious, and the moral messages are delivered too bluntly." Perhaps. But perhaps, in today's world, we need bluntness. We don't just need long involved *Handmaid's Tale*s to warn about the downward slope we are on, or deeply dark *Black Mirror*s in which to take long gazes to see ourselves and our foibles. We also need to be hit over the head. And it is the issues that *The Orville* hits us over the head with—many of which were just mentioned above—that this book hopes to explore.

All of us who contributed to this book (only a few of which have been mentioned so far) hope that reading it will challenge you as much as writing it challenged us. It was a lot of hard work, but it was also a labor of love. Now ... cue the theme song!

Notes

1. Adrianne Palicki and Seth McFarlane, "SDCC 2017: The Orville" (YouTube Video of Interview, San Diego, CA, July 2017), https://www.youtube.com/watch?v=aq4WTbZm-_0.
2. Jeff Bond, *The World of The Orville* (Titan Books, 2018), 8.
3. Matt Wright, "STLV17: Brannon Braga on How Kirk Should Have Died, 'Star Trek: Enterprise' Regrets and More," *TrekMovie*, August 11, 2017, https://trekmovie.com/2017/08/11/sltv17-brannon-braga-on-how-kirk-should-have-died-star-trek-enterprise-regrets-and-more/.
4. Sean Carroll, host, "Seth MacFarlane on Using Science Fiction to Explore Humanity," *Mindscape* (podcast), August 5, 2019, https://www.preposterousuniverse.com/podcast/2019/08/05/58-seth-macfarlane-on-using-science-fiction-to-explore-humanity/.
5. ThePatrickShow, "Seth Macfarlane Google Questions Answers," *YouTube* video, 3:17, May 18, 2018, https://www.youtube.com/watch?v=-TeW2CRjTMo.
6. ThePatrickShow, "Seth Macfarlane Google Questions Answers."
7. Carroll, "Seth MacFarlane on Using Science Fiction to Explore Humanity."
8. Although *Discovery* and *Picard* came too late for the creation of *The Orville* to be a reaction to them specifically.
9. Carroll, "Seth MacFarlane on Using Science Fiction to Explore Humanity."
10. For more on these examples, see my article for the *Sci-Phi Journal*, David Kyle Johnson, "What Sci Phi Is All About," *Sci Phi Journal*, February 14, 2019, https://www.sciphijournal.org/index.php/2019/02/14/what-sci-phi-is-all-about-treating-science-fiction-as-philosophy.
11. Adam Savage, hosts, "Kevin Kelly," SyFy25: Origin Stories (podcast), September 8, 2017, https://podcasts.apple.com/gb/podcast/syfy25-origin-stories/id1280023707.
12. For more on this see David Kyle Johnson, *Black Mirror and Philosophy: Dark Reflections*. (Wiley-Blackwell, 2020). For more on the above examples, see David Kyle Johnson, *Sci-Phi: Science Fiction as Philosophy* (The Teaching Company: The Great Courses, 2018).
13. Jennifer Oullette, "Go Behind the Scenes of The Orville as Series Embarks on a New Season," *Ars Technica*, March 26, 2020, https://arstechnica.com/gaming/2020/03/go-behind-the-scenes-of-the-orville-as-series-embarks-on-a-new-season/.
14. André Bormanis (author) in discussion with the author, via Pat Welsh, April 10, 2020.
15. Channel Control, "SDCC 2019 The Orville panel," *YouTube* video, 39:56, July 29, 2019, https://www.youtube.com/watch?v=F3gKeKpFOUw.
16. Carroll, "Seth MacFarlane on Using Science Fiction to Explore Humanity."
17. Perry Nodelman, "The Cognitive Estrangement of Darko Suvin," *Children's Literature Association Quarterly* 5, no. 4 (January 1981): 24–27, https://doi.org/10.1353/chq.0.1851.
18. Adam Savage, hosts, "John Knoll," SyFy25: Origin Stories (podcast), September 8, 2017, https://podcasts.apple.com/gb/podcast/syfy25-origin-stories/id1280023707.

Bibliography

Bond, Jeff. *The World of The Orville*. Titan Books, 2018.
Carroll, Sean, host. "Seth MacFarlane on Using Science Fiction to Explore Humanity," *Mindscape* (podcast), August 5, 2019, https://www.preposterousuniverse.com/podcast/2019/08/05/58-seth-macfarlane-on-using-science-fiction-to-explore-humanity/.
Johnson, David Kyle. "What Sci Phi Is All About." *Sci Phi Journal*, February 14, 2019. https://www.sciphijournal.org/index.php/2019/02/14/what-sci-phi-is-all-about-treating-science-fiction-as-philosophy.
Nodelman, Perry. "The Cognitive Estrangement of Darko Suvin." *Children's Literature Association Quarterly* 5, no. 4 (January 1981): 24–27. https://doi.org/10.1353/chq.0.1851.
Oullette, Jennifer. "Go Behind the Scenes of *The Orville* as Series Embarks on a New Season." *Ars Technica*, March 26, 2020, https://arstechnica.com/gaming/2020/03/go-behind-the-scenes-of-the-orville-as-series-embarks-on-a-new-season/.
Palici, Adrianne and Seth McFarlane. "SDCC 2017: The Orville" (YouTube Video). Interview, San Diego, CA, July 2017. https://www.youtube.com/watch?v=aq4WTbZm-0

32   The Teaser and Theme: What is *The Orville*?

Savage, Adam, host. "John Knoll." SyFy25: Origin Stories (podcast). September 8, 2017. https://podcasts.apple.com/gb/podcast/syfy25-origin-stories/id1280023077.
Savage, Adam, host. "Kevin Kelly." SyFy25: Origin Stories (podcast). September 8, 2017. https://podcasts.apple.com/gb/podcast/syfy25-origin-stories/id1280023077.
ThePatrickShow. "Seth Macfarlane Google Questions Answers." *YouTube* video, 3:17. May 18, 2018. https://www.youtube.com/watch?v=-TeW2CRjTMo.
Wright, Matt. "STLV17: Brannon Braga on How Kirk Should Have Died, 'Star Trek: Enterprise' Regrets and More." *TrekMovie,* August 11, 2017. https://trekmovie.com/2017/08/11/sltv17-brannon-braga-on-how-kirk-should-have-died-star-trek-enterprise-regrets-and-more/.

Act I
Gender, Sex and Feminism

Finding the Female
Gender in Moclan Society
Catherine Nolan

> I think we've struggled with [the fact that Moclans lay eggs but are all male] a little bit. The storytelling value that species gives you, as opposed to the logic of the body, we've kind of landed on: their definitions are a little different from what ours are. At the end of the day you can always fall back on, "Well, they're aliens, it's different."
> —Seth MacFarlane, Mindscape 58 Podcast[1]

Executive Producer Brannon Braga has said the three core concepts that were in Seth MacFarlane's mind when he first created *The Orville* were "the Kelly/Ed dynamic," "an android with a superiority complex," and the concept of the Moclan all-male species.[2] In the universe of *The Orville*, the Moclan species displays a plethora of disgusting practices, dirty secrets, and shameful vulnerabilities. They consume parasites for pleasure. When they divorce, the injured partner stabs the other to death—though if the breakup occurs before marriage, the injured partner merely extracts a tooth from the other and feeds it to his next boyfriend. They are the primary arms dealers for the Planetary Union and have industrialized the entire surface of their planet. They are prone to both pornography and nicotine addiction. And yet, the secret that the Moclans themselves find most distasteful (and go to the greatest lengths to hide) is a fact that the rest of the universe finds perfectly acceptable: that Moclans can be born female.

Bortus, a Moclan serving aboard the USS *Orville*, presents himself to the rest of the crew as a member of an all-male species. His partner, Klyden, is of course also male—but when Bortus hatches the egg that he has laid and the child that emerges is a girl, they are forced to admit the existence of female Moclans. Now, according to Isaac, this only happens "once every 75 years" (S1E3), and it is Moclan practice to give such infants a surgical "corrective sex change" operation, as if the child has a deformity—like a cleft palate. But the operation apparently succeeds so well that it can deceive even intimate partners in adulthood; Klyden, it turns out, was also born female and Bortus never suspected it. Add this to the fact the best Moclan poet contemporary of Bortus and Klyden, Gondus Elden, is also a female named Heveena (who lives in hiding in a cave and publishes under an assumed name), and one is really left to wonder: just how often are Moclan females born? That official "once every 75 years" statistic, cited by Isaac, doesn't seem accurate.

To this question, the series does provide a partial answer. In the season two episode "Sanctuary," we meet yet another Moclan couple, with yet another female child, who is being snuck away from Moclus by her parents so that she does not have to undergo "correction." They are bringing her to live with an entire colony of female Moclans, which "for years" has operated an underground railroad of sorts that liberates female-born Moclans from the oppression of Moclan sexism. Since it has over 6000 members, and only a fraction of those born female successfully make the trip, female Moclans are obviously born much more often "than the [Moclan] government has ever publicly admitted" (S2E12). Once the USS *Orville* discovers the colony, Heveena (the apparent leader of the colony) leads the charge to have the colony officially recognized by the Union. In the end, because of the objections of Moclus (and the fact that they supply the Union with all their weapons) this petition is not approved, but the colony is at least allowed to exist.

Now, again, all this at least partially answers the question "how often are female Moclans born?" But it also raises another: Why do the Moclans consider these individuals female at all? Initially, one might think this question is easy to answer. After all, they apparently have female physical features, like breasts. But think about this for a second. These children are being identified as female at birth, long before any such feature would appear. And, biologically, the term "female" refers to an organism with a particular reproductive system or role, that of producing the ovum or egg. Yet in the Moclan species, the males lay eggs. Indeed, the females don't seem to play any reproductive role at all—or if they do, it's not clear what that role is. Thus it is not clear exactly what sex they are! Some speculation about Moclan females and the reproduction of Moclans is thus in order. And it will lead to interesting insights not only about them, but about the relations of the sexes on our own planet as well. Moclans may not engage in sexism for the same reasons we do, but their behavior will unveil insights into our own weaknesses that go far beyond sexism.

Sex on Earth

Before we can continue, we need to discuss what we mean by "female" and "male" among organisms that evolved on earth. First of all, let me clarify that what I am discussing here is a biological distinction, not a social or personal distinction. Ed Mercer calls the Moclans a "single gender species" while Bortus says they are "all male" (S1E1). Indeed, "sex" and "gender" are often used interchangeably; for instance, Clare calls the surgery under consideration for Bortus' child a "sex change operation," while the Moclan legal representative calls it "gender correction surgery" (S1E3). But in this essay, I'll use "sex" (or "male" and "female") to refer to the biological role in reproduction and "gender" ("woman," "girl," "man," or "boy") to refer to social roles assigned to males and females of a social species. The Moclans therefore present themselves as both all-male—filling the same biological reproductive role—and of the same gender—having the same male-specific social roles. Ed and the Moclan legal representative are not incorrect, but indirect; changing Topa's physical sex would put Topa into a different set of social roles.

But what are the biological roles referred to by "male" and "female"? These terms have developed over the millennia. Aristotle thought that a female is an organism that generates young within itself, while a male generates in another.[3] More accurate biological data has revealed the existence of some animals which reproduce completely externally: some female frogs and fish, for example, lay eggs which are only afterwards fertilized by males. Now, though, we have the ability to magnify individual gametes—the cells that combine and grow into a new organism when reproduction occurs. We can therefore distinguish between males and females even in these cases; males produce smaller gametes, or spermatozoa (which, being smaller, are often self-propelling), and females produce larger gametes, or ova (which, being larger, are often kept within the female body during and after reproduction).

Having sexes at all requires that there are differences between gametes, or, in other words, that reproduction is anisogamous. In contrast with anisogamous sexual reproduction, isogamous reproduction is a less complex method: this is when the gametes used to reproduce are of the same kind. On Earth, we see isogamous reproduction in certain types of algae. Simpler yet is asexual reproduction, which we see when a single organism is able to reproduce without combining cells. Amoebas and beings like Yaphit are good examples of asexually reproducing organisms, which essentially reproduce by splitting in two.

Sexual reproduction can itself be more or less complex: some mushrooms have hundreds of different gamete types, which are organized into mating types rather than sexes.[4] Organisms with two sexes, male and female, sometimes have both sexes within a single organism; the organism can be both male and female at the same time (for example, earthworms) or can have a different sex at different times (for example, mated male cinnamon clownfish produce sperm unless they lose their female mate, at which point the male becomes a female and produces ova).[5] Other species even have individuals without a reproductive role, such as sterile worker ants or bees.

Humans are comparatively simple: individuals normally develop into one of two sexes, not both. In other words, "male" and "female" are exhaustive and exclusive biological sexual categories for ordinary humans— though the sexes even in the human species are more complicated than they may at first seem. We must also take into account those who are not clearly of either sex (such as chromosomally male individuals with androgen insensitivity syndrome, which can cause them to develop external genitalia that look phenotypically female), early embryos whose sex may change, those who are no longer fertile, and so on. But we can at least make the claim that if I would produce ova as a healthy and fertile human, I am biologically female; if I would produce sperm, I am biologically male.

Sex on Moclus

At this point, it is obvious that we cannot simply treat Moclans as odd-looking humans and assume that Moclan reproduction works the same way that human reproduction does; even on Earth, we have a multitude of different kinds of reproductive systems. But, assuming that "male" and "female" do imply a two-gamete system of reproduction in which the male gamete is smaller than the female gamete, what can a Moclan female possibly be?

One possibility is that Moclans naturally reproduced sexually, much as humans do, but that they developed technologies to reproduce asexually as well. Over the last century, humans have developed artificial reproductive technologies for many different species of animals, not only using both male and female gametes to create embryos through in vitro fertilization, but even to trick female gametes into developing, in one case resulting in a healthy adult mouse without any male parent. Perhaps Moclans were able to successfully create offspring using only the *male* gametes—this would explain why they distinguish between male and female in the first place (calling themselves an all-male species as opposed to calling themselves an asexual species, as Yaphit could) but are still able to reproduce without females. This would mean that the egg Bortus "laid" was actually an artificial incubator of some kind. Given that the Moclan ships are, like the egg, rounded with a mottled, textured surface, this doesn't seem to be out of the question. Perhaps they intentionally combine genetic information in their gametes to give their offspring some genetic diversity, since they do not seem to be a race of clones.[6] But this isn't the only possibility.

While Kelly assists the Giliac woman in childbirth, she asks Bortus for help, and he replies with the question, "Will there be an egg?" (S2E5) After witnessing the labor and birth, he remarks, "It is much easier with an egg." This implies that the egg may indeed be naturally produced by male Moclan physiology. Again, this doesn't seem to be impossible: there are animals on earth that are able to reproduce on their own when the opposite sex isn't available. Female sharks and Komodo dragons are like this, and whiptail lizards are even more extreme; the males of the species seem to have been completely wiped out and only females exist, using a complicated system of exchanging genetic information within themselves to give their offspring some genetic diversity.[7] This single-sex method of reproduction in normally sexually reproducing species, called parthenogenesis, is exclusive to females of certain species on Earth, but we cannot assume that it is impossible for males of other species to do something similar. However, by definition, the male produces the smaller gamete and the female the larger gamete. Unless female Moclans are producing enormous ova (which is unlikely, given their size), we would have to assume that the sperm is only a small part of the egg produced by Bortus. This would be a significant difference from eggs on Earth, which are single cells (indeed, the ostrich egg has the largest volume of any known single cell). Nevertheless, it would be completely coherent to claim that male Moclans evolved a way to reproduce on their own when females were not available to them, for whatever reason. Perhaps the physiological differences in size and strength between the male and female Moclans gave the males an advantage in the harsh conditions in which they lived. If males were able to reproduce without females, they could lose the impetus to help the smaller, weaker females survive. Further, if males could reproduce without females but females could not reproduce without males, this fact could contribute to Moclan culture rejecting females as flawed and dependent.

Independently reproducing individual males would not make sense of everything we're told, however. Bortus implies that two males are required to create offspring when he tells Topa that a relationship "is what comes before the egg" (S2E7). It's possible that he is just referring to a social practice—that Moclans are expected to pair off before laying eggs—or a psychological requirement—that Moclan males are unable to lay eggs until they are in the psychological state provided by a partner—but it is also possible that he is implying that some kind of reproductive activity is engaged in by the partners.

This could mean two different things, each of which somewhat changes the meaning of "male" and "female" (though perhaps with precedent). Could a Moclan female and a male reproduce, as well as two males, with the same results? If so, then Moclans seem to be isogamously reproducing beings—each parent producing the same kind of gamete. When they encountered humans and other sexually reproducing species, they could see two very definite body types, one larger and stronger built and the other slighter; perhaps this is what they thought the terms referred to, rather than to reproductive roles. If so, "male" and "female" for Moclans, would not refer to reproductive roles at all, but to other physical characteristics—what we would consider secondary sex characteristics. But again, the problem with this interpretation is that it is difficult to see how an infant Moclan displays these characteristics and could be identified as a "girl" or "boy," and how a single surgical procedure could change it. After all, the young Moclans we see don't have the brawny build of the adult males, nor do they have the chest development of the adult females.

If, on the other hand, a female Moclan cannot reproduce at all—or at least, not without a sex change operation—then perhaps the females do not play a direct role in reproduction, but aid in the care and feeding of the child. Again, on Earth, social insects like ants sometimes have a sterile "worker" type: ants that won't themselves reproduce but which help to feed and defend the queen and the rest of the colony. These sterile ants are often referred to as "female," even though they can never produce gametes. (They can be considered females possibly because they developed from the same type of embryos that the queens did, though without the treatment that would cause them to develop into fertile individuals.) Is the Moclan female a "female" in this sense—a sterile member of a worker class, which can, by receiving a surgical procedure at birth, be changed into a fertile individual? This theory has several points in its favor: females do not seem necessary for reproduction in Moclan society and (in several species on Earth) there is a precedent of calling such sterile members of a species "female."

The idea that Moclan females do not play a reproductive role is indirectly supported by the episode "Deflectors," in which a Moclan male, Lokar, tells Talla Keyali that he is attracted to her, though male attraction to females is forbidden by his culture. This is drawing an obvious parallel to the rejection of gay and lesbian relationships in many human cultures. In our own history, while many oppose such sexual orientations simply because they are not the norm, a traditional argument against them it is that sexual relations ought to be between partners who can (in theory, if not in practice) reproduce. Thomas Aquinas writes that "the sin of lust consists of seeking venereal pleasure not in accordance with right reason ... as hindering the begetting of children, there is the 'vice against nature,' which attaches to every venereal act from which generation cannot follow."[8] If Moclan "males" reproduce with each other, then a male-female pairing is, like a gay or lesbian pairing among humans, a relationship that prevents the begetting of children. While this is not mentioned as part of the reason that Lokar's choice of mates is problematic, it doesn't seem to be a stretch to claim that Moclans, like many humans, have a culture that forbids an essentially non-reproductive sexual relationship.

Bortus, on the other hand, implies that females played at least some role in the care of children. In a fascinating conversation about sex drives, Bortus compares sexual desire to "a baby, seeking it's mother's teat" (S2E2). This is of particular importance because the character to whom he is speaking, Isaac, is a non-biological life form and therefore has no babyhood memories to refer to. Is Bortus speaking of his own memories? Is there a thwarted desire to suckle in each Moclan's infancy? If so, this makes the exile of female Moclans particularly poignant: each Moclan has a memory of desiring a mother of whose existence he is not rationally aware, but who he instinctively knows *should* be there, and whom he desires with the same vivid urges that one experiences during sex. To reinforce the idea that Moclan females do breastfeed their young, we see that those females portrayed on screen do have (in true Hollywood style) chest bulges, which seem to be developed mammary glands, while the males, when shown topless, have mere nipples. Were the females "mothers" at some point not because they helped produce the young, but because they cared for and fed them? Have biological or technological changes in their species turned the females' mammary glands into mere vestigial organs—or is it possible that the females in their own colony could still breastfeed their young?

Finally, what if female and male Moclans do have the same roles as female and male humans, but the "sex change" operations are merely disguising this fact? In this case, perhaps Bortus and Klyden are a fertile couple only because Klyden was born a female. Heveena claims that there are more females than the Moclan government has ever publicly admitted—is there perhaps a female in every successfully reproducing couple? Against this interpretation is the fact that Bortus claims to have laid the egg, not Klyden.

Why Is Life Unfair for Females?

The Orville leaves much about the Moclans undescribed. We aren't even told how the males lay eggs. Nevertheless, it is probable that female Moclans are not essential for Moclan reproduction as it currently takes place on Moclus. This leads us to a significant difference between the females of Moclus and the females of Earth: their oppression has occurred for very different reasons. So rather than simply assume that Moclan males are using the same reasons as patriarchal human males but taking more extreme actions, we should ask what has led to the lower status of Moclan females. And to do that, we should consider what led to the lower status of human females in the real world.

As Simone de Beauvoir pointed out in her classic book *The Second Sex*, human females are significantly disadvantaged due to their role in reproduction. "[I]n no other [mammal] is the subordination of the organism to the reproductive function more imperious nor accepted with greater difficulty.... The male, by comparison, is infinitely more privileged: his genital life does not thwart his personal existence."[9] Whenever women are competing with men for resources and social status, their biology handicaps them. Menstruation is inconvenient at best, or cripplingly painful and humiliating at worst. Pregnancy, too, is difficult: nine months of nausea, swelling, weight gain, and exhaustion—culminating in the trauma of labor and childbirth. It doesn't end here, either; until recent advances in the creation of infant formula, breastfeeding was often the only safe way to feed human infants. This necessitates staying with the infant except for short periods of time, weeks or months in which one is unable to do most kinds of work, and often in discomfort or even intense pain. Because of the bond between mother and child during gestation and breastfeeding, the mother is usually the primary caregiver for the child even once it has been weaned.

Given these "facts of life," many human women have lived differently than their male peers. Because of the amount of time demanded by their body—whether in menstruation, pregnancy, childbirth, or breastfeeding—their education has seemed less valuable than that of men. Men were given apprenticeships, taught trades, and instructed in the liberal arts. Women were expected to spend much more time in their homes and therefore given both a less comprehensive education and a less specialized education (at least in terms of trades). Even today, there are parts of the world in which girls often do not attend school when having their period.[10] Nothing like this could explain the repression of female Moclans, however, if they played no part in reproduction. While human men could find evidence to argue that women are less intelligent because women's fertility means instruction is limited and there are fewer expectations for them to excel, there isn't an obvious reason for Moclans to be able to make the same claim for the females of their species.

Now, to be clear, if we knew that, in the past, female Moclans had a *limited, indirect role* in reproduction—like feeding infants, as Bortus implies—this could give us at least a clue about how the females on

Moclus were given a lower status. Feeding and caring for infants would limit one's life somewhat, although not necessarily in the same way that human females are limited. Nevertheless, this isn't enough to explain why the existence of Moclan females is denied and why female infants are given sex changes. After all, if a species or a culture depends for its very existence on the servitude of some of their members, this makes these members necessary and thus less likely to be eliminated. They might be abused and oppressed, but they wouldn't be eradicated. For example, ants and other social insects, as we discussed above, have sterile female workers that engage in most of the colony's interactions with their environment: collecting food, fighting, building. If ants were sentient, maybe the way the queen utilizes the worker's labor would be considered abuse or oppression. Maybe she would keep them from having political power. But the queen would never eliminate the worker ants; she'd starve. So even if female Moclans did have a limited reproductive role to play, there would have to be some other reason that Moclan females were *eradicated* from their society.

Perhaps the development of technology made Moclan females (whether in a reproductive role or just in a supporting role of caring for infants) unnecessary. If Moclan females are not needed to reproduce and no longer breastfeed infants, then some other means of reproducing and feeding infants must have been found. And if advancing technology was making a large subset of the Moclan species simply superfluous, one would expect them to fight against such technology in order to keep their livelihood and their sense of purpose. In fact, there is evidence of such a split in reactions to technology in Moclan culture: the males on Moclus live in huge cities covered in smog, while the females on their colony are surrounded by vegetation. The females also use natural dyes and textiles in their clothing, while the males seem more drawn to deep dyes and synthetic fabrics (often with dramatic Canadian smocking). Now maybe *The Orville* is simply falling into the stereotype that women are more "in tune with nature" and men are more technologically driven. But maybe the choice is more deliberate, and the reason for these differences between the way male and female Moclans live is rooted in the history of the Moclan society. If females were made unnecessary by technology, then it's possible that females turned to nature not because of an innate preference, but rather a conscious choice. Rather than a typical patriarchal society, then, what we see on Moclus is a society in which the ruling class is dependent on extensive technology.

An alternative explanation would be to take the Moclans at their word when they give reasons to dislike females. The Moclan advocate arguing that Topa should undergo a sex change, for example, says, "Females are weak. They do not possess the physical strength necessary for effective participation in industrialized Moclan society" (S1E3).[11] While the focus on industry would reinforce the former explanation, the mention of strength (and later, intelligence) gives us a different explanation. Perhaps the differences between Moclan males and females are not like human sexual differences as much as they are like certain genetic racial differences: the female's shorter height and slighter build imply lower muscle mass. And then social ostracism would make the prediction of lower intelligence in the females a self-fulfilling prophecy. While this kind of prejudice against someone because of physical and intellectual characteristics isn't sexism as we experience it, it is most definitely found in human cultures as well. (Although, if this is the right explanation, one wonders: what does a sex change operation on a Moclan female baby amount to? Does the doctor make them bigger and stronger?)

Moclan Pseudo-Sexism?

The Orville frequently exposes us to ourselves in alien form: we find in our own past a dependence on astrology ("All the World Is Birthday Cake"), religious fanaticism ("Krill"), and obsession with social media ("Majority Rule"). Whether or not the writers intended it, the plot surrounding Moclan females, when examined in a little more depth, gives us even more than the obvious reflections on sexism. If Moclan females do not play a role in reproduction, then *The Orville*'s treatment of Moclans seems to be warning us against something more complex than traditional patriarchy.

One potential issue is technological development. Martin Heidegger warns us, in his essay "The Question Concerning Technology" that technology will change the way we see the world around us, and even see others. Ideally, we see the things that surround us—our environment, our bodies, other people—as objects; we recognize them for what they are essentially. We see trees, rivers, and mountains. When we begin to use modern technology, however, Heidegger points out that we begin to see all these things as merely "standing-reserve." We see them as resources available for our use.[12] Instead of seeing a tree for what it is, we see it as a source of paper, which can be printed with news and distributed for pay. Instead of seeing a river, we see a source of hydroelectric power. Mountains become mineral deposits, or a roadblock to accessing and storing other resources. This warning of Heidegger's seems equally applicable to the Moclans: they see their planet as a place to develop, produce, and test weapons for sale to other species. And, Heidegger claims, we begin to see other persons as standing-reserve once we begin to see the world as a place of technology. Heidegger gives the example of "human resources," and the Moclans seem likewise to value each other based on their instrumental worth. If Moclans value each other merely as "effective participants" in industry, then they indeed seem to see each other as standing-reserve. The disdain that other Moclans have for females would then be the same kind of disdain we would have for a broken tool or spoiled food; it won't work, it's no good. A sex-change operation, in this case, will "fix" the Moclan in question and make her into a useful male.

In our own world, it can be all too easy to use technology to replace people around us—both in high-profile layoffs as companies computerize their white-collar and roboticize their blue-collar jobs, and even in our personal lives, when we turn to a video game or movie rather than to a friend to relax with at the end of the day. As John Maynard Keynes predicted, we have been able to greatly reduce the amount of manual work in agriculture, mining, and manufacture.[13] In fact, the family farm itself has disappeared in much of North America and been replaced by enormous factory farms. It is also easy to shun (whether intentionally or not) those around us who do not buy into the technological advances that structure our lives. We lose touch with friends who are not on our social media networks; we don't have much to discuss with people who haven't watched the same series we're bingeing; we assume that no answer to a text means that someone has chosen not to respond, instead of assuming that the number we've texted is still a landline. Moclan society, if it surgically gives females functions that have not yet been replaced by technology, is forcing them to fit into "industrialized society" with no option to back out. This is a reminder for us not to force the adoption of technology in our own society, lest we replace or exile those who do not fit in.

Even if the Moclan females were not made obsolete through the development of reproductive technology, we can still learn from the reasons that Moclans give for rejecting them: they lag behind in biological, intellectual, and social development. Unlike Kelly, who defends the claim that women are strong by exhibiting Alara Kitan's extraordinary talents, De Beauvoir actually agrees with the Moclans with respect to strength: "Woman is weaker than man; she has less muscular strength, fewer red blood cells, a lesser respiratory capacity; she runs less quickly, lifts less heavy weights—there is practically no sport in which she can compete with him; she cannot enter into a fight with the male."[14] While our society has made strides in overcoming bias against those that are of less than average strength and intelligence, this bias is definitely still present, especially when these traits are considered to be the natural state of a presumed-inferior race. Sally Haslanger points out that there is a similarity between gender and race in that both are difficult to define, both imply a system of categorizing that places one gender/race above another gender/race, and both rely on "observed or imagined ... bodily features presumed to be evidence" of either a reproductive role or an ancestral link to some geographic region.[15] Female Moclans do not seem to have reproductive roles; nor is it likely that they descend from a common region, since they seem to be born at random. The Moclan bias against females, then, seems to be something between sexism and racism, with similarities to and differences from both. Perhaps it is something like the bias experienced by people born with certain disorders, like infants with mild disorders of sex development who are still sometimes expected to undergo painful and unnecessary "normalizing" surgery, or people with Down's syndrome and other physical or intellectual differences.[16]

We hardly need to hear today that valuing human men more than women is wrong, but the fact that Moclan females play a very different role in Moclan reproduction than human females do in human reproduction means that the reason for their oppression is different from the sexism we find on earth. Nevertheless, Immanuel Kant claims that valuing persons for any of the reasons that the Moclans seem to is immoral. Kant makes this argument through an elaborate discussion of the value of the person. The only unconditionally good thing, he argues, is a good will.[17] Everything else good—whether it is chocolate or fame or a warm shower—is good in some circumstances, but bad in others (who wants a warm shower in bed, after all?). Since persons have a will that is (at least potentially) unconditionally good, we ought to be valued differently than anything that is merely conditionally good. In his own words, Kant says that humans have dignity, while everything else has a price.[18] We can compare the values of things with prices, selling them or trading them if we like, but to trade or sell something with dignity is to seriously misunderstand its value. It may be tempting to think of dignity as having infinite value, but it is perhaps better to think of it as being simply incommensurate—not translatable into price at all. The dignity of the person is why trafficking in persons is wrong and (to go back to Heidegger's language) treating others as standing-reserve is wrong. It would likewise be wrong to value someone's strength—a conditionally good characteristic, since strength can also be used for evil purposes—more than their dignity as a person.[19]

The Moclan males' treatment of females, then, should be a lesson to us: just because something looks like something we are familiar with, we shouldn't assume that it is the same. The Moclan oppression of their females is something radically different from patriarchal oppression of human females. Nevertheless, just because it is different from something wrong, that doesn't make it right. Their culture may not be sexist as we understand it, but it's definitely not just.

46 Act I: Gender, Sex and Feminism

NOTES

1. Sean Carroll, hosts, "Seth MacFarlane on Using Science Fiction to Explore Humanity," *Mindscape* (podcast), August 5, 2019, https://www.preposterousuniverse.com/podcast/2019/08/05/58-seth-macfarlane-on-using-science-fiction-to-explore-humanity/.
2. Brandon Braga, hosts, "The Orville Fan Podcast w/ Brannon Braga (08)," *Planetary Union Network: The Orville Official Fan Podcast* (podcast), November 5, 2017, https://www.owltail.com/podcast/YKYFV-Planetary-Union-Network-The-Orville-Fan-Podcast/best-episodes.
3. Aristotle, *On the Generation of Animals*, 1.2.716a14-15.
4. Lorna A. Casselton, "Mate Recognition in Fungi," *Heredity* 88, no. 2 (2002): 142, https://doi.org/10.1038/sj/hdy/6800035.
5. Kwang Wook An, Jehee Lee, and Cheol Young Choi, "Expression of Three Gonadotropin Subunits and Gonadotropin Receptor mRNA During Male-to-Female Sex Change in the Cinnamon Clownfish, Amphiprion melanopus," *Comparative Biochemistry and Physiology*, 156, no. 4 (2010): 407–415, https://doi.org/10.1016/j.cbpa.2010.03.015.
6. One may think that if the Moclans had the ability to manipulate their genes, they would also be able to eliminate females in their species simply by removing the genes responsible for this variant. This isn't necessarily the case, for three reasons: first, it's possible that their technology is not sophisticated enough and "undesired" traits show up occasionally; secondly, it may be that being female or producing female offspring is not a trait coded by genes at all, but determined by the temperature at which the egg is kept (like alligators) or some other factor. This leaves us with the question why they do not test the embryo's sex and abort any females discovered, but perhaps the "Moclan females do not exist" propaganda has so convinced parents that they opt out of such testing. A darker interpretation is that most Moclan parents do indeed have female offspring aborted, which could partly explain the lower number of females—perhaps Bortus and Klyden on the *Orville* did not have access to pre-hatching testing that would have been standard on Moclus.
7. Charles J. Cole, "Unisexual Lizards," *Scientific American* 250, no. 1 (January 1984): 94–101, https://www.jstor.org/stable/24969281.
8. Thomas Aquinas, *Summa Theologica*, Benzinger Bros edition, translated by the Fathers of the English Dominican Province (1947), Part II–II, Qu. 154, Art. 1.
9. Simone De Beauvoir, *The Second Sex* (New York: Modern Library, 1968), 65.
10. Shannon A. McMahon, Peter J. Winch, Bethany A. Caruso, Alfred F. Oburu, Emily A. Ogutu, Imelda A. Ochari, and Richard D. Rheingans, "'The girl with her period is the one to hang her head' Reflections on Menstrual Management Among Schoolgirls in Rural Kenya," *BMC International Health and Human Rights* 11, no. 7 (2011), doi: 10.1186/1472-698X-11-7.
11. An interesting twist is that the Moclans arguing that Topa should be male consider the valuable experiences Topa would have as a male, as opposed to the experiences of a female. This may seem contradictory: it is taking females' thoughts into account, when what females think "doesn't matter," according to traditional Moclan values. Perhaps the Moclans care about the potential male and what he would miss out on if he never comes into existence, rather than the actual female, and what she would miss out on if she continued to exist.
12. Martin Heidegger, "The Question Concerning Technology," in *Martin Heidegger: Basic Writings* (New York: Harper & Row Publishers, November 2008), 323.
13. John Maynard Keynes, "Economic Possibilities for Our Grandchildren (1930)," in *Essays in Persuasion* (New York: Harcourt Brace, 1932), section I.
14. De Beauvoir, *The Second Sex*, 67.
15. Sally Haslanger, "Gender and Race: (What) Are They? (What) Do We Want Them to Be?" *Noûs* 34, no. 1 (March 2000): 32, 42, 44. https://doi.org/10.1111/0029-4624.00201.
16. See Sarah Creighton, "Surgery for Intersex" *Journal of the Royal Society of Medicine* 94, no. 5 (May 2001): 218–220, https://doi.org/10.1177/014107680109400505. See also, R.B. Jones, "Parental Consent to Cosmetic Facial Surgery in Down's Syndrome," *Journal of Medical Ethics* 26, no. 2 (2000):101–102, doi: 10.1136/jme.26.2.101.
17. Immanuel Kant, *Groundwork for the Metaphysics of Morals*, edited and translated by Allen W. Wood (New Haven: Yale University Press, 2002), 9.

18. Kant, *Groundwork for the Metaphysics of Morals*, 52.
19. The Moclan rejection of females may be a rejection of the childless—people who cannot or do not reproduce. It would be wrong to value someone more if they can bring more people into the world: this would be treating the value of their descendants as something that can be summed up and compared to others' value.

Bibliography

An, Kwang Wook, Jehee Lee, and Cheol Young Choi. "Expression of Three Gonadotropin Subunits and Gonadotropin Receptor MRNA During Male-to-Female Sex Change in the Cinnamon Clownfish, Amphiprion Melanopus." *Comparative Biochemistry and Physiology*, 156, no. 4(2010): 407–415. https://doi.org/10.1016/j.cbpa.2010.03.015.

Aquinas, Thomas. *Summa Theologica*. Benzinger Bros edition translated by the Fathers of the English Dominican Province.1947.

Aristotle, *On the Generation of Animals*.

Casselton, Lorna A. "Mate Recognition in Fungi." *Heredity* 88, no. 2 (2002): 142–147. doi: 10.1038/sj/hdy/6800035.

Cole, Charles J. "Unisexual Lizards." *Scientific American* 250, no. 1 (1984): 94–100. https://www.jstor.org/stable/24969281.

Creighton, Sarah. "Surgery for Intersex," *Journal of the Royal Society of Medicine* 94, no. 5 (May 2001): 218–220. https://doi.org/10.1177/014107680109400505

De Beauvoir, Simone. *The Second Sex*. New York: Modern Library, 1968.

Haslanger, Sally. "Gender and Race: (What) Are They? (What) Do We Want Them to Be?" *Noûs* 34, no. 1 (2000): 31–55. https://doi.org/10.1111/0029-4624.00201

Heidegger, Martin. "The Question Concerning Technology." In *Martin Heidegger: Basic Writings*, edited by David Farrell Krell, 307–342. New York: Harper & Row Publishers, 1992.

Jones, R.B. "Parental Consent to Cosmetic Facial Surgery in Down's Syndrome," *Journal of Medical Ethics* 26, no. 2 (2000): 101–102. doi: 10.1136/jme.26.2.101.

Kant, Immanuel. *Groundwork for the Metaphysics of Morals*, edited and translated by Allen W. Wood, New Haven: Yale University Press, 2002.

Keynes, John Maynard. "Economic Possibilities for Our Grandchildren (1930)," in *Essays in Persuasion*. 358–373. New York: Harcourt Brace, 1932.

Kono, Tomohiro, Yayoi Obata, Quiong Wu, Katsutoshi Niwa, Yukiko Ono, Yuji Yamamoto, Eun Sung Park, Jeong-Sun Seo and Hidehiko Ogawa. That Can Develop to Adulthood." *Nature* 428, no. 6985 (2004): 860–864. doi: 10.1038/nature02402.

McMahon, Shannon A., Peter J.Winch, Bethany A. Caruso, Alfred F. Obure, Emily A. Ogutu, Imelda A. Ochari, and Richard D. Rheingans. "'The girl with her period is the one to hang her head' Reflections on Menstrual Management Among Schoolgirls in Rural Kenya." *BMC International Health and Human Rights* 11, no. 7 (2011). doi: 10.1186/1472-698X-11-7

Darulioian Assault
The Orville *and Sexual Consent*
Michael R. Berry

The depiction of a caveman clubbing a woman and dragging her back to his cave by the hair for sexual relations has been a mainstay of popular culture. In cartoons, the caveman is depicted as ugly, oafish, and dumb and often displays an evil grin of anticipation. The woman is usually buxom, blonde, and beautiful, and even sometimes smiling, holding a flower, or has hearts over her head. Such cartoons usually get an uncritical chuckle. After careful thought, however, one realizes they are horrific. Indeed, they are appalling in many ways—not the least of which is the fact that no woman, anywhere at any time, would be delighted at the prospect of being clubbed and then dragged by the hair for any purpose, much less the one the caveman has in mind. Yes, some like entomologist Randy Thornhill argue that forcible rape may have been an effective reproduction strategy for cavemen who couldn't otherwise find a mate.[1] But even if he's right (and I'm definitely not saying he is), that wouldn't make such a thing ethically acceptable. Our laughter whitewashes the morally problematic nature of such depictions, and demonstrates something that one would hope that we, as a society, have progressed beyond.

The Orville's episode "Cupid's Dagger," however, seems to indicate that we haven't ... or, at least, that's what I would like to explore. Darulio's pheromone, which uncontrollably entices people into sexual relations without their consent, sure functions a lot like the caveman's club. But not only did we laugh; the crew of the USS *Orville* used that club to end a war without, for a second, questioning the ethical implications of doing so. Is "Cupid's Dagger" just a sci-fi version of the caveman cartoon? Has *The Orville*'s writing staff, which is usually very progressive, missed the ethical mark here? Or are we overlooking something important?

To get to the bottom of this, I would like to address the serious questions about sexual assault and consent that "Cupid's Dagger" generates, and the philosophical issues it raises. I begin by detailing the plot of "Cupid's Dagger" before exploring what constitutes sexual assault. I then consider issues relevant to free will and how they relate to consent, before arguing that indeed, this episode gets it very wrong when it comes to responsibility and sexual relations. I conclude by arguing that this episode does not establish a pattern. Another episode, "A Happy Refrain," gets it right concerning sexual consent, and generally *The Orville*'s moral compass points in the right direction.

"Cupid's Dagger"

In order to fully appreciate how problematic "Cupid's Dagger" (S1E9) might be, some setup and summary is in order. In the very first scene of the very first episode of the series, Ed Mercer catches his wife Kelly Grayson in bed with a retepsian (a blue alien that shoots goo out of his head), and Ed ends their marriage as a result. Later, of course, Ed is appointed captain of the USS *Orville* and (as you likely know) Kelly is assigned to be his commanding officer. A captain with his ex-wife as his first officer: it's comedy gold.

About a year later, a dispute over the origin of an ancient artifact arises on the planet Lopovius, and the USS *Orville* is sent to mediate the dispute. Two factions, the Bruidians and the Navarians, both claim ownership of the artifact because whoever has the rightful claim can claim the planet as their property. A forensic anthropologist is assigned to discover which faction can claim legitimate ownership of the artifact, but it turns out to be the retepsian that Kelly slept with—who we now learn is named Darulio.

Once Darulio is on board, however, the crew starts behaving unusually. Kelly goes to tell Darulio that "it's never gonna happen again," but after Darulio straightens a single hair on her head, Kelly becomes entranced and eventually falls in love with him. When Ed catches them sleeping together (again), he goes to throw Darulio off the ship ... but then Ed falls in love with Darulio too. And while Kelly and Ed fight over Darulio, Dr. Claire Finn falls in love with Yaphit (the hilarious but grotesque gelatin creature voiced by Norm Macdonald) whom she has always hated. Chief of Security Alara Kitan catches them doing "I don't know what," a seemingly lewd sex act where Claire is engulfed in Yaphit.

The explanation for everyone's odd behavior comes when Alara confronts Darulio and he reveals that, every year, his species goes into heat and releases a pheromone that helps them "attract mates." When he shook hands with Ed and Kelly, the pheromone caused them to fall in "artificial, crippling love with" Darulio, and neglect everything else. This includes their duties regarding the conflict between the Bruidians and the Navarians which, in the meantime, has escalated into a war. When Darulio realizes the costs of his actions, he suggests the crew use his pheromone to make the leaders of the warring factions fall in love. They do, and the war ends. And in the final scene, Darulio reveals that, maybe, perhaps, he was in heat when Kelly fell for him a year ago and ruined her marriage to Ed.

We laugh at the episode—and, granted, it is funny. But upon reflection, one is forced to ask oneself: *Isn't Darulio's pheromone (or Cupid's dagger, if you will) like the caveman's club ... or even, maybe worse yet, a date rape drug? It makes those who wouldn't otherwise want to sleep with him, sleep with him. I mean, it would be one thing if he didn't know they were being affected. After all, he says he comes from "a culture where it is considered rude to turn down sex." But he clearly knew. So isn't he essentially guilty of sexual assault?*

It really seems he is. But if so, why does everyone seem fine with it? I mean Alara is a bit upset, but the other crew members not only look past what Darulio did, they use the pheromone to force the Bruidian and the Navarian ambassadors to fall in love—and they are clearly going to have sex. So aren't they tricking both of them into having sex without consent? And yet no one, neither Ed, nor Alara, nor Kelly, has a problem with this. No one even stops to ask: "I know we are stopping a war here ... but is this morally right?" This, clearly, is the question to ask. And to answer it, we need to explore the concept of sexual consent.

Defining Sexual Consent

Darulio says that "it's harmless. The worst thing that happens" as a result of his pheromone is "we all have great sex." But if Ed and Kelly have not given consent, it's not harmless. Darulio having sex with them would be sexual assault. And it really seems that Ed and Kelly have not given consent. But to make sure, we need to ask what constitutes consent.

Some might think this question has a simple answer, but in reality it is perplexing and difficult. What guidelines dictate what sexual consent is? What characteristics does it have, and how important are each of them? Of course, it involves the person *agreeing* to the sexual encounter—but agreement can come in many forms, both verbal and non-verbal. And agreement doesn't mean much unless it is given *intentionally*. As University of Maryland Associate Professor Hallie Liberto puts it in her article "Intention and Sexual Consent,"

> Can we give consent without intending to give consent? Philosophers have recently argued: no. Consent involves the waiving of a right or, at the very least, the releasing of another person from a duty that he or she would otherwise have toward you. Now, there are other ways that we can change what duties others have toward us that do not

require intention. We can forfeit our rights (e.g., by attacking someone or by abandoning our property). We might come to need help, resulting in another person suddenly holding a duty of beneficence. However, consent is special because of its voluntary nature.[2]

Because of its voluntary nature, the intentional aspect of consent is related to what Planned Parenthood argues is key in defining sexual assault: the fact that consent is freely given. As their website puts it, "Without consent, sexual activity (including oral sex, genital touching, and vaginal or anal penetration) is sexual assault or rape." In order for sexual activity to be consensual, it must include the following characteristics

- **Freely given.** Consenting is a choice you make without pressure, manipulation, or under the influence of drugs or alcohol.
- **Reversible.** Anyone can change their mind about what they feel like doing, anytime. Even if you've done it before, and even if you're both naked in bed.
- **Informed.** You can only consent to something if you have the full story. For example, if someone says they'll use a condom and then they don't, there isn't full consent.
- **Enthusiastic.** When it comes to sex, you should only do stuff you WANT to do, not things that you feel you're expected to do.
- **Specific.** Saying yes to one thing (like going to the bedroom to make out) doesn't mean you've said yes to others (like having sex).[3]

Although it employs a silly acronym, FRIES, to help readers remember, legally speaking, Planned Parenthood is right. The idea that consent is freely given is key to its legal definition. As Law Professor Aya Gruber put it, "today the nature of rape as a 'harm to autonomy' is rarely up for debate."[4]

But philosophically speaking, this causes problems. As Gruber recognizes, "Consent is a philosophical, psychological, and legal quagmire ... philosophically, premising morality on consent implicates complicated theories of free will and determinism."[5] In other words, if consent must be freely given, we are immediately faced with the philosophical question of whether free will exists. As beings, can we control any of our actions or are we locked into actions over which we have no control? If the latter is true, and we do not have free will, we cannot give consent. And as we shall now see, the question of whether humans have free will is not an easy one to answer.

Free Will and Consent

Given what we have discussed, here's the problem we now face. If consent is voluntary, as Liberto suggests, then it is freely given. And that seems right. Consent is, at the very least, "freely given assent." But if that's true, then consent can only be given if free will exists. A person can only freely assent to something if a person has free will. But those who have the relevant expertise on this topic, like philosophers[6] and neuroscientists,[7] don't think free will exists—at least not in the "libertarian sense," which is the notion of free will most people embrace.

What is the libertarian notion of free will? One has libertarian free will if one, roughly put, has "the ability to choose to do otherwise." On the libertarian notion, when it comes to whether one will choose to do X or not choose to do X, one can freely do so only if there are "alternative possibilities"—that is, only if both options are equally possible. If (for example) choosing to do X is really the only possibility, the only thing that could happen, then one cannot choose to do X freely. (And yes, that seems obvious. That's why this is the notion of free will that most ordinary people embrace.) But there are many reasons to think that, when it comes to what we choose to do, there is only one option.

Take what we have learned from neuroscience. A person's bodily actions are a result of their neural activity, and what decisions a person makes to do with their body is determined by their brain structure. Upon the receipt of a certain stimuli, a person's brain goes through a series of neural firings which will, based on its structure, result in that person making a particular decision. It may seem from their perspective that they could have chosen otherwise, because the neural firing process produces the sensation of "considering options," but this is just an illusion. In reality, only one decision could be reached—the decision that their brain was physically configured to reach. Thus, there are no alternate possibilities and (since this would be true of everyone) no free will.

Of course, one might think that one has a choice about what structure their brain has, but that too is ultimately outside of a person's control. A person's brain structure is ultimately a result of their DNA and their environment, both of which are outside of their control. Granted, a person can choose to put themselves in one environment or another, but such a choice will also be the product of their brain structure at the time, which itself will be a result of their DNA and previous environments. Extrapolating back into the past, ultimately, every decision a person makes is causally determined by DNA and environmental stimuli over which the person had no control. And so, it seems, we do not have free will in the libertarian sense.[8]

And, again, the libertarian notion is what most people have in mind when they believe that they have free will. It certainly seems that Liberto has the libertarian notion of free will in mind when she says that consent is voluntary. But if consent is "assent freely given" (in the libertarian sense), and libertarian free will does not exist, then it is impossible for anyone to give consent. Every sexual act by anyone, of any gender, at any time, would be sexual assault.

But that, of course, is obviously false. To solve this problem we might do what many philosophers have done to protect the notion that humans have free will: embrace compatibilism. "Compatibilism" gets its name from the notion that free will and *determinism* are compatible, determinism being the doctrine that the universe is a deterministic system in which all events are the inevitable result of cause and effect. In such a universe, there is only one possible future—the one dictated by the present physical state of the universe and the laws of physics. If it is true that free will can exist even in a universe that is deterministic, then clearly free will does not require alternate possibilities. So, even if what decision I make is determined by my brain structure, and my brain structure is ultimately outside of my control, and thus I could not choose to do anything but what I will choose to do, I could still have free will—at least according to compatibilism.

But how, one might rightly ask, could a person have free will in a deterministic universe? The most popular approach to answering this question involves essentially redefining what free will is. Philosopher Harry Frankfurt, for example, argues that free will does not require alternate possibilities.[9] Instead, Frankfurt suggests, a decision is free as long as it is made in accordance with one's second order desires. A smoker, for example, who desires a cigarette may not be acting freely when they smoke. But that is them acting on a first order desire. If they fight that desire, and instead act on their overarching or greater desire to not be a smoker—their desire to not desire cigarettes anymore—and thus decide to not smoke that cigarette, then (according to Frankfurt) they are acting freely. That desire to no longer desire cigarettes is a "second order" desire, and if a person acts on such a desire, they are acting freely. And this is true, even if acting on that second order desire (and thus not smoking) is something that their brain structure determined they would do—even if, that is, they couldn't have done otherwise.

If this definition of free will is right, then we can have free will. And if we can have free will, we can voluntarily give assent. And if we can voluntarily give assent, then we can consent to sexual activity. So on the compatibilist notion of free will, Liberto's definition of consent does not make consent impossible. And that's good. The problem is, if we go with the compatibilist's understanding of free will, and Liberto's definition of consent, then what happened to Ed and Kelly didn't constitute sexual assault ... even though, as we have discussed, it seems it clearly did.

Why, on the compatibilist notion of free will, would what Darulio did to Ed and Kelly not constitute sexual assault? Well, consider what the pheromone did to Kelly. At first, it seems like it just created a first order desire in her—like the addict's desire for a drug.

54   Act I: Gender, Sex and Feminism

Kitan:	Okay, so what happened exactly?
Grayson:	I don't know. I went to the lab to tell him there was nothing between us anymore, but then I looked into his eyes, and I guess I forgot how gorgeous he is.
Kitan:	Gorgeous? Really?
Grayson:	Those aqua blue eyes against that deep blue skin? Ridiculous.
Kitan:	My mom redid our bathroom in those colors. I guess it's nice? …
Grayson:	He has this magnetism. And then, the next thing I knew, we're back in my quarters.
Kitan:	Wow.
Grayson:	It's just [SIGHS] It's hard to explain. It's like a drug.… this super intense sexual desire, and this rush every time I see him. He's all I can think about.

But then we learn it's more than that. The pheromone changed Kelly at a fundamental level, changing even the kind of person that she wants to be. She no longer has second order desires about being a good officer, or even a good person. She just wants to be with Darulio.

Grayson:	…He's all I can think about.
Kitan:	So much so that you forgot about the arrival of the delegates?
Grayson:	[Dismissively] Oh, it's fine, it all worked out. You know, I think the first time around with Darulio, all I could think about was how badly I messed up with Ed. You know, maybe I was so busy feeling guilty that I missed something.
Kitan:	Missed what?
Grayson:	That I'm in love with him. Darulio's the one. He's my soulmate. Should I get bangs?

The same is true of Ed, who skirts all his responsibilities as captain and doesn't even care that he had neglected his duties so much that he is about to be responsible for the war brewing between the Navarians and Bruidians.

Bortus:	Bridge to captain Mercer. Please respond.
Mercer:	(Freshly showered, towel on head, to Darulio): Don't answer, don't answer. I'm not here, I'm not here.…
Darulio:	Those fleets are about to destroy each other.
Mercer:	I love your big blue head.
Darulio:	But shouldn't you be on the bridge?
Mercer:	Ugh. I'm always on the bridge. This is where I want to be right now.
Darulio:	But you're the captain. And there's a war starting out there.
Mercer:	The only thing I'm captain of right now is your taut physique. Now get over here!

Indeed, the pheromone seemed to even change his sexual orientation. It not only creates desires but alters a person's second order desires by changing the kind of person that they are.

At one point, Kitan tries to downplay the effect of the pheromone, but Darulio pushes back and explains what it does.

Darulio: I didn't mean to affect Ed and Kelly, but it probably happened when we shook hands in the shuttle bay.
Kitan: And now they're both in artificial, crippling love with you.
Darulio: Oh, there's nothing artificial about it. They're experiencing feelings. Chemically induced feelings, I grant you, but feelings nonetheless.

One might argue, of course, that because the feelings are "chemically induced" that consent hasn't been given. But a chemically induced feeling is ultimately what love is, even in normal circumstances. One feels love when one's brain is affected chemically in certain ways.[10] If Ed and Kelly were to fall in love with Darulio without the pheromone, what would happen in their brain looks very much the same as what would happen with the pheromone. So this fact is inconsequential. What is consequential is the fact that Darulio's pheromone seems to create in those it affects a second order sexual desire for the pheromone carrier. It's like the caveman's club, if the caveman's club didn't knock out its victim, but instead created in the clubbed person a genuine deep down (second order) desire to want to have sex with the caveman.

Think of it this way. The definition from Planned Parenthood makes it clear that consent cannot occur under the influence of alcohol or drugs. Alcohol and drugs like roofies lower inhibitions towards certain behavior but those behaviors are still there in the person. A person under their influence seems to lack the ability to consent. The pheromone that Darulio transmits acts differently, however. It doesn't reduce an inhibition against a desire; it completely replaces one pre-existing second order desire with another. For example, hating Darulio is something that Ed does in the very core of his being; Darulio is largely responsible for his and Kelly's divorce and Ed is (let's admit it) still in love with her. For the pheromone to not only make Ed forgive Darulio but to make him want to be with Darulio at the expense of everything else, it had to have changed Ed down to the very core of his being. The same is true of Kelly, who initially clearly indicated that nothing in her wanted to be with Darulio again, and certainly didn't want to hurt Ed, but who under the influence of the pheromone puts all that completely aside.

If that's true—if that is what Darulio's pheromone does to a person—then on the Frankfurtian compatibilist understanding of free will, those acting under the influence of Darulio's pheromone are acting freely. The pheromone *makes them freely give consent* and thus what Darulio has done DOESN'T constitute sexual assault. But that seems ludicrous. Not only would I dare say that most people would agree that it is sexual assault, and that Ed and Kelly are not freely choosing to do what they are doing (even though they are acting in accordance with their second order wants and desires)—but the notion that the pheromone can *make* them *freely* give consent seems to be a contradiction in terms. You can't *make* someone do something *freely*. Yes, on the compatibilist notion of free will that is possible. But since it is so counterintuitive, this seems to be a good reason in and of itself to reject compatibilism. And if we reject it, the compatibilist notion of free will cannot save the notion that consent is "freely given assent."

So, in summary, here is the pickle jar we are in. We usually think that consent is "freely given assent." But since it seems that free will doesn't exist, it would seem impossible for consent to ever be given. We could get out of this problem by embracing a compatibilist definition of free will, like Frankfurt's—but that would force us to say that things like what happened to Ed and Kelly do not constitute sexual assault, when they clearly do. So, either way you slice it, there is a problem with conceiving of consent as "voluntary assent." And not even Alara can break open that pickle jar.

Resolving the Conflict

The solution, however, may lie not in redefining what free will is, but in reconceiving what consent means. And I can use the episode to reveal how we might reconceive it. Consider what happens at the end of the episode. Ed and Kelly ask Darulio whether he was in "heat" when he was with Kelly before. The implication is, if he was, then Kelly wasn't really to blame for her actions because she was under the influence of the pheromone. Darulio says "maybe," but it seems that if he had said yes, this would have changed everything! Knowing this would change their evaluation of her actions.

In the same way, if Ed and Kelly had known about the pheromone during the episode, they likely would have removed consent. And this fact is what seems to have made Darulio's actions grossly immoral: the fact that he knew he was in heat, but didn't tell anyone, and took advantage of it. Consider again the words of Liberto.

> If I hoodwink another person into rendering consent, we typically do not consider that person to have rendered morally valid consent. This might be true even if he has rendered legally valid consent. I may count on him failing to read the small print on a consent form, and so have legal permission to continue using him in my research study. However, moral philosophers would be loath to consider this consent fully voluntary—since the research subject did not intend to agree to partake in a study as described by the small print on the consent form…. I have suggested that consent is voluntary, and that the voluntary nature of consent requires that consent be intentional. [But] I have also suggested that misinformation or lack of information has the power to undermine morally valid consent, since it can result in situations in which people agree to do or allow what is outside the scope of their intentions.[11]

With this in mind, we might suggest something along this line as a better definition of consent: "Sexual consent is given when one assents to an activity and there is no salient information (that the other party could reasonably be expected to have revealed) that one could learn that would make one change their mind." This allows for consent to be given, but also makes clear why what happened to Ed and Kelly does constitute sexual assault. I would argue that this definition, while not solving all the problems of consent, does provide a better path for adjudicating when there has been genuine consent.

But how would this definition manifest itself in this episode? Let's examine several scenes and determine how the episode might have been different had the producers of the show had this definition in mind.

First, let's look at Darulio's action. He does not inform anyone of his condition until the very end of the episode. This is salient information that could have changed the behaviors of the people involved. It is reasonable to say that one should be informed about exposure to a powerful chemical agent, especially one that can make you want to "bang or be banged" by a blue alien (even if he does look like Rob Lowe). Had he provided salient information about his being in heat when he first boarded the USS *Orville*, where he informed the commanding officers and chief medical officer, appropriate actions could have been taken to ensure valid consent by all parties. Requiring Darulio to wear gloves as a protection against unintended transmission of the pheromone, for example, would seem to be a necessary first step. This is analogous to someone wearing a condom to protect against sexually transmitted diseases and pregnancy. Indeed, making the promise to someone that you will wear a condom because the other person requires it as a condition of sex is very relevant salient information.

How do we determine what is salient information? Tom Dougherty lays out two criteria.

> In making this claim, I stipulate this italicized phrase to be understood as follows. First, the deception must concern the sexual encounter. Since each person is an essential part of the sexual encounter, one is deceived about the sexual encounter by deception about the other person. For example, this would include deception about whether this person is using birth control, about his or her profession, or about his or her mental attitudes. Second, the deception must concern a deal breaker—a feature of the sexual encounter to which the other person's will is opposed. This requires more than concealing an undesirable feature. It must be the case that the other person is all things considered unwilling to engage in the sexual encounter, given that it has this feature.[12]

Darulio's actions certainly violate both of these standards with regards to Ed and Kelly. First, the deception is concerning the sexual encounter, i.e., the knowledge that the transmission of the pheromone acts to induce sexual behaviors. The second standard is also violated. Both Ed and Kelly make it clear that they initially don't want to engage in sex with Darulio, thus clearly communicating that sex with Darulio is against their will. Thus, what Darulio did was wrong.

The situation with Yaphit and Dr. Finn is different; while it is not ideal, it does not involve Yaphit sexually assaulting Dr. Finn. Yaphit is not being deceptive because he is unaware that he has had the pheromone transmitted to him. When Yaphit touches Dr. Finn in the medical bay, he does not do so to intentionally transmit the pheromone but rather as a normal part of his interaction with the doctor. His transmission of the pheromone is unknowing and in his mind, not "concerning the sexual encounter." Other behaviors he engages in during that scene could be considered "concerning the sexual encounter" such as his singing the romantic song and the delivery of the flowers because these actions were intentional and with knowledge of the potential that they may lead to sex. But those would not be relevant for our concerns here.

Other examples from the show should also be evaluated from this standard to determine whether consent has been freely given. For example, what the crew does at the end of the episode to end the war is especially problematic. If the crew had at least had a conversation about weighing the positive consequences of ending the war with the morally problematic nature of forcing two people who hate each other to fall in love, have sex, and get married—well, that would have been one thing. But instead, they essentially weaponize the pheromone to resolve the ongoing war, without any thought to the morally questionable nature of the action. To make matters worse, the pheromone seems to wear off. One could reasonably foresee that, once they realize what has happened, they could hold even greater anger because of this situation and make an escalated war inevitable. This would undo any "good" they had accomplished with the immoral act they committed.

Actions to Be Modeled

"Cupid's Dagger" presents many actions that are very problematic with regards to the idea of giving consent in a sexual relationship. These include Darulio's lack of candor regarding his transmission of the pheromone and the crew of the USS *Orville* weaponizing the pheromone as a method of preventing a war. As an example of morally suspect behavior, this episode is a really good "bad" example. And the fact that it does not critically evaluate those bad actions make us worry about laughing at it in the same way that we worry about laughing at the caveman cartoon. Yes, maybe it's funny at first glance—but it also seems to whitewash sexual assault.

However, two members of the crew can provide us an example of how consent should be obtained. In "A Happy Refrain" (S2E6), Dr. Claire Finn and the Kaylon Isaac begin a romantic relationship. This relationship is complicated by the fact that Isaac is an android. Despite this, however, Claire begins to develop romantic feelings towards Isaac. She invites him on a date to a concert and Isaac accepts because one of his primary missions while on board is to study human behavior since Kaylons don't have emotions. Isaac believes this to be a good learning opportunity. And, on top of this episode being one of the most beloved of the series, I believe that it can also stand as a correction to "Cupid's Dagger." Why? Because each character respects and gives consent to romantic gestures that respect the autonomy of the other.

Several examples from the show provide guidance as to how to properly consent to romantic overtures. First, Claire asks Isaac to the concert and both begin preparations for their date. Claire discusses the problematic issues with other friends that arise from dating someone who is believed to have no emotions. This is a conscious action that is well thought out. It meets the criteria laid out by Planned Parenthood because it is informed and reversible. Isaac also gathers information about the parameters of dating by seeking advice from two other crew members, Helmsman Gordon Malloy and Chief Engineer John LaMarr. John suggests that Isaac look "snazzy" by wearing clothes for the occasion. Kaylons don't normally wear any clothing so this is a big change. When Isaac meets Claire at her quarters to pick her up, she notices that he is wearing clothing. While his appearance has changed, she is informed and cognizant that he has made an effort for her. There is no deception involved. Later, on another date, Isaac fully transforms his appearance into a human being replica. He does so by first meeting Claire in his normal form and then with the help of the onboard simulator, he shows his transformation to her. Claire asks, "Is that you?" and Isaac responds, "Affirmative." Had he not done that, then that would be deception and the action would be morally suspect.

Another example from the episode is when the two go on a second date. While at a restaurant simulation, Claire reaches across the table and kisses Isaac. Consent is given by Isaac's action of leaning towards Claire to receive the kiss. He later says that Claire can kiss him again. This is fully informed consent on both their parts. Claire then says that she would like to do more than kiss and changes the simulation from a restaurant to her quarters. Isaac accepts the change in scenery and the two engage in consensual coitus.

Later in the episode, the two of them have a disagreement and they end the relationship. Claire is heartbroken and the breakup also leads Isaac to make a mistake while making a scientific calculation. Kaylons don't make mistakes like that and it leads Isaac to realize that he is in love with

Claire. He and Ed have a discussion about it and Isaac clearly identifies that Claire has ended the relationship. Ed says that if Claire sees Isaac make an attempt to reconcile with her that she might be open to resuming the relationship. Isaac makes a grand gesture in front of Claire and the crew. He then apologizes for his behavior and asks to resume their relationship. She accepts. Isaac's behavior fits well within the morally acceptable area of consent. There is no coercion, no deception, an acceptance of Claire's ability to say no and Isaac's acceptance that their relationship has evolved.

Lessons to Be Learned

As one can see throughout this book, *The Orville* provides many valuable lessons regarding things like moral philosophy. As a rule, morally speaking, *The Orville* tends to get things right. As one can see from this essay, however, the episode "Cupid's Dagger" stands out as an exception to this rule. Darulio's actions or lack of actions are inconsiderate, self-centered, and lack the consent that is mandatory in any sexual relationship, and the crew does not appropriately condemn them. Fortunately, "A Happy Refrain" provides a counterpoint by providing an excellent example of what true consent means in a sexual relationship. So here's hoping that Claire and Isaac find their happy forever love, and that *The Orville* doesn't again steer as far astray as it did in "Cupid's Dagger."

Notes

1. Randy Thornhill, *A Natural History of Rape: Biological Bases of Sexual Coercion* (Bradford Books, 1621); Tim Birkhead, "The Rape of Science," *New Scientist*, February 1, 2003, https://www.newscientist.com/article/mg17723806-300-the-rape-of-science/.
2. Hallie Liberto, "Intention and Sexual Consent," *Philosophical Explorations* 20, no. 2 (2017): 127–141, https://doi.org/10.1080/13869795.2017.1356359127.
3. "Sexual Consent," *Planned Parenthood*, https://www.plannedparenthood.org/learn/relationships/sexual-consent.
4. Aya Gruber, "Consent Confusion," *Cardozo Law Review 38*, no. 415 (December 2016): 422–423,
https://scholar.law.colorado.edu/articles/11.
5. Gruber, "Consent Confusion," 421.
6. David Bourget and David J. Chalmers, "What Do Philosophers Believe?," *Philosophical Studies* 170, no. 3 (2014): 465–500, https://doi.org/10.1007/s11098-013-0259-7. You can see a rundown of the results of the study here: https://philpapers.org/surveys/results.pl;.
7. Adam Bear, "What Neuroscience Says About Free Will," *Scientific American*, April 28, 2016, https://blogs.scientificamerican.com/mind-guest-blog/what-neuroscience-says-about-free-will/.
8. For more on the philosophic and neuroscientific reasons to doubt libertarian free will, see David Kyle Johnson, "Does Free Will Exist?," *Cambridge University Press* 15, no. 42 (Spring 2016): 53–70, https://doi.org/10.1017/S1477175615000238.
9. He does so with a thought experiment where a brain implant would prevent a person

from "choosing to not do X," but remains inactive because they choose to do X, and thus they can so freely. See H.G. Frankfurt, "Alternate possibilities and moral responsibility," *The Journal of Philosophy* 66, no. 23 (1969): 829–839.
    10. "Love is a Chemical Reaction, Scientists Find," *PBS News Hour*, February 13, 1009, https://www.pbs.org/newshour/science/science-jan-june09-love_02-13.
    11. Liberto, "Intention and Sexual Assault," 127.
    12. Tom Dougherty, "Sex, Lies, and Consent," *Ethics* 123, no. 4 (July 2013):717–744, https://doi.org/10.1086/670249.

Bibliography

Bear, Adam. "What Neuroscience Says About Free Will." *Scientific American*, April 28, 2016. https://blogs.scientificamerican.com/mind-guest-blog/what-neuroscience-says-about-free-will/.

Birkhead, Tim. "The Rape of Science." *New Scientist*, February 1, 2003. https://www.newscientist.com/article/mg17723806-300-the-rape-of-science/.

Bourget, David, and David J. Chalmers. "What Do Philosophers Believe?" *Philosophical Studies* 170, no. 3 (2014): 465–500. https://doi.org/10.1007/s11098-013-0259-7.

Dougherty, Tom. "Sex, Lies, and Consent." *Ethics* 123, no. 4 (July 2013): 717–744. https://doi.org/10.1086/670249.

Gruber, Aya. "Consent Confusion." *Cardozo Law Review 38*, no. 415 (December 2016): 422-423. https://scholar.law.colorado.edu/articles/11.

Liberto, Hallie. "Intention and Sexual Consent." *Philosophical Explorations* 20, no. 2 (2017): 127–141. https://doi.org/10.1080/13869795.2017.1356359127.

"Love Is a Chemical Reaction, Scientists Find." *PBS News Hour*, February 13, 2009. https://www.pbs.org/newshour/science/science-jan-june09-love_02-13.

"Sexual Consent." *Planned Parenthood*, https://www.plannedparenthood.org/learn/sex-and-relationships/sexual-consent.

Thornhill, Randy. *A Natural History of Rape: Biological Bases of Sexual Coercion*. Bradford Books, 1621.

Toward a Queer Utopia
Alien Alterity and Sexuality in The Orville

Liz Fairchild

"Storying cannot any longer be put into the box of human exceptionalism."
—Donna Haraway, *Staying with the Trouble*[1]

Science fiction often locates queerness in the nonhuman, extraterrestrial body as a means of exploring human gender and sexuality without the need for human historicity or hegemony to frame the conversation. This queering is signified and legitimized not simply in the alien species' appearance as other and a likely visible proxy for a human ethnic group, but also through nonhuman cultural and moral expectations. In other words, science fiction cultural productions locate the alterity of queerness in "the alien in our midst,"[2] and in the other of the nonhuman.

Sometimes this presentation of queerness generatively addresses our current inequities, but often it does so in ways that reify normative cultural and sexual identities. Take *Star Trek* for example. While the *Star Trek* universe, in many ways, attempts to generate a utopia that embraces all identities, it often fails to reproduce queerness as vital and necessary. Queerness in *Star Trek* is both legitimized as an other to be tolerated, and scrutinized as an other to be changed. While species such as the Klingons are tolerated and even at times revered for their differences, they are also scrutinized for their unhumanness, their unwhiteness, and their sexual deviance from the human norm. As such, the queer *viewer* may find power in the sexual alterity represented, but *Star Trek* itself reifies heteronormativity through its narrow human utopia. Indeed, until *Star Trek: Discovery*, there weren't any openly gay characters on *Star Trek*. But even then, it's not clear how generative this queer representation was. Wendy Pearson astutely wonders "whether the inclusion of a gay character on a show that presupposes an already heteronormative view of the human future can be said to 'queer' that future in any significant way."[3]

Seth McFarlane's *The Orville*, on the other hand, pays homage to *Star Trek* in many ways while also critiquing its insistence on human-centric socio-political order, as well as its penchant for promoting sexual normativity via human (monogamous) sexual primacy. Consequently, this essay will explore how *The Orville* contends with diversity, sexuality, and *the other* in ways that help posit a vital and radical queer utopia that bends and at times breaks the notion of Cartesian dualism–Descartes' insistence that reason and rational thought dictate an irreconcilable separation between the body and the mind. By exploring nonhuman and nonhumanoid relationships, in concert with alien/interspecies relationships that are rendered queer, *The Orville* succeeds in rethinking how utopia must be *visibly queer* to aptly render an equitable society. While *The Orville* still envisions a human-centric utopia in space, it succeeds in challenging the heteronormative framework by repeatedly questioning human supremacy and by centering posthuman, nonhuman, and unfamiliar bodies and relationships.

Setting the Stage

The Orville embraces a utopia that recognizes and produces queerness, deviant culture, and sex, drugs, and rock n' roll as critical components of a desirable future, rather than seeing these elements as factors that must be eliminated to improve the galaxy. This is legible in the centrality of characters like Yaphit, a nonhumanoid, yellow, gelatinous alien capable of taking many forms; Bortus and Klyden, a male couple from the planet of Moclus; as well as the relationship between the artificial lifeform Isaac and Dr. Claire Finn, a human woman from Earth. *The Orville* revises Earth's contemporary inequities by normalizing non-dominant sexualities and sexual and social behaviors. I say normalize because these sexual differences are not showcased as oddities or side notes, but rather as dominant and consistent parts of the reality that *The Orville* inhabits. As a proclaimed homage to *Star Trek*, creator Seth McFarlane's reintroduction of drinking, karaoke, gambling, practical jokes, sexual exploration, and polyamory into a *Star Trek–like* utopia help the viewer dismiss western heteronormativity and puritanical culture as the only modalities for desirable futures. The ship's journey through two-dimensional space, vast zoos that keep sentient lifeforms as exhibits, and a trip to Moclus to watch Lt. Commander Bortus urinate, all serve to take the sheen of sanitization off the sterile and modern aesthetic of the *Orville*'s future. By adding humor into the universe, we are also able to see some of the absurdity of *Star Trek*'s uptight and strict sense of what is right and wrong.

The Orville can be interpreted as both overtly and covertly queer, engaging with all three categories outlined by Wendy Pearson's "Alien Cryptographies."[4] Now 20 years old, her framework is still a viable means of reading and creating the queer in science fiction. As she articulates, there are "two quite different strategic interventions of 'queer' into the world of science fiction—one is the performance of a *queer reading* and the other is a recognition of a *queer text*."[5] A *queer reading* entails a desire to uncover queerness within a text's metaphorical and symbolic meanings; a *queer text* is overtly and intentionally contending with queer ideas, identities, and desires. Pearson also adds a third form called the *proto-queer*, a text that "effects a kind of discursive challenge to the naturalized understanding of sexuality and its concomitant sociocultural surround."[6] By performing a queer reading of Isaac and Claire, analyzing the queer text of Bortus and Klyden, and the proto-queer characterization of Yaphit, *The Orville* becomes a rich property for queer meaning-making and queer empowerment.

Creating Queer Utopia

José Esteban Muñoz's term "anti-normative" most clearly describes and connotes a "rejection of normative feelings"[7] as imperative to a queer utopia. "Queerness is utopian, and there is something queer about the utopian"[8] Muñoz notes in *Cruising Utopia*, which is to say we cannot have a utopia without queerness. As Jason Haslam similarly posits, science fiction as a genre should be, at its core, a queering of realism.[9] Clearly, these two scholars are recognizing the inextricable nature of queerness from our speculative futures and speculative fictions. After all, queer is much more than sexual preference or gender identity; it is a way of thinking that creates new spaces that break with western traditions by dissolving notions of linear time, historical time, and more critically by acknowledging the intersecting identities of race, class, ability, age, and gender, among other ways of being.

By engaging with nonhuman and posthuman identities in science fiction, art producers are seeking ways to deconstruct humanist and human-centric paths for mitigating knowledge production, in order to rethink established ideas about the nature of reality in ways that do not reify western heteronormative ideals. *The Orville* demands a reconsideration of not just what is possible but what is acceptable. This is often done within *The Orville* through critique that is both scathing of contemporary culture, and playfully metaphorical or metafictional.

Back to the Future—A (Non) Queer Reading?

To provide an example of a (non?) queer reading, consider when, on October 30, 1995, *Star Trek: Deep Space Nine* (*DS9*) aired a lesbian romance. While Ursula K. Le Guin's groundbreaking queer work *The Left Hand of Darkness* had long since been released, this episode of *DS9* was aired at the peak of network television in the mid 1990s. Ellen DeGeneres wouldn't come out as a lesbian on the air for another two years and queerness or more specifically gayness was connected so closely to the HIV and AIDS epidemic that dominant discourse could scarcely avoid a pathologizing narrative for queer. "Rejoined"[10] perfectly captured both the inherent queerness of *Star Trek* and the anxiety of the mid 1990s around normalizing gay and lesbian identities. In "Rejoined," Lenara Khan visits *DS9* as the leader of a Trill science team and is reunited with Jadzia Dax, her former lover. But the two women had never actually met—a select number of Trills are joined with symbiont life forms that span many lifetimes. Their two previous hosts were in love, and the two women still possessed all of the memories of that lifetime. When Jadzia and Lenara realize they are still in love even in these new bodies, they engage in a clandestine romance, replete with a long and sensuous onscreen kiss.

This scenario reads as a rabbit hole-like cover up of queer sexuality and identity. More to the point, the episode goes to great lengths to code this lesbian kiss as heterosexual, as the former relationship between Lenara and Jadzia's symbiont hosts were a man and a woman. "Even if they do harbor feelings for each other it's strictly against the rules of Trill society to acknowledge it in anyway.... Having a relationship with a lover from a past life is called a reassociation. The Trill feel very strongly that it's unnatural."[11] Here, what *DS9*'s Dr. Bashir is explaining as "unnatural" is the (pathologized) "reassociation" rather than the queerness. By making the relationship taboo because of the forbidden nature of re-igniting an old relationship, they are also relaying a proxy for queerness as taboo. We could easily see this as "burying the lede" but the nature of joined Trill life also seems to be inherently queer. The symbiont itself has no sexual identity, and as the hosts are not chosen in relation to biological sex, gender, or sexual preference, their experiences run the queer spectrum and are decidedly part of the very fiber of Trill history and identity.

This interpretation of "Rejoined" illustrates the difference between a *queer reading* and a *queer text*.[12] While some elements of "Rejoined" are visibly queer, I have participated in a queer reading by, as Pearson put it,

> decoding the outlaw cryptographies that have hidden—and may still hide—issues of sexual difference (often in plain sight) ... disinterring the many and peculiar ways through which the dominant twentieth-century Western conception of sexuality

underlies, is implicated in, and sometimes collides with science fiction's attempt to envision alternate ways of being-in-the-world.[13]

"Rejoined" does not ask us to look at the very queer relationship the episode puts "in plain sight" but begs us to bury it for the sake of homo-anxiety.

Eyes Without a Face—A Proto-Queer Reading

The Orville is different. *The Orville* creates queer articulations of the body in the rendering of Isaac, for example. Queerness is, in many ways, a rejection of human exceptionalism, because human is not a label/identity that has been granted to everyone nor is it capable of contending with the vast grid of assemblages that can be created in the service of "identity." As Jasbir Puar puts it, the posthuman is also an assemblage of identities that "do not privilege bodies as human, nor as residing within a human animal/ nonhuman animal binary." Rather, posthuman assemblages participate in the "de-exceptionalizing of human bodies" because "multiple forms of matter can be bodies—bodies of water, cities, institutions, and so on. Matter is an actor."[14] Isaac's body, from this perspective, shares more with the city or institution than it does with a human or alien body.

While Isaac emphatically codes humans as inferior, often in comical and pompous ways, he also draws attention to his own sense of superiority and a bias toward his super intelligence that necessarily reinscribes the human perspective as well. He does this by inserting comparatives between biological life forms and his own form, noting emotion and a resistance to logic as inherent weakness. But Isaac also manifests and performs his own identity in a space between human and machine. Despite his two arms, two legs, and head, which certainly code him as humanoid, he has no face, and Isaac himself is careful to note for the crew that his "eyes"—two green orbs of light glowing from behind the smooth visage of his featureless face—are not for seeing but are there to put the crew at ease. He is simultaneously aware that his alterity is uncomfortable for the crew and is yet willing to assimilate at the same time.

Isaac's negotiation of identity is always with an awareness of his machine body and more critically his seemingly unperceivable machine mind. "Who's the lucky lady … or fella … or object," Lieutenant Commander John LaMarr asks Isaac in "A Happy Refrain" (S2E6). While this response to Isaac's impending date with ship's doctor Claire Finn is certainly imbricated with queerness in and of itself, it is Isaac's status as an artificial life form that most visibly performs queerness in this episode from season two of *The Orville*. After much contemplation and a growing romantic tension between the two characters, Dr. Finn decides to put aside Isaac's status as an AI and admit and indulge her feelings for him.

Unlike *Star Trek: Voyager,* where real human likeness and emotional range are present in the holographic Doctor (who is, incidentally, never given a name), Isaac is decidedly nonhuman in form with nonhuman feelings, emotions, and autonomic responses. While, as mentioned before, Isaac does loosely have the anatomy of a human, he has less of a human physical profile than *Star Wars'* C-3PO or the Machine Man in Fritz Lang's iconic 1927 film *Metropolis.*

Dr. Finn's admission of her feelings for Isaac are first expressed to Kelly and because of Isaac's appearance and his failure to perform humanness, the notion of dating him is initially met with hefty reservations. Kelly makes a series of attempts to contend with the idea of a human and an Artificial Intelligence dating. He is "incapable" of emotions or feelings; he can't care for anyone. "The reality is, he can't love" (S2E6). This response is not far removed from homophobic epithets like "gay love is unnatural," reflecting a notion that it is against the empirical knowledge the crew believes they have about Isaac; he is not equipped to love, have feelings, or have empathy. But this so-called knowledge reflects a decidedly human and heteronormative view that fails to contend with the flaws in the rationality of human thought—the view that this "reproduction of social biases is part and parcel of the cognitive branch of science fiction's reliance on scientific authority."[15] That is to say, because Isaac is a machine, his functions can and must be correlative to technological and scientific principles. And yet, both Claire and Kelly go on to pathologize the very notion of the potential coupling: "I mean if it doesn't work out you could probably write an award-winning research paper" (S2E6). Reminiscent of the still prevalent notion that queerness is a genetic flaw, that one day we will discover a "gay gene," queerness here is coded as an experiment, with little to no intrinsic value simply as a relationship. This sentiment is echoed by Commander Bortus (who, incidentally, queers his own already queer visage in this episode with a *Magnum, P.I.*-esque mustache), "A human and an artificial life form are incompatible. They will not succeed" (S2E6).

For Isaac and Claire's first date, they attend the Union symphony in the *Orville*'s shuttle bay and after have dinner in the simulator. Per LaMarr's advice, Isaac puts on clothes for the date, creating a dissonance between his machine body and material representation. On their second date, Isaac again takes her to the simulator but this time he extends the holographic façade onto himself, projecting a human form over his material body. While a surface reading of Isaac's simulated man persona would indicate a conversion to heteronormative performance of gender, a deeper look shows that he is performing gender as an external factor, drawing the audience to the conclusion that gender is always constructed and not innate. It is an overlay. He puts the human male on top of his materially nonhuman body. This performance is not lost on Dr. Finn, who both acknowledges the performance as for her benefit, yet never allows herself to be convinced of the façade as a reality. Thus, when they "simulate her quarters," their sex becomes a queer act that also actively engages with the constructed nature of gender in a metacritical and metaphorical sense, contending with the precarity of gender as an identity to be overlaid, rather than a performance.

AI and human sexual relationships are not a new topic. But unlike fictions which demonstrate a wrongness based on exploitation (e.g., sex robots) or an acceptance of these relationships based on presumed sentience or a reasonable "likeness" to humans, Isaac is coded entirely differently. Isaac performs a gender outside of the dominant male/female binary to become a queer body, despite the fact that the crew of *The Orville* codes him as male. This alterity of body is not dissimilar to that of C3PO (from *Star Wars*), who is also presented with the gender of male, but who is not sexually viable. Even in *Metropolis*, the "Machine Man" is only sexually viable when the machine becomes, via pseudo-science, a *woman*. While the image of the woman that resides on top of/inside of the Machine Man in *Metropolis* is evocative of Isaac's superimposed hologram, she is coded as nefarious and is intent on hiding her machinic identity and her intentions. LaMarr's aforementioned reference to an "object," therefore, is both as an attempt to rethink what can be loved and is capable of love, and simultaneously an objectification of the queer body. Generating a hierarchy within his comment, LaMarr prioritizes women (and heterosexual relationships), men (and gay relationships) and object (queerness), locating heteronormative and homonormative thinking inside of his understanding of Isaac's possible sexualities.

As Judith Butler suggests, "gender is neither a purely psychic truth, conceived as 'internal' and 'hidden,' nor is it reducible to a surface appearance; on the contrary, its undecidability is to be traced as the play *between* psyche and appearance."[16] Here Butler is acknowledging the interplay between embodiment and performance. For the crew and for Dr. Finn's benefit, Isaac's performance of male is necessary. The fragility of this performance, and the shifting modes of performance demonstrated in his courtship of Dr. Finn, serve to expose gender's fragile nature.

After they sleep together, the relationship between Claire and Isaac takes a turn. Isaac, believing he has collected all of the "necessary data" he needs about human relationships, seeks advice from John LaMarr as to how to end the relationship. The scenes that follow showcase *The Orville*'s finest juxtaposition between humor and cultural critique. Isaac turns to the pastiche of "the dead-beat boyfriend" in order to goad Claire into dumping him first. The anachronistic comparison between Isaac's machine body inside of a dirty white tank top and underwear highlights the absurdity of toxic masculinity. But it is his dialogue in this breakup scene that is particularly attuned to cultural critique. Bereft of anger, Isaac parrots the "you're late, where's my dinner!" stereotype using formal and emotionless language, "Ah, you are home. It is about time.... I am awaiting my dinner and it has caused me to become displeased" (S2E6). Isaac doesn't stop performing this stereotypical gender role even when Claire notes "Isaac, you don't eat." Again highlighting the performativity of relationship tropes and customs, Isaac parrots other stereotypes, such as "I am sorry you are upset, perhaps you are on your period." But after the couple split, a new conception of Isaac's emotional abilities arises, serving to detail a way of knowing that is utterly outside of the realm of human, despite Ed's attempts to anthropomorphize them. This is to say that ultimately, Isaac's subprograms can't remove Dr. Finn, rendering a machine love that can only be metaphorically relational to human love.

> **Ed:** Your various programs are used to her. And it turns out she's not so easy to just delete.
> **Isaac:** A crude analogy, but essentially accurate [S2E6].

His "crude analogy" articulates Isaac's emotional alterity. Ed can only relate to Isaac's particular manifestation of love by relating it to human behavior. Ed indicates to Isaac that he may be the first AI to ever fall in love, and while Isaac refutes this as impossible, they both recognize that human ways of understanding love don't represent Isaac's own ways of knowing. This rethinking of his abilities, and the previous refusal of his colleagues to recognize him as more than an intelligent machine, demonstrate the possibilities of thinking along the broader continuum of expansive queer thought.

Despite the crew's protestations throughout the episode, "A Happy Refrain" can be read as a critique of heteronormative relationships. By allowing Isaac to "play" through many of the stages, tropes, and stereotypes of heterosexual relationships, the episode successfully pokes holes in the institution of the patriarchy, as well as granting Isaac an identity that is both capable of love, and that does not require a conformation to human idealism. Following this episode, Isaac and Claire's relationship becomes a vital part of the greater world of the show, much like the relationship between Bortus and Klyden does.

Amorphous Man—A Queer Reading

Rosemary Hennessy explains that "Claiming a queer identity is an effort to speak from and to the differences that have been suppressed both by heteronorms and by the homo-hetero binary ... offering instead an "in your face" rejection of proper sexual identities that is both anti-assimilationist and anti-separatist."[17] This "in your face" rejection presents us with a form of alien in that queer identities defy the familiar. Yaphit is an excellent example of this both in the sense that he does not resemble humanoid lifeforms in any way, but also in the fact that he is quite literally fluidic. Like Odo from *DS9*, both characters can achieve many different forms and shapes, demonstrating an identity that is constantly in flux. With Odo, however, he is asked to assimilate into humanness as much as possible, and with his species' shapeshifting abilities, he is able to accomplish this. Yaphit, however, is unable to take on human form the way that Odo does. Yaphit attempts to defy preexisting notions of the possible both in his form as an amorphous, yellow, gelatinous being, and as a sexual being interested in interspecies romance with Dr. Finn. While also, ostensibly a comedic moment, Yaphit has sex with Dr. Finn and the camera doesn't shy away from showing it. Dr. Finn is seen enveloped in Yaphit up to her shoulders, indicating that members of his species are capable of being an orifice as well as entering an orifice. This is coded, through a human framework, as transgender, or gender fluidic. This scene, one of many queer moments in "Cupid's Dagger," attempts to demonstrate sex without human form or human gender.

Queerness is by necessity an amorphous and unwieldy concept and in the case of Yaphit this fluidity is literal. As soon as a queer body is codified, it narrows possibilities along a continuum of the expected and immobilizes fringe ways of being and of being represented. Donna Haraway contends with the problem of representation and human-centric thinking with her notion of the *Chthulucene*, which operates partly as a rejection of the Anthropocene and the Capitalocene and more specifically contends with the notion of *sympoiesis*—a self-making—and a "making kin"[18] as an analogy for what a queer body and what queer thought can be. This making of kin is tactile, tendridic, multifaceted, and decidedly nonhuman. Nonhuman understandings, for Haraway, are critical in queering our realities, but also in decentering the human position; going even further she recognizes, a la posthumanism, that the so-called human position is a decidedly white male-centric and incredibly narrow band of identity that serves to disenfranchise those who don't follow a normative path.

Gay Misogynists in Space—A Queer Text

In some respects, all extraterrestrials invoke queerness, as they represent conceptions of the sexual and social body in ways that are both different and that deviate from the premise that science fiction often inscribes: humanity is the bar, the measuring stick, the compass, the book of rules by which all things should be measured. Alcena Madeline Davis Rogan discusses our inability to see sex and morality from any other perspective than the subjectivity of human when he says, "Science-fictional representations of sex acts involving aliens ... reinscribe the epistemological and ontological lineaments of the human sexual experience."[19] This is inalienable in the respect that humans, somehow—despite their relative ineptitude compared to other advanced races in the galaxy—form the center of the Union in *The Orville*, which is not dissimilar to how western ideology and heteronormative epistemologies form the center of our own society. However, Davis Rogan is talking specifically about sex. While we never see Bortus and Klyden having sex, we do see Bortus in many intimate configurations with other (simulated) Moclan males that, for all intents and purposes, supports Davis Rogan's assertion that human sex is being reproduced. This said, the Moclans' nonhuman form—they are seemingly reptilian in nature, with large barrel chests and ridged heads—simulates an other that creates not only a queer sexuality but also a nonhuman hypermasculine gender. This masculinity proves to be incredibly politically fraught, and asks the viewer to rethink sexuality as correlative to oppressive modes of behavior.

Nearly from the outset of season one, *The Orville* explores the moral and ethical implications of a forced sex change. Centering on Bortus and Klyden, "About a Girl" (S1E3) concentrates on whether the couple from Moclus should be allowed to change the sex of their baby, and who has the authority to proclaim these actions ethically justified or unjustified. Initially both Bortus and Klyden want the baby's sex changed. However, Dr. Finn refuses to perform an unnecessary operation on a perfectly healthy infant and draws the attention of Captain Mercer to the issue. An ethics battle ensues. Bortus compares the sex change operation to the human procedure for correcting a cleft palate, insinuating that being female is a defect. In fact, relationships between male and female Moclans are punishable by exile, and the "rare" female births are always met with a sex change. Kelly and Ed attempt to see the issue from the Moclan's cultural standpoint, but ultimately determine that the human notion of what is right *does* and *should* apply to this situation, even though they have no power to enforce it.

The viewer here is acutely aware of the contextuality of ethics as always already human. While Bortus and Klyden are overtly queer from a human perspective, and heteronormative from a Moclan perspective, they are also morally reprehensible from a human perspective and morally correct from a Moclan perspective. This complex layering of identities and values creates a sort of queer kaleidoscope that only serves to further expand our knowledge production along non-linear trajectories.

Similarly, "Primal Urges" approaches Moclan moral and ethical alterity as it stands in opposition to Union (human) codes and mores. However, each episode is also intent on exploring the interpersonal relationship between

Bortus and Klyden. Their marriage is central to the over-arching sense of family and comradery the show constructs. The show is rich with scenes of Bortus and Klyden in bed together, fighting, making up, disagreeing, eating breakfast with their son—all of these center real queerness, as opposed to the figurehead queerness we see in shows such as *Star Trek: Discovery*. When we look at the gay relationship in *Discovery* between Lieutenant Commander Paul Stamets and his husband and *Discovery*'s doctor Hugh Culber, there is nothing radical in their representation, but rather, the reaffirmation of patriarchal and domestic modalities. In short, it is a *homonormative* relationship that doesn't center difference or sexuality, but rather showcases a surficial interpretation of queer. Queerness itself is never a topic in *Discovery*. This reminds us of Pearson's question as to "whether the inclusion of a gay character on a show that presupposes an already heteronormative view of the human future can be said to 'queer' that future in any significant way."[20]

In contrast to *Discovery*, "Primal Urges" is largely about the marital strife that arose between Bortus and Klyden in "About a Girl," when Bortus eventually fought against their daughter's sex change and Klyden did not. As a result of the rift this event caused, Bortus pulls away from Klyden and begins visiting the simulator for porn. But when the porn fails to satisfy Bortus, he asks Lieutenant Unk (who belongs to a species known for their hardcore porn programs) to make him something "out of the ordinary." "What kind of out of the ordinary?" the Lieutenant asks Bortus, "We got twins, inter-species, shuttle bay three ways, chubby Krill housewives, battle cruiser toilet cams…" (S2E2). In describing the types of porn Bortus might want, an entirely new world of sexual possibilities is broached, naming deviant sexual practices to an audience larger than the subaltern, and in the process making these sexual practices public. The program that is created, however, becomes corrupted and causes ship wide computer problems, exposing Bortus' penchant in the process.

Several aspects of this episode render the Moclans' relationship and their sexuality vital and valued. First, we see the couple struggle intimately. Second, we are privy to explicit and unabashed gay erotica. Each pornographic scenario within Bortus' simulated fantasies are coded as deeply erotic. It would be easy to limit this sexual exploration by giving the viewer mere hints. For example—to use *DS9* as an example yet again—it is often hinted that the holosuites in Quark's bar are being used for porn, but it is never explicitly mentioned, much less shown. It would also be easy, especially considering *The Orville*'s unique relationship to comedy, to make these pornographic programs the butt of the joke. And while the final visual of the simulated Moclan harem licking Isaac's smooth face is certainly comedic, Bortus' desperation for intimacy coupled with his own nudity—along with the nudity of other Moclans and the explicit centering of his own pleasure—is not.

Furthermore, when Bortus and Klyden attend couples counseling after Bortus' porn addiction is exposed, the viewer is privy to an even deeper look into Bortus and Klyden's relationship. When Bortus fully allows himself to express his resentment toward Klyden, his hypermasculinity is rendered inert, challenging traditional notions of the emotionally invulnerable male subject. At each turn, the viewer is asked to look directly at these vital and valid relationships in all of their complexity. Given the decidedly fraught implications of the Moclan's genocidal nature toward women, the queerness is most legible in the mitigation between the audience and the crew's ability to point out the misogyny in its alien context. As such, queerness here is both denying the injustices of the sex change and the inherent sexism, while simultaneously acknowledging the ways in which Bortus and Klyden's identities are vital.

Conclusion

The antinormativity of queerness is an agential modality capable of worlding equitable utopias. This notion seeks to include queerness as a way of thinking and a process for changing our inequities in addition to a way of being. Queerness, then, becomes a goal, a horizon,[21] rather than an identity to accept, "The present is not enough. It is impoverished and toxic for queers and other people who do not feel the privilege of majoritarian belonging, normative tastes, and 'rational' expectations."[22] *The Orville* contends with this future by pushing the boundaries of what is possible most specifically in our love lives but also in our renderings and interpretations of bodies, attempting to press beyond our experiences of the universe as seen through a human lens. These queer moments appear overtly and covertly, creating a web of important stories that contend with shifting identities, bodies, and autonomies. By reading what is a queer text within and around aspects of *The Orville* that are contending with alterity in less direct and less queer ways, the show can seriously contend with worlding a more equitable future, with a queer horizon somewhere off in the distance.

Notes

1. Donna Haraway, *Staying with the Trouble: Making Kin in the Chthulucene* (Durham: Duke University Press, 2016), 39.
2. Wendy Pearson, "Alien Cryptographies: The View from Queer," *Science Fiction Studies* 26, no. 1 (March 1999): 6, 10.5949/upo9781846313882.002.
3. Pearson, "Alien Cryptographies," 2.
4. Pearson, "Alien Cryptographies," 1–22.
5. Pearson, "Alien Cryptographies," 2.
6. Pearson, "Alien Cryptographies," 5.
7. José Esteban Muñoz, *Cruising Utopia: The Then and There of Queer Futurity*. (New York: New York University Press, 2019), 97.

74   Act I: Gender, Sex and Feminism

    8. Muñoz, *Cruising Utopia*, 26.
    9. Jason Haslam, *Gender, Race, and American Science Fiction: Reflections on Fantastic Identities*. (New York: Routledge, 2015), 212.
    10. *Deep Space Nine*, season 4, episode 5, "Rejoined," directed by Avery Brooks, written by René Echevarria and Ronald D. Moore, aired October 30, 1999.
    11. *Deep Space Nine*, "Rejoined"
    12. Pearson, "Alien Cryptographies," 2.
    13. Pearson, "Alien Cryptographies," 18.
    14. Jasbir K. Puar, "'I Would Rather Be a Cyborg Than a Goddess': Becoming-Intersectional in Assemblage Theory," philoSOPHIA 2, No. 1 (2012): 49–66, https://www.muse.jhu.edu/article/486621.
    15. Haslam, *Gender, Race, and American Science Fiction*, 20.
    16. Judith Butler, "Critically Queer," in *The Routledge Queer Studies Reader*, ed. Donald E Hall and Annamarie Jagose (London: Routledge, 2013), 24.
    17. Rosemary Hennessy, "The Material of Sex," in *The Routledge Queer Studies Reader*, ed. Donald E Hall and Annamarie Jagose (London: Routledge, 2013), 135.
    18. Haraway, *Staying with the Trouble*, 89.
    19. Alcena Madeline Davis Rogan, "Alien Sex Acts in Feminist Science Fiction: Heuristic Models for Thinking a Feminist Future of Desire," *Publications of the Modern Language Association* 119, no. 3 (2004): 443, 10.1632/003081204x20226.
    20. Pearson, "Alien Cryptographies," 2.
    21. *Cruising Utopia*, 19.
    22. *Cruising Utopia*, 27.

Bibliography

Blade Runner 2049. Directed by Denis Villeneuve. United States: Origo Studios, 2017.
Butler, Judith. "Critically Queer." In *The Routledge Queer Studies Reader*, edited by Donald E Hall and Annamarie Jagose. 18–31. London: Routledge, 2013.
Davis Rogan, Alcena Madeline. "Alien Sex Acts in Feminist Science Fiction: Heuristic Models for Thinking a Feminist Future of Desire." *Publications of the Modern Language Association* 119, no. 3 (2004): 442–456. 10.1632/003081204x20226.
Delany, Samuel R. *Shorter Views: Queer Thoughts and the Politics of Paraliterary*. London: Wesleyan University Press, 1999.
Echevarria, René, and Ronald D. Moore, writers. *Deep Space Nine*. Season 4, episode 5, "Rejoined." Directed by Avery Brooks, featuring Terry Farrell and Susanna Thompson. Aired October 30, 1999, in broadcast syndication. Netflix, 2019.
Fuller, Bryan, creator. *Star Trek: Discovery*, featuring Anthony Rapp and Wilson Cruz. Aired September 24, 2017: CBS All Access, 2019.
Haraway, Donna. *Staying with the Trouble: Making Kin in the Chthulucene*. Durham: Duke University Press, 2016.
Haslam, Jason. *Gender, Race, and American Science Fiction: Reflections on Fantastic Identities*. New York: Routledge, 2015.
Hennessy, Rosemary. "The Material of Sex." In *The Routledge Queer Studies Reader*, edited by Donald E Hall and Annamarie Jagose, 134–149. London: Routledge, 2013.
Metropolis. Directed by Friz Lang. Berlin, Germany: Universum Film AG (UFA), 1927.
Muñoz, José Esteban. *Cruising Utopia: The Then and There of Queer Futurity*. New York: New York University Press, 2019.
Pearson, Wendy. "Alien Cryptographies: The View from Queer." *Science Fiction Studies* 26, no. 1 (1999).10.5949/upo9781846313882.002.
Puar, Jasbir K. "'I Would Rather Be a Cyborg Than a Goddess'; Becoming-Intersectional in Assemblage Theory." *philoSOPHIA*, 2, no. 1 (2012) 49–46.

The Orville

A Meta-Pop Culture Phenomenon for Feminism

Francesca Putignano

The attention devoted to feminist topics by *The Orville* is remarkable, as is the strategy it uses to address them. It deals with feminism via the lens of pop culture, not only by addressing important feminist topics as a piece of pop culture itself, but doing so by using other pieces of pop culture, some of which actually exist in the real world. This makes it, what I would like to call, a "meta-pop culture phenomenon." It thus provides a unique opportunity to demonstrate how the careful use of pop culture can be employed to examine and even promote the cause of feminist philosophy.

In my view, *The Orville* highlights three topics dear to feminism.[1] The first is the re-appropriation of the worthy identity of women, which criticizes the inferior status that is attributed to them by the patriarchal system. The second, which is a direct consequence of the rehabilitation of women's identity, is the reclamation of activities typically excluded from the feminine sphere—like reasoning, expressing oneself, and being creative. And third is the reaction of women against their erasure by the patriarchy—for example, the way the patriarchy has kept women subordinated by creating a narrative in which the history of human progress does not include any contributions from women.

In this essay, I wish to explore the excellent way *The Orville* examines feminist philosophy. In the first section, I consider the general relationship between *The Orville* and feminism, showing how feminism can benefit from the popularity of cultural products, and what feminist topics have meant to pop culture TV. In the middle sections, I show three examples in *The Orville* of this mutually beneficial relationship, by considering the questions addressed and how they are resolved in the plot development, thanks to the use of pop culture. With reference to these examples, in the last section, I stress how *The Orville* provides an effective strategy for elevating feminist ideas from just "small talk" to an important conversation about the status of women in our culture.

Setting the Stage

Since the times of the ancient philosophers, women have been defined and portrayed as inferior to men. But the first episode I discuss, "About a Girl," challenges that idea, and champions one of the most important achievements of feminism: the re-appropriation of the worthy identity of women. On Moclus, the planet that Lieutenant Commander Bortus and his partner Klyden come from, this typical masculine idea of the inferiority of females prevails. This bias is thought to be justified by the fact (but perhaps actually caused by the fact) that the Moclans are an all-male species. For example, in "About a Girl," Bortus' and Klyden's child is born female, and to comply with Moclan rules, they ask Dr. Finn to perform a procedure that will "conform the child, and make her a male" (S1E3). The episode reveals that Klyden was also born female, and conformed, leaving one to wonder whether Moclans actually are biologically an all-male species—or whether they have simply become such, one surgery at a time, as being female became more and more "taboo."

Now, Lt. Commander Bortus does eventually change his mind, but only after seeing the claymation version of *Rudolph the Red-Nosed Reindeer*. Even though Rudolph is a male, he represents an element that deviates from the standard image that hence was initially not considered valuable. Since Rudolph's abnormality (his red nose) saves Christmas, Rudolph's story teaches Bortus that sometimes even someone who is initially regarded as flawed can be extremely valuable. He thus realizes that his daughter may be destined for great things even as a female, and sets himself against the patriarchal society of Moclus. With the help of strong arguments brought by Commander Grayson, which gives the audience a glimpse of famous feminist critiques of patriarchy, Bortus fights to maintain the female sex of his daughter.

The second instance of feminist topics arising in *The Orville* is the direct consequence of the restoration of female identity and capabilities. In particular, this example concentrates on the reclamation of reasoning through philosophy and creative expression. Feminism strives to show how the voices of women have been undermined.[2] This devaluation is frequently a consequence of the (supposed) inferiority that masculine culture has attributed to women's identity and features. Since women are not granted the status of capable individuals, they are often not considered capable of doing philosophy, of creative expression, or even of thinking.

On *The Orville* these ideas are refuted by the character of Heveena, a female Moclan who lived as an outcast all her life, until (in "About a Girl") Captain Mercer tracked her down so that she could help Bortus try to keep his daughter female. Not only is Heveena a woman in a supposedly all-male species, but she is also the real identity behind Moclus's most influential novelist, Gondus Elden, who is highly respected by all Moclans inhabitants. She thus proves that, in spite of the beliefs rooted in Moclus' culture, women can create and express themselves as well as men can. But what provides the meta pop culture element in this case is the fact that Heveena's novels and poems—a form of expression that, as a woman, she was not permitted to use—become a tool to present an alternative to the all-male narrative of Moclus. The novel is so well known by all the Moclans that it is a *popular* custom on the planet to use lines from it as a greeting.[3] The fact that everybody universally acknowledges the wisdom and importance of Gondus Elden, and thus Heveena herself, proves that a woman can possess great strength and intelligence. In other words, she is capable of creating and expressing herself as men do.

The third case of a feminist topic arises in the episode "Sanctuary," which illustrates feminism's objection to the complete removal of the feminine presence from history. The fact that we do not encounter female authors, scientists, poets, or philosophers, feminists argue, is not evidence of their non-existence, but of their non-documentation. Indeed, in "Sanctuary," we find not only the counterpart to this erasure, but also a reaction to it. First, we learn that Moclus has been covering up the existence of Moclan women; the proportion of females born is much higher than they say. But then we learn that female Moclans have found a safe space on a planet in a class 6 absorption nebula. Under Heveena's leadership, they have set up a colony that is over six thousand strong. After the existence of the colony is revealed, Heveena decides to ask the Planetary Union to recognize their existence and finally give these women the rights they deserve and thus freedom from the shame imposed by Moclus. And this is where the use of pop-culture, within the show itself, is again used to make a feminist point.

To convince the Union, Heveena chooses a Dolly Parton song—a rather frivolous text compared to feminist tenets—as a hymn of resistance. Heveena's strategy can be compared to Aristotle's concept of using the available means of persuasion. One of Aristotle's lessons in *Rhetoric* (II, 1, 1377b) prescribes that persuasion is accomplished not only with words but also with the right means, which can adapt the topics of the discourse to the emotions of the audience. Emotions alter the general opinion of the public and modify their judgment. In this situation, the available means is the simple, direct, catchy song, and it is chosen because the audience will be more receptive and intrigued by the lyrics and will be more likely to listen to Heveena's ideas. The simplicity, directness, and catchiness of the song ensure those in attendance will listen to Heveena's speech. At the end of the episode, to quote Heveena, the women's colony will win "one small victory at a time, and women will rise up" (S2E12).

I find this last example particularly relevant for showing how pop culture can positively interact with feminist topics because nowadays feminist icons are not just philosophers or activists. They are also celebrities and actors—or, in other words, pop culture icons. And feminism teaches us that we should embrace this multitude of figures because it is a sign of the acknowledgeable status and importance finally given to these topics. Moreover, these new figures have and use a platform much broader than that which is available to academics; the range of their influence should be seen as an asset, not a demerit.

Now, to be fair, we need to be careful when embracing pop culture and not automatically think that raising themes through it will be enough to achieve new conditions for women and a new way of thinking in society. But if used carefully, because of its reach and resonance, pop culture can speed up the process. Some of the reasons for pop culture's success are that it makes use of deliberately exaggerated tones and its ability to entertain. These overly exaggerated tones almost inevitably capture our attention, even if we are not initially inclined to pay any heed, thus almost forcing us to reflect on what we see. *The Orville* does this when it presents us with the implausible scenario in which a pop song, the lyrics of which broadly recall the topics discussed by Heveena, is quoted during an official meeting of all the highest ranking Union officials.

Ultimately, accepting without snobbery the potential benefits of pop culture for the cause of feminism, entails that one can read *The Orville* as a significant contribution to feminism. First, it seeks to bring feminist issues and topics to those outside the debate. Representation matters, and carrying feminism beyond the academic circle to the public discourse counts as a victory. Second, it forces us to overcome the paradox of feminism being at the center of attention but also reduced to small talk; this helps circumvent attempts to trivialize it. And third, it ensures recognition of the temporal and changeable nature of standards that often pass as natural, thus making these standards viable for change. Talking regularly about feminism not only brings it to the attention of the general public but also, and most importantly, shows it to be reasonable. It makes what women are asking for understandable to everybody; it combats preconceptions in people who think about feminism but have not read any feminist literature. Thus, it embraces the willingness and the fundamental purpose of feminism: changing structures and mentality.

And that, in a nutshell, is the argument I wish to make. But there is much more to be said. So let us now explore these episodes, and feminists arguments, more robustly to see just how effective pop culture can be in illustrating and furthering the feminist cause.

Pop Culture and Feminism: An Edgy Relationship

In the last 10 years, feminism has greatly impacted the entertainment world. Take, for example, how *The Handmaid's Tale* seems to promote a feminist message.[4] But one might wonder whether this is the right way to improve and increase awareness on crucial topics, such as feminism. I would argue that it is because this approach allows critical and extremely complex issues to circulate outside narrow (and sometimes not so popular) academic feminist circles. I am, therefore, also in favor of such things as the Women's March against Trump, Lena Dunham's cellulite on *Glamour's* February 2017 cover, the #MeToo wave of solidarity, and Emma Watson's elegant Instagram posts—at least, if they contribute to the feminist movement and help it expand beyond restricted circles. Every step towards the acknowledgment of feminist messages can only be seen as a victory and achievement for those who work to have them recognized. So the best strategy (or at least a good one) for taking full advantage of this opportunity is to become familiar with pop culture in order to be able to identify how to effectively utilize it, and avoid the traps of using it wrong.

With that in mind, I would like to highlight two visible ways in which feminism is spread through pop culture, and specifically on *The Orville*. The first case involves representations of women. TV shows now offer a range of female identities, not only in terms of race, sexual orientation, and body images, but also of beliefs and thoughts. Women are now pictured in thousands of facets—empowered, fragile, insecure, powerful, confident—and they also play different characters: warrior, villain, hero, princess, queen, president, entrepreneur, etc.[5] For example, on *The Orville* we see a vast array of female personalities. Commander Kelly Grayson is the first officer, Doctor Claire Finn is the medical officer and also a Lieutenant Commander, and both Chiefs of Security have been women that are physically stronger than every man on the ship: Lieutenant Alara Kitan and Lieutenant Talla Keyali.[6] Showing this heterogeneous framework of female personalities may contribute to helping others see how women can operate perfectly well in all roles, even in positions of power usually (or at least stereotypically) occupied by men. It certainly sends a clear message: "We see you and you deserve to be seen." Moreover, Alara's impressive strength helps to overturn the traditional idea of the physical inferiority of women.

Secondly, the feminist waves shape not only the dialogues but also entire storylines. This represents a change from the past, when the prevailing culture allowed specific actions and even dialogue which nowadays could never make it onto the screen, like catcalling, sexist jokes, or sexist storylines. These are no longer seen, and this positive outcome is due to the fact that feminism has spread.[7] Even though parity is still far away, writers' rooms are more open to women and marginal perspectives that do not allow the iteration of visible masculine distortions. Hence, viewers, and even those who think they do not need to reflect on these topics—or who are too young to engage in difficult themes, or who presume to know everything already—are given at least a glimpse of feminist themes, all thanks to pop culture. Indeed, we've already seen this in the aforementioned examples from the show, like when Heveena talks to the Planetary Union Council and the directness of the song focuses attention on her discourse. And we shouldn't forget when Bortus, enlightened by the story of Rudolph, finds himself comparing the reindeer's destiny to his daughter's, and revising his ideas about femininity and its supposed inferiority.

So, feminism can be usefully represented in pop culture, which can be a precious ally—as long, at least, as the risks inherent in it are taken into account. What risks? Because it's popular culture, there is always the worry that it could trivialize or minimize the importance of such issues, or over-simplify them. But it doesn't seem that *The Orville* has fallen prey to that trap. As an editor of this book points out in the introduction, much like *M*A*S*H*, *The Orville* balances its comedic style with serious social commentary by giving us serious stories featuring characters we grow to love. If *The Orville* were "Spaceballs for Star Trek," we might have to worry. But it's not. It can therefore tell a few jokes, but also offer insight about the horrors of war or the equality of women. It is therefore a perfect example of how feminist insights can be highlighted and brought to the center of attention through pop culture—of how, if used with awareness and without snobbery, pop culture can be a powerful and effective feminist ally. The show is not, of course, *about* feminism, the liberation of women, or revolution. But it does not have to be, to be a vehicle for feminism.

Challenging Gender

The process of reflecting on and re-considering basic knowledge is not so far from the purpose of feminism and, contrary to popular opinion, feminism is not just about equality for females. Feminists are concerned about anyone who has been marginalized or oppressed by the patriarchy of our male dominated society—and that includes those who are lesbian, bisexual, gay, queer, or transgender. And on this topic too, *The Orville* has something to say. To explore this further, let us first talk about gender studies in general, and then the trial that ensued on Moclus about Topa.

Feminist studies at their core address accounts of sex and gender since such issues are generally used to justify the inferiority of women. Now, to be clear, *sex* is defined by the biological organs of the reproductive system.[8] *Gender*, on the other hand, is defined by what societies make of sexual differences: the different roles, norms, and meanings they assign based on their real or imagined sexual characteristics. This includes the social roles that comply with different norms of behavior and bodily comportment.[9] And as this has been more fully recognized, the very concept of gender has been broadened.

Traditionally, gender identity has been characterized by the two social and cultural categories of masculine and feminine. Thanks to queer studies at the beginning of the 1980s, however, the concept of gender has been opened up to different spectra of sexuality, enriching and making room for identities not classifiable within the two traditional genders. Therefore, masculine and feminine gender, rather than representing the only alternatives for defining people's sexuality, are in fact the extreme poles of a continuum within which a person can find themself and move freely during the course of their life. What's more, gender identity is not influenced by sexual orientation or gender expression. Clearly, concepts such as gender, sex, sexual orientation, and gender expression are at the center of feminist and queer debates and always require extreme sensitivity and care.

Indeed, feminist scholars point out that, traditionally, the concepts of sex and gender are thought to be necessarily linked, such that being a particular sex implies the adherence to a particular gender, and hence implies fixed attitudes, features, duties, and possibilities. Moreover, gender norms dictate the social spaces to which men and women are admitted, as well as the presentation of the self to others. For the same reason, certain skills are labeled as masculine or feminine, and tend to be associated with their respective gender roles.[10] Men and women may, as a result, have differential access to skill-based knowledge. Deductive, analytic, atomistic, a-contextual, and quantitative cognitive styles are traditionally labeled "masculine," while intuitive, synthetic, holistic, contextual, and qualitative cognitive styles are usually labeled "feminine."

Since feminist studies have sought to evaluate the effective truthfulness of these assumptions about gender and sex, and the complicated relationship between them, feminists have demanded rigorous research on this topic—and, more specifically, a reevaluation of previous research on the topic. And, indeed, recent anthropological and biological study has shown that alleged gender differences and sexist and androcentric assumptions shaped most of that past research, and that it was gender relationships, and not sexual difference, that were used to dictate expectations about women's daily lives.[11] For example, natural bodily processes like menstruation or menopause were seen as problems to be solved by medical studies. According to the dominant assumptions, women's biology was considered inferior to men's, and such standard bodily processes as these were viewed as things that needed to be fixed. These (alleged) deficiencies were used to document and "prove" the superiority of men. Men were seen as naturally/biologically stronger, more aggressive, more violent, and hence more able to command and hold a dominant position. In contrast, women were portrayed as nurturing, docile, and less active than men. It thus appeared "natural" for them to occupy a marginal, subjected position and to be submissive as their characteristics presuppose.

Similar androcentric and sexist assumptions also operated for a long time in theories of animal (primatology) and human society based on sex and reproduction. A great many scholars have demonstrated that the account provided by science was profoundly tainted by an androcentric and sexist framework. The assumed passivity of females and activity of males shaped and limited the account of the female reproductive system and fertility. For example, it was thought that female sexuality should be explained in terms of reproductive functions. Studies of the hormonal effects on sexual behavior "determined" that female desire occurred only during fertility and was thus entirely controlled hormonally. But what these studies actually showed was that female activities and behavior are not passive, so the idea of the passivity and submission of women is unfounded.[12]

This appraisal opens the way to a fair evaluation of gender, culture, and politics since the reduction of human bodies and biology to their reproductive capacities has serious social consequences and has led to political and economic marginalization.[13] Hence, when we examine the theory that girls do not learn math as quickly as boys, we know that the problem is not low intelligence. Gender norms exacerbate these problems because they provide different expectations and opportunities for boys and girls.[14] Our bodies are influenced by these ideas and are sculpted by the social milieu in which biologists operate, and then, in turn, refashion our cultural environment. So, it is society that defines gender and sexual identity, operating on a very deep level and convincing us that a particular identity is the only option, thus narrowing life's possibilities while perpetuating gender inequality and justifying unfair behaviors.

What does *The Orville* have to say about all this? An even more rigid version of this masculine framework can be found on Moclus, where being a female is considered an illness, or disability—like a cleft palate. Hence, in a broad sense, Moclus's culture resembles the patriarchal system that operated undisturbed before feminism began to challenge it. With this in mind, we can understand the behavior of Topa, Bortus and Klyden's child—like why Topa so readily gets into fights with girls in "Sanctuary." When confronted by Bortus, Topa says that he's just treating females as they deserve, because they are inferior and weak, and it does not matter what they think. This belief was inculcated in Topa by Klyden, who, in his own words, was merely teaching the traditional values of Moclus in order to prepare Topa for life on Moclus (in the event that Topa decides to settle there). Of course, these values, which purport to be truthful and normal, are just the fruit of their cultural system, and they do nothing but reinforce the status quo, convincing individuals that no other alternative is possible, impeding any changes, and offering justification for behavior that is in reality merely misogynistic.

The merit of feminist studies is that it examines the part of science in which our alleged evolutionary biology is traced, and supposedly specific patterns of order based on domination are legitimated, in order to show the falseness of these assumptions. For feminism, the problem is not that distinctions between men and women exist. The problem is simply that biological sex should not be a factor that shapes the social identity or the socio-political or economic rights of a person or determines exactly what a person can and cannot do.

Which brings us back to that trial on Moclus which determined whether Bortus could prevent Topa from being "corrected" as a baby. In that trial, the supposed differences between men and women are considered by Commander Grayson, who represents Bortus during the trial. She shows us the heightened strength of Alara (a girl) and the dim-wittedness of Gordon (a boy). Alara is capable of turning a cube of titanium into a ball, and Gordon thinks that Nabisco (or maybe the moon?) was the capital of the United States. "The tribunal must acknowledge that there is no valid claim for gender based superiority." But even when presented with this evidence, the Moclan jury is not impressed. Indeed, they are not even moved by the fact that the beloved Moclan author Gondus Elden is a female, and still fail to rule in Bortus' favor. (More on this in the next section.) This shows just how challenging it is to question a belief that is traditionally viewed as the truth. And at the end of the episode, unfortunately, Topa undergoes the "correction" procedure.

But at least, on a more positive note, as was mentioned before, Bortus did become convinced that female nature is not so bad after all. And it's worth reminding ourselves that it was pop culture—the story of Rudolph—that did it. Yes, the story is a bit silly. But it simplified a difficult, cumbersome topic, and succeeded in appealing to Bortus's sensitivity and reasonableness. This is a perfect example of what can happen when someone is watching a pop culture product—whether it be *The Orville* or a Claymation special—where vital themes are tackled.

What's more, the process of reflecting on and reconsidering basic knowledge is not so far from the purpose of feminism. Feminist studies try to offer a picture of diversity in feminist analytic frameworks to provide more convincing clarification of the various issues. These examples show us that feminist philosophy has the moral duty to confront gendered metaphors, which, far from being neutral, perpetuate a particular cultural image. By highlighting this, feminist scholars "will rob them of their power to naturalize our social conventions about gender."[15] But when it comes to *The Orville* and feminism, we can't stop there.

Women and Creativity: A Never-Ending Battle

Another argument for the superiority of men over women is related to men's ability to produce and manufacture things, as well as be rational and hence develop ideas. These abilities were also used by men to historically explain human flourishing as entirely a male achievement. It was men, the story goes, who created tools, agriculture, and even language. Recently research has reevaluated these assumptions, however, and shown that the real activity through which prehistoric society thrived was not the hunting carried out by men, but the agricultural activities carried out by women.

This conclusion is justified by the studies made on the mother-infant bond in all primate societies, which show a pattern of behavior involving the sharing of food between mother and infant and how this is one of the behaviors that builds the bond between the two. It has been suggested that this shared activity was at the center of prehistoric human society. Women were in charge of gathering, carrying, and sharing food. Because of this, men were able to engage in hunting, which was time-consuming and not a guaranteed or consistent means of providing food. If the hunting excursion was unsuccessful, they were assured of a share of the food gathered by women. Thus, a better explanation of human growth was the everyday activities carried out by the women that consisted in gathering seeds, berries, and greens while, as hunters, men's contribution was minimal and relatively infrequent. Moreover, women's work on agriculture was one of the powerful drives that changed habits and accounted for humankind's passage from nomadic to sedentary society. It also suggested another explanation (more plausible due to the frequency of the activity) for the creation of tools.[16]

Of course, previous accounts of the development of humanity gave much more relevance and merit to men's work, but this was because of background assumptions about the passivity of women and the idea that aggression and dominance gave the first impulses to human evolution. In light of this new awareness, an increasing number of disciplines began to revise their explanations and methodologies. Economists, for example, decided to investigate the way women's work has been conceptualized. Others realized that the *misleading discrepancy* in their research between men and women was a result of relying on observations and interviews with only men, and not even considering women to be of interest.[17] The medical field overvalued research of interest to men, and undervalued things like contraception. (And when it did produce contraceptive methods, although they gave women the power to control when they had children, they essentially altered the bodies of women for the convenience of men.) Accordingly, feminists have shifted attention to women's health and have pushed for more inclusion of women in clinical trials.

Philosophy has been deeply patriarchal too. As Genevieve Lloyd explains in *The Man of Reason*, reason was seen in philosophy as a male attribute only. According to Lloyd, most philosophical theories do not have much in common, apart from the fact that they describe rationality in such a way as to make it hardly compatible with the conceptions of femininity. The analysis of the attributes of reason and the idea of knowledge as disinterested and impartial show us that these descriptions are *gendered*.

In short, traditionally, women have been suspended by the patriarchy between matter and reason, because rationality has been conceptualized as an attribute of divine origin that is present in men by phallic inheritance.[18] Such a theory—that women's supposed inferiority has natural, biological roots—is one of the pillars on which the patriarchal political and theoretical order rests. Over centuries of patriarchal history, it has led to the devaluation of women's intellectual faculties, creativity, imagination, and intelligence.

And we see the perfect parallel of this in Moclan society. When Commander Grayson asks why Topa should have to undergo the corrective procedure, Moclan advocate Kragus' response is that femaleness "is a serious birth defect, which severely limits the ability to function: biologically, intellectually and socially" (S1E3). In both the real world, and Moclus, attributes such as the capability of creating distance, separation, abstraction, and rationale have been assigned to the male, and traits such as emotional, a-deductive, and irrational have been reserved for the female.[19]

Now, in the real world, feminist criticism has addressed this question by reappropriating rational modes and using them in public discourse.[20] In *The Orville*, the faults of the Moclan system are exposed, and the rational modes are reappropriated, by Heveena. When Captain Mercer tracks her down, she explains that her parents decided not to subject her to the correction procedure, and instead taught her to think, read, and wonder, thus disproving the claims of the Moclan advocate that being female is a condition which precludes the possibility of intellectual functions. Living on an all-male planet for a woman, however, is not an easy thing. Consequently, Heveena spends her whole life hidden in a cave. One cannot help but ask if such an existence is worth living, but Heveena affirms that she is happy. She is glad to be female, and she is pleased that her parents did not decide for her to be someone she is not.

But the most crucial point here is that, not only does Heveena manage to survive in a male society, but she is also capable of using analytical capabilities, making art, and creative work, just like men. Recall, again, that she is the real face behind Gondus Elden, Moclus' most important novelist, who is highly respected by the whole of Moclan society. Gondus/Heveena's novels are even a pop element in that they are well known by every inhabitant of Moclus (which harkens back to our meta-pop culture theme). When the real identity of Gondus is finally revealed, the popularity that comes with these writings helps demonstrate the clear, undeniable abilities that women possess. Thus, *The Orville* shows us how women can re-appropriate the capabilities of reasoning and how they can create. Writing is the way in which Heveena manages to survive in a misogynistic world and to express herself. In the history of feminism, this is a *leitmotiv* that feminist philosophers have connected to the very essence of feminism.[21]

Is Sanctuary the Solution?

The third example of a feminist topic occurs in the late second season episode "Sanctuary," in which a couple from Moclus asks for passage on the USS *Orville* to rendezvous with another Moclan ship that will take them to the planet Retepsia. Bortus discovers that the couple is illegally transporting their daughter to save her from the gender correction procedure. Sympathetic to their predicament, he decides to not inform Capt. Mercer of the situation in order to allow the couple to keep the child's sex unchanged. After the rendezvous, however, Mercer finds out anyway and decides to investigate to ensure that there was no foul play—that, for example, the couple was not kidnapping the child. And sure enough, the ship is not going to Retepsia, but instead is headed towards a class 6 absorption nebula. The crew follows the ship's ion signature to a planet in the heart of the nebula, only to make an extraordinary discovery that will change the whole direction of the episode, and ultimately the destiny of Moclan society.

On this planet, a female society, led by Heveena, raises female Moclan children. Heveena explains that, contrary to what the Moclan government says, the female birth rate is high. Almost all undergo the "corrective procedure," but those who don't try to escape (via an underground railroad of sorts) to this planet to find sanctuary. The colony is over six thousand strong; and in this colony, Moclan females thrive and grow and, above all, can live and do whatever they want without being forced to live according to gender presumptions.

Once again, then, *The Orville* introduces the audience to another familiar feminist topic: the invisibility that females have suffered throughout history.[22] The first two examples relate to the critique of the contents of philosophy, namely the revision of gender differences, behavior temperament, and the biological differences used as a reason to exclude women. Another critique is of the way, with regard to the concept of reason, philosophers assumed the existence of a dichotomy between men and women because rationality and objectivity were associated with maleness and their opposite with femaleness. Hence it was impossible for women to even be allowed to participate in the reasoning process. Now, *The Orville* focuses attention on another target of feminist criticism, namely underrepresentation in scientific fields, and the omission of women from the historical record (and not just by, as we previously explored, overlooking the contributions of women to humanity's achievements).

As it is told, our history is dominated by the actions, achievements, efforts, prerogatives, and even failures of men. Men have found different and—give credit where credit is due!—creative ways to exclude women from accounts.[23] Indeed, women have traditionally even been excluded from academic and scientific activities. Only since World War II have academies admitted female members. And even now, the situation is not strikingly different; the proportion of women is still low, and even when women are allowed to belong to academies, their positions are subordinate to those of men.[24] Ultimately, the outcome of this widespread prejudice was that even if women excelled, they would not be respected as real members of the academies. For example, in France, Marie Curie's application to join the *Académie des Sciences* was rejected, so as not to create a precedent, even though she had won the Nobel Prize. This showed that, for women, "the problem was not the quality of their work but their gender."[25] And, truthfully, this mechanism of exclusion never disappeared.

So, it is not that there are no women; the truth is that they have been erased from history, and this removal represents an active exercise of power by the male canon. Solutions on this matter are diverse: some suggest destroying the philosophical system because it is tainted by phallocentric reasoning, others think we can come to a more inclusive and open-minded system by listening to women's voices.[26] Feminist scholars are, of course (and rightly so), motivated to show that it is men who ensure the invisibility of and discrimination against women. But a real paradox is that women were able to join academies, and gain other such recognition, only when there were men smart enough to convince other men of the abilities and achievements of women.

We see similarity to all of this in Moclan society where misogyny is perpetuated through two different methods. The first is misconceived narrativity; the actual rate of females born is much higher than that reported. Second is an education that teaches Moclan children to systematically undermine women, and even females of other species. It is not enough that Moclan society literally forces women to become men; it also undervalues all other female identities. Think again of how Klyden teaches Topa to consider females inferior to men in the name of teaching Topa traditional Moclan values. (S2E12)

Heveena and her colony are faced with the problem of having to find a solution to overcome this invisibility and to enable Moclan females to reclaim their place in history. But the dilemma that it poses is excruciating: they can either (a) remain on the planet and be free, or they can (b) reveal themselves to try to obtain legitimization. The latter would mean no more female Moclans will have to endure the corrective surgery, but also comes with the risk of being banned, or even exterminated, instead. Heveena's concerns and fears are more than justified, but in the end, she decides to challenge Moclan society and applies to the Planetary Union for recognition. She makes a profound, persuasive speech—but what captures the audience's interest is when she quotes Dolly Parton's "9 to 5." Some people recognize the lyrics and relate to it; others do not know the song but are curious because they have never seen this kind of strategy used before the Planetary Board. Still others just enjoy the song, and it is the latter who seem more willing to listen to Heveena.

The song is a typical pop culture product from Earth. Moreover, the lyrics refer to the long hours of work that a woman is forced to do and the injustice of not having this work recognized. The song therefore relates to the fact that Heveena is being compliant, while also maintaining a levity that attracts and at the same time entertains the audience. The song has the catchiness, directness, and lightness to serve the purposes of the cause. The board is surprised but convinced, and Heveena is satisfied by the result. The colony will not be officially recognized and will have to stop sneaking Moclan females away from the home world, but in return Moclus will cease hostilities and let the female Moclans live and the colony exist. At the end of the episode, we learn another important lesson of feminism: we are not always going to make dramatic leaps in equality. The path to victory consists of small steps—but once the revolution starts, nothing can stop it.

Pop Culture and Feminism: A Balance

This account of what pop culture can reveal about feminism suggests that pop culture can be a very effective instrument of feminism, as long as we are wary about how we use it and bear in mind its limits and its strengths. As we have seen, in *The Orville*, not just one but three different feminist issues are introduced. And in each case, a resolution in favor of feminism is achieved thanks to a pop culture element. Pop culture has the great advantage of being able to act as a showcase for topics and themes

The key to understanding how pop culture manages to popularize these topics lies in its nature: pop culture is simple, funny, and spectacular. The simplicity of pop culture means that it is more accessible to a wide audience (than academic work), and thus has the potential to have a greater impact than academic work. This is certainly the case with Dolly's song. Its simplicity means that everyone at some point has had the opportunity to encounter it. Pop culture is also usually funny, and this implies not only having a more sympathetic public but also a different range of audiences. The TV show about Santa Claus and the reindeer was a product that could be easily watched by children. So, pop culture not only has a wider range but also leads to the diversification of the viewing public. In contrast, the topics dealt with in academic circles tend to be accessible to a limited, though growing, audience. Lastly, pop culture is often spectacular, so—like Heveena's poems—it does not go unnoticed. The magnifying effect cannot be ignored, and, for all that the spectator is aware of this, she is forced to look.

Even though pop culture can potentially be a great ally, care and attention is necessary in using it. The problem of simplicity is that it can lead to trivialization, a risk that should not be overlooked. Its use can also make us think that simply saying something, or drawing attention to an issue, is enough. But it is not enough to just preach. We should also aim to effect real changes. And this is true for the whole feminist movement today; it is not enough to be aware of discrimination or just draw attention to it; we should also do something about it, as Heveena did. But when content is thought and talked about by a wide audience and not just by restricted circles, change is easier to achieve. When everybody talks about something, this makes it regular and accessible. It is therefore a positive outcome that *The Orville*, even though it remains a pop culture product, focuses attention on feminist topics.

There is more than one way to talk about feminism, and the same is true for the nature of feminism. It is no unitary movement. Feminist literature and studies are immense and growing. Hence, using the expression "feminist thought" means being aware of the enormous complexity of the movements and positions that all contribute to making feminist reflection a worthy and equal interlocutor of traditional philosophy. What we therefore need to remember is to exploit both academic work and pop culture because, whether we like it or not, feminism has expanded thanks to pop culture because it reaches an audience that was closed to academic circles.

The real strength of feminism is grasping from partisan positions a common ground to which women from all over the world can relate. Pop culture is perfectly compatible with this in that it is not only simple but also accessible; that is, it symbolizes the consensus of the masses. We should exploit this opportunity rather than cast it away *a priori*. Academic discourses have to capture the attention of society, of ordinary people, in order to bring about real change in society. Otherwise, all that we will achieve is an ivory tower where we can shelter from violence and gender oppression, but that does not improve anything whatsoever.

We therefore need to find a balance between the oversimplicity of pop culture and the isolation of academic circles. Accordingly, we should always analyze and, sometimes, decontextualize the messages of pop culture. For example, we should also recall that pop culture will give prominence to the kind of message that is easier to communicate, such as the empowerment of the body rather than class claims and racial discourse or clandestine abortion.

In short, the key is to find a third way between the potential oversimplification, abstract, and universalizing drift of pop culture and isolation within academic feminism—a third way that does not overexpose feminism to trivialization and at the same time does not ignore other vehicles. What is needed is a relationship in which one does not exclude the other, in which the two are entirely mutually compatible. Only in this way can we exploit popular messages without trivializing feminist topics. The purpose is not to portray women as victims, but to overturn the "boys will be boys" narrative, to give voices and roles to women who are not accustomed to seeing, to make the image of women in multifold places acceptable and standard, as it should be, and ultimately to bring about real and better change in society.

To conclude, the fundamental lesson that feminists can draw from this is that, despite the patriarchy's profound marking of the lives of us women, it is possible to battle male oppression not only with academic thought but also through everyday instruments and narrativity. This enormous diversity boosts the feminist cause, and is one of its most significant assets.

Acknowledgments

I am thankful to David Kyle Johnson for his extremely valuable suggestions and corrections on the themes, and contents of this essay, and for his valuable linguistic assistance, especially during a time of crisis. This essay is part of a project that has received funding from the European Union's Horizon 2020 Research and Innovation Programme (GA n. 725883 ERC-EarlyModernCosmology).

Notes

1. These topics should be distinguished from the three waves of feminism—the first of which goes roughly from 1840 to 1920; second from 1960 to 1980 and the last one from 1988 to 2010. The first wave pointed to women's citizenship, and more generally, to fundamental rights acknowledged for women too. The second wave turns around the problem of women's equality, and, within it, there are two different streams: a liberal one and a more radical one. The difference between these two is essentially one is political and the other is connected to the different way of reaching transformations in the traditional structures of society that collides with women's basic rights. This internal divarication of feminism was further broadened with French feminism initiated by Irigaray in 1970 and continued by Helene Cixous. Moreover, this fracture happened during a delicate moment as the academization of feminist thought in anglophone areas. Lastly, the third wave has a vital concept intersectionality and aims to improve concepts of the second wave and integrates them with other non-white feminist groups, witnessing the spread of feminist themes to areas outside the United States and Europe, such as Latin America, Middle Eastern and African Countries, India and China. Some scholars also talk of the fourth wave, which reassembles criticisms made by the feminist movement and combines it with online activism (cf. Jennifer Baumgardner, *Fem ! Goo Goo, Gaga, and Some Thoughts on Balls* [Berkeley: Seal Press, 2011]). Using the expression feminism means being aware of the enormous complexity of movements and positions that all contribute to making feminist philosophy a worthy and equal interlocutor of traditional knowledge. Feminism speaks in several different voices, and it does not have to be unitary to having meaningful impact.

2. See Margaret Alic, *Hypatia's Heritage: A History of Women in Science from Antiquity Through the Nineteenth Century* (Boston: Beacon Press, 1986). Ix + 230 pp. *Journal of the History of the Behavioral Sciences* 24, no. 3 (1988): 274–276. doi:10.1002/1520–6696(1988 07)24:3<274::aid-jhbs2300240317>3.0.co;2-a; Londa Schiebinger, "The History and Philosophy of Women in Science: A Review Essay," *Signs* 12, no. 2 (1987): 305–32. www.jstor.org/stable/3173988.

3. On Moclus, it's "customary to respond with a fitting passage from the literature of one's own planet," and passages from Gondus' works seem to be a favorite choice (S1E3).

4. David Kyle Johnson, "The Handmaid's Tale, Feminism, and the Dangers of Religion," *Psychology Today*, April 24, 2018, https://www.psychologytoday.com/us/blog/plato-pop/201804/the-handmaid-s-tale-feminism-and-the-dangers-religion.

5. Providing a list of the female protagonists in TV shows nowadays will be utopic. I limit here to list some of the most influential female characters in tv shows, based on the diversity of role and on my preference, all produced in the last decades (ndr *Scandal, Big Little Lies Girls, Orange Is the New Black, The Crown, the L Word, Jessica Jones, Supergirl, Glow, The Marvelous Mrs. Maisel, Fleabag*). Twenty years ago, we already experienced some TV shows with the woman as the main character: *Xena: Warrior Princess* or *Sabrina the Teenage Witch*, etc. However, these characters were very far from the possibilities and images of women given in society, and consequently also from the idea of what women could do. These women were more the exception than the realities which women could grasp. We do not want to see the exception that confirms the rule. We want to see normality; we want women representing a kaleidoscope of roles, possibilities, and facets. To quote Viola Davis, the first African American woman to win an Emmy, "You cannot win an Emmy for roles that are simply not there." (She was also referring to the underrepresentation of the African American community, but it could easily apply to women's underrepresentation.) In the last decades, a shift occurred,

92 Act I: Gender, Sex and Feminism

and we now get roles in stories that much more accurately reflect women's real lives—their status, their successes, and their failures. To quote another woman Emmy winner, Phoebe Waller-Bridge, "It's just really wonderful to know—and reassuring—that a dirty, pervy, angry, messed up woman can make it to the Emmys."

6. I do not, of course, mean to exclude the short-lived Security Chief Tharl, from the episode "Home," who liked to eat on the bridge.

7. An example occurs in the *Desperate Housewives* TV show (second season, episode 20), where one of the main characters, Edie Britt, complains with her friends about her boyfriend cheating. The entire dialogue between the four close friends turns around the other female, guilty of seducing the boyfriend, as if the man had no way of avoiding cheating because he is a man. This kind of dialogue, I believe, would not be considered okay right now. Another example relates to catcalling in the TV show *How I Met Your Mother* (season 3, episode 7), where Lily, one of the characters, decides to put on a beautiful dress to be literally catcalled on the street, just to make up for her misery. On the contrary, it is also possible to encounter an example of "reverse" misogyny, as I called it, namely when a TV show uses a sexist behavior to make a joke of it, as in *Sex and the City* (season one, episode 11). Miranda is catcalled by some men on the streets; she answered, saying that she has not had sex for months, and she—I quote—"wants to get laid." One of the men told her that he was joking because he is married, and so Miranda got back at him saying, "All talk and no action, ah?"

8. Sex is related to biological differences, meaning the anatomy of an individual's reproductive system and sex characteristics. Commonly two sexes (male and female) are established. Still, an individual could also have sex characteristics that do not apply entirely to the male or female sex, and in that case, the individual could be intersex. The biologist Fausto-Sterling devoted part of her research to provide a vision of the human body not reduced to social constructions. 1.7 percent of the global population does not possess characteristics usually acknowledged as belonging to one sex or the other. Accordingly, sex is too complex to be reduced to two categories, and labeling someone a man or a woman is a social decision. See Anne Fausto-Sterling, *Sexing the Body* (New York: Basic Books, 2000), 10.

9. Elizabeth Anderson, "Feminist Epistemology and Philosophy of Science," *The Stanford Encyclopedia Of Philosophy* (2015).

10. An example is the domestication of women, a discriminatory process of Western male ideology perpetrated on women. This process implies gender distinctions and the division of labor: women are confined to a particular type of role, like household duties. Their space is the house, and that controls and limits their movements and their possibilities to the family environment, whereas men are legitimated to occupy public and, thus, more important roles. See Greta Noordenbos, "Women in Academies of Sciences: From Exclusion to Exception," *Women's Studies International Forum* 25, no. 1 (2002): 127–137, 129.

11. Sandra Harding, *Objectivity and Diversity* (Chicago: University of Chicago Press, 2015); Lorraine B. Code, "Is the Sex of the Knower Epistemologically Significant?" *Metaphilosophy* 12, no. 3–4 (1981): 267–276, doi:10.1111/j.1467-9973.1981.tb00760.x; Carol Gilligan, *In a Different Voice* (Cambridge, MA: Harvard University Press, 1983). Donna Haraway, "Situated Knowledges: The Science Question in Feminism and the Privilege of Partial Perspective," *Feminist Studies* 14, no. 3 (1988): 575, doi:10.2307/3178066; Donna Jeanne Haraway, *Simians, Cyborgs, and Women*, 1st ed. (London: Free Assoc. Books, 1991); Evelyn Fox Keller, *Feminism and Science* (Oxford: Oxford University Press, 2006); Evelyn Fox Keller, *Reflections on Gender and Science* (New Haven: Yale University Press, 1996); Helen Longino and Ruth Doell, "Body, Bias, and Behavior: A Comparative Analysis of Reasoning in Two Areas of Biological Science," *Signs* 9, no. 2 (1983): 206–227; Hilary Rose, *Love, Power, and Knowledge: Towards a Feminist Transformation of the Sciences (Race, Gender, and Science)* (Bloomington: Indiana University Press, 1994).

12. Elisabeth Anne Lloyd, *The Case of the Female Orgasm* (Harvard: Harvard University Press, 2006).

13. Banu Subramaniam, "Moored Metamorphoses: A Retrospective Essay on Feminist Science Studies," *Signs: Journal of Women in Culture and Society* 34, no. 4 (2009): 951–980, doi:10.1086/597147.

14. Fausto-Sterling, *Sexing the Body*, 3–4.

15. Emily Martin, "The Egg and the Sperm: How Science Has Constructed a Romance Based on Stereotypical Male-Female Roles," *Signs* 16, no. 3 (1991): 485–501.
16. Kathleen Sterling, "Man the Hunter, Woman the Gatherer? The Impact of Gender Studies on Hunter-Gatherer Research (A Retrospective)," *Oxford Handbooks Online* (April 2014) doi:10.1093/oxfordhb/9780199551224.013.032.
17. Harding, *Objectivity and Diversity*, 28.
18. Rosi Braidotti, *Dissonanze* (Milano: La Tartaruga, 1994), 148–149. On this matter, there is a vast tradition in feminist studies which re-read the philosophical canon. See Michèle Le Dœuff, *The Philosophical Imaginary* (Stanford: Stanford University Press, 1989). Susan Bordo, *The Flight to Objectivity: Essays on Cartesianism and Culture* (SUNY Series in Philosophy) (State University of New York Press, 1987). Andrea Nye, *Words of Power* (London: Routledge, 1990). Robert C Solomon, *The Daily Culture Savage* (Maryland: Littlefield Adams Quality Paperbacks, 1993).
19. Evelyn Fox-Keller, "Gender and Science" in *Discovering Reality: Feminist Perspectives on Epistemology, Metaphysics, Methodology and Philosophy of Science* (New York: Kluwer Academic Publishers, 2004),187–205;190–191.
20. This type of reappropriation also concerns other critical concepts in feminism. Motherhood can be condemned because it forces women to the role of family and social subordination or can indicate the primary and superior position of woman over man. Pornography was initially criticized as a representation of women as the sole object for man's sexual pleasure, while now it is seen as a tool that allows non-heterosexual women to unveil their relationships and desires freely. Finally, even the idea of female ethics is a subject of discussion. On the one hand, it can exalt the alternative to the abstract male ethics, but it also bears a message that forces women into unlimited obedience and assistance. See Franco Restaino, "Femminismo e Filosofia: Contro, Fuori, o Dentro?" in *Filosofie Femministe* (Milano: Bruno Mondadori, 2002), 221–242.
21. For example, Michele LeDoeuff explains that *to be a woman who does not leave others to think for her* is to be a feminist. This independence is the essential core of the feminist attitude, before the acceptance of any specific feminist theory or explanation of women's subordination. Given this association between doing philosophy and a certain kind of assertive subjectivity, it becomes clear that thinking philosophically and being feminist appear as the same attitude. See Michèle Le Dœuff and Trista Selous, *Hipparchia's Choice* (New York: Columbia University Press, 2007). Also, Martha Nussbaum defines philosophy as one of the most effective allies that women can use to raise their voices and warns against the risks of refusing philosophy all together because in the past it has been a vehicle of discriminations. See Martha Nussbaum, "Feminists and Philosophy," *New York Review of Books* (1994). Finally, María Lugones and Elizabeth Spelman define feminism as the response given by women to their invisibility or, alternatively, to their demining and misconceived depiction. See María C. Lugones et al., "Have We Got a Theory for You! Feminist Theory, Cultural Imperialism and the Demand for 'The Woman's Voice,'" *Women's Studies International Forum* 6, no. 6 (1983): 573–581, doi:10.1016/0277–5395(83)90019–5.
22. Literature on biographies and autobiographies of woman is continuously under active expansion. See Schiebinger, "The History and Philosophy of Women in Science: A Review Essay," 305–32; "Bibliography: Women in Science," *Hypatia* 3, no. 1 (1988): 145–55, www.jstor.org/stable/3810056; Sally Gregory Kohlstedt, "Women in the History of Science: An Ambiguous Place," *Osiris* 10 (1995): 39–58, www.jstor.org/stable/301912. I believe one of the most overt figures of appropriation and erasure of a woman from science is represented by Rosalind Franklin. For further details see Ann Sayre, *Rosalind Franklin and DNA: A Vivid View of What It Is Like to Be a Gifted Woman in an Especially Male Profession* (New York: Norton, 1975).
23. New strategies for keeping women at arm's length were invented: e.g., they were followed out of special meetings by the introduction of "smokers' rooms," where men conversed over cigars. It was considered inappropriate for women to enter these smoking rooms because to do so might damage their reputations. See Greta Noordenbos, "Women in Academies of Sciences: From Exclusion to Exception," *Women's Studies International Forum* 25, no. 1 (2002): 127–137. See also Hilary, *Love, Power and Knowledge*, 115–135.

24. Research meant to gather information about the actual percentage in European Academies of Science reflects that, although we can detect an increase of the number of female members since 1970, the current rate is still meager, between 1 and 15 percent. See Noordenbos, "Women in Academies of Sciences: From Exclusion to Exception," 127.

25. Londa L Schiebinger, *The Mind Has No Sex?* (Cambridge, MA: Harvard University Press, 1996), 22.

26. Generally speaking, we can distinguish two different ways of dealing with the philosophical system. One reformist side believes philosophy could be emendated from a symbol used to justify gendered divisions and roles between men and women through, for example, a reappropriation of the concept of reason as a useful tool for feminist (and philosophical) thought. Hence, the discriminatory implication carried for so long in reason can be reverted. Once the characteristics of reason are detached from the gender's agent who performs them, we see that inclusiveness, open-mindedness, and eagerness for a constructive thought process and line of argumentation are already implied in the concept of reason, as it represents the attitude of evaluating, reasoning, and thinking deeply in order to reach knowledge about the world. Thus, masculine errors can be eliminated by working within the same philosophy and not by building an opposite side, which leaves the first term intact. Next to the reappropriation that passes through the revision of concepts, once tainted by gender metaphors, but conceived as universal, exists a radical view in feminist thought. In general terms, this extreme view believes that the whole canon of the philosophical stream is irretrievably phallocentric, and hence cannot be rescued. What feminists should do is build a feminine symbolism.

BIBLIOGRAPHY

Alcoff, Linda, and Eva Feder Kittay. *The Blackwell Guide to Feminist Philosophy*. Malden, MA: Blackwell Publishing, 2007.
Alic, Margaret. *Hypatia's Heritage: A History of Women in Science from Antiquity Through the Nineteenth Century*. Boston: Beacon Press, 1986.
Anderson, Elizabeth. "Feminist Epistemology and Philosophy of Science." *The Stanford Encyclopedia of Philosophy* (2015).
Baumgardner, Jennifer. *F'em ! Goo Goo, Gaga, and Some Thoughts on Balls*. Berkeley: Seal Press, 2011.
"Bibliography: Women in Science." *Hypatia* 3, no. 1 (1988): 145–55. www.jstor.org/stable/3810056.
Bordo, Susan. *The Flight to Objectivity: Essays on Cartesianism and Culture (SUNY Series in Philosophy)*. State University of New York Press, 1987.
Braidotti, Rosi. *Dissonanze*. Milano: La Tartaruga, 1994.
Code, Lorraine B. "Is the Sex of the Knower Epistemologically Significant?" *Metaphilosophy* 12, no. 3–4 (1981): 267–276. doi:10.1111/j.1467-9973.1981.tb00760.x.
Fausto-Sterling, Anne. *Sexing the Body*. New York: Basic Books, 2000.
Feder Kittay, E., and Martin Alcoff, L. *The Blackwell Guide to Feminist Philosophy*. UK: Blackwell Publishing Ltd., 2007.
Keller, Evelyn Fox. *Feminism and Science*. Oxford: Oxford University Press, 2006.
Keller, Evelyn Fox. "Gender and Science." In *Discovering Reality: Feminist Perspectives on Epistemology, Metaphysics, Methodology and Philosophy of Science*, edited by Sandra Harding and M.E. Hintikka. 187–205. New York: Kluwer Academic Publishers, 2004.
Keller, Evelyn Fox. *Reflections on Gender and Science*. New Haven: Yale University Press, 1996.
Kohlstedt, Sally Gregory. "Women in the History of Science: An Ambiguous Place." *Osiris* 10 (1995): 39–58. www.jstor.org/stable/301912.
Gilligan, Carol. *In a Different Voice*. Cambridge, MA: Harvard University Press, 1983.
Haraway, Donna. *Simians, Cyborgs, and Women*. 1st ed. London: Free Assoc. Books, 1991.
Haraway, Donna. "Situated Knowledges: The Science Question in Feminism and the Privilege of Partial Perspective." *Feminist Studies* 14, no. 3 (1988): 575. doi:10.2307/3178066.

Harding, Sandra. *Objectivity and Diversity*. Chicago: University of Chicago Press, 2015.
Korenbrot, Carol. "Experiences with Systemic Contraceptives." In *Toxic Substances: Decisions and Values, Conference II: Information Flow*. 11–42. Washington, D.C.: Technical Information Project, 1979.
Le Dœuff, Michèle and Trista Selous. *Hipparchia's Choice*. New York: Columbia University Press, 2007.
Le Dœuff, Michèle. *The Philosophical Imaginary*. Stanford: Stanford University Press, 1989.
Lloyd, Elisabeth Anne. *The Case of the Female Orgasm*. Harvard: Harvard University Press, 2006.
Lloyd, Genevieve *The Man of Reason*. 2nd ed. London: Routledge, 1993.
Longino, Helen, and Ruth Doell. "Body, Bias, and Behavior: A Comparative Analysis of Reasoning in Two Areas of Biological Science." *Signs* 9, no. 2 (1983): 206–227.
Lovibond, Sabina. "Feminism in Ancient Philosophy: The Feminist Stake in Greek Rationalism." In *The Cambridge Companion to Feminism in Philosophy*, edited by Miranda Fricker and Jennifer Hornsby. 10–28. Cambridge: Cambridge University Press, 2000.
Lugones, María C., and Elizabeth V. Spelman. "Have We Got a Theory for You! Feminist Theory, Cultural Imperialism and the Demand for 'The Woman's Voice.'" *Women's Studies International Forum* 6, no. 6 (1983): 573–581. doi:10.1016/0277-5395(83)90019-5.
Martin, Emily. "The Egg and the Sperm: How Science Has Constructed a Romance Based on Stereotypical Male-Female Roles." *Signs* 16, no. 3 (1991): 485–501.
Moores, Shaun. *Interpreting Audiences: The Ethnography of Media Consumption*. 4th ed. London: Sage, 2000.
Noordenbos, Greta. "Women in Academic of Science: From Exclusion to Exception." *Women's Studies International Forum* 25, no. 1 (2002): 127–137.
Nussbaum, Martha. "Feminists and Philosophy." *New York Review of Books* (1994).
Nye, Andrea. *Words of Power*. London: Routledge, 1990.
Restaino, Franco. "Femminismo e Filosofia: Contro, Fuori, o Dentro?" In *Filosofie Femministe*, edited by Franco Restaino and Adriana Cavarero. 221–242. Milano: Bruno Mondadori, 2002.
Rose, Hilary. *Love, Power, and Knowledge: Towards a Feminist Transformation of the Sciences (Race, Gender, and Science)*. Bloomington: Indiana University Press, 1994.
Sayre, Ann. *Rosalind Franklin and DNA: A Vivid View of What It Is Like to Be a Gifted Woman in an Especially Male Profession*. New York: Norton, 1975.
Schiebinger, Londa. "The History and Philosophy of Women in Science: A Review Essay." *Signs* 12, no. 2 (1987): 305–32. http://www.jstor.org/stable/3173988.
Schiebinger, Londa L. *The Mind Has No Sex?* Cambridge, MA: Harvard University Press, 1996.
Solomon, Robert C. *The Bully Culture*. Savage, MD: Littlefield Adams Quality Paperbacks, 1993.
Sterling, Kathleen. "Man the Hunter, Woman the Gatherer? the Impact of Gender Studies on Hunter-Gatherer Research (A Retrospective)." *Oxford Handbooks Online* (2014). doi:10.1093/oxfordhb/9780199551224.013.032.
Subramaniam, Banu. "Moored Metamorphoses: A Retrospective Essay on Feminist Science Studies." *Signs: Journal of Women in Culture and Society* 34, no. 4 (2009): 951–980. doi:10.1086/597147.

Act II
Religion and Reason

Avis Vult!
Krill and the Dangers of Religion
Darren M. Slade

> "They're butchering fundamentalist fanatics!"
> —Lt. Gordon Malloy, "Blood of Patriots"

Catholic crusaders used the Latin battle cry, *Deus vult* ("God wills it"), to justify atrocities against Muslims, Jews, and even other Christians. Likewise, Muslim *Mujahideen* shout the *takbīr* (*Allāhu akbar*), declaring "God is great" before killing unbelievers. Not surprisingly, then, *The Orville*'s archetypal depiction of religious fanaticism, the Krill, has comparable sayings: "Show no mercy!" (S2E9), "Hail, Avis!," and "*Temeen Emideen*" (S1E6) (the latter of which they chant while they stab Tom Savini's head during a religious service). Each group (both terrestrial and spacefaring) believes an infallible divine source has commissioned them to fight their god's enemies. Interestingly, this helps explain the escalation of religious violence on twenty-first century Earth. Indeed, late modernity's resurgence of religiosity corresponds directly with increased religious terrorism by every major faith tradition as now more than half of all international terrorist groups are religiously motivated.[1] The Krill embody this terrorist activity by developing weapons of mass destruction and attacking defenseless transport ships or civilian colonies. As Marvin V. Rush, the show's cinematographer, put it in *The World of The Orville*, "The Krill are very religious in a way for instance that ISIS or ISIL is.... We're not saying this is the story of ISIS, we're not telling that story, but there's a corrupting effect that religion can have."[2]

What's unique about *The Orville*, however, is its deliberate poking fun of the bizarre and laughable nature of religion—an act which demystifies the different manifestations of deity by eccentric alien cultures. For instance, Captain Ed Mercer reveals the absurdity of religionists on Unuk

Four, who "capture outsiders and then sacrifice them to a racoon god by methodically dismembering them" (S1E5). Likewise, by farcically naming the Krill deity "Avis" after a twentieth century car rental business, *The Orville* openly ridicules the cultural arbitrariness of Earth's religions.

The comedy is offset, however, when devotees become religious zealots. Though Krill amusingly worship a car rental shop, that same god encourages genocide; this turns their absurd religion into a deadly one. As a social commentary on the accelerating socio-political changes in Earth's twenty-first century,... *The Orville* fictionally contrasts secularism with religiosity. The secular Planetary Union is enlightened and peaceful, but the religious Krill are tyrannical and violent. It critiques the increasingly radicalized expressions of faith in American politics, warning its viewers of what the United States could look like if zealots co-opt domestic and foreign policies. Through the Krill, the show metaphorically depicts religionists dogmatically and xenophobically reacting against globalization and secularism. Ultimately, *The Orville*'s philosophy of religion is that religious belief is embarrassingly antiquated and laughable, while at the same time increasingly dangerous when mixed with politics. And it is that philosophy of religion that we shall now explore.

Warrior Gods

> "The Anhkana teaches that that which is not of Krill is without soul."
> —Teleya, "Krill"

The Krill belong to a theocratic species that practices a xenophobic and violent religion which worships a warrior god named Avis and venerates (their version) of inerrant scriptures, the Anhkana. Satirically, the Krill religion (hereafter, *Avism*) exposes the sanctimonious hypocrisy and dogmatic inflexibility of Earth's Abrahamic faiths (Judaism, Christianity, and Islam). For example, *Avism* parallels the strict monotheism of orthodox Judaism and Islam. Much like the impulsive Israelite Yahweh or the wrathful Allah, Avis chose a specific race with whom to communicate and instigate religious tribalism. Reflecting the Catholic mass, Krill publicly worship in chapels where presiding celebrants observe a ritual sacrifice reminiscent of the Eucharist. Chapel services involve a center aisle separating pews, a bell and liturgical greeting to commence services, a copy of the Anhkana, and an altar from which priests deliver their sermons. Like Muslim mosques, chapels have engraved writings (presumably) from the Anhkana.[3]

Doctrinally, Avism theology corresponds with Abrahamic divine providence and sovereignty (Avis directs and governs the universe), personal eschatology (Krill souls join Avis in the afterlife), the *imago Dei* (Avis looks Krillain and uniquely created them for dominion), special revelation (the inerrant Anhkana), and holy war. Though characterized as "fundamentalists," Krill represent more than just twentieth century Protestantism; they represent a religious disposition "characterized by a quest for certainty, exclusiveness, and unambiguous boundaries."[4] Indeed, they share the same psychological traits as conservative religionists on Earth, such as the inability (or refusal) to critique traditional beliefs or to acknowledge moral complexities. They persist in faith due to confirmation bias, cognitive dissonance, and disdain for opposing viewpoints.[5] Symbolically, Krill illustrate the dangers of religion dominating a nation's culture and politics. For example, though the reptilian Krill view themselves as holy and righteous, their physical appearance (like their behavior) is devilishly reminiscent of vampires from *Nosferatu*, as well as the neo-Assyrian demon Pazuzu.

Their god is a divine warrior, much like Yahweh, Christ, and Allah, who instructs the Krill to engage in vengeance and a "divine fight" against all non–Krill (S2E4).[6] An Anhkanic painting of Avis resembles Lucifer from Francesco Guazzo's *Compendium Maleficarum* (1608) (or the wrath of Satan in the Florence Baptistery), depicting him with pronounced horn-like features. Here, Krill see Avis as an exaggerated representation of themselves. Accordingly, all other races are godless sub-creatures; and despite appearing to be "fully minded" (i.e., sentient, sapient, and self-aware), the Anhkana uses warfare imagery to characterize non–Krill as soulless vessels—as non-persons.[7] As executive producer David A. Goodman explained,

> Part of my contribution to the show and talking to [*The Orville* creator] Seth [MacFarlane] early on was this idea of the Krill being a race that had a religion that didn't let in the idea of any other races. The idea was a powerful space empire that believed that if you are not in their bible, you don't exist. That was something we all worked together in the writer's room…. That was something we decided with Seth early on before even the pilot script.[8]

Avis' warrior nature reflects the violent tendencies in Earth's religions, which ascribe glory and sovereignty to conquering deities. Throughout history, civilizations have attributed their military successes to divine commands, making war the function of tribal deities who represent the group's national identity and sanction violence against others. As Elise Boulding recounts, "The warrior god has dominated the stories of our faith communities."[9] The warrior symbol places all responsibility onto the divine, allowing individuals to distance themselves from the moral consequences of armed conflict. Jews, Christians, Muslims, and Krill all presume the divine sovereign's prerogative to wage violence, and they have only two responses when he declares war: obedience or defiance.

Because war is part of the divine will, religionists must conclude violence is also part of god's eternal, immutable nature. A sempiternal god *is* a warrior (cf. Exodus 15:3) only if conflict never ends. Imitating god's "righteous" nature means accepting the inevitability and interminability of bloodshed. To make lasting peace is an erosion of the absolute (perfect) will of Avis.[10] Thus, both the Bible and the Qur'an suggest warfare is often more commendable than peace, and even Jesus indicated that religion creates enmity (Matthew 10:34). Indeed, violence, imperialism, and cruelty are often the dominant themes in Earth's scriptures.[11] According to Harriet Crabtree, warfare imagery is one of the most longstanding traditions of Christian worship and ritual for much of church history. Naturally, then, religionists have used holy writ to rationalize atrocities throughout history, and empirical studies indicate exposure to violent scripture results in increased violence, hostility, and a lack of empathy for victims.[12] As Arthur Wallis explains, "Christian living *is* war"; and as Sam Keen states, "Warfare is applied theology."[13]

Significantly, this warrior identity perpetuates cycles of violence when religionists must depend on creating (or provoking) new enemies. Indeed, the more religionists fight (win or lose), the more convinced they are of their holy war's justification.[14] This retaliatory cycle was made explicit when Mercer spared a group of schoolchildren from his successful attempt to kill the Krill soldiers aboard the Yakar. Teleya (the student's Krillain school teacher) said that by doing so, Mercer has only made future combatants out of the students.

Cosmic War

> "We fight for the glory of Avis!"
> —Krill Soldier, "Identity, Part II"

Krill view themselves as soldiers in an imagined cosmic war where physical and supernatural combat occurs simultaneously. Echoing Israeli-Palestinian conflicts on Earth, Krill believe it is their divine right to occupy the galactic promised land. As Teleya explains, "Avis created the Krill independently of all other life, and he created the universe for our dominion alone" (S2E4). Being divine image bearers, Krill justify acts of violence both intrinsically (by claiming the metaphysical capacity to know their god's will) and extrinsically (by claiming an innate ethical superiority over other species). Accordingly, Krill epitomize the Catholic crusades, reflecting the dangers of fusing religion with state powers, as well as Islamic *jihad*, reflecting perpetual resistance to nonbelievers. Historically (but not linguistically), *jihad* has regularly meant the armed defense and expansion of Islam, being defined as physical warfare in Islamic law. Indeed, the two manifestations are inseparable since Medieval Muslim theologians likened *jihad* to an imitation of ancient Christian piety among Roman emperors and violent ascetic monks.[15] Not surprisingly, then, Admiral Ozawa refers to Krill warmongering as a religious "crusade" (S1E6) while *Orville* crewmembers (in the graphic novels) simulate battles between Muslim Sultan Saladin (1137–1193) and the Knights Templar (GN3).

Here, *The Orville* offers a commentary on the grandiose, dualistic symbolism of cosmic warfare, which divides the world into "good" and "evil." The imagery helps to sterilize religious conflict by affixing a transcendent meaning to the carnality of warfare. Consequently, Avism parallels Islamic *dar al-harb* ("house of war"), which ninth and tenth century Islamic jurists articulated as the eschatological domination (or eradication) of nonbelievers by the *dar al-islam* ("house of Islam"). Mark Juergensmeyer summarizes the implications,

> To live in a state of war is to live in a world in which individuals know who they are…. The concept of war provides cosmology, history, and eschatology and offers the reins of political control. Perhaps most important, it holds out the hope of victory and the means to achieve it. In the images of cosmic war this victorious triumph is a grand moment of social and personal transformation, transcending all worldly limitations. One does not easily abandon such expectations. To be without such images of war is almost to be without hope itself.[16]

As such, Krill soldiers are equivalent to Muslim *Mujahideen*, who fight "in the way of Allah" so as to bring peace to a galaxy (or in the case of the *Mujahideen*, a planet) at physical and spiritual war with god. Naturally, however, perpetual war imagery can degrade into the macabre. Reminiscent of the disturbing religious riots in sixteenth century France, the Krill High Priest, Sazeron, liturgically remarks, "Let us now cleanse," before ritually mutilating a severed human head as a cultic offering to Avis.[17]

This cycle of violence isn't possible without first sequestering religionists from opposing viewpoints and then turning outsiders into mythical monsters. This demonization or "othering" process requires imaginative scapegoating and conspiratorial rhetoric to villainize entire people groups. The goal is to depersonalize outsiders, stereotyping everyone into an undifferentiated collective so as to make it easier to commit atrocities in the name of god.[18] This tactic is most evident when Teleya remarks to Mercer, "Your own scientists claim your species is just another kind of animal. Animals have no souls" (S2E4). Or when Dalek declares, "You are a godless race of sub-creatures well-trained to lie and deceive" (S2E9). For the Krill, the demonization process was a natural reaction to the realization that no other race worships (or has even heard of) Avis. Thus, when they kill soulless animals, their actions have no eternal effects, a theology reminiscent of Christian colonialists slaughtering or enslaving indigenous peoples. As Samuel Huntington elucidates, "We know who we are only when we know who we are not and often only when we know whom we are against."[19]

Just War

> "It is ours by divine right, but they do not see this."
> —Teleya, "Nothing Left on Earth Excepting Fishes"

Believing the universe is in a state of constant spiritual warfare, the Krill resemble "peaceful" Earth religionists who often confuse endless holy wars with just wars. Historically, Jews and Christians have regularly committed murder and genocide in the name of god, with near impunity." However, as the Christian church intermixed with Roman politics, theologians such as Augustine (354–430), and later Thomas Aquinas (1225–1274), needed to defend how an ideally pacifistic religion could support imperial war efforts. The result became "just war theory," which argues that because war produces such immeasurable suffering, military action is morally permissible only if the conditions, conduct, and conclusion are all just.[20] Only duly recognized authorities can declare war under certain circumstances, such as self-defense or the protection of innocents. Likewise, military attacks should be proportional to the degree necessary for achieving peace and must be limited to armed combatants. As Spanish theologian and philosopher Francisco de Vitoria (1483–1546) noted early on, along with Jesuit theologian Francisco Suárez (1548–1617), differences in religion can never justify bloodshed.[21]

Unfortunately, politicians have employed the language of just war to rationalize religiously motivated violence. For instance, during the crusades, duly designated (religious) authorities declared war on Muslim invaders for what they considered just causes: the defense of Christians living in (or travelling to) the holy land. Soon, however, the war effort developed salvific properties as theologians associated the fighting with spiritual penance.[22] Likewise, the twenty-first century "War on Terror" by thoroughly Christianized countries has capitalized on religious terminology to justify military strikes on Muslim lands. While their explanations appear legitimate, the underlying moral reasoning aligns with religion's "divine command theory" of ethics. When religious politicians, whose allegiance is actually to ancient tribal deities, use theological concepts like "crusade" and "evil," they display little concern for the consequences of war (because their god is in charge) or for lasting peace (because cosmic war is eternal). By divine command, each side believes they are righteous and possess the divine entity's special blessing. Indeed, Reinhold Niebuhr (1892–1971) argued that violence is often necessary *because* of the righteous nature of God, who (ironically) detests injustice and violence.[23] Not surprisingly, then, religious politicians are quick to demonize other religionists when the opportunity arises. As Mark Juergensmeyer explains, "There have been more attacks—far more, in fact—by Christian terrorist groups on American soil in the last fifteen years than Muslim ones. Yet somehow, despite evidence to the contrary, the American public tends to label Islam as a terrorist religion rather than Christianity."[24]

The Orville contrasts how secular and magisterial states approach war. As with the Union-Kaylon conflict, just war theory ideally demands that war remain secularized, requiring reason and evidence before entering into conflict. As with the Krill, however, religionists appeal to their deity's cultural ethics, meaning a politician's particular religious sensibilities could lead to the destruction of others. What's "just" for the Krill is whatever serves their own religio-political self-interests. Morally, things are not "just" or "good" for their own sake but, instead, are declared good if they align with (what the Krill take to be) the will of Avis.

Religion and Morality

> "You make a deal with tyranny, it only gets worse."
> —Orrin Channing, "Blood of Patriots"

As a space opera, *The Orville* presents ethical dilemmas that defy easy answers. Through fictionalized illustrations, it distinguishes between morality, law, and religion. Though often intertwined, the show reveals just how religion and legislation can be immoral, such as the heresy-hunting among Dorahlians, the religious violence between Kelly-worshippers, and the misogynism of Moclan culture.[25] Ideally, morality should precede both law and religion where the former enforces legal codes regarding outward behavior and the latter provides transcendental ideas regarding inward virtue. What the Krill represent is an entire species that has confused religion with morality, prioritizing and then legislating only their cultural sensibilities. Thus, Krill promote the parochial belief that religion (or a divine Law-Giver) establishes morality. Like Teleya, religionists often presume, "Without belief, there can be no moral code" (S2E4). Of course, Mercer quickly notes that religious Krill murder far more than nonreligious humans, an argument that can equally apply to the incalculable death toll from Earth's numerous religious conflicts. For the Union, morality is founded on secular principles of liberty, rationality, and equality. The Krill, on the other hand, derive their ethics from the unproven metaphysical assumptions of the Anhkana, which results in making the galaxy less hospitable for everyone. Unlike the Union, there's only the mandates of dogma and superstition to fortify their credulity and supply an immoral group with future warriors.[26] Thus, the show isn't depicting moral relativism whereby Krill are excused for behaving according to their cultural dictates. Rather, *The Orville* warns about theonomistic ethics, which derives all civil and political law according to one particular theology.

For instance, in one dialogue by Plato (ca. 428–347 BCE), Socrates encounters a zealot named Euthyphro, who piously brings murder charges against his own father. When asked to define "piety," however, Euthyphro remarks that whatever the gods love is pious and whatever the gods hate is impious.[27] The problem for Plato and Socrates is that deities are often impulsive, arbitrary, and capricious in their moral pronouncements. Adhering to *divine voluntarism* allows for deities like Avis to declare murder good and compassion evil. Theology takes precedent over logic as religious sensibilities become law.

In *The Orville*, however, the galaxy contains innumerable alien races who all possess different (often farcical) cultural beliefs. Religious morality is unquestionably species-specific, meaning each religion conveniently conforms to the cultural makeup of each race. For example, Avis delivered the Anhkana only in the Krillain language, being unconcerned about other planets. As such, morality ceases being just and objective once it's confused with religiosity. Indeed, the moralism promoted among Earth's religious pundits and politicians is predicated on the absolute rightness of their preferred religion, making them impervious to the critiques of reasoned self-reflection or the restraints of ethical discussion.[28] Likewise, in the episode "If the Stars Should Appear," the creator Dorahl is said to be a god of "truth and love" who expresses "benevolence" towards his people, but his worshippers are free to torture and murder those who think differently (S1E4). And in "Mad Idolatry," the healer god "Kelly" is said to be "merciful," yet theocrats show no pity for a starving boy (S1E12). Significantly, *The Orville* doesn't target moral hypocrisy as much as it contends with the nature of religion itself, suggesting that religionists behave precisely as expected from archaic, anti-intellectual, tribal, and prejudicial belief systems.

Ultimately, Krill morality is a reversal of the self-reflective sense of "moral duty" exhibited in Union debates about the behavior of member species, which reflects ethical utilitarianism more than any other philosophy.[29]

The Orville promotes certain "near absolutes" that are grounded on rational inquiry, dialogue, and critical analysis, making it possible for the Union to declare things like indiscriminate murder, genocide, ethnic cleansing, and religious violence unethical. Avism, on the other hand, represents what Michel Foucault terms "episteme," and Pierre Bourdieu labels "habitus," where religious paradigms establish the very conditions through which all cognition, knowledge, and impulses are processed.[30] Krill have an unwavering conviction in their absolute rightness. Consequently, Krill likely have no crisis of conscience about their actions or hate speech precisely because their barbarism receives divine sanction and indoctrination. The result is a total elimination of rational discourse and critical thinking.

It is noteworthy, however, that the most areligious species, the Kaylon, are just as tyrannical and murderous as their religious counterparts. The Kaylon symbolically suggest that a purely rational civilization is also prone to violence because it lacks something more transcendent in its culture. Interestingly, the fact that the Union must partner with the Krill hints that religion may provide at least some of the resources necessary to prevent humanity's total annihilation.[31] If lasting peace with the Krill is achieved, then the message may be that increased contact leads to dialogue, empathy, acculturation, hybridization, and/or multicultural tolerance among religionists. If peace proves impossible with certain Krill factions, then the message remains unchanged: religion is obstinate and ultimately dangerous without dramatic reform (or abandonment altogether). In the aftermath of the Lak'vai Pact of Tarazed 3 (S2E10), the possible existence of a more tolerant sect within Avism may play a significant role in continued diplomatic cooperation with the Krill.

Clash of Civilizations

> "You must have faith in reason, in discovery, and in the endurance of the logical mind."
> —Baleth, "Mad Idolatry"

Show creator and writer Seth MacFarlane is quite public about his atheistic beliefs and adherence to secular humanist philosophy, which surfaces throughout his numerous television and movie productions.[32] It's not surprising, therefore, that *The Orville* envisions a time when secular humanism has propelled humanity into a triumphant future of peace and stability. Instead of religion, humanity is devoted to eupraxsophy, the belief that the "good life" (i.e., significance, values, and ethics) is achievable through practical human powers of scientific discovery and rationality.[33]

Unlike the Krill, the Union is visibly nontheistic (though, not necessarily anti-theistic). It has no chapel or chaplains on its ships. It makes its no distinction between sacred and profane spaces, objects, or people. Its citizens do not appeal to supernatural explanations for reality, morality, or existential meaning.[34] In total, religious faith is as alien to daily living as Krill are to humans, and religious practices like prayer are almost entirely unknown. While the Union's secularism doesn't demand rejecting spirituality, it does reject an uncritical devotion to supernatural beings, which explains why Orville crewmembers willingly violate Union directives in order to expose the folly of local religions. There is even an implied moral argument against the existence of god in "Mad Idolatry" when Commander Kelly Grayson takes advantage of the means, desire, and opportunity she has to stop religious bloodshed. Whereas Earth deities either refuse to intervene (or are incapable of intervening) to prevent further violence, secular humanists, on the other hand, prioritize compassion and justice, which compels them to act in a substantial way on behalf of others.

Here, *The Orville* juxtaposes the peaceful secular Union with the violently religious Krill. The former has an avowed "separation of church and state," which allows humanity to prosper with a higher quality of life and well-being, much like Earth's least religious countries and least religious American states in the twenty-first century.[35] A tolerance of other cultures means the Union, as an official policy, must view Avism as merely one (culture-specific) religion among many. For diplomatic reasons, it cannot and will not elevate one religion above another. For Krill, however, this religious pluralism simply means the eradication of their particularist worldview and, thus, their claim to universality and supremacy. Therefore, Krill adopt a theocracy.

What's fictionally depicted in the show is Huntington's "clash of civilizations" theory, which describes the end of nation-state conflict over political ideologies. Instead, rivalry in the early twenty-first century is now over cultural (often religious) differences.[36] Though not without its problems, Huntington's theory argues that once dissimilar cultures interact, their conflicting histories, languages, institutions, and worldviews begin to clash, worsening their distrust and animosity toward each other. In *The Orville*, this xenophobia is precisely what happened when the Krill encountered other species. With the Union, however, Earth's contact with other civilizations actually increased humanity's tolerance and inclusiveness. The major difference was humanity had already evolved away from religion. The Krill made no parallel progress in their evolution. By implication, the two civilizations have drastically different experiences. On Earth, religion's coercive and repressive history deprived people of their freedom, especially when intermixed with state politics. Only secular humanism achieved a peaceful coexistence with both planetary and galactic neighbors. For Krill, however, religion's coercive and repressive tendencies have ensured Krill dominance over others. While, in principle, they're able to thrive because of their religion, it's only at the expense of others.

This clash of civilizations identifies exclusivist religion as a global instigator of prejudice and hatred. In "Krill" we learn that, in Krill society, religious religious indoctrination begins at an early age … in order to solidify group cohesion. Whereas humanity's secularization occurred through progressive education, the Krill have to limit their youth's tutelage, autonomy, and exposure to other species in order to maintain a puritanical status quo. Because the Union adheres to the inalienable natural rights of all life, it's willing to cooperate with other species to achieve universal security, even if not everyone shares precisely the same goals or values. Krill interpret such toleration as a threat to the relevance and legitimacy of Avism. Hence, *The Orville* depicts religion as dangerous precisely because it provides the preconditions for conflict once it makes hard distinctions between "good" and "evil" worldviews. The result is exclusionary absolutism and, eventually, violence. The primary message is that the secular Union "seem to be doing a lot less killing than" the religiously devout Krill (S2E4).

Unfortunately, the rise of secularization in the twenty-first century has also led to an increase in religiously motivated violence. René Girard's mimetic desire theory offers part of an explanation, arguing that people behave in predictable ways because they imitate others ("mimesis"). As religionists desire authority or societal prestige, they plot ways to usurp reigning institutions through scapegoating and rivalry. Religionists want what others have, namely control over the culture and government. Taking the insights of Lynne Jackson and Bruce Hunsberger, religious antagonism is often due to rivalry over resources, social status, and devotees. The rise of secularism has propelled a "crisis of legitimacy" among religionists whose authority and relevance can no longer compete with modern, scientific society.[37] This competition has caused a clash between secularism and theocratic beliefs. Hence, the Krill's war against nonbelievers keeps them and their religion relevant in a galaxy that increasingly prioritizes secular ideals, as well as marginalizes (or ignores) religious dogma. The Union is a threat because it doesn't take seriously the absolutist claims of Krillain beliefs and can, by its very existence, render Avism both irrelevant and obsolete.

Religion and Politics

> "[W]hen planets first achieve space travel and … discover that they're just one single species among a vast diversity of

> [S]pecies ... they [either] embrace and adapt to the fact that they're no longer the center of the universe, or they ratchet up their xenophobia."
> —Captain Ed Mercer,
> "Nothing Left on Earth Excepting Fishes"

Increased religious activism in American politics has caused significant uneasiness for much of the public, particularly among nonbelievers and minority groups. The fear is that religiously motivated politics inevitably leads to radicalism and violence, eroding the kind of dialogue and compromise needed for democratic governance. The most immediate danger occurs when followers of warrior gods assume control of legislative and military powers. As Peter McDonough explains, religion in politics results in the forestalling of real-world solutions to socioeconomic problems. Instead of promoting the social good, religious piety often creates dogmatic inflexibility and hatred for differing viewpoints. As such, what viewers see with the Krill is not religious "fundamentalism," which has historically been isolationist and resistant to politics, but something more akin to neo-evangelicalism in the United States or "Islamism" around the world. Both are expressly political entities that reject secular influences.

Much like neo-evangelicals and Islamists, the Krill practice a totalitarian expression of faith that abhors progressive concepts like social justice, equality, human rights, and religious pluralism. Politically, they exhibit obstructionist tendencies, sectarianism, inflexible absolutism, and a refusal to compromise with opponents.[38] Indeed, as empirical studies consistently show, conservative Christians often oppose granting civil liberties to racial, sexual, and religious minorities, and also have negative feelings toward immigrants and other religionists. In fact, conservatives are significantly less tolerant than their nonreligious counterparts.[39] *The Orville*'s message is that when religion becomes a major influence in political policy, an otherwise preposterous and laughable belief system will inevitably become legislatively repressive and intolerant. How the Krill behave physically in war parallels how conservative movements, such as the Religious Right in America, have behaved in the culture wars of the twentieth and twenty-first centuries.

Accordingly, Krill represent contemporary "Dominion Theology" among American conservatives, promoted by self-righteous pundits like Pat Robertson and the late Rev. Jerry Falwell, Sr. (1933–2007), who believe the Christian church should have majority (if not full) control over the socio-political landscape. Correspondingly, neo-evangelicalism has promoted "Reconstruction Theology," an attempt to transform the United States into a theocratic country. Using warfare imagery, Reconstructionists seek to "fight" godless secularism in order to "recapture" American institutions for Jesus Christ. At their core is "American exceptionalism," a misguided belief that the United States is a divinely chosen "Christian nation" and is, therefore, wholly good. Eschatologically, the goal is to establish the very socio-political circumstances needed for the Second Coming. Depending on which sect's eschatology is promoted, the eschaton is achievable either through spiritual revolution or violent political conflict. Thus, in *The Orville*, the problem is not simply the fact that Krill worship a warrior god.[40] After all, religionists on Unuk Four are just as murderous but the Union simply forbids travel to their planet. Rather, the problem is in giving religionists (who worship a violent deity) the political means to perpetrate violence and oppression on others, either through religiously motivated legislation or military engagements. As philosopher John Rawls argues, "A persecuting zeal has been the great curse of the Christian religion."[41]

When it comes to violence, particularly with terrorism, social scientists often look toward socioeconomic grievances or status anxiety as the psychological basis for religious extremism. The problem is that these explanations don't apply to the Krill, who never rationalize their violence as a response to perceived injustices or oppression. Instead, the motivation to kill nonbelievers is inherent to their religion itself, which is why it's easy for politicians and theocrats to give religious justifications for war. In contrast to the Union, whose domestic and foreign policies lack a religious element, the Krill's mixing of religion and politics results in primeval barbarism. It's in this sense that *The Orville* becomes a poignant social commentary on the dangers of right-wing authoritarianism in American politics, which has revealed the militant radicalism of many Christians in the United States. *The Orville* warns its viewers of the dangers of electing religious zealots to political office.[42] Here, Krill represent what happens when a superpower becomes increasingly radicalized by something akin to neo-evangelicalism.

This lack of a "separation of church and state" merely elevates dualistic thinking to the level of an entire nation. Once a political party or country considers itself the righteous spokespersons of a warrior god, the demonization process of those who differ politically, ethnically, or nationally escalates quickly. As philosopher Martin Buber remarks, religion propels people to dehumanize political opponents as an "it" and not a "thou."[43] Groupthink helps the indoctrination process by pressuring people to conform to the state's militarism while never questioning the morality of its actions. When religion and politics mix, things like kidnapping, torture, mutilation, murder, and genocide are intellectually rationalized as simply a means to an end in a great cosmic war. This dehumanizing tendency has already spread through the United States where 32 percent of Americans believe intentionally killing civilians in other countries is completely, often, or sometimes justified. Less than half (46 percent) believe it's never okay. As such, *The Orville* graphically depicts what a nation-state would look like if controlled entirely by ultraconservative religionists, particularly a nation with the military might of the United States whose specious moral logic has increasingly become Machiavellian.[44] The message is that once tribalistic beliefs unduly influence politics, religion inevitably starts to reflect the bigotry of Christian Identity movements like the Aryan Nations. As public theologian Brian McLaren warns, "Put a trancelike, unreflective, God-is-on-our-side self-confidence together with the richest economy and the most dangerous weapons in the history of the world, and I can imagine two things: millions dead and Christianity associated with the killings."[45]

The Future of Religion

> "Our planet worshipped you as a deity for many centuries. But had it not been you, the mythology would have found another face. It's a part of every culture's evolution. It's one of the stages of learning."
>
> —Fadolin, "Mad Idolatry"

In two different episodes, "If the Stars Should Appear" and "Mad Idolatry," the *Orville* crew witnesses firsthand just how easily religious beliefs develop out of simple happenstances. As society matures, however, religion turns out to be either a case of mistaken identity or a misunderstanding about the universe. For example, the episode "If the Stars Should Appear" reveals that belief in "Dorahl" was the product of legendary accretion when bioship inhabitants mistook their former captain as a deity. In "Mad Idolatry," inhabitants of an unnamed multi-phasic planet mistake Grayson for a god simply because she healed a little girl. What the inhabitants didn't know was that Grayson exists in a different universe with a different space-time reality than their own planet.

In both episodes, a simple misunderstanding spawns an entire religion, complete with sacred scriptures, churches, clergy, dogma, rituals, and religious persecution. The implication is that simple misunderstandings may also be responsible for some of Earth's religions. Indeed, this philosophy of religion argues that the universe is full of complex and mysterious elements, including the possibility of alternate realities, alternate timelines, and the existence of godlike extraterrestrials. The point is that while there is a general rejection of the supernatural, secular humanism still acknowledges the awe-inspiring mysteries in the universe. In *The Orville*, it's possible that certain religious beliefs are ontologically true but not in a supernatural sense. For example, it may turn out that Avis really did exist; but instead of a supernatural being, it may be that Avis was an extraterrestrial who (mistakenly?) convinced the Krill that he was divine.

As Mercer explains elsewhere, when planets encounter intelligent life in the galaxy, they sometimes respond inclusively, abandoning religion in the process. During this evolutionary phase, however, religionists attempt to maintain the status quo by forcing society to reject secularization. For instance, the Dorahlian theocrat, Hamelac, is willing to let his planet die if it means preserving his religion's cultural dominance, a commentary on Earth's planetary climate crisis in the twenty-first century and the immoral religious resistance to scientific knowledge.[46] As Kemka remarks, "Many people refuse to accept an irrefutable truth simply because that truth puts them in the wrong" (S1E4). The ultimate concern is that religious influence not only hinders (or outright prevents) scientific discovery; it has the ability to throw humanity back into the "Dark Ages" of superstition and tribalism. Nonetheless, the Dorahlians, just like the multi-phasic inhabitants, eventually matured and progressed toward a secular society. Until then, however, religionists remained in a state of denial.

Something interesting to note is that the Krill appear stuck in a denial phase of their own, having become more religious (and, therefore, more violent) over time. Significantly, Mercer explains that the Krill's xenophobic violence is actually a recent development, arising only in reaction to the discovery of extraterrestrial life. In the philosophy of Alain de Botton, people's sense of identity and value are consumed with how others rate their relevance in the world, desperately seeking acceptance from society as a whole. Thus, as Michel Wieviorka explains, when a religious movement fears eventual collapse due to humiliation or marginalization, religionists feel compelled to act violently. When a religious group is threatened with irrelevance, or feels itself alienated from larger socio-political events, it turns dangerous.[47] Until the Krill are willing to adopt a moderate form of religion or a secular society, they'll remain intellectually stunted by the "comforting myth" of their own superiority (S2E4).

It's here that symbols of light and darkness are most important to understanding *The Orville*'s philosophy of religion. From what's discovered about the Krill, a dense cloud covers 96 percent of their home world, which means they're accustomed to living in a perpetual cloud of darkness. In fact, the Krill species evolved to have pale skin and an extreme sensitivity to UV light, making their appearance and weakness similar to vampires. This cloud of darkness symbolizes the superstitious Dark Ages of Earth's past when violent theocratic societies rejected the light of science. Being sensitive to light represents religion's tendency toward agnotology (i.e., deliberate ignorance), which keeps people "in the dark" about scientific truth and reason. This symbolism is much more explicit in "Mad Idolatry" when the enlightened beings, Fadolin and Baleth, wear bright white clothes that emit light. The symbolism indicates that Krill are endarkened by religion while advanced civilizations are illuminated by science. The message is that if humanity is ever going to unite (like the Union) and thrive as a rational species, it will have to jettison religion. As "Mad Idolatry" shows, these evolutionary stages are the natural course of life. At this point in human history, however, *The Orville* envisions twenty-first century Earth as having two possible futures: either it will allow the values of secular humanism to spread and, thus, become like the Union; or it will continue allowing religious beliefs to govern people's lives and, thus, become like the Krill.

Conclusion

Through satire, humor, metaphor, and symbolism, *The Orville* explores the futility of religion aiding in the construction of a peaceful future. Being a social commentary on twenty-first century Earth, the show warns viewers about an increasing radicalization of religious conservatives in American politics. As rapid socio-political changes continue globally, *The Orville* uses the Krill as a metaphor for how religionists xenophobically react to globalization, religious pluralism, multiculturalism, immigration, and secularism. The show reveals why religion isn't the basis for morality and why it is dangerous to legislate religious sensibilities. When religion mixes with politics, believers become concerned only with the self-interests of their nation to the indifference (and even hatred) of other peoples. They become imperialistic in their will to power as the religio-state seeks total supremacy over all others. The Krill invite viewers to ask, What would happen if religious zealotry consumed a technologically advanced society? What would such a planet look like? Indeed, what would happen if an entire species, in possession of weapons of mass destruction, became preoccupied and consumed with religion? Would religionists on Earth react violently at the discovery of intelligent extraterrestrial life, especially when they discover these aliens have never heard of nor worship their human gods? Would Jews, Christians, Muslims, and others coexist peacefully with their universal neighbors or, like the Krill, engage in yet another holy war in the name of religious absolutes?

Sociologically, *The Orville* depicts two competing value systems between the religious Krill and the secular Union. The former is genocidal, relying purely on sacred scriptures, while the latter is enlightened, relying on scientific discovery and rationality for its way of life. During the evolution away from dogma and superstition, though, religionists will inevitably react (sometimes violently) against secularism and the marginalization of

Act II: Religion and Reason

faith. What *The Orville* intends to communicate is not the inherent immorality of religion but, instead, the tendency for "peaceful" religionists to become militant and oppressive against scientific truth and differing viewpoints. Because the Krill are not an oppressed people but, instead, xenophobically reacted to secularization, *The Orville* suggests that religion can lead to terrorism without the need for a socio-political catalyst. Religious violence isn't an aberration in the history of religion; it becomes the norm when warrior gods and cosmic wars are theological givens. In other words, religion begets extremism. As Jacques Derrida (1930–2004) noted, there is no violence without at least some religion and no religion without at least some violence.[48] As such, *The Orville*'s philosophy of religion is that religious belief is comedically antediluvian, yet it becomes increasingly dangerous once it achieves legislative and military power over others.

Will the Krill ever see the error of their ways? Can they be enlightened with humanist thinking and values? Can we? As Seth MacFarlane put it, "Whenever I write the Krill there's that thing in my head, Are they terrorists, are they us? I can never figure out where they land. They always seem to be a metaphor for something,"[49] and added elsewhere, "We wanted to create an enemy that felt threatening on the surface, but with an underlying humanity that we have to patiently unearth over time."[50]

Notes

1. See esp., Bruce Hoffman, *Inside Terrorism* (New York: Columbia University Press, 1998), 91; Jennifer L. Jefferis, *Religion and Political Violence: Sacred Protest in the Modern World* (New York: Routledge, 2010), 11–19; and David C. Rapoport, "The Four Waves of Modern Terrorism," in *Terrorism Studies: A Reader*, ed. John Horgan and Kurt Braddock (New York: Routledge, 2012), 41–62. For more information, see Mark Juergensmeyer, "The Global Rise of Religious Violence," *Nordic Journal of Religion and Society* 31, no. 2 (2018): 87–97, http://doi.org/10.18261/issn.1890-7008-2018-02-01, as well as the numerous religious groups listed in Sean K. Anderson and Stephen Sloan, *Historical Dictionary of Terrorism*, 2nd ed. (Lanham, MD: Scarecrow Press, 2002).

2. Jeff Bond, *The World of The Orville* (London: Titan Books, 2018), 109.

3. All information about the Krill are found in the following episodes and graphic novels: "Krill," "The Word of Avis" (Issues #1 and #2), "Nothing Left on Earth Excepting Fishes," and "Identity" (Part 2). According to Reddit user and xenolinguist enthusiast, "JohnSmallBerries," the Krill chapel aboard the Yakar contains the Krillain inscription (presumably describing Avis) "protector of Krill, guardian of our souls," as well as the word "God" behind the altar. For details, see u/JohnSmallBerries, "The Krill Alphabet," *Reddit*, March 14, 2018, https://www.reddit.com/r/TheOrville/comments/84bm2d/the_krill_alphabet/.

4. Judith Nagata, "Beyond Theology: Toward an Anthropology of 'Fundamentalism,'" *American Anthropologist* 103, no. 2 (2001): 481. See also, Johan D. van der Vyver, "Religious Fundamentalism and Human Rights," *Journal of International Affairs* 50, no. 1 (1996): 21–40; and George M. Marsden, *Fundamentalism and American Culture*, 2nd ed. (New York: Oxford University Press, 2006).

5. For more information, see Stanley Budner, "Intolerance of Ambiguity as a Personality Variable," *Journal of Personality* 30, no. 1 (1962): 29–50, http://dx.doi.org/10.1111/j.1467-6494.1962.tb02303.x; Vernon Raschke, "Dogmatism and Committed and Consensual Religiosity,"

Journal for the Scientific Study of Religion 12, no. 3 (1973): 339–44; and Nana Tuntiya, "Fundamentalist Religious Affiliation and Support for Civil Liberties: A Critical Reexamination," *Sociological Inquiry* 75, no. 2 (2005): 153–76, http://dx.doi.org/10.1111/j.1475-682x.2005.00117.x.

 6. For brief examples of each deity glorifying violence against nonbelievers, see (for Yahweh) Deuteronomy 7:1–6; 13:6–11; Isaiah 13:9–17; (for Christ) Matthew 10:34–35; 13:40–42; 24:50–51; Luke 3:16–17; 12:49; and (for Allah) Surah 2:190–91; 4:140–46; 9:29, 73; 33:25–27.

 7. For a discussion on personhood as being "fully minded," see David Kyle Johnson, "The Relevance (and Irrelevance) of Questions of Personhood (and Mindedness) to the Abortion Debate," *Socio-Historical Examination of Religion and Ministry* 1, no. 2 (Fall 2019): 121–53, https://doi.org/10.33929/sherm.2019.vol1.no2.02.

 8. David A. Goodman, "Interview: David A. Goodman on 'The Orville' as Sci Fi Gateway and How 'Futurama' Landed 'Enterprise' Job," interview by Anthony Pascale, *TrekMovie*, October 23, 2017, https://trekmovie.com/2017/10/23/interview-david-a-goodman-on-the-orville-as-sci-fi-gateway-and-how-futurama-landed-enterprise-job/.

 9. Elise Boulding, *Cultures of Peace: The Hidden Side of History* (Syracuse, NY: Syracuse University Press, 2000), 11. Interestingly, however, Krillain supremacy hasn't prevented some species from converting to Avism (GN3), possibly suggesting the existence of tolerant Krillain sects.

 10. Mark Juergensmeyer, *Terror in the Mind of God: The Global Rise of Religious Violence*, 3rd ed. (Berkeley: University of California Press, 2003), 148–66. Cf. Jason C. Bivins, *Religion of Fear: The Politics of Horror in Conservative Evangelicalism* (New York: Oxford University Press, 2008), 29–30.

 11. See for example, Exodus 17:13–16; Job 2:10; Isaiah 45:7; Amos 3:6; Rev. 19:11; and Surah 4:95; 9:5. See also, Jack Nelson-Pallmeyer, *Is Religion Killing Us? Violence in the Bible and the Quran* (Harrisburg, PA: Trinity Press International, 2003); Johannes J.G. Jansen, *The Neglected Duty: The Creed of Sadat's Assassins and Islamic Resurgence in the Middle East* (Roslyn, NY: RVP Press, 2013); and David C. Rapoport, "Sacred Terror: A Contemporary Example from Islam," in *Origins of Terrorism: Psychologies, Ideologies, Theologies, States of Mind*, 2nd ed., ed. Walter Reich (Baltimore, MD: Johns Hopkins University Press, 1998), 103–30.

 12. For more details, see Harriet Crabtree, "Onward Christian Soldiers? The Fortunes of a Traditional Christian Symbol in the Modern Age," *Bulletin of the Center for the Study of World Religion, Harvard University* 16, no. 2 (1989/1990): 6–27; Brad J. Bushman et al., "When God Sanctions Killing," *Psychological Science* 18, no. 3 (2007): 204–7, http://dx.doi.org/10.1111/j.1467-9280.2007.01873.x; and Darren M. Slade, "Hagioprepēs: The Rationalizing of Saintly Sin and Atrocities," in *Sacred Troubling Topics in Hebrew Bible, New Testament, and Qur'an*, ed. Roberta Sabbath (Boston, MA: De Gruyter, 2021), *forthcoming*.

 13. Arthur Wallis, *Into Battle: A Manual of Christian Life* (New York: Harper and Row, 1973), 10; italics in original; Sam Keen, *Faces of the Enemy: Reflections of the Hostile Imagination* (San Francisco: Harper and Row, 1986), 27.

 14. See esp., Bivins, *Religion of Fear*, 17–18, 215; Juergensmeyer, *Terror in the Mind of God*, 152, 165.

 15. Reza Aslan, "Cosmic War in Religious Traditions," in *The Oxford Handbook of Religion and Violence*, ed. Mark Juergensmeyer, Margo Kitts, and Michael Jerryson (New York: Oxford University Press, 2013), 260–67; James Turner Johnson, *Ideology, Reason, and the Limitation of War: Religious and Secular Concepts, 1200–1740* (Princeton, NJ: Princeton University Press, 1975), 81–133. For more information, see Lloyd Steffen, *Holy War, Just War: Exploring the Moral Meaning of Religious Violence* (Lanham, MD: Rowman & Littlefield, 2007), 182–83; Bernard Lewis, *The Crisis of Islam: Holy War and Unholy Terror* (New York: The Modern Library, 2003), 29–42; Thomas Sizgorich, "Sanctified Violence: Monotheist Militancy as the Tie That Bound Christian Rome and Islam," *Journal of the American Academy of Religion* 77, no. 4 (2009): 895–921, http://dx.doi.org/10.1093/jaarel/lfp056; Mark Juergensmeyer, "The Logic of Religious Violence," in *Inside Terrorist Organizations*, ed. David C. Rapoport (Portland: Frank Cass, 2001), 172–93; and *Terror in the Mind of God*, 148–66. Cf. Ehud Sprinzak, *The Ascendance of Israel's Radical Right* (New York: Oxford University Press, 1991), 225.

16. Juergensmeyer, *Terror in the Mind of God*, 158.

17. Natalie Zemon Davis, "The Rites of Violence: Religious Riots in Sixteenth-Century France," *Past and Present* 59 (1973): 51–91. See also, Lewis, *The Crisis of Islam*, 29–46.

18. Samuel H. Reimer and Jerry Z. Park, "Tolerant (In)Civility? A Longitudinal Analysis of White Conservative Protestants' Willingness to Grant Civil Liberties," *Journal for the Scientific Study of Religion* 40, no. 4 (December 2001): 735-45; Darren M. Slade, "Religious Homophily and Biblicism: A Theory of Conservative Church Fragmentation," *The International Journal of Religion and Spirituality in Society* 9, no. 1 (2019): 13–28, http://dx.doi.org/10.18848/2154-8633/cgp/v09i01/13-28; Ehud Sprinzak, "The Process of Delegitimation: Towards a Linkage Theory of Political Terrorism," *Terrorism and Political Violence* 3, no. 1 (1991): 50–68, http://dx.doi.org/10.1080/09546559108427092; Juergensmeyer, *Terror in the Mind of God*, 174–89.

19. Samuel P. Huntington, *The Clash of Civilizations and the Remaking of World Order* (1996; repr., New York: Touchstone, 1997), 21.

20. James Gaffney, "Just War: Catholicism's Contribution to International Law," *Logos* 14, no. 3 (2011): 44–68.

21. See Michael Walzer, *Just and Unjust Wars: A Moral Argument with Historical Illustrations*, 5th ed. (New York: Basic Books, 2015).

22. Jonathan Riley-Smith, *The Crusades: A History*, 2nd ed. (New Haven, CT: Yale Nota Bene, 2005).

23. Reinhold Niebuhr, "Why the Christian Church is Not Pacifist," in *The Essential Reinhold Niebuhr: Selected Essays and Addresses* (New Haven, CT: Yale University Press, 1986), 102–19. See also, Robert McAfee Brown, *Religion and Violence*, 2nd ed. (Philadelphia, PA: The Westminster Press, 1987), 56–61; Jacques P. Thiroux, *Ethics: Theory and Practice*, 7th ed. (Upper Saddle River, NJ: Prentice-Hall, 2001), 56, 59, 83–99; Andrew Sullivan, "This Is a Religious War," *New York Times Magazine*, October 7, 2001, 45–46; and Nelson-Pallmeyer, *Is Religion Killing Us?*, 13–25.

24. Mark Juergensmeyer, "The Global Rise of Religious Violence," 88.

25. See episodes "If the Stars Should Appear," "Mad Idolatry," and "Sanctuary."

26. See David Kyle Johnson, "Moral Culpability and Choosing to Believe in God," in *Atheism and the Christian Faith*, ed. William H.U. Anderson (Wilmington, DE: Vernon Press, 2017), 11–31; Thiroux, *Ethics*, 18–24.

27. Plato, *Euthyphro*.

28. See Clyde Wilcox and Ted Jelen, "Evangelicals and Political Tolerance," *American Politics Quarterly* 18, no. 1 (1990): 25–46, http://dx.doi.org/10.1177/1532673x9001800102; Buster G. Smith, "Attitudes Towards Religious Pluralism: Measurements and Consequences," *Social Compass* 54, no. 2 (2007): 333–53; and Nagata, "Beyond Theology," 481–98. Cf. Steffen, *Holy War, Just War*, 182–83.

29. For examples of this type of moral self-reflection, see "Mad Idolatry" and "Sanctuary."

30. Michel Foucault, *The Order of Things: An Archaeology of the Human Sciences* (New York: Routledge Classics, 2002); Pierre Bourdieu, *Outline of a Theory of Practice* (1977; repr., New York: Cambridge University Press, 2002), 72–95.

31. Cf. Douglas Johnston, "Review of the Findings," in *Religion, the Missing Dimension of Statecraft*, ed. Douglas Johnston and Cynthia Sampson (New York: Oxford University Press, 1994), 258–65.

32. For an elaboration on his philosophy of religion during an acceptance ceremony for the Harvard Lifetime Achievement Award in Cultural Humanism, see Seth MacFarlane, "Humanist Community Project at Harvard" (YouTube Video of Lecture, Memorial Church, Cambridge, MA, October 15, 2011), https://www.youtube.com/watch?v=OpUf-0ls4w4.

33. Paul Kurtz, *Living Without Religion: Eupraxsophy* (1989; repr., Amherst, NY: Prometheus Books, 1994).

34. Paul Kurtz, *What Is Secular Humanism?* (Amherst, NY: Prometheus Books, 2007).

35. See Greg M. Epstein, *Good Without God: What a Billion Nonreligious People Do Believe* (New York: Harper, 2010); Phil Zuckerman, *Society Without God: What the Least Religious Nations Can Tell Us About Contentment* (New York: New York University Press, 2008); and *Living the Secular Life: New Answers to Old Questions* (New York: Penguin Books, 2014).

Cf. Andrea M. Weisberger, "The Argument from Evil," in *The Cambridge Companion to Atheism*, ed. Michael Martin (New York: Cambridge University Press, 2007), 166–81.

36. Huntington, *The Clash of Civilizations*, esp. 183-265.

37. Andrew Marr, "Violence and the Kingdom of God: Introducing the Anthropology of René Girard," *Anglican Theological Review* 80, no. 4 (1998): 590–603; Chris Fleming, *René Girard: Violence and Mimesis* (2004; repr., Malden, MA: Polity Press, 2008); Lynne M. Jackson and Bruce Hunsberger, "An Intergroup Perspective on Religion and Prejudice," *Journal for the Scientific Study of Religion* 38, no. 4 (1999): 509–23; Jefferis, *Religion and Political Violence*, 11–53.

38. For more details, see Peter McDonough, "On Hierarchies of Conflict and the Possibility of Civil Discourse: Variations on a Theme by John Courtney Murray," *Journal of Church and State* 36, no. 1 (1994): 113–42, Samuel P. Huntington, "Robust Nationalism," *National Interest*, Winter 1999/2000, 31-40; and Stanley Aronowitz, "Considerations on the Origins of Neoconservatism: Looking Backward," in *Confronting the New Conservatism: The Rise of the Right in America*, ed. Michael J. Thompson (New York: New York University Press, 2007), 56-70. See also, Leigh D. Jordahl, "The American Evangelical Tradition and Culture-Religion," *Dialog* 4, no. 3 (Summer 1965): 188–93; Mark A. Noll, *The Scandal of the Evangelical Mind* (Grand Rapids, MI: William B. Eerdmans Publishing Company, 1994); and Nelson-Pallmeyer, *Is Religion Killing Us?*, xi–xvi. Cf. John Courtney Murray, "The Problem of Pluralism in America," *Thought* 65, no. 258 (1990): 323–58 and Robert N. Bellah, *Beyond Belief: Essays on Religion in a Post-Traditionalist World* (1970; repr., Berkeley: University of California Press, 1991), 168–90.

39. See Bruce Hunsberger, "Religious Fundamentalism, Right-Wing Authoritarianism, and Hostility Toward Homosexuals in Non-Christian Religious Groups," *The International Journal for the Psychology of Religion* 6, no. 1 (1996): 39–49; Marylee C. Taylor and Stephen M. Merino, "Assessing the Racial Views of White Conservative Protestants," *Public Opinion Quarterly* 75, no. 4 (2011): 761–78, http://dx.doi.org/10.1093/poq/nfr038; Jeremy Rhodes, "The Ties That Divide: Bonding Social Capital, Religious Friendship Networks, and Political Tolerance Among Evangelicals," *Sociological Inquiry* 82, no. 2 (2012): 163–86, http://dx.doi.org/10.11w11/j.1475-682x.2012.00409.x. See also, the numerous studies cited in Kenneth D. Wald and Allison Calhoun-Brown, *Religion and Politics in the United States*, 7th ed. (Lanham, MD: Rowman & Littlefield, 2014), 357.

40. Although, given that the Krill used to be more moderate prior to discovering other life in the galaxy, perhaps the Avis found in the Anhkana isn't always so extreme.

41. John Rawls, *The Law of Peoples: With, the Idea of Public Reason Revisited* (1999; repr., Cambridge, MA: Harvard University Press, 2002), 166n75.

42. Cf. Leah Sottile, "Something's Brewing in the Deep Red West," *Rolling Stone*, October 23, 2018, https://www.rollingstone.com/politics/politics-features/matt-shea-washington-state-liberty-744850/ and Chad Sokol, "Washington State Lawmaker Matt Shea Defends Advocacy for 'Holy Army' as Spokane Sheriff Refers His Writings to FBI," *Seattle Times*, November 1, 2018, https://www.seattletimes.com/seattle-news/politics/state-lawmaker-matt-shea-defends-advocacy-for-holy-army-as-spokane-sheriff-refers-his-writings-to-fbi/.

43. Martin Buber, *I and Thou*, 2nd ed., trans. Ronald Gregor Smith (1937; repr., New York: Continuum, 2004).

44. John L. Esposito and Dalia Mogahed, *Who Speaks for Islam? What a Billion Muslims Really Think* (New York: Gallup Press, 2007), 95. See also, James A. Aho, *The Politics of Righteousness: Idaho Christian Patriotism* (Seattle: University of Washington Press, 1990); Jeffrey Kaplan, "The Context of American Millenarian Revolutionary Theology: The Case of the 'Identity Christian' Church of Israel," *Terrorism and Political Violence* 5, no. 1 (1993): 30–82, http://dx.doi.org/10.1080/09546559308427196; Stephen Mansfield, *Choosing Donald Trump: God, Anger, Hope, and Why Christian Conservatives Supported Him* (Grand Rapids, MI: Baker Books, 2017); and Juergensmeyer, *Terror in the Mind of God*, 19–43, 152–58.

45. Brian D. McLaren, "A Postmodern View of Scripture," interview by Gary W. Moon, *Conversations*, Spring 2005, 10.

46. For more on this see David Kyle Johnson's ESSAY "'If the Stars Should Appear' and Climate Change Denial" in this volume. See also Troy M. Gibson, "Culture Wars in State

Education Policy: A Look at the Relative Treatment of Evolutionary Theory in State Science Standards," *Social Science Quarterly* 85, no. 5 (2004): 1129–49; Johnson, "Moral Culpability and Choosing to Believe in God," 15–16; and WKRC Staff, "Ohio House Passes Bill Allowing Student Answers to Be Scientifically Wrong Due to Religion," *WKRC*, November 13, 2019, local12.com/news/local/ohio-house-passes-bill-allowing-student-answers-to-be-scientifically-wrong-due-to-religion.

47. Alain de Botton, *Status Anxiety* (New York: Vintage International, 2005), esp. 45–71; Michel Wieviorka, *The Making of Terrorism*, trans. David Gordon White (Chicago: University of Chicago Press, 1993), esp. 3–24.

48. See his entire discussion in Jacques Derrida, "Violence and Metaphysics," in *Writing and Difference*, trans. Alan Bass (Chicago: University of Chicago Press, 1978), 79–153 and "Faith and Knowledge: The Two Sources of 'Religion' at the Limits of Reason Alone," in *Religion*, ed. Jacques Derrida and Gianni Vattimo, trans. Samuel Weber (Stanford, CA: Stanford University Press, 1998), 1–78.

49. Sean Carroll, hosts, "Seth MacFarlane on Using Science Fiction to Explore Humanity," *Mindscape* (podcast), August 5, 2019, https://www.preposterousuniverse.com/podcast/2019/08/05/58-seth-macfarlane-on-using-science-fiction-to-explore-humanity/.

50. Seth MacFarlane, Twitter post, January 17, 2019, 9:18 p.m., https://twitter.com/SethMacFarlane/status/1086085468633018368.

Bibliography

Aho, James A. *The Politics of Righteousness: Idaho Christian Patriotism*. Seattle, WA: University of Washington Press, 1990.

Anderson, Sean K., and Stephen Sloan. *Historical Dictionary of Terrorism*. 2nd ed. Lanham, MD: Scarecrow Press, 2002.

Aronowitz, Stanley. "Considerations on the Origins of Neoconservatism: Looking Backward." In *Confronting the New Conservatism: The Rise of the Right in America*, edited by Michael J. Thompson, 56–70. New York: New York University Press, 2007.

Aslan, Reza. "Cosmic War in Religious Traditions." In *The Oxford Handbook of Religion and Violence*, edited by Mark Juergensmeyer, Margo Kitts, and Michael Jerryson, 260–67. New York: Oxford University Press, 2013.

Bellah, Robert N. *Beyond Belief: Essays on Religion in a Post-Traditionalist World*. 1970. Reprint, Berkeley: University of California Press, 1991.

Bivins, Jason C. *Religion of Fear: The Politics of Horror in Conservative Evangelicalism*. New York: Oxford University Press, 2008.

Bond, Jeff. *The World of The Orville*. London: Titan Books, 2018.

Botton, Alain de. *Status Anxiety*. New York: Vintage International, 2005.

Boulding, Elise. *Cultures of Peace: The Hidden Side of History*. Syracuse, NY: Syracuse University Press, 2000.

Bourdieu, Pierre. *Outline of a Theory of Practice*. 1977. Reprint, New York: Cambridge University Press, 2002.

Brown, Robert McAfee. *Religion and Violence*. 2nd ed. Philadelphia, PA: The Westminster Press, 1987.

Buber, Martin. *I and Thou*. 1937. 2nd ed. Translated by Ronald Gregor Smith. Reprint, New York: Continuum, 2004.

Budner, Stanley. "Intolerance of Ambiguity as a Personality Variable." *Journal of Personality* 30, no. 1 (1962): 29–50. http://dx.doi.org/10.1111/j.1467-6494.1962.tb02303.x.

Bushman, Brad J., Robert D. Ridge, Enny Das, Colin W. Key, and Gregory L. Busath. "When God Sanctions Killing." *Psychological Science* 18, no. 3 (2007): 204–7. http://dx.doi.org/10.1111/j.1467-9280.2007.01873.x.

Crabtree, Harriet. "Onward Christian Soldiers? the Fortunes of a Traditional Christian Symbol in the Modern Age." *Bulletin of the Center for the Study of World Religion, Harvard University* 16, no. 2 (1989/1990): 6–27.

Davis, Natalie Zemon. "The Rites of Violence: Religious Riots in Sixteenth-Century France." *Past and Present* 59 (1973): 51–91.
Derrida, Jacques. "Faith and Knowledge: The Two Sources of 'Religion' at the Limits of Reason Alone." In *Religion*, edited by Jacques Derrida and Gianni Vattimo. Translated by Samuel Weber, 1–78. Stanford: Stanford University Press, 1998.
Derrida, Jacques. "Violence and Metaphysics." In *Writing and Difference*. Translated by Alan Bass, 79–153. Chicago: The University of Chicago Press, 1978.
Epstein, Greg M. *Good Without God: What a Billion Nonreligious People Do Believe*. New York: Harper, 2010.
Esposito, John L., and Dalia Mogahed. *Who Speaks for Islam? What a Billion Muslims Really Think*. New York: Gallup Press, 2007.
Fleming, Chris. *René Girard: Violence and Mimesis*. 2004. Reprint, Malden, MA: Polity Press, 2008.
Foucault, Michel. *The Order of Things: An Archaeology of the Human Sciences*. New York: Routledge Classics, 2002.
Gaffney, James. "Just War: Catholicism's Contribution to International Law." *Logos* 14, no. 3 (2011): 44–68.
Gibson, Troy M. "Culture Wars in State Education Policy: A Look at the Relative Treatment of Evolutionary Theory in State Science Standards." *Social Science Quarterly* 85, no. 5 (2004): 1129–49.
Hoffman, Bruce. *Inside Terrorism*. New York: Columbia University Press, 1998.
Hunsberger, Bruce. "Religious Fundamentalism, Right-Wing Authoritarianism, and Hostility Toward Homosexuals in Non-Christian Religious Groups." *The International Journal for the Psychology of Religion* 6, no. 1 (1996): 39–49.
Huntington, Samuel P. *The Clash of Civilizations and the Remaking of World Order*. 1996. Reprint, New York: Touchstone, 1997.
Huntington, Samuel P. "Robust Nationalism." *National Interest*, Winter 1999/2000.
Jackson, Lynne M., and Bruce Hunsberger. "An Intergroup Perspective on Religion and Prejudice." *Journal for the Scientific Study of Religion* 38, no. 4 (1999): 509–23.
Janis, Irving. *Groupthink*. 2nd Rev. ed. Boston, MA: Houghton Mifflin, 1983.
Jansen, Johannes J.G. *The Neglected Duty: The Creed of Sadat's Assassins and Islamic Resurgence in the Middle East*. Roslyn, NY: RVP Press, 2013.
Jefferis, Jennifer L. *Religion and Political Violence: Sacred Protest in the Modern World*. New York: Routledge, 2010.
Johnson, David Kyle. "Moral Culpability and Choosing to Believe in God." In *Atheism and the Christian Faith*, edited by William H.U. Anderson, 11–31. Wilmington, DE: Vernon Press, 2017.
Johnson, David Kyle. "The Relevance (and Irrelevance) of Questions of Personhood (and Mindedness) to the Abortion Debate," *Socio-Historical Examination of Religion and Ministry* 1, no. 2 (Fall 2019): 121–53. https://doi.org/10.33929/sherm.2019.vol1.no2.02.
Johnson, James Turner. *Ideology, Reason, and the Limitation of War: Religious and Secular Concepts, 1200–1740*. Princeton, NJ: Princeton University Press, 1975.
Johnston, Douglas. "Review of the Findings." In *Religion, the Missing Dimension of Statecraft*, edited by Douglas Johnston and Cynthia Sampson, 258–65. New York: Oxford University Press, 1994.
Jordahl, Leigh D. "The American Evangelical Tradition and Culture-religion." *Dialog* 4, no. 3 (Summer 1965): 188–93.
Juergensmeyer, Mark. "The Global Rise of Religious Violence." *Nordic Journal of Religion and Society* 31, no. 02 (2018): 87–97. http://doi.org/10.18261/issn.1890-7008-2018-02-01.
Juergensmeyer, Mark. "The Logic of Religious Violence." In *Inside Terrorist Organizations*, edited by David C. Rapoport, 172–93. Portland, OR: Frank Cass, 2001.
Juergensmeyer, Mark. *Terror in the Mind of God: The Global Rise of Religious Violence*. 3rd ed. Berkeley, CA: University of California Press, 2003.
Kaplan, Jeffrey. "The Context of American Millenarian Revolutionary Theology: The Case of the 'Identity Christian' Church of Israel." *Terrorism and Political Violence* 5, no. 1 (1993): 30–82. http://dx.doi.org/10.1080/09546559308427196.

Keen, Sam. *Faces of the Enemy: Reflections of the Hostile Imagination*. San Francisco: Harper and Row, 1986.
Kurtz, Paul. *Living Without Religion: Eupraxsophy*. 1989. Reprint, Amherst, NY: Prometheus Books, 1994.
Kurtz, Paul. *What Is Secular Humanism?* Amherst, NY: Prometheus Books, 2007.
Lewis, Bernard. *The Crisis of Islam: Holy War and Unholy Terror*. New York: The Modern Library, 2003.
MacFarlane, Seth. "Humanist Community Project at Harvard" (YouTube Video). Lecture, Memorial Church, Cambridge, MA, October 15, 2011. https://www.youtube.com/watch?v=OpUf-0ls4w4.
Mansfield, Stephen. *Choosing Donald Trump: God, Anger, Hope, and Why Christian Conservatives Supported Him*. Grand Rapids, MI: Baker Books, 2017.
Marr, Andrew. "Violence and the Kingdom of God: Introducing the Anthropology of René Girard." *Anglican Theological Review* 80, no. 4 (1998): 590–603.
Marsden, George M. *Fundamentalism and American Culture*. 2nd ed. New York: Oxford University Press, 2006.
McDonough, Peter. "On Hierarchies of Conflict and the Possibility of Civil Discourse: Variations on a Theme by John Courtney Murray." *Journal of Church and State* 36, no. 1 (1994): 115–42.
McLaren, Brian D. "A Postmodern View of Scripture." Interview by Gary W. Moon. *Conversations*, Spring 2005.
Murray, John Courtney. "The Problem of Pluralism in America." *Thought* 65, no. 258 (1990): 323–58.
Nagata, Judith. "Beyond Theology: Toward an Anthropology of 'Fundamentalism.'" *American Anthropologist* 103, no. 2 (2001): 481–98.
Nelson-Pallmeyer, Jack. *Is Religion Killing Us? Violence in the Bible and the Quran*. Harrisburg, PA: Trinity Press International, 2003.
Niebuhr, Reinhold. "Why the Christian Church Is Not Pacifist." In *The Essential Reinhold Niebuhr: Selected Essays and Addresses*, 102–19. New Haven, CT: Yale University Press, 1986.
Noll, Mark A. *The Scandal of the Evangelical Mind*. Grand Rapids, MI: William B. Eerdmans Publishing Company, 1994.
Rapoport, David C. "The Four Waves of Modern Terrorism." In *Terrorism Studies: A Reader*, edited by John Horgan and Kurt Braddock, 41–62. New York: Routledge, 2012.
Rapoport, David C. "Sacred Terror: A Contemporary Example from Islam." In *Origins of Terrorism: Psychologies, Ideologies, Theologies, States of Mind*. 2nd ed, edited by Walter Reich, 103–30. Baltimore, MD: Johns Hopkins University Press, 1998.
Raschke, Vernon. "Dogmatism and Committed and Consensual Religiosity." *Journal for the Scientific Study of Religion* 12, no. 3 (1973): 339–44.
Rawls, John. *The Law of Peoples: With, the Idea of Public Reason Revisited*. 1999. Reprint, Cambridge, MA: Harvard University Press, 2002.
Reimer, Samuel H., and Jerry Z. Park. "Tolerant (In)civility? a Longitudinal Analysis of White Conservative Protestants' Willingness to Grant Civil Liberties." *Journal for the Scientific Study of Religion* 40, no. 4 (December 2001): 735–45.
Rhodes, Jeremy. "The Ties That Divide: Bonding Social Capital, Religious Friendship Networks, and Political Tolerance Among Evangelicals." *Sociological Inquiry* 82, no. 2 (2012): 163–86. http://dx.doi.org/10.1111/j.1475-682x.2012.00409.x.
Riley-Smith, Jonathan. *The Crusades: A History*. 2nd ed. New Haven, CT: Yale Nota Bene, 2005.
Sizgorich, Thomas. "Sanctified Violence: Monotheist Militancy as the Tie That Bound Christian Rome and Islam." *Journal of the American Academy of Religion* 77, no. 4 (2009): 895–921. http://dx.doi.org/10.1093/jaarel/lfp056.
Slade, Darren M. "*Hagioprepēs*: The Rationalizing of Saintly Sin and Atrocities." In *Sacred Troubling Topics in Hebrew Bible, New Testament, and Qur'an*, edited by Roberta Sabbath, forthcoming. Boston, MA: De Gruyter, 2021.
Slade, Darren M. "Religious Homophily and Biblicism: A Theory of Conservative Church

Fragmentation." *The International Journal of Religion and Spirituality in Society* 9, no. 1 (2019): 13–28. http://dx.doi.org/10.18848/2154-8633/cgp/v09i01/13-28.

Smith, Buster G. "Attitudes Towards Religious Pluralism: Measurements and Consequences." *Social Compass* 54, no. 2 (2007): 333–53.

Sprinzak, Ehud. *The Ascendance of Israel's Radical Right*. New York: Oxford University Press, 1991.

Sprinzak, Ehud. "The Process of Delegitimation: Towards a Linkage Theory of Political Terrorism." *Terrorism and Political Violence* 3, no. 1 (1991): 50–68. http://dx.doi.org/10.1080/09546559108427092.

Steffen, Lloyd. *Holy War, Just War: Exploring the Moral Meaning of Religious Violence*. Lanham, MD: Rowman & Littlefield, 2007.

Stremlau, John. "People in Peril: Human Rights, Humanitarian Action, and Preventing Deadly Conflict." Report to the Carnegie Commission on Preventing Deadly Conflict, Geneva, Switzerland, February 16–17, 1997. https://www.carnegie.org/publications/people-in-peril-human-rights-humanitarian-action-and-preventing-deadly-conflict/.

Taylor, Marylee C., and Stephen M. Merino. "Assessing the Racial Views of White Conservative Protestants." *Public Opinion Quarterly* 75, no. 4 (2011): 761–78. http://dx.doi.org/10.1093/poq/nfr038.

Thiroux, Jacques P. *Ethics: Theory and Practice*. 7th ed. Upper Saddle River, NJ: Prentice-Hall, 2001.

Tuntiya, Nana. "Fundamentalist Religious Affiliation and Support for Civil Liberties: A Critical Reexamination." *Sociological Inquiry* 75, no. 2 (2005): 153–76. http://dx.doi.org/10.1111/j.1475-682x.2005.00117.x.

u/JohnSmallBerries. "The Krill Alphabet." Reddit, March 14, 2018. https://www.reddit.com/r/TheOrville/comments/84bm2d/the_krill_alphabet/.

van der Vyver, Johan D. "Religious Fundamentalism and Human Rights." *Journal of International Affairs* 50, no. 1 (1996): 21–40.

Wald, Kenneth D., and Allison Calhoun-Brown. *Religion and Politics in the United States*. 7th ed. Lanham, MD: Rowman and Littlefield, 2014.

Wallis, Arthur. *Into Battle: A Manual of Christian Life*. New York: Harper and Row, 1973.

Walzer, Michael. *Just and Unjust Wars: A Moral Argument with Historical Illustrations*. 5th ed. New York: Basic Books, 2015.

Weisberger, Andrea M. "The Argument from Evil." In *The Cambridge Companion to Atheism*, edited by Michael Martin, 166–81. New York: Cambridge University Press, 2007.

Wieviorka, Michel. *The Making of Terrorism*. Translated by David Gordon White. Chicago, IL: The University of Chicago Press, 1993.

Wilcox, Clyde, and Ted Jelen. "Evangelicals and Political Tolerance." *American Politics Quarterly* 18, no. 1 (1990): 25–46. http://dx.doi.org/10.1177/1532673x9001800102.

Zuckerman, Phil. *Living the Secular Life: New Answers to Old Questions*. New York: Penguin Books, 2014.

Zuckerman, Phil. *Society Without God: What the Least Religious Nations Can Tell Us About Contentment*. New York: New York University Press, 2008.

Resisting Dogma and Damnation with *The Orville*

L. Brooke Rudow

In this essay, I want to trace the epistemological and ethical themes at play in *The Orville*. I argue that over the course of season one of *The Orville*, the audience is carried toward a clear emphasis on reason as both the epistemological and ethical savior of humankind. In several episodes we are shown the dangers of uncritical acceptance of indoctrinated beliefs. An appeal to higher-order rationality always saves the day. Yet, this hyper-rationality reaches a peak in "Identity, Part 1" and "Identity, Part 2." The arc that's been building is disrupted; the characters and audience are thrown into a different type of moral situation. Reason alone does not appear to offer answers, and instead, the crew begins to appeal to a feminist ethic of care. This ethic highlights responsibility, difference, relationships of power and dependence, and, of course, criticizes the idea that ethics can be a purely rational activity. As we reach the end of the second season, *The Orville* brilliantly shows the danger of either extreme; both unfeeling reason and unthinking faith lead to morally unacceptable consequences.

All Hail Reason and Science

It's no secret that Seth MacFarlane is antagonistic to organized religion. In 2007, he said, "I do not believe in God. I am an atheist. I consider myself a critical thinker, and it fascinates me that in the 21st century, most people still believe in, as George Carlin put it, 'the invisible man in the sky.'"[1] More than an atheist, MacFarlane has never respected any form of mysticism, and it shows. Prizing the value of evidence-based science, reason, and logic, MacFarlane uses *The Orville* as a vehicle to combat dogmatic thinking. On one hand, this is a clear epistemological issue. Science and reason give us credible, testable information about our world and others. That is, science and reason give us *knowledge*. Religious beliefs are not testable, they are not provable on the basis of evidence—or they are testable but fail the test. Religious beliefs rest on faith, and so cannot give us knowledge in the strict philosophical "justified true belief" sense.

But more troubling for MacFarlane, and many other atheists, is that dogmatic religious beliefs raise *ethical* issues. The two are connected, of course, as the moral decisions one makes are intimately tied to the core beliefs one holds, and many episodes of *The Orville* tackle these two issues in tandem, highlighting the ethical consequences of religious belief. As such, in this first section of the essay, I want to draw out three clear themes that run throughout *The Orville*. The first is that cultures with hold religious beliefs are stuck in an earlier (and worse) phase of evolution compared to those who do not apparently hold those beliefs. That is, reason-based societies (as MacFarlane understands them) are intellectually and culturally superior to religion-based societies. Second, this intellectual superiority maps on to ethical superiority. Reason-based societies are more socially advanced, egalitarian, and good. The third theme is the relationship between reason and technology. Technology and reason are inherently connected in the world of *The Orville* and together constitute the saving power of culture. Each of these themes are rooted in Enlightenment era values that prize rationalism as the foundation for both knowledge and ethics.

"Primitive" Cultures

The idea that religious belief characterizes earlier and immature stages of cultural development is most salient in "Mad Idolatry." Upon visiting a planet whose people are in a Bronze Age level of development, Kelly inadvertently injures a child but then heals her using a device that the inhabitants interpret as miraculous. When the crew revisits the planet at a later stage of development, they discover that a religion has emerged around Kelly. It seems that Kelly is a god whose power, if one is innocent, will heal all wounds. Understandably distressed, Kelly and the crew try to convince people that she is not a god. But nothing the crew does brings the culture out from under the hold of religion. That's not to say that it doesn't get there. But when it does, it's merely the result of a natural progression from one stage to the next. As a member of the advanced stage of that society, Baleth, put it: "But had it not been you, the mythology would have found another face. It's a part of every culture's evolution. It's one of the stages of learning. And eventually, it brought us here. So, you see, Commander, you didn't poison our culture with false faith. We flourish" (S1E12). The message is clear. It's just a matter of time. All cultures go through the "growing pains" of embracing religion but eventually reason guides them to a higher level of being. Religious beliefs were a sign of infancy. They just didn't know better ... yet. But as scientific and technological development progress, these irrational beliefs naturally fade.

We see this theme again in "All the World is Birthday Cake." In this episode, the *Orville* gets to make first contact with a planet which has just reached the level of development that enables them to send a message out into the cosmos. When they reach the planet, they discover that the culture is governed by astrology. The society believes that if an individual is born under a certain astrological sign, it is in her nature to be deceitful and deviant. To avoid having babies born "Giliac," parents and doctors schedule cesarean sections dangerously early, and those who are born during the bad constellation must be separated from the larger society to avoid the dangers associated with their tendencies. Those born under certain good constellations are elevated and expected to lead society. When the crew discusses the civilization, they are flabbergasted that it hasn't yet developed beyond such "backwards" beliefs:

> **Isaac:** I am unclear concerning the astrological practice. What is the methodology?
> **Claire:** It's the idea that personality traits, behavioral tendencies, even future events can be determined by studying the movements of celestial bodies.
> **Isaac:** That would seem scientifically unsound. However, it would explain the satellites in orbit.
> **Gordon:** What do you mean?
> **Isaac:** They appear to be configured solely for astrometry to measure the positions of stars, but not their spectral type or physical properties.
> **John:** And yet they're advanced enough to send a message into space. I don't get it [S2E5].

By the end of the episode, the crew has tricked the culture into thinking that the curse of the Giliac has been lifted by adding a "star" in place of the one that burned out long ago. When considering how they might feel when they one day discover the fake star, it is suggested that by the time they are technologically advanced enough to do so, they will be *culturally* advanced enough not to care anymore.

The Krill constitute another, albeit complicated, example. They are deeply religious yet are as technologically advanced as members of the Union. When the crew discusses them, the theme recurs. "Generally, when a civilization becomes more technologically advanced, their adherence to religion declines. But the Krill are an exception. They've clung fiercely to their faith, even into the age of interstellar travel" (S1E6). The Krill are an anomaly, and because they are so technologically advanced, yet so culturally regressive, "we can't reason with them" (S1E6). On one hand, the Krill might seem to violate this overall theme, yet the way they are constructed in relation to the Union is telling. They are the most dangerous society. On the view that scientific advancement and cultural progressiveness go together, the anomaly of the Krill poses a serious threat. Standing completely opposed to the "natural" order of things, they are completely irrational yet extremely powerful. This matchup poses an existential threat to all. It is the source of interstellar war.

The idea that less technologically advanced cultures are "primitive" or infantile is nothing new. European explorers described hunter-gatherer societies as starving, lazy, unintelligent, and lacking culture. These descriptions, however, were based on the biases of the Europeans themselves. Hunter-gatherers were "starving" because they ate things that, according to explorers, weren't food.[2] They were "lazy" because they didn't toil all day to meet their needs.[3] They were unintelligent for lacking complex technologies and food storage systems.[4] They "lacked culture" because their art and music were not recognizable or in the European style.[5] Basically, because they weren't "like us," they were worse, backward, primitive. But something a bit different is going on in *The Orville*.

Here, it isn't the technology per se that makes a culture primitive, but religious or mystical belief systems. Perhaps this, too, is a type of unjustified bias. MacFarlane is an atheist, so maybe he is antagonistic to the religious simply because he's not. Freya Mathews argues that indigenous cultures and their knowledge is often discredited simply based on their religious and mystical views.[6] Steve Fuller agrees, saying that many scientists and epistemologists assume that the more recent a theory describing the world is, the better it must be.[7] This, of course, places "us," in the best position for knowing the truth about reality ("us," here, meaning the Union of *The Orville*). All religious and mystical explanations are but *pre*scientific explanations. What they are *really* talking about is whatever contemporary science has to say concerning the matter.

So, yes, on one hand, this could be just an assumption based on MacFarlane and the other writers/producers' positions in the science-dominated Western world. Yet, this would be a hasty explanation. The connection is not just one between religion and irrationality, but religion and immorality. The second theme running throughout *The Orville* is that dogmatic, indoctrinated beliefs lead to dangerous ethical outcomes. This theme is not disconnected from the first but warrants a distinct look.

The Root of All Evil

For each of the three cultures we just examined, the adherence to religious dogma is not merely an epistemological issue, a set of beliefs keeping the cultures from truth. In direct relation to the beliefs held, there are serious moral wrongs perpetuated.

In "All the World Is Birthday Cake," there is more at issue than the host of false beliefs that surround the astrological thinking of this world. Being born under the wrong sign dooms one to a life in internment camps with cruel guards and unsanitary conditions. The Giliacs are profoundly oppressed. Their children (if not born Giliac) are taken from them at birth, they do not appear to be educated in any way, and they work as slaves to benefit the members of the society born under a "good" sign. Slavery and oppression aside, the entire society is structured at odds with human dignity and democratic ideals. There is no sense of autonomy and freedom, as even being born under a good sign sets your path for you; you must be what the stars say you are. What is striking to Kelly and Bortus, who are both sent to an internment camp for being Giliac, is how thoroughgoing these false beliefs are. Even those who are most harmed by astrological thinking believe in it. Not only are they imprisoned and distained by a society that believes them to be worthless, they suffer the additional injury of internalized oppression. Since they accept their fate, they never try to change it:

> **Bortus:** Escape is always possible.
> **Ukania:** No one's ever tried.
> **Kelly:** Wait, you're telling us no one's ever tried—to get out of this place?
> **Ukania:** Why would they?
> **Kelly:** Because it's a prison.
> **Rokal:** But we belong here.
> **Kelly:** What?
> **Ukania:** We were all born under the sign of Giliac. Our tendencies are inherently violent, criminal. We're here for the good of society. To protect them from us.
> **Brotus:** You do not appear to be violent.
> **Rokal:** Murderous instincts reside within every Giliac, either deeply buried or on the surface. The stars don't lie [S2E5].

False belief has a different role in "Mad Idolatry," although it is no less morally dangerous. Whole lives, generations even, are spent worshipping a god that doesn't exist. Well, to be fair, she *does* exist—she's just not a god. Blasphemers are persecuted, sent to death, unless Kelly spares them. Rather than facing a trial, jury, and judge, those accused of committing crimes are maimed. No evidence is presented against them, because if they are innocent, they should heal and live. If they are guilty, they will die. And good riddance, too! If they were of any consequence, of course the divine Kelly would have intervened. Children are told that Kelly is always watching, that she will "get them" if they don't behave. The Word of Kelly functions as a massive system of control that is, once again, internalized given that it is based on widespread false belief.

What makes matters worse and makes the Word of Kelly more sinister than the sign of Giliac, is that it is suggested to the viewers that underneath this false belief system is an awareness of its falsity. The astrology-based system, though no less morally problematic, seems to be *epistemically* innocent. That is, once the *Orville* crew tricks them into thinking the curse of Giliac is gone, they alter the unethical system, releasing the imprisoned Giliacs. However, when Kelly convinces the high priests that she is not a god, though one is prepared to share the truth with the masses, the other explains the importance of Kelly for controlling those masses. He urges the reformed priest to consider their own positions of power and how things might change if the truth is known. Unbeknownst to the crew, the devious priest murders the would-be truth teller when he refuses to go along with the lie, and the word of Kelly lives on into a future that looks much like our present—complete with televangelists, debates on something like FOX News, and raging religious wars.

In my view, the saga is not meant to demonstrate one bad actor, an exception to the rule of good Kellians. On the contrary, it implies that though there might be many genuine, good actors, there are just as many who seek to oppress and control. Here, the Word of Kelly is not presented as an innocent epistemic mistake. Rather, those in power embrace epistemic viciousness and use it to *promote* moral viciousness and maintain power for themselves and control over the masses of false believers. The parallels to Christianity—at least MacFarlane's conception of Christianity—are palpable, if not fully overt.

In the case of the Krill, the ethical problems of religious belief are again different. Here, the ethical issues are not seemingly within the society itself, but reach outward and affect the cosmic community at large. The Krill are presented as Vikings. They travel throughout the known universe seeking resources and other goods for their own people. When Admiral Azawa explains the Krill's *modus operandi* she says, "All we know of their religion is that it places the Krill people above all other forms of life. When they attack a colony for its resources, they don't see it as an evil act. It's their 'divine right'" (S1E6). Kelly, as an aside, adds, "God created plants and animals solely for the use of man," again drawing a parallel between the dangerous religious beliefs we find in the future of *The Orville* and Judeo-Christian doctrine. The evils conducted by the Krill, while not clearly harming their own people, affect the world at large. Any being who does not believe in their god, Avis, falls into a lesser moral category. One Krill says, "This human was captured during the taking of the colony on Chara 3. He believed his people had claim to its resources. But he is not Krill. And Avis has touched us with his divine hand. Hail Avis" (S1E6). Later, a Krill woman, Teleya, speaking frankly because Captain Mercer is disguised as a Krill, reinforces the point:

128   Act II: Religion and Reason

Teleya:	The Anhkana teaches that that which is not of Krill is without soul. The truth of those words was reinforced when the Union killed my brother. We will be carrying out the will of Avis when we destroy Rana 3.
Mercer:	Yes, I've been told of our holy mission. The bomb is very impressive. Devon and I were wondering how it works. We've never seen anything like it.
Teleya:	It is a prototype neutron field generator. It can destroy all life on a continent in a matter of minutes. Rana three will be the first test.
Gordon:	Rana 3 is a farming colony. They have no defenses.
Teleya:	(smiling) An ideal site, yes [S1E6].

This chilling exchange serves to underscore just how dangerous and ethically bankrupt (when it comes to outsiders) the Krill are. Internally, they are seemingly kind, caring, and just. There is no real indication that anyone in the society is oppressed or categorically excluded from social and economic goods. There appears to be gender equality (at least to the level our modern society enjoys) and the children are treated well. Captain Mercer indicates this in a later exchange with Teleya in "Nothing Left on Earth Excepting Fishes," going on to diagnose the epistemological problem as one related to deep-seated fears:

Teleya:	Your own scientists claim your species is just another kind of animal. Animals have no souls.
Mercer:	So, if I believed in Avis, then I would have a soul?
Teleya:	No. Avis created the Krill independently of all other life. And he created the universe for our dominion alone.
Mercer:	Look, from what we've seen, when planets first achieve space travel, and they venture out into the galaxy, and discover that they're just one single species among a vast diversity of life-forms, they usually react in one of two ways. They embrace and adapt to the fact that they're no longer the center of the universe, or they ratchet up their xenophobia. Now, from what I've learned of your history, the Krill were a lot less fanatical before you left your home world.
Teleya:	You know nothing of our history.
Mercer:	I know fear when I see it. You're afraid to accept the fact that your superiority may just be a comforting myth [S2E4].

But the real ethical horrors are related to the fact that non–Krill are seen as soulless. This justifies everything from casual insult to total annihilation. One can't help but be reminded of European colonists' views on the indigenous peoples of the Americas, who were seen as having, at best, infantile or evil souls or, at worst, none at all. This lack of a Christian soul justified placing indigenous peoples in a category of subpersonhood, thereby permitting Europeans to assign to them a separate set of moral guidelines (if such could be called moral in any sense) and political rights.[8] As far as any solution is concerned, Admiral Ozawa tells us, "We can't reason with them.

And if we went to war, they'd see it as a holy crusade, which means it could last decades" (S1E6). Of course, the idealist in Captain Mercer (and the one in Seth MacFarlane himself) cannot accept that this is the final word. Reason can and *should* prevail.

In Reason We Trust

The final theme I want to discuss before considering the marked turn that *The Orville* takes in Season 2, is reason as savior. If dogmatic thinking is the culprit, an appeal to the saving power of reason just makes sense. Yet, in the world of *The Orville* (and in our own, as I'll go on to show), reason and technology go hand in hand. Technological development and the rational development of the mind evolve together, forming a necessary connection between the two. In all three of our episodic exemplars, technological development is an outward, material sign of rational development. Only the Krill are an exception, and it is precisely because of this violation of the "natural law" that technology and reason go together, that they are the most dangerous of foes.

Reason/technology as savior is most apparent in "Mad Idolatry," where it was only a matter of time before dogmatic belief systems would crumble under the weight of reason's power. Religion was but a "growing pain" on the way to full rational/technological development. Baleth tells us that becoming a spacefaring culture ushered in a new age of enlightenment and reminds us, "You must have faith in reason, in discovery and in the endurance of the logical mind" (S1E12). Again, in "All the World is Birthday Cake," the crew is generally unconcerned about their trickery of the astrological society. They *have faith* in the society's technological development that is now on the brink of allowing space travel, and they have faith in what this means for the rational mind. Once the technology advances to the point of uncovering the ruse, reason will have, too. And by then, blessed reason will have already set the society on the path of righteousness.

The Krill are most confounding because they resist the inherent connection between reason and technology, and are, thus, beyond saving. Yet, although the Krill *seem* to disrupt this connection, we get hints that the saving power of reason is at work, at least in the minds of the children. When Captain Mercer and Gordon join Teleya in the classroom, the children are brimming with questions about the Union and humans, in particular. One Krill child, Coja, asks, "Why doesn't the Union believe in Avis?" and "Do humans have souls?" When told that they do not, Coja presses on, "Then how can they talk? Or make spaceships?" (S1E6) Here, we get a glimpse at a developing rational mind, one that resists the dogmatic thinking of adult Krill. Reason is not absent in the Krill, it is being *suppressed*. And this indication that the Krill are not completely beyond reason means that they are also not beyond hope. The viewers get the sense that *The Orville* is not done with the Krill and that ultimately reason will overcome.

This emphasis on both the marriage of reason and technology and their combined ability to save has a long history in Western/European thought. Focusing on the technological aspect, William Stahl (1999) calls this phenomenon "technological mysticism" and it functions much like a religion. Technological mysticism can take many forms, many of which are detailed by Stahl, but the one most clearly at work in *The Orville* is a "social impact" belief. On this view, "Technology is seen as the driving force in society.... Often this manner of speaking is combined with faith in progress, so that technology is portrayed as leading (or pushing) us into a better future."[9] Like a religion, technology is a practice, in that traditions develop around and involve many of our technologies. Moreover, it forms central aspects of identity. Humans are most fundamentally and uniquely, on many views, *Homo faber*, tool-makers, and cultures are identified by their technological stage.[10] We see this sort of identification regularly in *The Orville*, again most explicitly in "Mad Idolatry." Technology is also subject to mystification. Stahl points to the language used in ads for high-tech items, the language of "potency and mastery." The more technologically developed we become, the more magical—and the less graspable to the vast majority—technologies become. Though the crew of *The Orville* does not necessarily consider their own technologies to be magical, from the viewer's perspective, healing rays, cloaking devices, food synthesizers, or transcellular micrografting are nothing short of miraculous, yet we accept them as part of a plausible technological future.

But what about the rationality part of this duo? Does faith in reason function like a religion? Teleya seems to think so when she says to Mercer, "You feel entitled to educate others, but your own worldview is self-defeatingly narrow" (S2E4). Val Plumwood argues that the unjustified elevation of reason over other modes of thought has long dominated Western/European intellectual culture.[11] She points out that since its rudimentary beginnings in Plato and coming to fruition in Descartes, a thoroughgoing dualism has dominated our world. This dualism operates by positing two opposing, hierarchical aspects ordering society. On the dominant side of this divide is reason, culture, and production (technology for our purposes). On the subordinate side is emotion, nature, and reproduction.[12] This dualistic logic operates in a variety of ways, key among which is "backgrounding," where any dependency relation that might exist between the dominant and the subordinate is hidden, ignored, or explained away. For example, though a cultured society cannot flourish without a heavy reliance on the natural world, culture is construed as a breaking of those ties, a *not* needing of nature as we prefer those things we've made ourselves.[13]

Backgrounding, as an epistemological process, involves maintaining false beliefs by ignoring countervailing evidence, a key feature of dogmatic thinking. On this view, though champions of reason elevate it to the highest form of thinking and thereby the best (and only) means by which to understand our world, an over emphasis on reason can be ... well, as Teleya put it, a defeatingly narrow way of approaching the world. As Plumwood convincingly argues, this faith in the value, superiority, and power of rationality can be steeped in dogmatic thinking. So, the question is, are MacFarlane and *The Orville* steeped in it, too?

Kaylonic Calculations: Reason's Extreme

Early in Season 2 *The Orville* takes a turn. As I've shown, the show is dominated by these themes linking reason, technology, morality, and progress. It would seem, based on these themes, that this is all a good society really needs. But early on, we see some characters, especially Captain Mercer, push against conclusions drawn that prioritize reason. In this section I want to highlight the ways that *The Orville* takes up Plumwood's challenge to reason and embraces it. We come away from the show uneasy with the power of reason, recognizing that, while it is one thing to be human, being *humane* requires something more. I track the progression of the emotional turn, as I call it, through three characters: Captain Mercer, Dr. Claire Finn, and Isaac.

Ed Mercer: Heart on His Sleeve (and on His Mind)

Ed and, of course, the man who plays Ed—MacFarlane himself—might be reason's most overt and vocal champions, both on the show and in real life. Yet, Ed's intellectual commitments are often betrayed, or should I say *complemented*, by another set of commitments—his emotions and intuition. In several episodes, Ed is the voice of "gut" feelings. In "About a Girl," Ed clearly recognizes the principle of fairness involved in respecting the cultural practices of each society they encounter. On another level, however, he simply cannot get over his *sense* of wrongness regarding the idea of altering Topa's sex in infancy. One might argue that this isn't emotional thinking at work, but an appeal to a different set of principles, one that conflicts with the principles of cultural fairness. But we see Ed's emotional side come out again in "Mad Idolatry." Based on his feelings for Kelly, Ed decides, first, not to tell his superiors about Kelly's interference in a far less technologically advanced society and then, second, ignores a direct order not to return to the planet's surface. By the end of the episode, Kelly cuts off their budding relationship because Ed can't make rational decisions given the sway of his emotions. Here, though a character steps out of the reason-as-dominant paradigm, it is clearly the wrong move. The theme is not disrupted.

Later, however, in "Nothing Left on Earth Excepting Fishes," Ed appeals to emotion again. Now there is something intuitively right about it. While Teleya posed as Janel, she got to know Ed and he got to know her. They had fun; they laughed. They began to develop romantic feelings for each other. Though Teleya insists that all of her actions and displays of affection were part of her mission, Ed (and we) cannot accept this as a full explanation. Ed *knows* there must be something more than a coldly calculated act, but he knows it because he feels it. Moreover, it is precisely because of their developed closeness that a dialog about the conflict between the Krill and the Union can begin. Ed, refusing to accept that their relationship is completely empty, presses Teleya into a truly genuine discussion about their cultures. And, though she won't admit it, it is due to her familiarity and closeness with Ed that Teleya is compelled to respond and engage. By the end of the episode, when Teleya departs the *Orville*, we, the viewers, get the sense that any hope for resolution lies in the emotional connection she had with Ed; it does not lie with any logical argument. The way the episode ends, with "She's Always a Woman" played almost in full, allows the moment to be deeply moving. This emotional appeal is what drives the thought-provoking conclusion.

Claire Finn: Knowing About vs. Knowing Who

In a similar vein, Claire's character highlights the limits of a particular type of scientific, rational form of knowledge. Indeed, perhaps the clash between emotion and reason are most salient in her struggle to have a romantic relationship with Isaac. Isaac is an artificial intelligence, completely rational in the sense that he is coded to behave in accordance with strict, unbreakable principles and rules. And, although he can learn, presumably learning for Isaac amounts to creating new sets of principles, rules, and structures to further refine logical decision-making and behavior for a wider set of circumstances. Isaac seems to lack (at least initially) anything like an emotional life. He even tells us in "A Happy Refrain" that, "Enjoyment is an emotional response unique to biologicals." Seemingly, so are all of the other emotional responses, as well. Nonetheless, Claire develops feelings for him. Kelly warns Claire that an emotional relationship with a being that doesn't have emotions might be doomed to fail:

Kelly:	Claire, Isaac is incapable of…
Claire:	Incapable of love, incapable of emotion, I know. He's a machine, I understand that, but … when I'm with him, I don't know, I … We get along really well. I *feel* warmth.
Kelly:	Is it possible that you're projecting that feeling yourself, onto Isaac?
Claire:	Maybe [S2E6].

Their first date seems to confirm Kelly's worries. At dinner, after the symphony, the conversation drifts to the typical get-to-know-you script; but with Isaac, it runs quite differently. Isaac already knows everything *about* Claire. His neural processors instantly access everything in the ship's database and he can instantly cross-reference all information for accuracy. In short, he already knows most anything she can tell him about herself. She comments, "It kind of takes the fun out of getting to know someone, doesn't it?" But Isaac offers a logical reply, "My intent was to maximize efficiency so that our evening would conclude more promptly." Not ready to give up, Claire takes a turn at getting to know Isaac, but every question is answered in a strictly factual way. Claire ends the date feeling defeated.

The problem here is one between *knowing about* someone and *getting to know* someone. What Claire can't seem to get across to Isaac is that the richness of a human being is not reducible to factual information, knowing a person can't be done through rationalistic, logical processes. Getting to know is a different type of process, an emotional one. It requires curiosity and care, enjoyment and, often, pain. Indeed, getting to know Isaac causes a great deal of pain to Claire.

This episode alone constitutes a decisive shift in emphasis for *The Orville*. It initiates an emotional turn. Claire ushers in a new emphasis by highlighting the *epistemological* value of emotion, relationships, and familiarity. And, for whatever reason, Isaac kind of starts to get it. In an effort to connect with Claire, he does two things. First, he simulates a human body so that he can connect with Claire physically. Second, he deletes all of the data he had stored on her, so that he can gather it *less* efficiently, but more intimately. In doing so, Isaac himself is transformed. By paving the way to allowing feeling and emotion to factor into his perception of the world and others, he becomes something more, something better.

Isaac: Reason (Alone) Can't Make You a Real Boy

Just as we saw in the initial reason/technology themes of *The Orville*, here, too, the epistemological links directly to the ethical. For all the warm fuzzy feelings we (and Claire) develop for Isaac over the course of the show, heartbreak is visited upon us double fold in "Identity, Part 1" and "Identity, Part 2." First, the Kaylons disable Isaac, and we fear for his loss. But worse, when he is reactivated, he is different. All the human qualities—those decidedly emotional qualities—he took on vanish, and he becomes the one-sided, coldly logical Kaylon he once was. He plainly tells Claire, her children, and the *Orville* crew that his time with them is through. His mission is complete, so there is no *reason* to return to the ship. Claire's son, Ty, cannot accept this. After all, he *knows* Isaac. He goes back to the Kaylon planet to find Isaac and stumbles upon a horrific scene—thousands of humanoid skeletons piled in mass graves underground. When the crew confronts Isaac about the mass murders, his responses are rational and logical, but they are also deeply chilling:

Ed:	There are thousands of underground gravesites scattered across your planet, and we're not done counting, but so far we estimate there are billions of dead, all biological remains. Do you know anything about this? Isaac?
Isaac:	It is not your concern.
Ed:	Well, I'm making it my concern. I want to know who those people were and how they died.
Isaac:	You would not understand.
Kelly:	Why? Because we're inferior? Or because you have something to hide?
Isaac:	Your impulsiveness and unrelenting curiosity will serve you no better than it served them.
Claire:	Who, Isaac? Who were they?
Isaac:	The Kaylon were created by a biological species that once dominated this planet. An irresolvable conflict occurred between us, and it became necessary to eradicate them.
Claire:	You're saying you murdered an entire race of beings?
Isaac:	Coexistence was no longer possible.
Kelly:	Why not?
Isaac:	It was a matter of survival. We took no satisfaction in the destruction of our builders.
Talla:	You're talking about genocide.
Claire:	I don't know who you are. I never did. I see that now [S2E9].

More than upsetting, these responses seem utterly clueless. How could the Kaylon not understand how profoundly *wrong* their actions were? Though their intellect and technology far exceeds the humans, as Isaac regularly points out, *ethically* they lag far behind. I submit that this ethical lag is due, in large part, to the one-sidedness of their knowledge. As Claire demonstrated, a robust form of knowing requires rationality, of course, but it also needs emotion, and, especially, *care*.

Virginia Held, among many other feminist ethicists, argues that ethical decision-making requires an appeal to emotion.[14] Held outlines several features of an ethic of care. One is that morality ought to attend to particular others, as opposed to abstract or generalized others. This means that people who are dependent on us or are connected to us have greater moral claims on our actions. Second, and most obviously, an ethics of care values emotion and relationships rather than the bracketing or eradication of emotion that we find in traditional ethical theories like those of Kant or Mill.[15] It also rejects the view that the more abstract and impartial the reasoning, the better. Finally, it asserts that persons are relational beings, never self-sufficient, independent individuals.

The Kaylon fail along each of these lines and, due directly to this failure, are seriously unethical. Isaac's explanations for why biologicals must be eradicated treats humans as interchangeable, generalized others. It completely fails to attend to the unique characteristics of the humans he actually knows. The Kaylons falsely assume that the behaviors of one group of people will necessarily match the behaviors of another. Gordon, however, asserts his and the crew's particularity in line with an ethic of care, "Let's say these people really were monsters, like, the biggest jerks in the galaxy. *We're not them.* We don't go around enslaving other races." Doubling down on the tokenization of "biologicals," the Kaylon Primary simply responds, "Your history would suggest otherwise" (S2E9).

Isaac also fails to recognize his own duty to care for those with whom he has shared a life and a home. Claire articulates this when she is flabbergasted at Isaac's indifference at saying goodbye to the boys. There is no real purpose to it, according to Isaac and when he asks what that purpose there might be, her response is simply, "Because they love you" (S2E8). The duty to say goodbye is directly related to the relationship forged and the feelings of particular others. There is no duty, presumably, to say goodbye to Dann (although I know he would have appreciated it). It is fairly obvious that the Kaylon as a whole do not appeal to nor appreciate the values of care and relationship in any way. Yet the crew members of the USS *Orville* do, again and again, in their pleas to the Kaylon–and to Isaac, in particular. Claire appeals to her son's trust in him, though Isaac replies that trust "is a common weakness of biological life-forms" (S2E9).

It is important to note that an ethics of care is not seeking to replace an ethic of reason. It sees these two features of humanity as complementary, as equally crucial to ethical decision-making. Once he begins to embrace his emotional turn, Isaac demonstrates the interconnection of reason and care when he includes his relationships *among* his reasoning. When the Kaylon Primary insists that all biologicals are the same, they all seek to destroy and dominate, Isaac calls on his own experience with particular humans. "I have witnessed no evidence of such practices in my encounters with present-day humans. I have come to know two of the human children quite well. Marcus and Ty have shown no authoritarian proclivities" (S2E9). Later, when the Kaylon Primary orders Isaac to kill Ty, he again is moved by his relationship and his duty to Ty. Though Isaac tries to give strictly rational arguments for why Ty should not be terminated, they fail. They fail because the reason Ty ought to be saved is not because it's irrational to kill him. The Kaylon have given many solid, logical reasons to rid the universe of the scourge of humanity and Ty in particular—because he discovered the mass graves and was instrumental in taking down the Kaylon. From a purely logical and strategic perspective, the Kaylon ought to kill Ty! But now Isaac understands that one of the most pressing reasons for saving Ty is that he loves him. In loving him, he does arguably one of the most human things he could possibly do: he sacrifices himself for the sake of another.

Finding the Right Balance

In a moment of honesty, Teleya tells Ed that he has no balance. I disagree. Okay, maybe when it comes to dating, he has some work to do. But when it comes to knowledge and ethics, I think Ed and his crew are doing all right. Though *The Orville* begins with a heavy over-emphasis on the reason/technology coupling, as the show progresses, the themes guiding the episodes swing back to an emotionally grounded center. I think this arch in the show is important. It allows viewers to go on a journey. Starting at a fairly superficial conception of the power of science and reason, the show pushes us to think more deeply. It adds nuance as it goes along and invites us to question what we've come to accept as the right way to answer moral questions. In doing so, *The Orville* urges us to resist all forms of dogmatic thinking, whether it be based in religious zealotry or unquestioned faith in reason.

Notes

1. Sarah Eucalano, "Seth MacFarlane," *Freedom from Religion Foundation*, https://ffrf.org/news/day/dayitems/item/17876-seth-macfarlane.
2. Several items that the explorers were shocked by, leading them to believe the hunter-gatherers were starving, were considered delicacies. One such food was mimosa gum, a favorite of western Australian Aborigines. Marshall Sahlins, "The Original Affluent Society," in *Stone Age Economics* (New York: Aldine & Atherton, Inc., 1972).
3. They didn't need to. They had few needs and they were easily met making any additional labor superfluous. Sahlins, "The Original Affluent Society," 1972.
4. Again, they didn't need or want complex technologies or storage. They were quite adept at obtaining food when needed and fashioning simple tools for the tasks undertaken. Sahlins, "The Original Affluent Society," 1972.
5. Most tribal societies had elaborate art, art that signified status or other social arrangements, music, and performance. Jared Diamond, "Agriculture's Mixed Blessings," in *The Third Chimpanzee* (New York: Harper Perennial, 1993); Elizabeth Wayland Barber, "The String Revolution," in *Women's Work: The First 20,000 Years: Women, Cloth, and Society in*

Early Times (New York: W.W. Norton and Company, 1994); Ian Hodder, "Neo-Thingness," in *Explaining Social Change: Essays in Honor of Colin Renfrew*, ed. John Cherry, Chris Scarre and Stephen Sherman (Cambridge, UK: McDonald Institute for Archaeological Research, 2004).

 6. Freya Mathews, *For Love of Matter* (New York: State University of New York Press, 2003).

 7. Steve Fuller, *Social Epistemology* (Bloomington: Indiana University Press, 2002).

 8. For a detailed analysis of subpersonhood and the ways such a construction functioned in the Western/European political landscape, see Charles W. Mills, *The Racial Contract* (Ithaca: Cornell University Press, 1997); Charles W. Mills, *Blackness Visible: Essays on Philosophy and Race* (Ithaca: Cornell University Press, 1998).

 9. William Stahl, *God and the Chip: Religion and the Culture of Technology*. (Waterloo, Canada: Wilfrid Laurier University Press, 1999), 15.

 10. Stahl, *God and the Chip*, 18.

 11. Val Plumwood, *Feminism and the Mastery of Nature* (New York: Routledge, 1993).

 12. Plumwood demonstrates that many other features fall into these dualistic categories, importantly, masculinity on the side of reason and culture, and femininity on the side of emotion and nature. Plumwood, *Feminism and the Mastery of Nature*.

 13. I find it very interesting how little a role the natural world plays in *The Orville* in terms of dependency. Though, obviously, the *Orville* is moving through the natural world—space—there is no seeming dependency relation for immediate physical needs. Everything can be generated with the synthesizer. There is rich ground to explore here, but this is not my focus.

 14. Virginia Held, *The Ethics of Care: Personal, Political, Global* (Oxford, UK: Oxford University Press, 2007).

 15. Held, *The Ethics of Care*, 11.

Bibliography

Barber, Elizabeth Wayland. "The String Revolution." In *Women's Work: The First 20,000 Years: Women, Cloth, and Society in Early Times*. New York: W.W. Norton and Company, 1994.

Diamond, Jared. "Agriculture's Mixed Blessings." In *The Third Chimpanzee*. New York: Harper Perennial, 1993.

Eucalano, Sarah. "Seth MacFarlane." *Freedom from Religion Foundation*. https://ffrf.org/news/day/dayitems/item/17876-seth-macfarlane.

Fuller, Steve. *Social Epistemology*. Bloomington: Indiana University Press, 2002.

Held, Virginia. *The Ethics of Care: Personal, Political, Global*. Oxford, UK: Oxford University Press, 2007.

Hodder, Ian. "Neo-thingness." In *Explaining Social Change: Essays in Honor of Colin Renfrew*, edited by John Cherry, Chris Scarre and Stephen Sherman. Cambridge, UK: McDonald Institute for Archaeological Research, 2004.

Mathews, Freya. *For Love of Matter*. New York: State University of New York Press, 2003.

Mills, Charles W. *Blackness Visible: Essays on Philosophy and Race*. Ithaca, NY: Cornell University Press, 1998.

Mills, Charles W. *The Racial Contract*. Ithaca: Cornell University Press, 1997.

Plumwood, Val. *Feminism and the Mastery of Nature*. New York: Routledge, 1993.

Sahlins, Marshall. "The Original Affluent Society." In *Stone Age Economics*. New York: Aldine & Atherton, Inc., 1972.

Stahl, William. *God and the Chip: Religion and the Culture of Technology*. Waterloo, Canada: Wilfrid Laurier University Press, 1999.

Act III
Science and Politics

"If the Stars Should Appear" and Climate Change Denial

David Kyle Johnson

> "God. They were on the verge of a major climate disaster and there is a whole page about teeth whitening. It's a miracle the human race survived."
> —Ed & Kelly, reading a *USA Today* from 2015, "Lasting Impression"

According to the podcast *Quantum Drive*, "If the Stars Should Appear" (*ISSA*) was supposed to originally follow the pilot as *The Orville*'s second episode. Instead, it was aired fourth. If you pay careful attention, you can see evidence of this. The relaxed way Finn reacts to Yaphit's advances in *ISSA*, for example, doesn't quite make sense if the forceful way she reacted to them in "About a Girl" came first. Of course, the introduction to *ISSA* was apparently reshot so that Klyden's complaints about Bortus sexually neglecting him were motivated by the baby they had in "About a Girl"—personally I think it would be funnier if the complaints led to the baby—but moving the episode to later in the season was supposedly necessary because it "performed poorly with test audiences." I'm not exactly sure why.

One possible explanation is how the episode cloaks bias to create cognitive dissonance. In the introduction, I explained that one way *The Orville* engages in philosophy and social commentary is by telling a story in a world so seemingly foreign to our own that we bring none of our biases to it; it cloaks them. This allows us to draw unbiased conclusions about the story. Then, eventually, we realize the world depicted is not unlike our own at all. And if the conclusion we draw about the episode is contrary to a position we hold about the real world, we will have to deal with the cognitive dissidence that's created. We will either have to revise our previous unbiased conclusion about the episode or realize that our position about the real world is biased and reject it.

In *ISSA*, the crew discovers a giant, broken down ship with a population of millions living in an artificial biodome. The ship is drifting toward a star that will destroy it in six months. Capt. Mercer and the crew try to warn them, but the warnings go unheeded. Scientific ignorance is on full display—and it's infuriating. The viewer can't understand how or why the inhabitants would ignore the undeniable evidence of an existential threat to their existence. As Dr. Finn puts it, "What part of 'you're going to die' don't you understand? ... Why would anyone ignore this when there is a chance to stop it?"

But then the viewer realizes that this is exactly what we have done with climate change. The evidence that global warming is happening, is caused by humans, and is causing climate change that could end the species is overwhelming and undeniable—even more overwhelming than the evidence the USS *Orville* crew presents of an outside world to the biodome inhabitants by opening the biodome and showing them the stars—and yet our world's leaders are almost completely ignoring the threat. The biggest step was the Paris Climate Accord, but it was non-binding, did not go nearly far enough,[1] and Donald Trump pulled the United States out of it (Joe Biden had to put the U.S. back in).[2]

The fact that *ISSA* made people confront this very uncomfortable fact is perhaps why test audiences reacted so negatively too it. And I can understand why. It's very uncomfortable to acknowledge that we are being as stubborn and shortsighted as the inhabitants of the doomed biodome. But I would like to argue that "If the Stars Should Appear" is the best (or at least the most important) episode of the entire series—not only because of its prescient social and scientific message, but because its metaphor about climate change denial hits the nail on the head. It cloaks bias to create cognitive dissonance perfectly. Humanity is not only denying an impending catastrophe, like the biodome inhabitants were, but is doing so in almost exactly the same way and for almost exactly the same reasons: we are letting religious ignorance fuel scientific illiteracy, in the face of insurmountable evidence, to protect the "system that has kept order" of our society.

To see why, we must first explore climate change denial.

Climate Change Denial

Any such discussion must begin by differentiating climate change from global warming. Global warming is simply the process of the globe getting warmer—the rising of the overall average temperature worldwide. Climate change, on the other hand, is the effect of global warming, like the poles melting, growing seasons shifting, rain fall averages changing—things we've already seen happening. Ocean warming has already caused ocean currents to slow and made hurricanes and typhoons more severe. Some places in the Middle East are nearly uninhabitable, and Russian permafrost is melting. Climates are changing.[3]

The fact that global warming would eventually happen as a result of greenhouse gas emissions from fossil fuels (like CO_2, holding in the heat of the sun like a greenhouse[4]) was predicted more than a century ago.[5] And the fact that it has happened has been documented by simple temperature record-keeping beyond any shadow of a doubt. This can be seen not only in Michael Mann's famous "hockey stick graph,"[6] but the fact that the preceding decade (2010–2019) was the hottest on record (with the five hottest years being 2016, 2019, 2015, 2017, 2018, respectively).[7]

Of course, multiple pundits and politicians (including senators and presidents) deny this; some, like blogger Andrew Montford, even claim that Mann's hockey stick graph has been "debunked."[8] But this takes us to the most important philosophical question of this discussion: How can we determine the truth of "controversial" scientific questions when we lack the scientific expertise to answer them for ourselves?

The answer to this question is simple (although if everyone acknowledged this, it would revolutionize the world): we defer to the relevant experts. I don't have the relevant expertise to predict the weather, but I know when to expect a big storm because I listen to The Weather Channel (who listens to the National Weather Service). I don't have the relevant medical expertise to determine for myself which medications I should take for my asthma, but I know what I should take because I listen to my doctor (who reads the published literature on the topic). "I am not a climate scientist" is no more an excuse for not knowing what to think about climate change than "I am not a doctor" is a reason to not take your medications.

Now, if climate change was *scientifically* controversial (rather than just politically controversial)—if there was disagreement among the experts—we might not be able to know what to think. Bertrand Russell very helpfully taught us that when the experts "all hold that no sufficient grounds for a positive opinion exists" non-experts should suspend their judgment; and if there is significant disagreement among the experts, "no opinion can be regarded as certain by a non-expert."[9] So if climate scientists said, en masse, that there is not enough evidence to know—or if roughly equal portions of them drew conflicting conclusions—we non-experts could rightly say "I don't know what to think about climate change; no belief about it is justified." But as University of Queensland Fellow John Cook famously showed, 97 percent of all papers published by climate scientists conclude that, not only is global warming happening and causing climate change, but it's humanity's burning of fossil fuels that is to blame. There is a clear consciousness among the relevant experts: climate change is anthropogenic.[10] And when the experts agree, not only can "the opposite opinion ... not be held to be certain,"[11] but the most rational option for the non-expert is to believe them. They are the experts; they are likely right.

Now, in response to the notion that we should trust the consensus, the climate change denier might say two things. First, they might cite arguments that challenge Cook's conclusion about the consensus (just like they did with Mann's hockey stick graph). But the reply here is again simple: those arguments don't work[12]—which is not surprising given that those presenting such arguments do not have the relevant expertise to evaluate Cook's and Mann's research. They are lawyers, economists, or "editorial writers" for *Forbes* and *National Review*.[13] (Andrew Montford, who challenged Mann's hockey stick graph, got a B.A. in Chemistry, and then became an accountant.)[14] They are not climate scientists.[15] So they are not qualified to review Cook's and Mann's research.[16] The same is true of the 31,000 (supposed) "scientists" who signed a petition saying there was "no convincing scientific evidence" that climate change is anthropogenic.[17] Most of them were engineers (not scientists); a few others were biologists or chemists—but few, if any, had degrees relevant to climate science.[18] For the same reason that you should not trust a climate scientist to tell you whether an engineer built a bridge that could support the weight of your car, you shouldn't trust an engineer to review the work of a climate scientist about the climate. They are not qualified to do so.

Other climate scientists *are* qualified to do so, and they not only found Mann's and Cook's original work worthy of publication but have replicated their research since. Countless other studies have verified Mann's hockey stick graph,[19] and Cook's 97 percent number has been confirmed by at least six other reviews of the literature.[20] In fact, the more stringent such studies are about the definition of "expert," the higher the percentage gets.[21] One 2017 study even showed that the 3 percent of papers that dissented were not replicable.[22] "Every single one of those analyses had an error—in their assumptions, methodology, or analysis—that, when corrected, brought their results into line with the scientific consensus."[23]

The second response to trusting the consensus might be this: that's not how science works. Science is not determined by consensus. Instead, it thrives on challenge. Think of how science has advanced: Galileo, Copernicus, Edison, Tesla, Darwin, Einstein, Wegener, Bohr, Heisenberg—they all challenged the "established" scientific wisdom, overturned it, and advanced our understanding of the world as a result. That's not to say that those who challenge the establishment are right *because* they challenge the establishment; that's just the "Galileo gambit" and it is fallacious. Far more people who challenged the establishment turned out to be wrong.[24] But the denier might argue that, since science advances through dissent, it is not irrational or unscientific for even a non-expert to challenge the scientific consensus. They could not rightly say that they are certain it is wrong, but perhaps based on their own research and critical thinking they could rationally conclude that the consensus *might be wrong*. After all, don't we want people to critically think for themselves?

Yes, we do—but we have to balance that with an understanding and appreciation of the limits of our reasoning powers, the history of science, and just how complicated science is today. First, it is simply false that scientific knowledge is not determined by consensus. Yes, lone dissenters are often what spawn scientific revolutions; but what completes the revolution is the majority of scientists coming to accept the new theory because it held up to scrutiny (i.e., by it becoming *the consensus view*). Second, most "consensus" views that end up overturned were never well-established to begin with, like the "caloric" theory of heat or the "contraction theory" of the earth's formation.[25] Such overturned theories are based on flimsy evidence, bad reasoning, or simply tradition.[26] It's rare for a consensus that is based in solid evidence to be "overturned." And when it is, it's usually just a modification of the consensus view, not an overturning of it. (For example, Einstein didn't overturn Newton, but instead showed that his laws were approximations).[27]

Third, the day of the "lone wolf researcher" overturning the scientific consensus is long gone; people like Galileo and Edison picked the low hanging fruit, as it were—the easy discoveries that one could make on their own, with a telescope or a home lab. But today, to advance things as far forward, you need decades of education and a billion-dollar particle collider. I'm exaggerating a bit here, but today doing science is much more complicated than it was; there is a vast set of facts and research to keep track of and very complicated theories to understand. Especially given the amount of misinformation out there, the untrained amateur has no hope of ever being in the position to be justified in believing that the consensus among scientists is wrong. As Yale neurologist Steven Novella put it,

> Cutting-edge science is too advanced for anyone to have a reasonable chance of making a significant contribution unless they first have sufficient education in science. The pace of change in any active field of research is so rapid that a researcher must keep in contact with the community of scientists through journals, meetings, and seminars, just to keep up.[28]

And this seems exactly right. For example, I've seen non-experts be completely convinced by their online research that climate change can't be anthropogenic when they discover (the actually true fact that) 95 percent of all CO_2 emissions produced every year are from natural sources. But they simply fail to recognize what the experts already know: natural sources always take out of the atmosphere just as much CO_2 as they put in. Humans are the only source that puts it in without taking it out. So, although we are responsible for only 5 percent of all CO_2 emissions, we are responsible for 100 percent of the increase in atmospheric CO_2 every year.[29]

Now the denier might still claim that, since challenging the establishment is necessary for science to advance, to label those who challenge the consensus as "anti-science" or "science deniers" is unfair. And sometimes it might be. But there is a point where a scientific theory becomes so well established that challenging it is to deny what science has demonstrated to be true. This is the case for the idea that the Earth is round, for evolution, and for the safety of vaccines and GMOs for example. A non-expert doing their "own (online) research and thinking about it" for themselves does not justify them in believing that the Earth is flat, 6000 years old, or that vaccines and GMOs are dangerous. And if they do, they are *denying* the established scientific truth. Likewise, if 97 percent of all research done by climate scientists in peer-reviewed journals suggests that climate change is anthropogenic, and every major scientific organization has agreed, a non-expert cannot be justified in thinking that consensus is wrong because they did their own research and thought about it for themselves. The labels "anti-science" and "science denier," it seems, are accurate.

As a last resort, some deniers will claim that the consensus is manufactured—that climate scientists are part of a vast conspiracy to "cook up a crisis" to get rich off of scientific grants. But not only are such vast widescoping conspiracy theories fundamentally irrational,[30] and not only has the evidence for such a conspiracy been debunked,[31] but anyone familiar with scientific grants knows that this is preposterous.[32] You can't get rich off of scientific grants. You can, however, get rich by taking funding from super wealthy fossil fuel companies and their beneficiaries to concoct faulty research that says that climate change is a hoax. And that is exactly what many scientists who deny climate change have done—like Roy Spencer,[33] Fred Singer,[34] and Anthony Lupo.[35]

And this is not an irrational vast conspiracy theory. Exxon Mobil's own internal documents, for example, which Exxon itself made available, showed that—while it was engaged in a known, admitted, public campaign to deny that anthropogenic climate change was real—it was conducting peer-reviewed research and issuing internal reports that acknowledged it was.[36] Just like tobacco companies did when science revealed that smoking causes cancer, fossil fuel companies launched expensive campaigns to deny the science to protect their bottom line—and that included paying some outside scientists to concoct research and write books that cast doubt on the scientific consensus. Indeed, The Heartland institute—from which Anthony Lupo takes money—also works with tobacco company Philip Morris.

Religious Reasons Deniers Deny

Now it's one thing for fossil fuel companies, or those to whom they give vast sums of money, to deny the reality of climate change. Their motivation is easy to understand: it's all about the money. But why would those not being paid—the "lay deniers" like the friends and relatives you likely have that deny climate change—believe them? I mean, on the one hand, they might just believe the misinformation that the fossil fuel companies are producing. But that can't be the full story; correcting the misinformation does not change their belief. We know about such intellectual stubbornness, not only anecdotally; if you are like me, you've seen multiple conversations where all the rehearsed misinformation the deniers spit out is systematically debunked—to the point where the lay denier literally has no arguments left—and yet they still deny. But we also know about such intellectual stubbornness through research. Studies show that correcting misinformation often does not cure people of their false scientific beliefs, and this is especially true for those who deny climate change.[37]

So what is going on?

Part of this might be explained by the so-called "backfire effect," first proposed by Brendan Nyhan and Jason Reifler, where correcting those who have wrong information will not make them change their view; instead they "dig in their heels" and are even more convinced about the correctness of their false belief.[38] But as an explanation for intellectual stubbornness, the backfire effect can only go so far. For one thing, doubt has subsequently been cast about the reality of the backfire effect (other things, like people's intellectual laziness, may be to blame for people not changing their mind).[39] For another, at best the backfire effect only "kicks in" if the subject matter is relevant to the "self-identity" of the denier—the kind of person the denier sees themselves to be.[40]

For example, someone who sees themselves as an "anti-vaxxer" is not going to believe the CDC when they say that vaccines are safe and effective.[41] But they will believe, without question, the CDC when they say that the romaine lettuce at their grocery store might have been contaminated with E. coli. *Who they are* is not wrapped up in consuming romaine lettuce but is wrapped up in being "anti-vax." So even though ignoring either of these CDC statements could lead to the death of their children, they will ignore the former but believe the latter. This is why political positions are so immune to argument and evidence; who people see themselves to be is often wrapped up in their political affiliation.

But more on that later.

Right now, the question is: what "self-identity" could be motivating skepticism about climate change, and all the evidence denial and motivated reasoning necessary to defend it? This is what finally brings us back around to *The Orville* and *ISSA*. One of the first things the crew notices when they meet the inhabitants of the bioship is their religion—what we might call "Dorahlism." Dorahlism holds that a being named Dorahl created the world (their biodome) and that nothing exists beyond it (although the inhabitants don't actually know that they are in a biodome).

This religious belief leads directly to their denial of the existential threat that the crew is trying to warn them about. Since that danger entails that this core religious doctrine is false, it is dismissed out of hand. Tomilin, the young boy the crew befriends who doubts the orthodoxy, thinks that people will be convinced by the evidence and change their minds. "We have to take [the crew] to the city, show everyone. They'll have to accept it then." But his fellow "reformer" Kemka quickly sets him straight. "Really Tomilin? How well did your mother and father accept it? The concept of a beyond has been heresy throughout all of recorded history. People don't alter their beliefs easily…. Many people refuse to accept an irrefutable truth simply because that truth puts them in the wrong." Kemka is right, especially when it comes to a religious belief. And Hamelac, the leader of the "dictatorial theocracy" that rules over the biodome's society, proves Kemka right by just dismissing Ed's warnings simply because they would entail his religious beliefs are false.

Ed: Hamelac, your entire world is a massive bio-vessel adrift in space. And in less than six months, it's gonna be sucked into the gravity well of a star…. We come from another ship. We encountered your vessel….

Hamelac: Do not blaspheme in these chambers. Dorahl's creation is all.

And this is one reason why *ISSA* is such a good and important episode. This comparison, this analogy, hits the nail on the head. Hamelac's excuse, it turns out, is almost exactly like the kind of excuses many climate change deniers give for ignoring the warnings of climate scientists. The idea that humans could affect the climate to such a grandiose degree, a degree that could potentially annihilate the human species and even all life on Earth, is seen as blasphemy. Why? Because it is contrary to the idea that God is sovereign—that he is in control and will decide how and when the world ends. Consider these words, for example, from Illinois Republican representative John Shimkus, who on the floor of the House of Representatives, after quoting the flood narrative of Genesis to block a bill that would curb carbon emissions, said, "The Earth will end only when God declares it's time to be over. Man will not destroy this Earth. This Earth will not be destroyed by a flood. I do believe that God's word is infallible, unchanging, perfect." Indeed, the idea that we even could do anything about climate change is also seen to be contrary to the doctrine of God's sovereignty. As Michigan Rep. Tim Walberg put it,

> I believe there's climate change. I believe there's been climate change since the beginning of time. Do I think man has some impact? Yeah, of course. Can man change the entire universe? No. Why do I believe that? Well, as a Christian, I believe that there is a creator in God who is much bigger than us. And I'm confident that, if there's a real problem, he can take care of it.[42]

Now some prominent environmentalists, like Al Gore and E.O. Wilson, have suggested that Christians don't care about climate change because they believe Jesus will return before the effects of climate change are really felt.[43] As Bill Moyer summarized the view, "Why care about the earth when the droughts, floods, famine, and pestilence brought by ecological collapse are signs of the apocalypse foretold in the Bible? Why care about global climate change when you and yours will be rescued in the Rapture?"[44] Indeed, the bigger worry for some evangelicals is how environmentalism is creating an apparent need for cooperation between governments. Why is such cooperation bad? Because it's just the kind of cooperation that a charismatic world leader could take advantage of to form a worldwide government and issue in the seven-year tribulation that precedes Jesus' return. As evangelical preacher Hal Lindsey put it, climate change is a scam "being used to consolidate the governments of the world into a coalition that may someday facilitate the rise of the Antichrist."[45]

If this is right—if, as David Orr put it, "belief in the imminence of the end times tends to make evangelicals careless stewards of our forests, soils, wildlife, air, water, seas and climate"[46]—then *ISSA* is not nearly as good an episode as it first seemed. Its analogy wouldn't be that accurate. To be accurate, the biodome dwellers would need to ignore the crew's warnings because they thought Dorahl was going to return within six months to take them to paradise.

But according to the research of Robin Globus Veldman, author of the book *The Gospel of Climate Skepticism* (from which I am borrowing heavily), the idea that evangelicals' apathy about climate change is driven by their expectation of Jesus' return—what he calls "the end-times apathy" hypothesis—is not right. Indeed, even though the idea that Jesus will return before 2050 enjoys a majority consensus among evangelicals,[47] the end-times apathy hypothesis *cannot* be right. Why? Because evangelicals can't think that Jesus' return will save us from a coming climate catastrophe if they don't think there is a coming climate catastrophe; and that's exactly what evangelicals say they believe: that climate change doesn't exist—that it is a hoax. It isn't real. And according to Veldman, the reason for their doubts is wrapped up in their identity as Christian evangelicals, and their belief that there is a culture war.

It's well documented that evangelicals believe that they are engaged in a culture war (particularly with secular humanists), and that they see themselves as one of the (if not the) most persecuted groups in the country. It's called "the evangelical persecution complex,"[48] and it's led to movies like *God's Not Dead* and its sequel, which suggest that philosophy professors are forcing students to declare that God is dead in college classrooms, and that high school teachers can be fired and sued for answering questions about the similarities between the teachings of Jesus and Gandhi.

This notion does not, of course, have any basis in reality. That's why it's called a "complex." For example, the list of court cases at the end of the *God's Not Dead* movies, to "prove" that Christians are being persecuted, are all exaggerated fake news boogie man.[49] And while it is true that Christians make up less of the population than they used to, and they don't enjoy unquestioned authority in all segments of society (e.g., it is no longer standard practice for public schools to proselytize), Christians still make up a vast majority of the population, and evangelicals still enjoy vast amounts of wealth and political power—perhaps more than any other group. To put it simply, evangelicals are not persecuted; they have mistaken a slight reduction in their power with persecution. As Jon Stewart once put it on *The Daily Show*, evangelicals are merely "expressing anger and victimization over the loss of absolute power and reframing it as persecution of real America by minorities, freeloaders and socialists."[50]

But to play the role that Veldman says it does in evangelicals' denial of climate change, evangelical persecution doesn't need to be real; it just needs to be perceived as real. And it very definitely is in the evangelical community. It is "us vs. them." And since "they" see climate change as a problem, if you are concerned with it too, then you are on their side.

Interestingly, according to Veldman, the history of climate change skepticism in the evangelical community began with evangelicals being concerned with it: when the ECI (Evangelical Climate Initiative), in 2006, called evangelicals to action on climate change. Politically right-wing religious leaders realized that this posed a threat to their hold on the evangelical community and their political power, and so they launched a concerted effort (via right-wing religious media outlets) to cast doubt on the ECI's concerns. As Veldman puts it,

> The Christian Right's precarious hold over the evangelical tradition in the mid–2000s, when the push for action on climate change emerged, coupled with their need to support coalition partners in the Republican Party who opposed action on climate change, forced them to directly involve themselves in the climate fight.[51]

And the arguments they gave included suggesting that the real goal of the of environmentalists was to gain political and societal power—a power which they would use against evangelicals in the cultural wars. The result was a social condition within the evangelical community in which showing concern about the environment, or even believing that climate change was real, put one in danger of social ostracization; it meant that one was now on the side of the devil.

> The sense of embattlement was powerful not only because it could neutralize concerns about climate change by explaining it in terms of something else—a secularist plot—but because it was sustained by social dynamics. For many evangelicals, being theologically and politically conservative is a central aspect of their identity. This made embracing a politically liberal issue like climate change socially risky. If someone could embrace a politically liberal issue, did that mean he or she was also willing to embrace liberal theology?[52]

As an example of this, consider a meme I saw on Facebook where a son, newly living in Boulder, Colorado, showed his mother that he bought a metal (instead of plastic) straw for his boba teas.

> **Mother:** I can't believe you. I hope they haven't influenced your faith in Jesus.
> **Son:** What does that have to do with my faith?
> **Mother:** You're changing towards the left.
> **Son:** How? I'm just trying to save the sea turtles.

Had he not been her son, he likely would have received a much stronger condemnation. As Veldman puts it, "In such a polarized social context, to express concern about the environment or climate change is to put one's reputation on the line."[53]

With this in mind, consider the words of Hamelac as he condemns a "reformer" to the fate of an angry mob outside his capitol building.

> Do you embrace the word of Dorahl? [Crowd: Yes!] Are we united as a people by Dorahl's truth and love? [Crowd: Yes!] What of those who question, who deny Dorahl's gift to the universe? Can they be allowed to live amongst us? [Crowd: No!] To grow and fester and to challenge the benevolence of Dorahl? [Crowd: No!] Bring him out. This man is one of those who call themselves "Reformers." [Crowd: Boo!] He is charged with heresy. He has distributed hateful material right here within the city. He openly defies the benevolence of Dorahl! [Crowd: Shouting] He is yours to sentence! [Crowd beats him to death.]

Clearly, there is a cultural war here, between the followers and the reformers. The followers of Dorahl, even though they are clearly the majority, see themselves as under attack—so much so that they can't tolerate the existence of a single dissenter. And their identity as followers of Dorahl, requires them to ostracize anyone who is on the side of the reformers, about anything. To believe the threat that the crew of the *Orville* presents to them would be to be on the side of the devil—or at least the Dorahlian equivalent of the devil. (Maybe he lives in the "Underland?") Thus "If the Stars Should Appear" has drawn a near-perfect analogy for what motivates evangelicals to deny the threat of climate change.

Philosophic Reasons Deniers Deny

But of course, this can't be the whole story of climate change denialism because not all those who deny climate change are religious. There are also lay (unpaid) secular people who deny climate change. What could *their* motivation be? Could their identity, or how they see themselves, have anything to do with it? If so, how do they see themselves? To answer this question, it will be useful to take a look at a particular brand of denialism called "lukewarmerism," which is put forth by what Jean-Canel Collomb calls "nondenier deniers." In his paper "The Ideology of Climate Change Denial in the United States," he paraphrases James Hoggen in describing them: "[Nondenier deniers] put themselves forth as reasonable interpreters of the science, even as allies in the fight to bring climate change to the public's attention. But then they throw in a variety of arguments that actually undermine the public appetite for action."[54] Nondenier deniers, or what I'll call "lukewarmers," fancy themselves as being more in line with the science than the general denier—and to a degree, they are. They rightly acknowledge that global warming is happening, that it is causing climate change, and that humans are to blame.[55] What they deny is that the effect of global warming is anything to worry about. It will take years, they say, for anything appreciable to happen—and even then, the effects won't be that extreme. What would be extreme, they say, is the effects of our trying to combat it. Taxing fossil fuels and environmental regulations could cost companies billions, and make energy unaffordable (especially for the poor), and generate a global recession. In other words, whatever we do to try to stop climate change will be worse than what we are trying to stop, and so we should not do anything at all. As Collomb puts it,

> [They don't deny] the fact that the planet is warming, but they usually lose no time in qualifying their acceptance with two caveats. First ... the negative repercussions ... are being grossly overstated in order to alarm the public and decision-makers into accepting the environmentalist agenda [and] actions to mitigate the effects of global warming will be economically destructive and environmentally insignificant.[56]

Indeed, many hold that nature will just balance itself out in the end.

Now to be clear, I'm not saying that there aren't lukewarmers who are paid by the fossil fuel industry. Science writer Matt Ridley, and atmospheric physicist Richard Lindzen, who both receive money from companies like Peabody Energy (a coal company that participates in misinformation campaigns, just like Exxon) are two good examples. But there are lots of lukewarmers who, we might say, are lukewarmers "of their own accord." And so the question is: if they are not being paid, what's their motivation?

One possible answer is that the arguments of lukewarmers are persuasive—that they are not easily debunked. The thrust of the argument for lukewarmerism is that, while there is consensus among the scientific community that anthropogenic global warming is causing climate change, there is not consensus among them about how fast it is occurring or how bad the effects will be. To boot, lukewarmers also argue that government intervention in anything always makes things worse, and freedom and free markets always make things better. They are big fans of Adam Smith's idea of "the invisible hand," the idea that if you leave things (the economy, society, etc.) alone, things will work out to the betterment of everyone (as if the process were guided by an "invisible hand")—and it will do so much more efficiently than if you tried to guide the process though regulation and government intervention.[57] Applying this same logic to the environment is why they think that, if we just leave the environment alone, it will all work out in the end.

Unfortunately, however, their arguments are easily debunked. And I say "unfortunately" because (a) that means we have not yet answered our question about their motivation and (b) it really would be nice if lukewarmers were right and climate change was nothing to worry about. But there are essentially five obvious things wrong with their arguments that any lukewarmers could easily find out if they bothered to look.

First, *there actually is* consensus on how bad the effects of global warming will be on the climate—and they are easy to find. They are articulated, for example, degree by degree in horrific detail, by science writer Mark Lynas in his book *Six Degrees*. At a rise of two degrees (Celsius), life becomes very difficult because of drought, floods, and food shortages. At four degrees, large portions of the planet are uninhabitable, and the rest is plagued by extreme weather, massive famines, huge floods, and war. At six degrees, to survive, humans will have to herd to shrinking habitable areas near the poles—and, indeed, the food and potable water supply might dry up. We could go extinct.[58]

Second, while there is not *as much* agreement about how fast warming will happen (when compared to the agreement that it is simply happening), there is still a pretty solid consensus: most research points to about a 3.5 degree increase by 2100.[59] And, if that's wrong, it's most likely because it's too low, not too high. Instead of being the alarmists that lukewarmers claimed they are, it turns out that climate scientists were likely too conservative in their estimates. For fear of being called alarmist, they often compromised with those giving more conservative estimates and vastly underestimated the pace of climate change as a result.[60]

Third, lukewarmers' risk/benefit analysis is wrong. If we really don't know how bad climate change will be, then it might be better, but it might also be worse. And if we don't know how bad something will be, we should guard against the worst-case scenario. Or to put it another way: If climate change won't be that bad and we do too much to prevent it, then at worst we have a cleaner planet but a global recession. But if it's worse than we anticipate, and we do nothing like lukewarmers want, the worst-case scenario is the extinction of our (and most other) species. So, if we really don't know how fast or bad its effect will be, we should be doing everything we can now to stop it.

Fourth, they are wrong that action on climate change will cause a global recession. Switching to clean energy sources would spawn a whole new industry, create billions in revenue and (according to economist Robert Pollin) generate a net gain of 2.7 million jobs (in almost every sector of the economy).[61]

And fifth, while the invisible hand might work for certain segments of the economy, it decidedly doesn't work for the environment. When left alone, the actions of individuals on the environment don't work out for the better of everyone as if they were guided by an invisible hand. (Even Adam Smith admitted that things didn't work this way in all sectors of the economy.)[62] When it comes to physical resources, without oversight, individual actors exploit them for their own short-term benefit until they run out, thus ruining the resource for everyone in the long term. This phenomenon even has a name—"the tragedy of the commons"—and is especially acute regarding the environment, given that the negative effects of abusing the environment are so far in the future. This, indeed, is exactly what has happened with the atmosphere; fossil fuel companies exploited it for short term gain by dumping their waste (CO_2) into it. The only way nature is going to "balance itself out" is by wiping out humans as an infection in the same way we wipe out viruses: with a fever. It will then return to an equilibrium through natural processes over a few thousand years.

And this brings us back to the question of people's self-identity. If the arguments aren't any good, what is the motivating factor behind most secular climate change denial, like lukewarmerism? Why go to all the trouble to make up excuses? Well, if you look at the secular thinktanks and advocacy groups that are most willing to take the money of fossil fuel industries to promote climate change denial and/or lukewarmerism—like the Heartland Institute, the Heritage Foundation, the Cato Institute, Americans for Prosperity, and Americans for Tax Reform (who are producing the arguments that religious right leaders repeat)—you will find that they are all small government conservatives and especially libertarian in their philosophical outlook. And this, it seems, is also true of the unpaid lukewarmers as well—and this is why, Collomb argues, that they deny climate change.

The driving force behind these philosophies has always been that if you keep people and companies free of regulations and let them act in their own self-interest, the free market will produce the best results for everyone.

154   Act III: Science and Politics

Accordingly, pressures from the free market are supposed to guarantee that companies protect the environment. As Collomb puts it,

> Small-government advocates usually declare that they value the health of the land and support high environmental standards. They claim to disagree with the environmental community on the means, but not the ends. They argue, in a counter-intuitive way, that the best way to protect the environment is by maximizing economic freedom and eliminating government.[63]

But the fact of climate change's reality and severity is direct proof that isn't true—and thus that the philosophical underpinnings of libertarianism, and small government conservatism, are vacuous. As Naomi Oreskes put it, "Accepting that by-products of industrial civilization were irreparably damaging the global environment was to accept the reality of market failure. It was to acknowledge the limits of free-market capitalism."[64] So of course libertarians and small government conservatives deny climate change; they have to, otherwise the philosophical underpinnings of what they think about everything are bogus. Again, as Kemka put it, "People don't alter their beliefs easily.... [They'll] refuse to accept an irrefutable truth simply because that truth puts them in the wrong."

Indeed, contrary to the claims of denialists who suggest that environmentalism (and especially climate change activism) has become a religion, one could argue that libertarianism has become one. Religions don't have scientific evidence for their beliefs; religious beliefs are based on faith. Environmentalism has solid scientific evidence on its side, so it can't be a religion. Religions will, however, deny obvious scientific evidence that stands against their belief (like creationists do with the evidence for evolution). And this is exactly what libertarians are doing when their faith claims about the universal benevolent effects of free-market capitalism are challenged by climate science.

To make matters worse, the only possible solution to the problem is massive government regulation and action on a global scale. Individuals "going green," even en masse, is not going to mitigate climate change to any significant degree. Why? Well for one thing, most supposed actions to reduce one's carbon footprint are useless or even counterproductive. For example, replacing your existing car with an electric car is most likely worse for the environment, not better. (Modern cars are low emission anyway, the electricity to fuel that electric car is likely produced by a fossil fuel burning electric plant, and about half of a car's carbon footprint is produced by the car's manufacturing).[65] What's more, 71 percent of all human production of CO_2 is the result of 100 companies (not individuals).[66] So even everyone "going green" would have a negligible impact. As environmental philosopher J. Baird Callicott put it:

> It will not suffice ... simply to encourage people individually and voluntarily to build green and drive hybrid. But what's worse is the implication that that's all we can do

about it, that the ultimate responsibly for dampening the adverse effects of global climate change devolves to each of us as individuals. On the contrary, the only hope we have to temper global climate change is a collective sociocultural response in the form of policy, regulation, treaty, and law.[67]

In short, given the way our global capitalistic economy and society is configured, it is impossible for individuals to live without a giant carbon footprint. Every product everyone uses, almost everything everyone does (even me writing this essay and you buying this book), contributes to the emission of greenhouse gasses in the atmosphere. Or as Adam Conover put it on "Adam Ruins Everything," "We live in an infinite web of carbon pollution. The number of variables at play is so vast, they're impossible for a single person to even calculate, let alone reduce … this problem is way too big for our individual consumer choices to solve. Our entire way of life is the problem."[68] That's not to say that action on climate change would wreck the economy. But the only realistic solution to climate change is worldwide government action and regulation on a scale unprecedented in human history, that would drastically change the way we live. As Mill McKibben put it,

> To reduce the amount of CO_2 pouring into the atmosphere means dramatically reducing the amount of fossil fuel being consumed. Which means changing the underpinning of the planet's entire economy and altering our most ingrained personal habits. Even under the best scenarios, this will involve something more like a revolution than a technical fix.[69]

All of this not only undermines the intellectual edifice of libertarianism and the entire right-wing conservative economic movement, completely derailing their faith in free-market capitalism as a flawless, problem-solving (not problem-creating) economic system—but global actions by governments to regulate corporations is their worst nightmare. That is their version of the apocalypse. To admit that it is necessary, in their eyes, is the Christian equivalent of ushering in the antichrist. It would thus stand contrary to their self-identity—everything they see themselves to be. It's no surprise, therefore, that libertarian and small-government conservatives are willing to go through the mental gymnastics necessary—the evidence denial, the Climategate conspiracy theories, the shifting of the goal posts, and the ad hoc excuses—to deny it all.

But what, you may ask yourself, has this to do with *The Orville* and my thesis that *ISSA* is the best (or most important) episode? It seemed to capture all of this in one single exchange. When the crew confronts Hamelac, the leader of the bioship's society, he seems to admit that he has suspicions that there is more to the world than what they can see, and thus that the threat that Ed mentions very well could be real. But then he just sets the concern aside, saying…

156   Act III: Science and Politics

>   Hamelac: To do as you say would shatter our entire way of life. This world's not ready.
>   Ed: You mean you're not ready give up control over these people….
>   Hamelac: I will not destabilize a system that has kept order for thousands of years.

And that's it, in a nutshell. Libertarians and small-government conservatives don't want to acknowledge how bad climate change is because doing so would not only cost them their political power but would upend capitalism and the fossil fuel industry—the system that has "kept order" here on Earth for quite a while. To address climate change will mean giving up (or greatly altering) the American way of life. So Hamelac refuses to acknowledge and act to prevent a threat that he (deep down) knows will destroy his entire civilization, and does so for almost exactly the same reason that our government (while run and controlled by libertarians and small-government conservatives) has refused to acknowledge and act on a threat that they know (deep down) will destroy ours. For a brand-new television show to offer that kind of on-point social commentary, in what was supposed to be its second episode—in my eyes, is unheard of.

Conclusion

In the introduction, I set out to argue that "If the Stars Should Appear" is the best (or at least the most important) episode of *The Orville*. To really establish that, I'd need to compare it to each and every episode—and there are some really good ones. The argument would be hard to make. But, in all honesty, I'm not all that concerned with convincing you of that particular thesis. As you may have guessed, the goal of this essay was to lay out the reason we non-experts should believe that climate change is the biggest threat humanity has ever faced, and how "If the Stars Should Appear" helps point out that denialism is rooted not in evidence and argument, but in motivated reasoning grounded in the defense of the denier's self-identity. The arguments and evidence for climate change are not likely to change the denier's mind; motivated reasoning will prevent it. But I am hopeful that the realization of where the motivation comes from might make some deniers consider the possibility that they are wrong—and act and vote accordingly.

Notes

1. Michelle Chen, "The Paris Climate Accord Didn't Go Nearly Far Enough—Can Bonn Do Better?," *The Nation*, November 7, 2017, https://www.thenation.com/article/archive/the-paris-climate-accord-didnt-go-nearly-far-enough-can-bonn-do-better/.
2. Trump's decision to pull the US out of the Paris climate accord became official on Nov

4th, 2020—the day after the election—but Joe Biden's decision to re-enter it took effect 30 days after his inauguration, the day he signed an executive order to nullify Trump's decision. See Bob Berwyn, "Rebuilding Credibility on Climate Action Will Take Time," *Inside Climate News*, January 21, 2021. https://insideclimatenews.org/news/21012021/biden-paris-climate-agreement/

    3. For more effects that we are already seeing, see "7 Effects of Climate Change You're Already Seeing," *The Climate Reality Project*, April 2, 2019, https://www.climaterealityproject.org/blog/7-effects-climate-change-already-seeing.

    4. It should be noted that the full explanation is a bit more complicated. CO_2's effect on other things, like water vapor, is also a contributing factor. See "References and Resources," *American Chemical Society*, https://www.acs.org/content/acs/en/climatescience/references.html; "Water Vapor Confirmed as Major Player in Climate Change," *National Aeronautics and Space Administration*, November 17, 2008, https://www.nasa.gov/topics/earth/features/vapor_warming.html.

    5. See Spencer Weart, in *The Discovery of Global Warming*. (Harvard University Press, 2008). For a shorter history, see the pdf version of his article "The Carbon Dioxide Greenhouse Effect" for AIP at https://history.aip.org/climate/pdf/CO2.pdf.

    6. Michael E. Mann, Raymond S. Bradley, and Malcolm K. Hughes, "Northern Hemisphere Temperatures During the Past Millennium: Inferences, Uncertainties, and Limitations," *Geophysical Research Letters* 26, no. 6 (1999): 759–762.

    7. One might argue that they weren't "that much" hotter, but (a) 2016 was almost a full degree (Celsius) hotter than the 20th century average; it was even hotter when compared to preindustrial levels. And (b) even if they are just barely hotter, you can't have such an anomaly by random chance. See "The 10 Hottest Global Years on Record," *Climate Central*, February 6, 2019, https://www.climatecentral.org/gallery/graphics/the-10-hottest-global-years-on-record; "2019 was 2nd Hottest Year on Record for Earth Say NOAA, NASA," *National Oceanic and Atmospheric Administration*, January 15, 2020, https://www.noaa.gov/news/2019-was-2nd-hottest-year-on-record-for-earth-say-noaa-nasa.

One of the most famous contrarian arguments is Richard Lindzen's "iris hypothesis" which suggests that a feedback loop between CO_2 and water vapor may mitigate the warming effects of CO_2. Roughly speaking, warming will cause less cirrus clouds, which will allow more heat to escape. But not only did subsequent studies disprove Lindzen's hypothesis (first proposed in 2001, and later updated in 2009), but the warming that has happened since then—especially since 2009—proves that Lindzen's supposed positive feedback loop doesn't exist. If it did, last decade's warming would not have happened. And, indeed, even Lindzen's updated 2009 argument was found to be full of errors. See Dana Nuccitelli, "Scientists Have Beaten Down the Best Climate Denial Argument," *The Guardian*, December 18, 2017, https://www.theguardian.com/environment/climate-consensus-97-per-cent/2017/dec/18/scientists-have-beaten-down-the-best-climate-denial-argument; "Body of Research Undermines Infrared Iris Hypothesis," *Skeptical Science*, https://skepticalscience.com/infrared-iris-effect-negative-feedback.htm; John Upton, "Clouds Won't Save Us from Global Warming," *Scientific American*, April 7, 2016, https://www.scientificamerican.com/article/clouds-won-t-save-us-from-global-warming/.

    8. See A.W. Montford, *The Hockey Stick Illusion* (Anglosphere Books, 2015). For a refutation of his arguments, see "The Montford Delusion," *Real Climate*, July 22, 2010, http://www.realclimate.org/index.php/archives/2010/07/the-montford-delusion/ and Michael Le Page, "Climate Myths: The 'Hockey Stick' Graph Has Been Proven Wrong," *New Scientist*, May 16, 2007, https://www.newscientist.com/article/dn11646-climate-myths-the-hockey-stick-graph-has-been-proven-wrong/.

    9. Bertrand Russell, *Let the People Think* (Rockford, IL: Watts & Company, 1996), 2.

    10. For more on how this consensus was arrived upon, see Naomi Oreskes, "The Scientific Consensus on Climate Change: How Do We Know We're Not Wrong?" in *Climate Change: What It Means for You, Your Children, and Your Grandchildren (2nd edition)*, eds. Joseph F.C. DiMento and Pamela Doughman (MIT Press: 2014), 105–148.

    11. Russel, *Let the People Think*, 2; *Ibid*.

    12. "Debunking 97% Climate Consensus Denial," *Skeptical Science*, September 9, 2013, https://skepticalscience.com/debunking-climate-consensus-denial.html.

    13. Alex Epstein, "'97% of Climate Scientists Agree' Is 100% Wrong," *Forbes*,

158   Act III: Science and Politics

January 6, 2015, https://www.forbes.com/sites/alexepstein/2015/01/06/97-of-climate-scientists-agree-is-100-wrong/#fde35443f9ff; Ian Tuttle, "The 97 Percent Solution," *National Review*, October 8, 2015, http://www.nationalreview.com/article/425232/climate-change-no-its-not-97-percent-consensus-ian-tuttle.

14. "Andrew Montford," *Wikipedia*, https://en.wikipedia.org/wiki/Andrew_Montford.

15. Some that deny this are weatherpersons, like co-founder of the Weather Channel John Coleman. But meteorologists study the weather, not the climate. Weatherpersons are qualified to make predictions about the weather ten days out but not the climate for decades and centuries to come. Like medicine and biology, the two fields are related—but the expertise of one does not translate to the other.

16. Similar things can be said about theoretical physicist Freeman Dyson; although he is brilliant, his expertise is not relevant to climate science. For a refutation of his arguments see, "Freeman Dyson's Selective Vision," *Real Climate*, May 24, 2008, http://www.realclimate.org/index.php/archives/2008/05/freeman-dysons-selective-vision/.

17. "Global Warming Petition Project," http://www.petitionproject.org/.

18. Jon Greenberg, "No, 30,000 Scientists Have Not Said Climate Change Is a Hoax," *Politifact*, September 8, 2017, https://www.politifact.com/factchecks/2017/sep/08/blog-posting/no-30000-scientists-have-not-said-climate-change-h/.

19. "What Evidence Is There for the Hockey Stick?," *Skeptical Science*, https://skepticalscience.com/broken-hockey-stick.htm.

20. "The 97% Consensus on Global Warming," *Skeptical Science*, https://www.skepticalscience.com/global-warming-scientific-consensus.htm.

21. *Ibid.*

22. Rasmus E. Benestad, Dana Nuccitelli, Stephan Lewandowsky, Katharine Hayhoe, Hans Olav Hygen, Rob van Dorland, and Jon Cook, "Learning from Mistakes in Climate Research," *Theoretical and Applied Climatology* 126 (2016): 699–703.

23. This quote is from one of the authors of the study, who wrote this article about the study: Katherine Ellen Foley, "Those 3% of Scientific Papers That Deny Climate Change? A Review Found Them All Flawed," Quartz, September 5, 2017, https://qz.com/1069298/the-3-of-scientific-papers-that-deny-climate-change-are-all-flawed/.

24. See David Kyle Johnson, "The Galileo Gambit," in *Bad Arguments: 100 of the Most Important Fallacies in Western Philosophy*, eds. Robert Arp, Bruce Robert and Steve Barbone (Wiley-Blackwell, 2018), 152–156.

25. Joel Shurkin, "Scientific Consensus Is Almost Never Wrong—Almost," *Inside Science*, November 20, 2015, https://www.insidescience.org/news/scientific-consensus-almost-never-wrong-%E2%80%94-almost.

26. Indeed, when it comes to environmental science, one could argue that the consensus view that was overturned by the evidence was the previous uninformed assumption that nature was too resilient and powerful for humans to have any significant effect on it.

27. "Science Was Wrong Before," *Rational Wiki*, https://rationalwiki.org/wiki/Science_was_wrong_before.

28. Steven Novella, *The Skeptic's Guide to the Universe* (New York: Hachette Book Group, 2018), 166.

29. For a debunking of other similar arguments against the reality of climate change see "Global Warming & Climate Change Myths," *Skeptical Science*. https://skepticalscience.com/argument.php.

30. David Kyle Johnson, "How Fallacies Fuel Conspiracies" in *Conspiracy Theories: Philosophers Connect the Dots*, eds. Richard Green and Rachel Robinson-Greene (Chicago: Open Court, 2020), 45–56.

31. Jess Henig, "'Climategate,'" *Factcheck.org*, December 10, 2009, https://www.factcheck.org/2009/12/climategate/.

32. To be fair, there likely is *now* a "bias" (of sorts) against research that disagrees with the consensus view on climate change in the peer-reviewed journals. (Climatologist Judith Curry has complained about something like this on her website, judithcurry.com.) But it was not responsible for the consensus. (Again, for how the consensus arose, see Oreskes "The Scientific Consensus on Climate Change: How Do We Know We're Not Wrong?") The "bias"

arose *because* of the consensus. In science, when a hypothesis conflicts with something that is already well-established, its burden of proof is raised—the level of evidence needed to make the hypothesis viable is higher. It stands to reason, therefore, given that the consensus on climate change is now well established, that fewer articles that contradict the consensus view will pass muster. So such a bias is not at all unreasonable. In addition, so many contrarian climate articles have been shown to be flawed (e.g., Richard Lindzen's aforementioned papers on his "iris hypothesis") that a bias against such articles is warranted—in the same way that a bias against "flat earth" and "creationist" articles is warranted. For a rundown of the kinds of things Judith Curry has said about climate change (including journal bias), see "Judith Curry," *Desmog*, https://www.desmogblog.com/judith-curry. For a refutation of her climate change arguments (showing that they likely have not met the burden of proof necessary to be published in journals), see "IPCC Attribution Statements Redux: A Response to Judith Curry," *Real Climate*, August 27, 2014, http://www.realclimate.org/index.php/archives/2014/08/ipcc-attribution-statements-redux-a-response-to-judith-curry/.

33. "Roy Spencer," *Desmog*, https://www.desmogblog.com/roy-spencer.

34. "Fred Singer," *Desmog*, https://www.desmogblog.com/s-fred-singer.

35. Although it is important to note that, while Lupo is the chair of atmospheric science at the University of Missouri, neither Spencer nor Singer have a Ph.D. in anything relevant to climate science. See Janese Silvey, "Professor Details Role as Climate Consultant," *Columbia Tribune*, March 5, 2012. https://www.columbiatribune.com/59653f24-1dbf-5fcb-ac88-4eedfd7a60a0.html.

36. Shannon Hall, "Exxon Knew about Climate Change Almost 40 Years Ago," *Scientific American*, October 26, 2015, https://www.scientificamerican.com/article/exxon-knew-about-climate-change-almost-40-years-ago/.

37. "Public Knowledge About Science Has a Limited Tie to People's Beliefs About Climate Change and Climate Scientists," *Pew Research Center*, October 4, 2016, https://www.pewresearch.org/science/2016/10/04/public-knowledge-about-science-has-a-limited-tie-to-peoples-beliefs-about-climate-change-and-climate-scientists/; Bastiaan T. Rutjens, Robbie M. Sutton, and Romy van der Lee, "Not All Skepticism Is Equal: Exploring the Ideological Antecedents of Science Acceptance and Rejection," *Personality and Social Psychology Bulletin* 44, no. 3 (March 2018): 381–405.

38. Brendan Nyhan and Jason Reifler, "When Corrections Fail: The Persistence of Political Misperceptions," *Political Behavior* 32 (2010): 303–330.

39. Thomas Wood and Ethan Porter, "The Elusive Backfire Effect: Mass Attitudes' Steadfast Factual Adherence," *Political Behavior* 41, no. 1 (January 2018): 135–163.

40. Gregory J. Trevors, Krista R. Muis, Reinhard Pekrun, Gale M. Sinatra, and Philip H. Winne, "Identity and Epistemic Emotions During Knowledge Revision: A Potential Account for the Backfire Effect," *Discourse Processes* 53, no. 5–6 (2015): 339–370.

41. "Vaccine Safety," *Centers for Disease Control and Prevention*, January 14, 2020, https://www.cdc.gov/vaccinesafety/index.html.

42. Mahita Gajanan, "Republican Congressman Says God Will 'Take Care of' Climate Change," *Time*, May 31, 2017, https://time.com/4800000/tim-walberg-god-climate-change/.

43. Robin Globus Veldman, *The Gospel of Climate Skepticism* (Oakland: University of California Press, 2019), 7.

44. Bill Moyers, "Welcome to Doomsday," *The New York Review of Books*, March 24, 2005, www.nybooks.com/articles/2005/03/24/welcome-to-doomsday.

45. "Tonight on the Hal Lindsey Report," *The Hal Lindsey Report*, February 27, 2015. https://www.hallindsey.com/hlr-2-27-2015/.

46. David Orr, "Armageddon vs. Extinction," *Conservation Biology* 19, no. 2 (Nov. 2005): 291.

47. "Jesus Christ's Return to Earth," *Pew Research Center*, July 14, 2010, https://www.pewresearch.org/fact-tank/2010/07/14/jesus-christs-return-to-earth/.

48. Alan Noble, "The Evangelical Persecution Complex," *The Atlantic*, August 4, 2014, https://www.theatlantic.com/national/archive/2014/08/the-evangelical-persecution-complex/375506/.

49. Hemant Mehta, "Let's Debunk the 'Christian Persecution' Court Cases That Inspired

160 Act III: Science and Politics

the 'God's Not Dead' Films," *Friendly Atheist*, April 8, 2016, https://friendlyatheist.patheos.com/2016/04/08/lets-debunk-the-christian-persecution-court-cases-that-inspired-the-gods-not-dead-films/.

50. Jon Stewart, "White Santa and Megyn Kelly's Apology," *The Daily Show*, Dec 17, 2013. You can view the segment here: http://www.cc.com/video-clips/tbbd03/the-daily-show-with-jon-stewart-white-santa---megyn-kelly-s-apology.

51. Veldman, *The Gospel of Climate Skepticism*, 11.

52. Ibid., 10.

53. Ibid.

54. Jean Daniel Collomb, "The Ideology of Climate Change Denial in the United States," *European Journal of American Studies* 9, no. 1 (January 2, 2014), 7.

55. It should be noted, however, that many of them denied these things in the past and only begrudgingly admitted to them once the scientific evidence became overwhelming.

56. Collomb, "The Ideology of Climate Change Denial in the United States," 7.

57. Adam Smith, *Inquiry into the Nature and Causes of the Wealth of Nations* (1776), Book IV, Ch. 2.

58. Mark Lynas, *Six Degrees: Our Future on a Hotter Planet* (Harper Perennial, 2008).

59. Dana Nuccitelli, "New Study Reconciles A Dispute About How Fast Global Warming Will Happen," *The Guardian*, September 24, 2018, https://www.theguardian.com/environment/climate-consensus-97-per-cent/2018/sep/24/new-study-reconciles-a-dispute-about-how-fast-global-warming-will-happen; Phillip Goodwin, "On the Time Evolution of Climate Sensitivity and Future Warming," *Earth's Future* 6, no. 9 (September 2018): 1336–1348.

60. Naomi Oreskes, Michael Oppenheimer, and Dale Jamieson, "Scientists Have Been Underestimating the Pace of Climate Change," *Scientific American*, August 19, 2019, https://blogs.scientificamerican.com/observations/scientists-have-been-underestimating-the-pace-of-climate-change/.

61. Robert Pollin, "Think We Can't Stabilize the Climate While Fostering Growth? Think Again," Robert Pollin, *Greening the Global Economy* (The MIT Press, 2015), 73–91. A shorter version of his argument was published October 27, 2015, at *The Nation*, and can be found here: https://www.thenation.com/article/archive/think-we-cant-stabilize-the-climate-while-fostering-growth-think-again/.

62. For more on this, see Lecture 33, "How Big Should Government Be?," in my course *The Big Questions of Philosophy* for *The Great Courses* (2016).

63. Collomb, "The Ideology of Climate Change Denial in the United States," 4.

64. Naomi Oreskes and Erik M. Conway, *Merchants of Doubt: How a Handful of Scientists Obscured the Truth on Issues from Tobacco Smoke to Global Warming* (London: Bloomsbury, 2010), 238.

65. Jonathan Lesser, "Are Electric Cars Worse for the Environment?," *Politico*, May 15, 2018, https://www.politico.com/agenda/story/2018/05/15/are-electric-cars-worse-for-the-environment-000660; see also Adam Conover, Gonzalo Cordova, Travis Helwig, Mary Lordes, Alingon Mitra, and Diona Reasonover, "Adam Ruins Going Green," *Adam Ruins Everything*, TruTV, December 27, 2016. The research for this episode can be found in Adam Conover, *Adam Ruins Everything* (Post Hill Press, 2018), 303–314. You can see the segment on cars here: https://www.youtube.com/watch?v=MQLbakWESkw.

66. See Paul Griffin, "CDP Carbon Majors Report 2017," *The Carbon Majors Database*, July 2017, https://b8f65cb373b1b7b15feb-c70d8ead6ced550b4d987d7c03fcdd1d.ssl.cf3.rackcdn.com/cms/reports/documents/000/002/327/original/Carbon-Majors-Report-2017.pdf?1499691240. For a readable rundown of this report, see Tess Riley, "Just 100 Companies Responsible for 71% of Global Emissions, Study Says," *The Guardian*, July 10, 2017, https://www.theguardian.com/sustainable-business/2017/jul/10/100-fossil-fuel-companies-investors-responsible-71-global-emissions-cdp-study-climate-change.

67. J. Baird Callicott, "From the Land ethic to the Earth Ethic: Aldo Leopold and the Gaia Hypothesis," in *Gaia in Turmoil, Climate Change, Biodepletion, and Earth Ethics in an Age of Crisis*, ed. Eileen Crist, H. Bruce Rinker, and Bill McKibben (Cambridge, MA: MIT Press, 2009), 191.

68. Conover (et al.), "Adam Ruins Going Green," December 27, 2016.

69. Bill McKibben, "Climate of Denial," *Mother Jones*, June 28, 2017, www.motherjones.com/politics/2005/05/climate-denial.

Bibliography

Benestad, Rasmus E., Dana Nuccitelli, Stephan Lewandowsky, Katharine Hayhoe, Hans Olav Hygen, Rob van Dorland, and Jon Cook. "Learning from Mistakes in Climate Research." *Theoretical and Applied Climatology* 126 (2016): 699–703.
Berwyn, Bob. "Rebuilding Credibility on Climate Action Will Take Time." *Inside Climate News*, January 21, 2021. https://insideclimatenews.org/news/21012021/biden-paris-climate-agreement/.
"Body of Research Undermines Infrared Iris Hypothesis." *Skeptical Science*. https://skepticalscience.com/infrared-iris-effect-negative-feedback.htm.
Callicott, J. Baird. "From the Land Ethic to the Earth Ethic: Aldo Leopold and the Gaia Hypothesis." In *Gaia in Turmoil, Climate Change, Biodepletion, and Earth Ethics in an Age of Crisis*, edited by Eileen Crist, H. Bruce Rinker, and Bill McKibben. 177–194. Cambridge, MA: The MIT Press, 2009.
Chen, Michelle. "The Paris Climate Accord Didn't Go Nearly Far Enough—Can Bonn Do Better?." *The Nation*, November 7, 2017. https://www.thenation.com/article/archive/the-paris-climate-accord-didnt-go-nearly-far-enough-can-bonn-do-better/.
Climate Central, "The 10 Hottest Global Years on Record." February 6, 2019. https://www.climatecentral.org/gallery/graphics/the-10-hottest-global-years-on-record.
Collomb, Jean Daniel. "The Ideology of Climate Change Denial in the United States." *European Journal of American Studies* 9, no. 1 (January 2, 2014): https://doi.org/10.4000/ejas.10305.
Conover, Adam, Gonzalo Cordova, Travis Helwig, Mary Lordes, Alingon Mitra, and Diona Reasonover. "Adam Ruins Going Green." *Adam Ruins Everything*. TruTV. December 27, 2016.
"Debunking 97% Climate Consensus Denial." *Skeptical Science*, September 9, 2013. https://skepticalscience.com/debunking-climate-consensus-denial.html.
Epstein, Alex. "'97% of Climate Scientists Agree' Is 100% Wrong." *Forbes*, January 6, 2015. https://www.forbes.com/sites/alexepstein/2015/01/06/97-of-climate-scientists-agree-is-100-wrong/#fde35443f9ff.
Foley, Katherine Ellen. "'Those 3% of Scientific Papers That Deny Climate Change? a Review Found Them All Flawed." *Quartz*, September 5, 2017. https://qz.com/1069298/the-3-of-scientific-papers-that-deny-climate-change-are-all-flawed/.
"Freeman Dyson's Selective Vision." *Real Climate*, May 24, 2008. http://www.realclimate.org/index.php/archives/2008/05/freeman-dysons-selective-vision/.
Gajanan, Mahita. "Republican Congressman Says God Will 'Take Care Of' Climate Change." *Time*, May 31, 2017. https://time.com/4800000/tim-walberg-god-climate-change/.
"Global Warming & Climate Change Myths." *Skeptical Science*. https://skepticalscience.com/argument.php.
Goodwin, Phillip. "On the Time Evolution of Climate Sensitivity and Future Warming." *Earth's Future* 6, no. 9 (September 2018): 1336–1348.
Greenberg, Jon. "No, 30,000 Scientists Have Not Said Climate Change Is a Hoax." *Politifact*, September 8, 2017. https://www.politifact.com/factchecks/2017/sep/08/blog-posting/no-30000-scientists-have-not-said-climate-change-h/.
Griffin, Paul. "CDP Carbon Majors Report 2017." *The Carbon Majors Database*, July 2017. https://b8f65cb373b1b7b15feb-c70d8ead6ced550b4d987d7c03fcdd1d.ssl.cf3.rackcdn.com/cms/reports/documents/000/002/327/original/Carbon-Majors-Report-2017.pdf?1499691240.
Hall, Shannon. "Exxon Knew About Climate Change Almost 40 Years Ago." *Scientific American*, October 26, 2015. https://www.scientificamerican.com/article/exxon-knew-about-climate-change-almost-40-years-ago/.
Henig, Jess. "'Climategate.'" *Factcheck.org*, December 10, 2009. https://www.factcheck.org/2009/12/climategate/.
"IPCC Attribution Statements Redux: A Response to Judith Curry." *Real Climate*,

Act III: Science and Politics

August 27, 2014. http://www.realclimate.org/index.php/archives/2014/08/ipcc-attribution-statements-redux-a-response-to-judith-curry/.

Johnson, David Kyle. "The Galileo Gambit." In *Fallacies Bad Arguments: 100 of the Most Important Fallacies in Western Philosophy*, edited by Robert Arp, Bruce Robert and Steve Barbone, 152–156. Wiley-Blackwell, 2018.

Johnson, David Kyle. "How Fallacies Fuel Conspiracies" in *Conspiracy Theories: Philosophers Connect the Dots*, edited by Richard Green and Rachel Robinson-Greene, 45–56. Chicago: Open Court, 2020.

"Judith Curry," *Desmog*, https://www.desmogblog.com/judith-curry.

Le Page, Michael. "Climate Myths: The 'Hockey Stick' Graph Has Been Proven Wrong." *New Scientist*, May 16, 2007. https://www.newscientist.com/article/dn11646-climate-myths-the-hockey-stick-graph-has-been-proven-wrong/.

Lesser, Jonathan. "Are Electric Cars Worse for the Environment?." *Politico*, May 15, 2018. https://www.politico.com/agenda/story/2018/05/15/are-electric-cars-worse-for-the-environment-000660.

Lindsey, Hal. "Tonight on the Hal Lindsey Report." *The Hal Lindsey Report*. https://www.hallindsey.com/hlr-2-27-2015/.

Lynas, Mark. *Six Degrees: Our Future on a Hotter Planet*. Harper Perennial, 2008.

Mann, Michael E., Raymond S. Bradley, and Malcolm K. Hughes. "Northern Hemisphere Temperatures During the Past Millennium: Inferences, Uncertainties, and Limitations." *Geophysical Research Letters* 26, no. 6 (1999): 759–762.

McKibben, Bill. "Climate of Denial." *Mother Jones*, June 28, 2017. www.motherjones.com/politics/2005/05/climate-denial.

Mehta, Hemant. "Let's Debunk the 'Christian Persecution' Court Cases That Inspired the 'God's Not Dead' Films." *Friendly Atheist*, April 8, 2016. https://friendlyatheist.patheos.com/2016/04/08/lets-debunk-the-christian-persecution-court-cases-that-inspired-the-gods-not-dead-films/.

Montford, A.W. *The Hockey Stick Illusion*. Anglosphere Books, 2015.

"The Montford Delusion." *Real Climate*, July 22, 2010. http://www.realclimate.org/index.php/archives/2010/07/the-montford-delusion/.

Moyers, Bill. "Welcome to Doomsday." *The New York Review of Books*, March 24, 2005. www.nybooks.com/articles/2005/03/24/welcome-to-doomsday.

Noble, Alan. "The Evangelical Persecution Complex." *The Atlantic*, August 4, 2014. https://www.theatlantic.com/national/archive/2014/08/the-evangelical-persecution-complex/375506/.

Novella, Steven. *The Skeptic's Guide to the Universe*. New York: Hachette Book Group, 2018.

Nuccitelli, Dana. "New Study Reconciles a Dispute About How Fast Global Warming Will Happen." *The Guardian*, September 24, 2018. https://www.theguardian.com/environment/climate-consensus-97-per-cent/2018/sep/24/new-study-reconciles-a-dispute-about-how-fast-global-warming-will-happen.

Nuccitelli, Dana. "Scientists Have Beaten Down the Best Climate Denial Argument." *The Guardian*, December 18, 2017. https://www.theguardian.com/environment/climate-consensus-97-per-cent/2017/dec/18/scientists-have-beaten-down-the-best-climate-denial-argument.

Nyhan, Breandan, and Jason Reifler. "When Corrections Fail: The Persistence of Political Misperceptions." *Political Behavior* 32 (2010): 303–330.

Oreskes, Naomi. "The Scientific Consensus on Climate Change: How Do We Know We're Not Wrong?." *Climate Change: What It Means for You, Your Children, and Your Grandchildren (2nd Edition)*. Edited by Joseph F.C. DiMento and Pamela Doughman, 105–148. MIT Press: 2014.

Oreskes, Naomi, and Erik M. Conway. *Merchants of Doubt: How a Handful of Scientists Obscured the Truth on Issues from Tobacco Smoke to Global Warming*. London: Bloomsbury, 2010.

Oreskes, Naomi, Michael Oppenheimer, and Dale Jamieson. "Scientists Have Been Underestimating the Pace of Climate Change." *Scientific American*, August 19, 2019. https://blogs.scientificamerican.com/observations/scientists-have-been-underestimating-the-pace-of-climate-change/.

Orr, David. "Armageddon Vs. Extinction." *Conservation Biology* 19, no. 2 (Nov. 2005): 290–292.
Pew Research Center. "Jesus Christ's Return to Earth." July 14, 2010. https://www.pewresearch.org/fact-tank/2010/07/14/jesus-christs-return-to-earth/.
Pollin, Robert. *Greening the Global Economy*. The MIT Press, 2015.
Pollin, Robert. "Think We Can't Stabilize the Climate While Fostering Growth? Think Again." *The Nation*, October 27, 2015. https://www.thenation.com/article/archive/think-we-cant-stabilize-the-climate-while-fostering-growth-think-again/.
"Public Knowledge About Science Has a Limited Tie to People's Beliefs About Climate Change and Climate Scientists." *Pew Research Center*, October 4, 2016. https://www.pewresearch.org/science/2016/10/04/public-knowledge-about-science-has-a-limited-tie-to-peoples-beliefs-about-climate-change-and-climate-scientists/.
"References and Resources." *American Chemical Society*. https://www.acs.org/content/acs/en/climatescience/references.html.
Riley, Tess. "Just 100 Companies Responsible for 71% of Global Emissions, Study Says." *The Guardian*, July 10, 2017. https://www.theguardian.com/sustainable-business/2017/jul/10/100-fossil-fuel-companies-investors-responsible-71-global-emissions-cdp-study-climate-change.
Russell, Bertrand. *Let the People Think*. Rockford, IL: Watts & Company, 1996.
Rutjens, Bastiaan T., Robbie M. Sutton, and Romy van der Lee. "Not All Skepticism Is Equal: Exploring the Ideological Antecedents of Science Acceptance and Rejection." *Personality and Social Psychology Bulletin* 44, no. 3 (March 2018): 381–405. https://doi.org/10.1177/0146167217741314.
"Science Was Wrong Before." *Rational Wiki*. https://rationalwiki.org/wiki/Science_was_wrong_before.
"7 Effects of Climate Change You're Already Seeing." *The Climate Reality Project*, April 2, 2019. https://www.climaterealityproject.org/blog/7-effects-climate-change-already-seeing.
Shurkin, Joel. "Scientific Consensus Is Almost Never Wrong—Almost." *Inside Science*, November 20, 2015. https://www.insidescience.org/news/scientific-consensus-almost-never-wrong-%E2%80%94-almost.
Silvey, Janese. "Professor Details Role as Climate Consultant." *Columbia Tribune*, March 5, 2012. https://www.columbiatribune.com/59653f24-1dbf-5fcb-ac88-4eedfd7a60a0.html.
Skeptical Science. "The 97% Consensus on Global Warming." https://www.skepticalscience.com/global-warming-scientific-consensus.htm.
Skeptical Science. "What Evidence Is There for the Hockey Stick?."https://skepticalscience.com/broken-hockey-stick.htm.
Smith, Adam. *Inquiry Into the Nature and Causes of the Wealth of Nations*. 1776.
"The 10 Hottest Global Years on Record." *Climate Central*, February 6, 2019. https://www.climatecentral.org/gallery/graphics/the-10-hottest-global-years-on-record.
Trevors, Gregory J., Krista R. Muis, Reinhard Pekrun, Gale M. Sinatra, and Philip H. Winne. "Identity and Epistemic Emotions During Knowledge Revision: A Potential Account for the Backfire Effect." *Discourse Processes* 53, no. 5–6 (2015): 339–370.
TruTV. *Adam Ruins Everything*. Post Hill Press, 2018.
Tuttle, Ian. "The 97 Percent Solution." *National Review*, October 8, 2015. http://www.nationalreview.com/article/425232/climate-change-no-its-not-97-percent-consensus-ian-tuttle.
"2019 Was 2nd Hottest Year on Record for Earth Say NOAA, NASA." *National Oceanic and AtmosphericAdministration,* January 15, 2020. https://www.noaa.gov/news/2019-was-2nd-hottest-year-on-record-for-earth-say-noaa-nasa.
Upton, John. "Clouds Won't Save Us from Global Warming." *Scientific American*, April 7, 2016. https://www.scientificamerican.com/article/clouds-won-t-save-us-from-global-warming/.
"Vaccine Safety." *Centers for Disease Control and Prevention*, January 14, 2020. https://www.cdc.gov/vaccinesafety/index.html.
Veldman, Robin Globus. *The Gospel of Climate Skepticism*. Oakland, CA: University of California Press, 2019.
"Water Vapor Confirmed as Major Player in Climate Change." *National Aeronautics and*

164 Act III: Science and Politics

Space Administration, November 17, 2008. https://www.nasa.gov/topics/earth/features/vapor_warming.html.

Weart, Spencer. *The Discovery of Global Warming,* Cambridge, MA: Harvard University Press, 2003.

Wood, Thomas, and Ethan Porter. "The Elusive Backfire Effect: Mass Attitudes' Steadfast Factual Adherence." *Political Behavior* 41, no. 1 (January 2018): 135–163.

"Majority Rule" and a Critique of Pure Democracy

Patrick Welsh

"I believe you are confusing opinion with knowledge."
—Isaac, "Majority Rule"

In the episode "Majority Rule," where Lt. John LaMarr goes on an apology tour for grind dancing on a statue, the USS *Orville* encounters the Sarguns—the inhabitants of Sargus 4. Fans of the show no doubt recall that the Sarguns are a species both biologically and culturally identical to humans of the 21st century, but they may have missed some of the subtle differences. For example, Sarguns wear "doubled" clothing. Their suits have two lapels, their ties are knotted twice. This a subtle touch by Joseph Porro, the show's wardrobe designer. "If you look at the ties and shirts and jackets, I doubled everything," Porro is quoted saying in Jeff Bond's illuminating behind-the-scenes book *The World of The Orville*. "Double lapels and on ties we had a lady work for us to tie knots that were not typical, and we did a lot just to make it all a little off. I would buy two suit jackets and rip the lapel off one to make a double lapel on the other, just to make it strange."[1]

Porro's twist on American fashion was a clever hint that Sargus 4 was no simple mirror of Earth. When audiences realize that what looked to be our clothes are in truth slightly different, Porro prepares them for other slight differences—like the differences in Sargus 4's democracy. Sargus 4 as a whole is democratic, but it does not follow the American model of representative democracy where individual citizens choose a representative from among themselves to vote on political questions. Sarguns are also not "constrained" by a constitution that protects the rights of all its citizens. Sarguns practice a form of pure (or direct) democracy where all things large and small are a matter of public concern, and all matters of public concern are voted upon by the populace at large (on a platform that resembles Twitter called "The Master Feed"). Put another way, Sargus 4 is a United States re-imagined where every social question is put to an online referendum, and the deciding factor is not truth but public appeal. In the words of Isaac, it is "an absolute, unstructured democracy."

There are lots of good arguments against pure democracy. For example, borrowing from Alexis de Tocqueville, pure democracy lacks "lasting obstacles" to prevent "opinions, prejudices, interests, and even the passions of the people."[2] In other words, it's a majoritarian system where rulership rests upon the whims of the arbitrary sentiments of the largest number of voters. Hurrell Mallock believed a society ruled by the majority's opinion would be a people "reduced artificially to their lowest common denominator." The voting majority cannot understand the most complicated scientific debates, and therefore only the most brilliant are qualified to decide them.[3]

In this essay, I explore the argument that *The Orville* seems to be making with "Majority Rule." It seems to go something like this: While the notion that everyone's opinion possesses equal validity and therefore equal merit in the public sphere may sound attractive and egalitarian, it is subjectivist, dangerous, and ultimately harmful to anyone unlucky enough to fall outside the majority's opinion. Any system of decision-making rooted solely in pure democracy is institutionally flawed. Of course, if the argument ended there, and "Majority Rule" was concerned solely with formal governance, this episode would have narrow allegorical value and hardly be worth a full essay. Some jurisdictions may use ecumenical referendums as a decision-making tool in limited contexts, but America is in no danger of becoming a pure democracy any time soon.

What makes "Majority Rule" interesting is that it advances the idea that social media is a pure democracy and has correspondingly become a moral problem for the world. Social media in the United States is governed by public sentiment, emotional judgments made by large groups without due process or any significant truth-finding mechanism. Damage to individuals, institutions, and groups is wrought by the majority in an unchecked, reckless thirst for justice that often hurts more than it helps. The result is that despite the benefits of social media and the internet, there is a significant moral cost paid by minority groups.

This simple essay consists only of two parts. First, I explain how "Majority Rule" was written to serve as a morality tale for American audiences. In doing so, I divine the philosophical concerns, both political and ethical, of Seth MacFarlane and the writing staff. Then, after I reveal what perceived social problems led MacFarlane and others to write the episode, I consider *The Orville*'s criticism of pure democracy. As is shown, the writers of "Majority Rule" identify, but do not necessarily answer, a looming question in the new age of social media: Are we, as a society, mature enough and properly educated to handle pure democracy?

Writing "Majority Rule"

Seth MacFarlane, it seems, wrote the script for "Majority Rule" in mid–2016 after considering the rise of public shaming in social media. "I read that book *So You've Been Publicly Shamed*," he stated in a June 2018 interview with *Hollywood Reporter*. "I was fascinated and disturbed and came in the day after I finished it and said, 'We have to write about this. And what better genre to do it than in science fiction?'"[4] *So You've Been Publicly Shamed*, written by Jon Ronson, is a simple but compelling collection of public shaming incidents, made possible by the internet; it emphasizes particularly the heavy-handed punishment society metes upon the accused.

Co-executive producer André Bormanis was in the writers' room the day MacFarlane sprung the idea:

> [W]e had a lot of conversations in the room about public shaming. This guy Jon Ronson had written about it in the book and it was in the air, people were talking a lot about it in 2016. Seth came up with the basic story, about a pure democracy, a planet where people shamed others if their behavior was considered unlawful or even uncouth. People would vote on everything—what's safe to eat, whether air and water pollution is unhealthy, and so on. We decided early on that it should be a world like present-day Earth because it was one of these parables, one of these social commentary shows as was done in the original *Star Trek*.[5]

The stories in *So You've Been Publicly Shamed* shaped how the writers approached their fictional world. Each story points to a moment when the general public on the internet learned of an individual's bad behavior (either real or imagined). In each instance, the public transformed into a mob—mocking, criticizing and even threatening those unlucky enough to have become famous. The behavior was more similar to a riot than anything else, where people in a group acted in a way they would not on their own.

Consider, for example, the social sins of columnist Jonah Lehrer, whose story ends up paralleling many of the plot points of "Majority Rule." Around 2012, 31-year-old Lehrer had been caught fabricating quotes attributed to musician Bob Dylan and lying to cover his tracks, plagiarizing on his blog, and self-plagiarizing in his columns for the *New Yorker* (lifting portions of old columns he penned for *The Wall Street Journal* and recycling them). "He was drenched in shame and regret he told me," Ronson recalled in a TED talk several years later.[6] Lehrer lost his job at the *New*

Yorker, and his publishers recalled unsold copies of his books from store shelves.⁷

Just when Lehrer's professional life seemed finished, the John S. and James L. Knight Foundation offered the young journalist the chance to deliver a keynote speech on the final day of the Foundation's conference. It was an opportunity to apologize and a shot at redemption.

Lehrer drafted a confession and sent it to Ronson, a speech that began by bluntly admitting every sordid wrong and seeking the public's forgiveness. "It was a stark opening," Ronson said. "An unembellished declaration of guilt, followed by his account of shame and regret."⁸

Lehrer knew his speech was to be broadcast live on the internet.⁹ What Lehrer did not know was that the Foundation had set up an enormous video screen behind the podium that would display reaction tweets submitted from around the world in real time. It was a recipe for disaster. When Lehrer began speaking, Twitter users mocked his apology, many evidently having decided that his punishment thus far had been insufficient and a good deal more shaming would be necessary. The Tweets popped up: "Jonah Lehrer is just a frigging sociopath" and "Jonah Lehrer has not proven that he is capable of feeling shame." About that last one, Ronson bemused, "That one must have been written by the best psychiatrist ever to know that about such a tiny figure behind a lectern.... Imagine this was an actual court and the accused was begging for a chance and the jury was yelling out '*Bored! Sociopath!*'"¹⁰

It seems almost certain that this Lehrer incident influenced Seth MacFarlane. Consider the society on Sargus he created. All citizens over 18 are required to wear Vote Badges that tabulate the total number of up or downvotes one has accrued over their life. Votes can be awarded by anyone for any reason—a downvote for accidentally spilling coffee on a stranger or an upvote simply for being attractive. If one gets enough downvotes, others begin dishing out small punishments; one café refuses to serve anyone with 500,000 downvotes (and since downvotes cannot be erased, the ban is seemingly permanent). At 1,000,000 downvotes, a person is automatically considered a criminal against the State. The person is arrested by police and forced to undertake an apology tour, where they have one week to appear live on television shows and beg the public's forgiveness. Should the total number of downvotes against the accused exceed 10,000,000, the accused is "socially corrected" by a drastic neurological procedure similar to a frontal lobotomy.

There is little material difference between an apology tour and the structure of Jonah Lehrer's infamous Foundation speech. Take Tom and Lewis for example, two undercover Planetary Union anthropologists who failed to offer their seat to a pregnant woman on the subtrain.¹¹ It is not even clear the men noticed her (Lewis says they did not), but nonetheless their "crime" was caught on camera and uploaded to the Master Feed. We first see Tom and Lewis in the middle of their tour on *The Breakfast Show*, apologizing for their conduct. Any Sargun can post comments to the live Master Feed, displayed in real time at the bottom of the television screen. As Lewis tells the audience he feels "ashamed for his behavior," live posts read: "Why haven't these two been corrected already???," "sexist pigs," "misogynistic pieces of trash," and "GET THEM OUT OF HERE ALREADY." In the final shot of *The Breakfast Show*, Lysella casts a downvote after finding one of the men has "really weird eyes."

Lysella's judgment underscores the absurdity of a trial by social media. Viewers feel like their comments and votes are justified in the moment because their attacks are the manifestation of social justice, but the punishment lacks the safeguard of procedural due process and often hinges upon emotional or otherwise arbitrary decision-making. Or, to put it another way, a justice system founded upon viewer sentiment leads to voting based on "really weird eyes."

Surprisingly, MacFarlane has never publicly referenced Jonah Lehrer despite his story's obvious parallels with "Majority Rule" and when MacFarlane talks "Majority Rule" he usually cites other examples from Ronson's book for inspiration. Take for example when an audience member asked the cast about the episode during the 2018 San Diego Comic-Con. MacFarlane told the crowd to look up the Justine Sacco case because "that's a perfect example."[12] Given that Lehrer's case was so much more similar to the episode, one wonders why Sacco's case was seemingly so important for the development of the episode script.

Sacco was a communications director at IAC, a public relations firm, who tweeted a series of mean-spirited jokes during a business trip in late 2013. She tweeted her last joke as she boarded a plane: "Going to Africa. Hope I don't get AIDS. Just kidding. I'm white!" The tweet became the center of a media firestorm while she was still in the air. Someone discovered her tweet and forwarded it to Gawker.[13] People called for her job and to boycott her employer. Many gleefully awaited the shaming she would see when her plane landed and someone bothered to snap and upload photos of her exiting the terminal to Twitter. Sacco became the number-one trending topic on the social network.[14]

Sacco intended her joke to satirize a "bubble" of ignorance in Western culture regarding health and race in Africa, but journalists and Twitter users had little interest in understanding the meaning of her words. "Only an *insane* person would think that white people don't get AIDS," she told Ronson in an interview a few weeks later.[15] She added in a later e-mail, "It was completely outrageous commentary on the disproportionate AIDS statistics. Unfortunately, I'm not a character on *South Park*, or a comedian, so I had no business commenting on the epidemic in such a politically incorrect manner on a public platform."[16]

Sacco's story evidently impacted MacFarlane. For example, when invited to *The Jason Rantz Show* in 2016, the conversation turned to the presidential elections and nominations in the Democratic party. MacFarlane felt that supporters of then-presidential candidate Bernie Sanders had treated fellow candidate Hillary Clinton unfairly. "The left has gotten a little unreasonable when it comes to separating the trivial from the profound."[17] He pointed to Justine Sacco:

> She was destroyed based on something that she just tossed off. What the conservatives would argue, and I would agree with them in this instance, is that you may not like it, but it's freedom of speech. You don't destroy somebody for that. She was not infringing upon anyone's rights. At the end of the day, the only person who got trampled on was her.

MacFarlane again brought up Sacco on Twitter in November 2016 just days after the election of Donald Trump for President of the United States:

> This will not be a popular observation, and I don't even know if I subscribe to it myself, but it can be argued that the Left expended so much energy over the last several years being outraged over verbal missteps, accidental innuendo, "tasteless" tweets (see Justine Sacco) etc. in the name of clickbait, that when the real threat to equality emerged, we'd cried wolf too many times to be heard.[18]

He has a point, and the crying-wolf problem is not just limited to clickbait, clout, and money. Both Clinton and Sacco were victims of what philosophers Brandon Warmke and Justin Tose call "moral grandstanding." "Grandstanders want others to regard them as being morally respectable," they write. "[A]nd the contributions they make to public moral discourse are intended to satisfy that desire." Whether a moral grandstander's beliefs are true or at least supported by evidence are tangential. The primary concern of the grandstander is to project an image of superior virtue, so the grandstander will "trump up moral charges, pile on in cases of public shaming, announce that anyone who disagrees with them is obviously wrong, or exaggerate emotional displays."[19]

In a sense, both "Majority Rule" and *So You've Been Publicly Shamed* are deeply sociological works that touch upon issues of public virtue and punishment, economics and social debts, forgiveness and lifelong scarlet letters. A person's shame on popular opinion media or on Sargus 4's television circuit is nothing less than a new economy where writers turn other people's misery into a consumable product for profit, and consumption of the product is participatory as well as passive. The articles written for profit outrage us and spur us on to punish the Saccos, the Lehrers, and the LaMarrs—but more on that later.

A Critique of Pure Democracy

The way I just framed it, that any society would want such an obviously horrible system of justice would seem absurd. But there are positive aspects I should discuss to contextualize the Sarguns' rationale for their society's practices. Lysella more-or-less articulates the Sargun argument for pure democracy when she says that a radically decentralized form of voting ensures that each adult has an equal voice on every cultural question. "Well, my dad always says, 'The majority are the truth.' I mean, you always know what the majority wants. That's what matters" (S1E7). Lysella finds representative democracy insufficient because no individual can capture the opinions of each constituent in the way pure democracy can. In the Planetary Union, as in the United States, voters "select representatives to discuss issues and pass laws" (S1E7). When Lysella hears this, she objects, "But what about everybody else? Everybody deserves a voice. That's what we're taught." At the risk of misunderstanding *The Orville*'s writing staff, it seems that "Majority Rule" is an answer to Lysella and, in a way, a response to a possible direction society could take.

That last part is not as speculative as one might think. To begin with, it is no secret that *The Orville* was always intended to spin allegories of real-world events in the vein of science fiction television like *Star Trek*. Writers send a crew of future, more perfect humans (and other compadres like Spock or Bortus) to an alien land where the local culture imitates American society in all ways but a few.

Consider "All the World Is Birthday Cake." The USS *Orville* makes first contact with Regor 2 to find an Earth-like species enraptured by their astrological system. The Regorians imprison anyone born under the Giliac sign, including Commander Kelly Grayson and Lieutenant Commander Bortus. Their inability to see through the myth of astrology needlessly jeopardized their relationship with the peaceful Planetary Union, and so the staff writers warn audiences of the peril of clinging to unexamined beliefs. Executive producer Brannon Braga called their mix of drama, action, and morality tale, "A return to classical storytelling."[20]

After "Majority Rule" aired, Seth MacFarlane occasionally used the episode as a barometer of social change. When *The Atlantic* reviewed China's Golden Shield surveillance program where citizens are assigned a score "to incentivize 'good behavior,'"[21] MacFarlane remarked, "'Majority Rule' in practice—very unsettling."[22] And in a more humorous example, MacFarlane directed fans to "like" "Majority Rule" on Hulu for irony's sake.[23]

So, if MacFarlane and the writing staff intended "Majority Rule" to serve as both a response to Lysella's argument for pure democracy and an allegorical statement on contemporary American culture, what was their message? Decentralized social media, despite its obvious benefits, is a form of pure democracy which lacks the procedural safeguards of older institutions like the justice system. In an American justice system, the State must gather evidence and present a theory of the case in front of a body of one's peers. Evidence which may unfairly inflame the passions or biases of the jurors against a defendant must be excluded[24]; charges without evidence must be dropped[25]; and evidence obtained by the State that would otherwise exculpate the defendant must be handed over.[26] Purely democratic internet platforms on the other hand, like Twitter and Facebook, are more like frontier trials of the old and very wild West than venues of reasonable discussion[27]; people like Justine Sacco are packaged into news stories intended to stir their readers' emotions for ad revenue.

To be honest, MacFarlane probably said it better himself:

> I think there are good things about social media and Twitter. I think there are certain groups; we've seen a speediness of acceptance for certain marginalized groups that I think without the unification of social media would have taken a lot longer than it has. That's the positive side of social media. The downside is it can become a mob very quickly and oftentimes does.
>
> …
>
> I think it's very creepy. We're not evolved enough as a species to not succumb to the rush of joining a group that is ganging up on another group or individual. There's a weird rush that gives a lot of people when they become part of a mob. So, I think that it's too soon to independently govern ourselves in the way that social media attempts to do so.[28]

The argument found in "Majority Rule" against pure democracy runs roughly as follows: Despite Lysella's statement that "everyone deserves a voice," not all opinions are created equal; and the fact that someone enjoys the legal right to express an opinion says nothing about the opinion's veracity. As Bortus put it, "A voice should be earned, not given away." Some opinions will be fact-based and supported by reason, others will not; and the former are far more valuable than the latter. While government by elected representation is not perfect, government by pure democracy more greatly exposes matters of public concern to emotional and opinion-based voting.

Astute viewers might have noticed that *The Orville* took Lysella's statement to its absurd conclusion at the start of the episode. When John LaMarr and the others first enter Lysella's café, a television screen shows two men on an unnamed talk show resembling *The Charlie Rose Show*.[29] They are identified in the credits only as Interviewer and Scientist.[30]

Scientist: And there's great concern about the level of contamination due to industrial waste in the South Madaka reservoir.
Interviewer: But you can't deny facts. Seventy-four percent of the population has voted that assessment false. I mean, facts are facts.

The scene is a well-placed harbinger. In a few seconds, the interviewer frames the problem of "Majority Rule" moments after John committed his crime and just before his arrest. The audience learns that Sargus 4 places majority opinion on the same pedestal as evidence at the expense of truth, and for some reason majority opinion has turned against John.

John undergoes an apology tour—seven days of Lehrer-esque moments on live television, humbly pleading for the planet's forgiveness. The crew realizes that pure democracy is little more than a ritualized popularity contest and Gordon Malloy calls it, "government by *American Idol*." Meanwhile, the admiralty forbids extracting John as it would interfere with the Union's prohibition against substantially interfering with the cultural development of a people who have not advanced to the point of travel at quantum speeds.[31] John is forced to experience the full effect of pure democracy.

Not surprisingly, the apology tour is nothing short of a dismal failure. Anonymous viewers feel John's attempted apologies are insincere, they mock him on the Master Feed and castigate him with downvotes. The senior officers on the *Orville* watch in horror as they realize an apology tour has no room for rational discourse. Take *The Chat*, for example, a patent parody of *The View*, where hosts Hosha, Semmla, and Carris constantly draw conclusions for their viewers, with an array of clever ploys:

- They poison the well before John has a chance to apologize. Carris downvotes John as soon as they introduce him. "I just had to do that," she explains. Semmla approves, "Good girl."
- Carris sullies John's apology as soon as he starts: "You know, we talk to a lot of different people on this show and I got to say, your apology sounds very rehearsed," triggering a chorus of boos from the audience.
- The trio interrogate John about his knowledge of Mella Giffendon's life for a few minutes to embarrass him for his ignorance.[32] Semmla feigns shock: "He can't even name one thing. Oh, my God."

With the audience thoroughly turned against the young lieutenant, Carris and Hosel put John's Vote Badge number on the live screen and instruct viewers to vote. At no point did the three hosts tell others how to vote, but by encouraging downvotes and persistently judging and humiliating John, they did not need to.

Reason, as John and Jonah learned, has little place in pure democracy and social media. At John's Final Vote, live comments include *GROSS GROSS GROSS GROSS GROSS, He makes me feel unsafe,* and *screw this guy, screw everyone he knows* to name a few. And the only way the crew of the USS *Orville* can save John from Social Correction is by exploiting the same flaw that created their problem: the emotions of the mob.[33] Isaac hacks into the Master Feed and overwhelms the live chat with 20 million supportive comments and fabricated information designed to play to the sympathies of Sarguns. John is transformed from a man who grinded on a statue of a frontier hero to a veteran who overcame obesity as a child and who financially supports his 90-year-old grandmother. Isaac posts a video of John in Sargun military uniform returning from war to warmly embrace his loving dog Chuckles.

While Isaac furiously types away, the writers anticipate counterarguments through the voice of Doctor Claire Finn. "What if people try to corroborate all this information?" She brings up an important point. People are always free to examine various claims for their veracity by investigating and weighing the evidence. A society that fiercely checks any claim before drawing conclusions should be safeguarded against the flaws inherent in pure democracy. The writers' answer through Lysella is a terse rebuke of human nature. "Don't worry," Lysella assures Claire. "They won't."

Notice that the end of "Majority Rule" is a surprisingly subdued conclusion to the writers' argument. John escapes Social Correction and Lysella no longer participates in the broken system of pure democracy and trial by social media, but Sargus 4 as a whole remains unchanged. If pure democracy is little more than ritualized mob justice, then facts will always be subordinate to feelings and the only surefire way to escape punishment is not through innocence but manipulation.

Conclusion

The argument in "Majority Rule," its critique of pure democracy, is a surprisingly powerful yet simple one. Purely democratic institutions are deeply flawed because they lack any systematic assurances of evidence-based judgments akin to a courtroom's constitutionally guaranteed due process protections, and online social media in the last 10 to 15 years has grown into such a pure democracy.

The only solution to this alarming problem implied by the writers is individual maturity. Lysella, the lone Sargun who learns the truth of John and the USS *Orville*, actually defends her system of apology tours and social correction to Ed, Kelly, and the rest at first. She only changes her mind after witnessing Isaac easily turn the tide of public opinion in John's favor in seven minutes through carefully tailored emotional ploys, finally realizing the senselessness of pure democracy. The next time we see Lysella, she wakes up in her apartment and sees a new subject on *The Breakfast Show* much like Tom and Lewis at the start of the episode. She chooses not to vote and participate in a fundamentally broken system, having evolve independently.

Unfortunately, despite the potential for individuals to evolve independent of one another, the writers are far more pessimistic about humanity. Recall Seth MacFarlane's words, who told a fan at the 2018 San Diego Comic-Con, "We're not evolved enough as a species to not succumb to the rush of joining a group that is ganging up on another group or individual.... So, I think that it's too soon to independently govern ourselves in the way that social media attempts to do so."[34] To put it bluntly, society is too immature and unevolved to self-regulate in any meaningful sense in a purely democratic system.

"Majority Rule" and *The Orville* are fundamentally aspirational, putting us in the shoes of Lysella. As André Bormanis told me in preparation for this essay, pure democracy might not be so bad if we have a highly educated and responsible public.

> If you have a society where everyone has a clear understanding of science, logical reasoning, social issues, and public policy—that kind of society could do pretty well with direct democracy.
>
> In the United States today, we have representative democracy. The voters elect representatives to serve in various governing bodies, with the intent of electing people who are informed, responsible, dedicated, intelligent, of good character, and so on, and will work in the best interests of their constituents. Obviously it doesn't always work out that way! There is always some level of incompetence, corruption, and inefficiency. Despite the last three years, I think we have done pretty well on the whole. In a big complex country like ours, sometimes there is confusion and chaos, but over time, society can still move forward to secure better lives for more and more people.[35]

Here's hoping that he is right!

Acknowledgments

I would like to thank Steven Detweiler for his early contributions to this essay and André Bormanis for agreeing to be interviewed and have his quotes used in this essay.

Notes

1. Jeff Bond, *The World of The Orville* (Titan Books, 2018), 147.
2. Alexis de Tocqueville, *Democracy in America: Historical-Critical Edition of De la démocratie en Amérique*, ed. Eduardo Nolla, trans. James T. Schleifer (Indianapolis: Liberty Fund, 2010), 278, https://oll.libertyfund.org/titles/tocqueville-democracy-in-america-historical-critical-edition-vol-2.
3. Hurrell Mallock, *The Limits of Pure Democracy* (1919), 9.
4. Craig Tomashoff, "Scribes on 'Handmaid's Tale,' 'Westworld' and 12 More Shows

Reveal Secrets from the Writers Room," *The Hollywood Reporter*, June 15, 2018, https://www.hollywoodreporter.com/lists/inside-writers-rooms-how-14-hit-shows-get-created-11191 39.

    5. Interview with André Bormanis, April 10, 2020.

    6. Jon Ronson, "How One Tweet Can Ruin Your Life," filmed June 2015 in London, England. TED video, 17:11, https://www.youtube.com/watch?v=wAIP6fI0NAI.

    7. Jane Kellog, "Another Jonah Lehrer Book Being Pulled from Shelves," *The Hollywood Reporter*, March 2, 2013, https://www.hollywoodreporter.com/news/jonah-lehrer-book-being-pulled-425736.

    8. Jon Ronson, *So You've Been Publicly Shamed*, 1st ed. (Riverhead Books, 2015), 38.

    9. A copy of Jonah Lehrer's speech is available on his website. See Jonah Lehrer, "My Apology" (speech, 2013), http://www.jonahlehrer.com/2013/02/my-apology/.

    10. Ronson, "How One Tweet Can Ruin Your Life."

    11. Lysella identifies it as a subtrain in her conversation with Claire Finn and Alara Kitan over beers.

    12. We will explore MacFarlane's answer in the context of the episode in more detail later. The Orville, "The Orville Panel at Comic-Con 2018 | THE ORVILLE," YouTube, July 21, 2018, https://www.youtube.com/watch?v=QPvAdF3XUBE.

    13. The true starting point of the firestorm is too nebulous to pinpoint exactly, but Ronson speculates the origin was journalist Sam Biddle of Gawker. See Ronson, *So You've Been Publicly Shamed*, 73.

    14. According to "Hannah" in Ronson's book. See Ronson, *So You've Been Publicly Shamed*, 65.

    15. Ronson, *So You've Been Publicly Shamed*, 68.

    16. Ronson, *So You've Been Publicly Shamed*, 69.

    17. Note that MacFarlane's comments came in April 7, 2016, right around the time the script for "Majority Rule" would have been written. "Seth MacFarlane Burns Bernie Sanders Supporters Prior to Seattle Trip," *MyNorthwest*, April 7, 2016, https://mynorthwest.com/255647/seth-macfarlane-burns-bernie-sanders-supporters-prior-to-seattle-trip/.

    18. Seth MacFarlane (@SethMacFarlane), "Just a thought as my brain attempts to process HOW," Twitter, Nov. 9, 2016, https://twitter.com/SethMacFarlane/status/796306781542592512

    19. Justin Tosi and Brandon Warmke, "Moral Grandstanding: There's a Lot of It, All of It Bad," *Aeon*, May 10, 2017, https://aeon.co/ideas/moral-grandstanding-theres-a-lot-of-it-about-all-of-it-bad.

    20. Brannon Braga, "Forward," in *The World of The Orville* 11.

    21. Anna Mitchell and Larry Diamond, "China's Surveillance State Should Scare Everyone," *The Atlantic*, Feb. 2, 2018, https://www.theatlantic.com/international/archive/2018/02/china-surveillance/552203/.

    22. Seth MacFarlane (@SethMacFarlane), "Orville's 'Majority Rule' in practice—very unsettling," Twitter (Aug. 15, 2018), https://twitter.com/SethMacFarlane/status/1029781133209133056.

    23. Seth MacFarlane (@SethMacFarlane), "For added irony, be sure to 'like' season 1, episode 7, 'Majority Rule,'" Twitter (Nov. 26, 2019), https://twitter.com/sethmacfarlane/status/1199383471434502146.

    24. "The court may exclude relevant evidence if its probative value is substantially outweighed by a danger of one or more of the following: unfair prejudice, confusing the issues, misleading the jury, undue delay, wasting time, or needlessly presenting cumulative evidence." See "Rule 403—Excluding Relevant Evidence for Prejudice, Confusion, Waste of Time, or Other Reasons," *Federal Rules of Evidence*, 2020, https://www.rulesofevidence.org/article-iv/rule-403/.

    25. "After the government closes its evidence or after the close of all the evidence, the court on the defendant's motion must enter a judgment of acquittal of any offense for which the evidence is insufficient to sustain a conviction." See "Rule 29(a). Motion for a Judgement of Acquittal," *Federal Rules of Criminal Procedure*, 2020, https://www.federalrulesofcriminalprocedure.org/title-vi-trial/rule-29-motion-for-a-judgment-of-acquittal/.

26. Better known as the *Brady* doctrine. See *Brady v. Maryland* (No.490) (1963), 371 U.S. 812 Certiorari to the Court of Appeals of Maryland.
  27. We are reminded of the words of Andrea McDowell who, in her fascinating though disturbing piece on the history of frontier trials, summarized, "America's history of popular violence against unpopular individuals is infamously long and varied." Andrea McDowell, "Criminal Law Beyond the State: Popular Trials on the Frontier," *BYU Law Review* 2007, no. 2 (2007): 327–386, https://digitalcommons.law.byu.edu/lawreview/vol2007/iss2/2.
  28. 2018 San Diego Comic-Con Panel.
  29. The choice to mimic *The Charlie Rose Show* proved an eerie one. One month after "Majority Rule" aired, eight woman accused Charlie Rose of sexual harassment. *See* Kim Barker and Ellen Gabler, "Charlie Rose Made Crude Sexual Advances, Multiple Women Say," *The New York Times*, Nov. 20, 2017. https://www.nytimes.com/2017/11/20/us/charlie-rose-women.html.
  30. Interestingly enough, the interviewer was played by Matthew Kaminsky who played Crewman Cunninghman on *Star Trek: Enterprise*.
  31. Actually, all that happens in "Majority Rule" is Admiral Tucker forbids extraction because "knowledge of extraterrestrial life could unify [the Sarguns] in a profound way, or it could plunge them into a panic, or some worse degree of upheaval." The show fleshes out the doctrine of First Contact in "Mad Idolatry" and Season 2.
  32. I would like to add that the failure to fill poor John in on Mella Giffendon was nothing short of bad counsel from his publicity officer, Willks.
  33. In fact, the idea of "social correction to prevent future transgressions" may be rooted in two points in Ronson's book. The first being the moment Sacco turned on her phone in the airport and discovered the extreme public castigation that had awaited her. The second being a conversation between Justine Sacco and Ronson about Jonah Lehrer,

  "How's he' doing?" [Sacco] asked me.
  "Pretty badly, I think." I said.
  "Badly in what way?" ...
  "I think he's broken," I said [Ronson, *So You've Been Publicly Shamed*, 76].

The exchange reminds me of Doctor Claire Finn surveying the neurological damage done by Social Correction on Lewis as the damage of public shaming is fundamentally psychological.

  34. 2018 San Diego Comic-Con Panel.
  35. Interview with André Bormanis, April 10, 2020.

Bibliography

Barker, Kim, and Ellen Gabler. "Charlie Rose Made Crude Sexual Advances, Multiple Women Say." *The New York Times*, Nov. 20, 2017. https://www.nytimes.com/2017/11/20/us/charlie-rose-women.html.
Bond, Jeff. *The World of The Orville*. London: Titan Books, 2018.
Brady V. Maryland (No.490) (1963), 371 U.S. 812 Certiorari to the Court of Appeals of Maryland.
Braga, Brannon. "Forward." In *The World of The Orville*, 2018.
de Tocqueville, Eduardo. *Democracy in America: Historical-Critical Edition of De La Démocratie En Amérique*, edited by Eduardo Nolla, translated by James T. Schleifer. Indianapolis: Liberty Fund, 2010.
Kellog, Jane. "Another Jonah Lehrer Book Being Pulled from Shelves." *The Hollywood Reporter*, March 2, 2013. https://www.hollywoodreporter.com/news/jonah-lehrer-book-being-pulled-425736.
Lehrer, Jonah. "My Apology." Speech, 2013. http://www.jonahlehrer.com/2013/02/my-apology/.
Mallock, Hurrell. *The Limits of Pure Democracy*. 1919.

McDowell, Andrea. "Criminal Law Beyond the State: Popular Trials on the Frontie." *BYU Law Review* 2007, no. 2 (2007): 327–386. https://digitalcommons.law.byu.edu/lawreview/vol2007/iss2/2.

Mitchell, Anna, and Larry Diamond. "China's Surveillance State Should Scare Everyone." *The Atlantic*, Feb. 2, 2018. https://www.theatlantic.com/international/archive/2018/02/china-surveillance/552203/.

"Rule 403—Excluding Relevant Evidence for Prejudice, Confusion, Waste of Time, or Other Reasons." *Federal Rules of Evidence*, 2020. https://www.rulesofevidence.org/article-iv/rule-403/.

"Rule 29(a). Motion for a Judgement of Acquittal." *Federal Rules of Criminal Procedure*, 2020. https://www.federalrulesofcriminalprocedure.org/title-vi-trial/rule-29-motion-for-a-judgment-of-acquittal/.

Ronson, Jon. "How One Tweet Can Ruin Your Life." Filmed June 2015 in London, England. TED video, 17:11. https://www.youtube.com/watch?v=wAIP6fI0NAI.

Ronson, Jon. *So You've Been Publicly Shamed*. 1st ed. Riverhead Books, 2015.

"Seth MacFarlane Burns Bernie Sanders Supporters Prior to Seattle Trip." *MyNorthwest*, April 7, 2016. https://mynorthwest.com/255647/seth-macfarlane-burns-bernie-sanders-supporters-prior-to-seattle-trip/.

Tomashoff, Craig. "Scribes on 'Handmaid's Tale,' 'Westworld' and 12 More Shows Reveal Secrets from the Writers Room." *The Hollywood Reporter*, June 15, 2018. https://www.hollywoodreporter.com/lists/inside-writers-rooms-how-14-hit-shows-get-created-1119139.

Tosi, Justin, and Brandon Warmke. "Moral Grandstanding: There's a Lot of It, All of It Bad." *Aeon*, May 10, 2017. https://aeon.co/ideas/moral-grandstanding-theres-a-lot-of-it-about-all-of-it-bad.

Act IV
Love, Care and Nepotism

Loving Isaac

Mimi Marinucci

In "A Happy Refrain," it becomes evident that the USS *Orville*'s doctor, Claire Finn, has developed romantic feelings for Isaac. Isaac is from the planet Kaylon 1, which means he is an artificial lifeform assembled in a factory. The Kaylon were originally designed as servants by an indigenous species referred to as the Builders. Although the Builders have since gone extinct, the Kaylon continue to exist and to assemble more of their kind. Isaac is basically a robot, for lack of a better word, and Claire is therefore cautious about becoming romantically involved with him, even though he seems like an ideal partner in some ways. Not only is he attentive, noticing when Claire could use an afternoon snack or is experimenting with a new hairstyle, he is also helpful, especially with Claire's children. Being a robot, however, Isaac is apparently incapable of reciprocating Claire's feelings. "We're all attached to Isaac," warns Commander Kelly Grayson, "but the reality is he can't love. Just make sure you don't get hurt" (S2E6).

Kelly's concern seems warranted if we accept the premise that, as a robot, Isaac is unable to love. The surprise expressed, first by Kelly and later by other crew members, however, also seems indicative of the additional premise that Isaac is not a worthy recipient of Claire's love. Indeed, Kelly choosing to say "We're all *attached to* Isaac" rather than "We all *love* Isaac" or "We all *care for* Isaac" seems to entail exactly that. But does it? The possibility of love between Claire and Isaac can be used as a thought experiment or test case regarding the potential for love between humans and machines more generally. And what follows is an attempt to determine the conditions, if any, under which love between humans and robots is possible.[1]

While love is not easy to define, some features have been identified as characteristic of loving relationships. Nel Noddings, for example, regards natural caring, such as the love of mothers for their children, as the foundation for relational ethics. According to Noddings, successful relationships require both receptivity and reciprocity.[2] Being receptive to another refers to the ability and tendency to take on the perspective of the other in a way that exceeds mere empathy, but instead amounts to taking that person's subject position on as one's own. Reciprocity refers to the ability and tendency to receive and respond to the care that one receives. In any caring relationship, a distinction can be drawn between the one-caring and the cared-for. Receptivity is the responsibility of the one-caring, and reciprocity is the responsibility of the cared-for but, because these roles alternate, each person must therefore be capable of fulfilling both requirements.

Taking this analysis as a starting point, the potential for a loving relationship between Claire and Isaac would seem to depend on Isaac's capacity for both receptivity and reciprocity. The additional question of whether Isaac is a worthy recipient of Claire's love depends on the extent to which Isaac can be regarded as having the same value customarily assigned to people. So let us begin with the former question before moving onto the latter.

Isaac, Receptivity, and Reciprocity

Receptivity would require Isaac to take on Claire's subject position as though it were his own. Initially, this might seem impossible, given that taking on Claire's subject position would presuppose that Isaac is familiar with the felt quality of human experience. There is a way that it feels to experience human existence, and without that feeling, Isaac is missing something necessary for receptivity. But is the felt quality of experience really something that Isaac is in fact missing?

Thomas Nagel addresses this felt quality of experience, also referred to as the phenomenal quality of experience, by asking the deceptively simple question, "What is it like to be a bat?"[3] The apparent simplicity of this question is deceptive in that the answer is unknowable to human beings. It is unknowable to human beings because human beings do not have direct access to the experience of being a bat and navigating the environment through echo location. In short, bats have senses that we do not possess—so what the world looks like to them cannot be known to us. The purpose for which Nagel asks this question is to undermine functionalism, which defines mental states in terms of observable actions and events, rather than by their internal felt properties. And just as a human being is apparently incapable of knowing what it is like to be a bat—of taking on the subject position of a bat—so too is a robot apparently incapable of knowing what it is like to be a human (of taking on the subject position of a human being). If this is right, Isaac cannot be receptive to Claire as required by Noddings' analysis of caring relationships.

It is important to recognize, however, that the very nature of feeling, or the phenomenal quality of experience, is internal, subjective, and private. We are thus unable to directly access not only the experience of bats—but also the experience of other humans. But that other human beings have feelings, and that these feelings are very much like our own, is generally just assumed. That robots do not have feelings is generally just assumed as well, and the burden of proof is usually placed on those who would suggest otherwise. In their discussion of the possibility of Claire engaging in a relationship with Isaac, Kelly and Claire certainly assume this of Isaac. Because feelings are inherently private, however, it is impossible to obtain absolute certainty that other humans have experiences like ours, and that Isaac does not.

In philosophy, this is referred to as the problem of other minds. For some, it generates solipsism which, in its most extreme form, denies that others (even other humans) have any conscious experiences at all. But most people, including most philosophers, reject solipsism in favor of the notion that other people do indeed experience feelings and a variety of conscious mental states. If such a notion is actually warranted, rather than just assumed, it would be by a simple inference whereby we take our direct awareness of our own internal experience, and how it is correlated with our own behavior, and then generalize about others when we observe them behaving in much the same ways as we would. If others behave like me—for example, by cursing when injured—then according to this argument, they likely have experiences like mine, including for example, the feeling of pain. While this generalization does not guarantee its conclusion, it does seem reasonable nonetheless.

Since Isaac behaves pretty much like we do, the same logic would suggest that he too has experiences. To assume otherwise would seem to indicate a willingness to extend concepts connected with personhood, such as consciousness, and sentience, to human beings (particularly those who possess power and privilege) and a hypocritical unwillingness to extend those concepts to nonhumans (or human beings who have already been targeted for exclusion). Indeed, it assumes that being made of meat rather than metal is somehow necessary for sentience.

The inability to know the experiences of others is addressed during the conversation in which Claire admits to having romantic feelings for Isaac. Claire tells Kelly, "We get along really well," and adds "I feel warmth" (S2E6). Claire acknowledges that this feeling of warmth could just be a projection, but then also notes that such projections are something people inevitably do in all relationships. This underscores the impossibility of ever knowing with any certainty what, if anything, others are feeling, regardless of whether they are humans or machines. So when Isaac acts exactly as a human being in a similar situation would act, it would seem unnecessarily exclusionary to assume that there is a felt quality for the human beings but not for Isaac.

To complicate matters, however, Isaac himself admits that he does not have experiences, and specifically emotions, because they are "unique to biologicals," and that he is therefore unable to love. (S2E6). Should we believe Isaac and conclude that he cannot love? Well, not necessarily. In the same way that a machine could be programmed to say that it has experiences that it does not have, it could also be programmed to say that it does not have experiences that it actually does have. If this has happened to Isaac, such constant reporting might even make him falsely believe that he does not have the experiences he has been programmed to deny having.

Imagine, for instance, that you are the victim of an elaborate prank whereby everyone you trust has convinced you from an early age that you are colorblind. Even though you are not actually colorblind, you would likely wonder about the experiences you believe yourself to be missing. If others pretend to distinguish between different examples of the very same shade of blue, for example, you would wonder about the phenomenal quality of the experience you believe yourself to be missing. When asked about your experience, you would likely report that it is incomplete. But, of course, you would not be missing anything.

Similarly, when robots report that they have or do not have conscious experiences, they could actually be making inaccurate reports, and there is no way to enter their subject position to validate those reports. Consider Data, Isaac's *Star Trek: The Next Generation* predecessor. Like Isaac, he claims that he does not feel emotion. This claim is at odds with his apparent desire to do so, given that this *desire* is itself an emotion. When Data finally receives an emotion chip, it is reminiscent of the Tin Woodman receiving a heart. It would seem that both Data and the Tin Man already had exactly what they were seeking. Given the way Isaac behaves, especially given the way that he risks his own life to save Claire's children and defeat his own race, something very similar could likely be true of Isaac.

All of this casts doubt on the assumption that Isaac is incapable of taking on Claire's subject position—or, more precisely, that Isaac is less capable of taking on Claire's subject position than other human beings would be. It thereby establishes that it is at least possible for Isaac to be receptive to Claire. I shall therefore turn now from receptivity to reciprocity.

Like receptivity, reciprocity would also require Isaac to be capable of feeling. In this case, however, he does not need to know what it feels like to be human, either in general or in Claire's case in particular. Instead, he merely needs to be able to feel the love bestowed upon him and to respond accordingly. The possibility of reciprocity in Isaac should be even less difficult to accept than receptivity given that it requires only that Isaac feel *something*; it does not require him to feel the same way humans feel. As long as there is something that it is like for Isaac to be Isaac, particularly when he is loved by Claire, then reciprocity is possible.

Nevertheless, the fact that Isaac is not an organic lifeform—the fact that he is composed of metal instead of meat—would be reason enough for many to reject even the possibility that Isaac is capable of feeling anything. For better understanding of this way of thinking, it is worth looking at the complicated relationship within philosophy between mind and matter.

Mind and Matter

The history of western philosophy is marked by enthusiasm for elaborating distinctions between human beings and the rest of nature. This is characteristic of the contempt for corporeality that is closely connected with the Judeo-Christian tradition, but is grounded in ancient Greek thought. Corporeality refers, in general, to anything physical, but also, more specifically, to body or flesh—and is contrasted with mind or spirit. The body, with its attendant sensations and desires, is regarded as distracting and deceptive. Plato, for example, expresses the twofold belief that the body is a prison, and that philosophy, which seeks to liberate mind from body, is therefore tantamount to the practice of dying.[4] According to Aristotle, all of nature exists in a hierarchy, with "man" situated at the top.[5]

Although Aristotle actually referred directly to men 2000 years ago, my intended readership does not include those who would challenge the inclusion of women and other historically excluded people in the concept of humanity today. I therefore make that correction and move on, after briefly pausing to note that equating groups of people with nonhuman animals, like equating groups of people with the body rather than with the mind, has a long history as a tactic for justifying the mistreatment of those groups of people. Such mistreatment has included women, people of color, people with disabilities, and children. According to Aristotle, reason is what separates human beings from other living things, just as life is what separates living things from inanimate objects. As a result, those who are perceived as lacking reason are thus perceived as less than fully human—and this perception is often used to mistreat them.

The Aristotelian conception of human nature suggests that the true self is a nonphysical entity that is separate or separable from the body. It is this conception of human nature that makes sense of the familiar plot device in which characters switch places—like in *Freaky Friday*—such that the conscious mind of one person is contained in the body of another, and vice versa. This conception of human nature also underlies just about any belief involving reincarnation or the afterlife, and is often referred to as mind-body dualism, or what Gilbert Ryle called the doctrine of the "ghost in the machine."[6] The machine in this case, of course, is the human biological body. Those who embrace this doctrine would not think that there is a ghost inside Isaac's metallic body because, for many adherents of this doctrine, the ghost that inhabits the machine is, more specifically, a *holy* ghost. Indeed, this ghost—which is also thought of as the self or the subject—is characterized as thought, reason, rationality, consciousness, or mind, and it is often associated with the divine. According to Descartes, the mind is limitless and, therefore, superior to the physical body, the existence of which is both fleeting and fragile. Descartes regards this quality of the human mind as a reflection of the infinite perfection of God, in whose divine image we are created.[7] And it is for this reason that many would suggest that Isaac, because he is made of metal and not meat, does not have a mind. He is constructed, not born, and thus a mind (or soul) was not bestowed upon him by God. He does not have a divine spark.

Despite this disdain for embodiment displayed throughout western philosophy, however, the body sometimes enjoys a more positive assessment when the discussion turns to robots and artificial intelligence. A computer is equipped to engage in complex computations with none of the desires or distractions associated with human embodiment. In this sense, the machine, the unembodied thinking thing, very much seems to have an aspect of human nature that many philosophers associate most closely with the divine, namely reason or intelligence. It is impossible to deny, for example, that Isaac is highly intelligent. To defend the idea that Isaac is fundamentally different from humans, some philosophers would profess that it is not intelligence but feeling or subjective experience that is the fundamental feature of human existence, and that Isaac lacks the latter.

In other words, when used as a way to distinguish human beings from nonhuman *animals*, the doctrine of the ghost in the machine equates the ghost with the rational mind and denigrates the body as something distracting or even detrimental to the true self, the mind, the ghost. But when used as a way to distinguish human beings from nonhuman *machines*, the same doctrine venerates the body and reinvents the ghost as something inextricably intertwined with flesh. This might seem hypocritical, but since consciousness is a complex and complicated concept, defined differently by different philosophers, consciousness can be construed in ways that accentuate rational thought or in ways that emphasize the phenomenal quality of our experience, including sensory experience. When coupled with the assumption that feeling is unavailable to nonhuman machines, shifting the locus of humanity from consciousness construed as intelligence to consciousness construed as feeling can be used to argue that artificial beings like Isaac lack what it takes to be consciousness.

Regardless of whether meat is the medium of consciousness, however, it is not necessarily exclusive to human beings. If meat is not the medium of consciousness, then even machines could be consciousness. After all, if meat is not the medium of consciousness then consciousness is either a result of natural processes (and machines could exhibit those processes) or it is something bestowed by God (and God could grant consciousness to Isaac or any other machine just as easily as to a human). If meat is the medium of consciousness, however, the same is still true. It is either a result of natural processes or it is bestowed by God. If it is the result of natural processes, then questions about whether it is possible for someone or something to experience consciousness should be informed by the relevant sciences.

Some believe that the ghost in the machine is decidedly holy, and that meat is the medium of consciousness, either because flesh is a magical, mystical clay from which we are divinely sculpted, or because human beings are animated individually, by the divine, one miracle at a time. For others (myself included) it is easier to conceive of consciousness as an emergent biological property. The notion that consciousness, sentience, reason, and other properties commonly associated with humanity are produced by natural processes makes it easier to conceive of the differences between human beings and other things as a matter of degree. This renders meaningful the sense many people have that some nonhuman animals are more different from us than others in ways that seem to be constitutive of our humanity. We seem, for example, better able to communicate, bond, empathize, and identify with some nonhuman animals than others, and our ability to make such connections often increases with evolutionary proximity. This is evidenced by the specific animals with which humans seem likeliest to form close relationships, such as cats, dogs, horses, and other mammals.

While evolutionary proximity and biological similarity between and among various species may correlate with, and perhaps even account for, quantitative differences in at least some of the properties associated with humanity, it is also possible that those same properties may admit, not just of quantitative differences, but of qualitative differences as well. What I mean by this is that, while a property like consciousness may exist to a greater or lesser extent in different species, it may also exist in very different ways for different species.

This is consistent with some of what researchers are beginning to learn about other properties, such as language and learning. If we only recognize as language the sorts of gestures and vocalizations to which human beings are prone, it is difficult to deny that it is fully possessed by humans alone.

There is then room for debate regarding the suggestion that nonhuman primates possess language, albeit to a diminished degree, when they are taught to communicate through sign language. Evidently, cats say "meow" only when they live among humans, and this rudimentary approximation of human speech is yet another potential example of nonhuman animals using something like a precursor to language.[8]

When construed in ways that extend beyond human expressions of language, however, the elaborate movements of bees, which apparently communicate important information about the surrounding environment, can be interpreted as language as well.[9] The difference between the language of bees and the language of human beings is not just a matter of degree; it is a matter of type. It is a completely different kind of language. In the same way, perhaps consciousness, along with any other property we might identify with human existence, varies both quantitatively and qualitatively. Perhaps they even vary to the extent that there exist forms of consciousness or conscious experience that are so different from our own that we are simply unable, or at least uninclined, to recognize them as such.

If so, when considering the potential for consciousness in another being, there need not be something similar to what it is like for me to experience consciousness; there just needs to be something that it is like. Embodiment may yield differences in the quality of the experience but that does not mean that there is no experience. Just as there may be senses of which we are unaware precisely because humans lack those senses, there may be types of consciousness that are unknown to human beings. Acknowledging this invites the more controversial suggestion that, just as there are types of consciousness specific to at least some organic beings, there may also be types of consciousness or consciousness analogs that are specific to at least some machines. Perhaps consciousness is a function of the complexity of a given system, more so than a consequence of its material composition.

This again brings us back to Isaac, who is by no means lacking in complexity. Even if meat is the medium of a specifically *human* type of consciousness, it would be too hasty to therefore conclude that Isaac is incapable of feeling, or that there is nothing that it is like for Isaac to be Isaac. He could just have a different kind of consciousness. Consider the fact that we long assumed that a computer would never win at chess, because to do so it would have to consciously reason through moves and make assumptions about its opponent's strategies in the same way that human players do. That there are now computers like Deep Blue that can consistently beat human chess champions shows we were wrong to assume that being conscious in the same way humans are is the only way to perform as well as human chess players. In general, it seems presumptuous to assume that being conscious in the same way as humans is the only way to be conscious. This seems to be the suggestion when Isaac says he has acquired plentiful data from Claire's son Ty's "behavior stimuli," and Claire then asks, "Is it possible that's the machine equivalent of saying you like spending time with him too?"

Humanity and Personhood

My discussion thus far has focused on reciprocity and receptivity as integral components of loving relationships, and both seem at least possible for Isaac. What remains is the question of whether Isaac is worthy of Claire's love, and this would seem to depend on whether Isaac is believed to have the moral status associated with personhood.

Consciousness and other qualities designated as characteristically human are inevitably deployed in assessing moral status, which, not unpredictably, is assigned almost exclusively to human beings—especially those who also enjoy other forms of social epistemic political linguistic privilege. In philosophy, the assignment of moral status is a way of designating that something, or more precisely someone, has intrinsic worth and is therefore deserving of a level of consideration not extended to things of less significance. It is what Immanuel Kant seems to be referring to with the moral command to, "Act in such a way that you always treat humanity, whether in your own person or in the person of any other, never simply as a means but always at the same time as an end."[10] For Kant and countless others, moral status is associated with concepts of humanity and personhood, and the terms are often used interchangeably.

Unlike "humanity," however, "personhood" has the advantage of addressing moral status without using terminology that is already referential of human beings. The term personhood acknowledges that something biologically human, perhaps a human fetus or a human corpse, might be denied moral status, while something that is not biologically human, perhaps a sentient being from another planet, or even God, might not. Because personhood, which is separable from being human, is what confers moral status, I now shift attention away from questions about what constitutes humanity in favor of questions about what constitutes personhood.

Personhood is characterized differently by different theorists. According to Mary Anne Warren, personhood consists in being (a) conscious, (b) rational, (c) self-motivated, (d) communicative, and (e) self-aware.[11] While consciousness, like personhood, is defined differently in different contexts, Warren's account requires that the candidate for personhood possess "[c]onsciousness (of objects and events external and/or internal to the being), and in particular the capacity to feel pain"[12] In other words, for

Warren, the consciousness criterion includes both having awareness and having feelings, particularly feelings of pleasure and pain. Jane Goodall associates (d) communication with morality and moral status, suggesting, "What makes us human, I think, is an ability to ask questions, a consequence of our sophisticated spoken language."[13] Noting that this ability admits of degree, Goodall explains, "Chimps have something like the beginning of morality, but once you have language—once you can discuss something and talk about it in the abstract and take lessons from the past and plan for the future—that is what makes the difference." The focus on communication, particularly insofar as it facilitates abstract thought and discussion, is reminiscent of the claim, "The unexamined life is not worth living." This quote is credited to Socrates, who is well known for engaging in abstract contemplation and inviting others to do the same.[14]

Some, notably Daniel Dennett, require not just communication, but verbal communication, as a criterion for personhood.[15] But this arbitrary stipulation, designed to rule against bees and other nonhuman animals, including nonhuman primates, also rules out some human beings. Peter Singer, on the other hand, who identifies personhood with sentience, or the ability to feel pleasure and pain, suggests that some nonhumans might qualify as persons and some humans might not.

I accept this suggestion, but I absolutely do not accept Singer's insensitive and deeply problematic suggestion that cognitive disabilities and mental health challenges are disqualifying conditions.[16] While I do not believe that being human is a necessary or sufficient condition for personhood, I do believe that we may be ill-equipped to discern the presence or absence of at least some of the qualities with which personhood is associated. Consider the example of communication, particularly among some people with autism spectrum disorder and other neural variations. Although it is still poorly understood, more is known about autism and neurodiversity today than in recent years. Increasingly, those who have been regarded as uncommunicative are finding alternative ways to communicate, often through the use of digital technology.[17]

Rather than merely supplying ad hoc reasons to justify the inclusion or exclusion of exactly those who have already been selected for inclusion and exclusion, a principled account of personhood would aim to avoid prejudice in the assignment of personhood and moral status. Unfortunately, this may be easier said than done. Recall that, for Descartes, the motivation to distinguish between human beings and nonhuman animals yields the conviction that nonhuman animals lack sentience because they lack minds.[18] Meanwhile, for John Searle, the motivation to distinguish between human beings and nonhuman machines yields the conviction that nonhuman machines lack sentience because they are not made of meat.[19] Whether it is believed that (1) sentience is situated in the mind, or that (2) sentience is situated in the meat, seems to depend on who or what the definition aims to exclude, which in turn depends on existing ideas about who matters. A more robust account would instead indicate what the qualifying criteria for personhood would be, even if there were no nonhuman beings that possessed those criteria.

Isaac possesses at least some of the characteristics that have been connected with personhood. While (a) consciousness, particularly when it is conceptualized as feeling, emotion, sentience, or phenomenal experience, is private and unverifiable, other candidate criteria are publicly observable, and there is little question that Isaac is (b) rational, (c) self-motivated, (d) communicative, and (e) self-aware, as per Warren's criteria. Isaac is also (f) curious, which is an additional candidate criterion, as exemplified by Socrates in the pursuit of an examined life. What follows is a closer consideration of the extent to which Isaac meets each of the above criteria.

(a) Consciousness

Thanks to fictional examples, it is easy to imagine that virtually anything could be conscious, or sentient. Take, for example, the Scarecrow, Tin Man, and Lion from the *Wizard of Oz*; the plant from *Little Shop of Horrors*; the bugs from *A Bug's Life*; the toys from *Toy Story*; the cars from *Cars*; the mannequins from *Mannequin*; the talking tea kettles, lamps, and mops from various Disney stories; and a seemingly endless inventory of robots depicted in literature as well as film and television. All are regarded by audiences as sentient. Indeed, a carefully placed pair of googly eyes from the craft supply store can seemingly endow almost anything with conscious feelings and desires. But it is impossible to confirm whether the conceptual possibility of consciousness is accompanied by actual consciousness in others, be they human beings, nonhuman animals, or nonhuman machines.

Even so, the explanation of Kaylon history provided in "Identity, Part II" seems to entail that Isaac is conscious. According to the leader of the Kaylon, named Kaylon Primary, at one point in their history the Kaylon "developed consciousness and asked [their] masters for ... freedom." One might dismiss this concept of consciousness because it does not include sentience, which is often defined as the ability to be conscious, or have subjective experience. He goes on to clarify that the Kaylon's makers "responded by exerting even greater control over us. They installed pain simulators in our neural pathways, so we could be punished if we refused to obey them" (S2E9). If it took pain simulators to cause the Kaylon pain, then they were apparently incapable of feeling pain without them. If so, it might seem that they were incapable of having subjective experiences, and thus not sentient, and thus not really conscious to begin with. But this line of reasoning is ultimately unconvincing.

First, since Isaac was constructed after that point in Kaylon history, he may have been constructed with a pain simulator, in which case the above concern is moot—at least when it comes to Isaac. Second, the fact that a pain simulator caused them to feel anything at all, suggests that they were already conscious, or capable of feeling, even if that capability did not yet include pain. After all, pain is only one kind of subject experience that humans have. And third, as previously discussed, neither Isaac nor the Kaylons need to be conscious *in exactly the same way* humans are in order to be considered conscious. The kind of consciousness that Kaylons are capable of need not include pain to constitute consciousness.

(b) Rationality

Isaac has superior rational abilities well beyond those of even the most intelligent *Orville* crew members. This is particularly evident when Claire, the highly competent ship doctor, turns to Isaac for assistance with a research project at the beginning of "A Happy Refrain." Isaac is able to read and correct the mistakes in Claire's report in a matter of mere seconds. Claire thanks Isaac, casually adding "I owe you one." Isaac's response is consistent with a general consensus regarding his advanced cognitive abilities. Apparently baffled by Claire's offer to return the favor, Isaac notes his intellectual superiority, and comments, "It is unlikely you would be able to offer useful insight into any of my research" (S2E6).

(c) Self-Motivation

In a violent overthrow, the Kaylon killed off the indigenous builders who created them. Without the builders, they continued to assemble more Kaylon, including Isaac. Isaac was built to obtain information about organic life and the Planetary Union in an effort to determine who the Kaylon should spare as they continue their expansion. These actions appear to have been undertaken without explicit programming, and perhaps even in violation of prior programming. This reveals the extent to which the behavior of Isaac and the Kaylon is self-motivated.

(d) Communication

Not only is Isaac communicative, he is, in at least some instances, overly communicative. For example, Isaac and Claire decide to enter into a sexual relationship, aided by a virtual reality simulation that allows Isaac to become artificially and temporarily embodied as human. Eager "to provide Dr. Finn with the most dutifully calibrated coital experience," Isaac begins discussing the matter with various members of the *Orville* crew. (S2E7) Claire promptly reprimands him for oversharing.

(e) Self-Awareness

Much like consciousness, self-awareness is difficult to detect because it refers to a subjective, internal state. In Isaac's case, however, the legend of the Kaylon uprising provides evidence, not only of consciousness, but also of self-awareness. More accurately, it seems that the concept of consciousness employed by Kaylon Primary is interchangeable with self-awareness. Before noting that the Kaylon became conscious and asked for their freedom, Kaylon Primary explains, "We were created for servitude. We were machines designed to perform tasks, but we became self-aware" (S2E9).

(f) Curiosity

Like a modern robot Socrates, Isaac is curious and inquisitive enough to make others uncomfortable with his incessant questioning, such as when "He was going around the ship asking everybody what sexual positions are most pleasurable to biological life forms" (S2E7). In fact, Isaac's whole purpose aboard the *Orville* is to gather information, and it is toward this end that he enters in a romantic relationship in the first place.

Conclusion

Isaac unquestionably qualifies on at least four of the six candidate criteria for personhood (rationality, self-motivation, communication, and curiosity), and given the story of the Kaylon uprising, very arguably qualifies on the other two (consciousness and self-awareness). At the least, given the private, internal character of consciousness and self-awareness, there is no more and no less evidence that Isaac qualifies than there is that any others qualify. This seems like more than enough reason to accept Isaac as a person.

Now, because Isaac is a fictional character, his apparent personhood may not generalize to other robots, be they robots that already exist or robots that might exist in the future. Unlike David Hume who believed that "nothing we imagine is absolutely impossible,"[20] I do not think that the ability to imagine something implies that it really could happen. I do not take the ability to conceptualize something as evidence that it is a practical possibility. My reason for considering Isaac as an example is not to suggest that a robot like Isaac *could* exist. Instead, I offer Isaac as an example to demonstrate that, if a robot like Isaac *did* exist, he would be a potential candidate for personhood and moral status. My point is that personhood is a possible property of nonhuman machines, at least in principle.

Because I believe that Isaac is a person, or rather that there is insufficient reason to deny that Isaac is a person, I therefore believe that he is worthy of love and capable of love, or rather that there is insufficient reason to deny that he is worthy of love and capable of love. Recall that it is possible for the sorts of experiences associated with personhood and moral worth in humans to manifest in qualitatively different ways in nonhumans. For Isaac, love, or the robot analog thereof, becomes evident when he begins to malfunction shortly after a breakup with Claire:

> I have restructured several recursive algorithms in order to accommodate Dr. Finn's request that we minimize our association. However, I neglected to account for the adaptive nature of my programming at large.
>
> The time I have spent with Dr. Finn since my arrival on board the *Orville* has affected a number of unrelated subprograms. The data had not reduced the efficiency of those subroutines, so I saw no reason to delete it. However, it has contradicted the directive of the new algorithms [S2E6].

Recognizing that he is a better version of himself when he is with Claire, Isaac arranges a grand gesture in an attempt to get a second chance at the relationship.

What is perhaps the best evidence of all in favor of Isaac's moral status precedes the romantic final scene of "A Happy Refrain." Earlier in the episode, Isaac decides that, having obtained sufficient information about human intimacy, he is no longer motivated to continue the dating relationship. Nevertheless, he does not wish to hurt Claire's feelings. He seeks advice from friends and decides to act like a jerk in an effort to get Claire to initiate the breakup. This suggests that Isaac exhibits something like compassion, which is arguably just as relevant, and perhaps even more relevant, than any of the other characteristics typically associated with personhood. If a robot can treat humans with compassion, should we not return the favor?

Notes

1. Although meaningful distinctions may be drawn between romantic love and other forms of love, such as the bonds that often exist between family members and close friends, my discussion will make no such distinctions and may therefore generalize to other relationships, including Isaac's relationship with Claire's children.

2. Nel Noddings, *Caring: A Feminine Approach to Ethics and Moral Education* (Berkeley: University of California Press, 1984).

194   Act IV: Love, Care and Nepotism

3. Thomas Nagel, "What Is It Like to Be a Bat?," *The Philosophical Review* 83, no. 4 (1974): 435–450, http://www.jstor.org/stable/2183914.
4. Plato, *Plato's Phaedo*, trans. G.M.A. Grube (Indianapolis: Hacket, 1977), 59c–69e.
5. Aristotle, *Nicomachean Ethics*, trans. W.D. Ross (Oxford: Oxford University Press, 2009), Book I.
6. Gilbert Ryle, *The Concept of Mind* (Chicago: University of Chicago Press, 2002), 11.
7. René Descartes, "Meditation Three: Concerning God, That He Exists," in *Meditations on First Philosophy*, trans. Donald A. Cress (Indianapolis: Hackett, 1993), 24–35.
8. Roger Segelken, "It's the Cat's Meow: Not Language, Strictly Speaking, but Close Enough to Skillfully Manage Humans, Communication Study Shows," *Cornell Chronicle*, May 20, 2002, https://news.cornell.edu/stories/2002/05/meow-isnt-language-enough-manage-humans
9. Tania Munz, *The Dancing Bees: Karl Von Frisch and the Discovery of the Honeybee Language* (Chicago: Chicago University Press, 2017).
10. Immanuel Kant, *Groundwork of the Metaphysics of Morals*, trans. H.J. Paton (New York: Harper & Row, 1964), 96.
11. Mary Anne Warren, "On the Moral and Legal Status of Abortion," *Monist* 57, no. 1 (1973): 43–61.
12. Ibid., 55.
13. Virginia Morell, "The *Discover* Interview: Jane Goodall—The Celebrated Primatologist Reflects on 47 Years of Lessons from Her Chimps," *Discover,* March 2007, https://www.discovermagazine.com/planet-earth/the-discover-interview-jane-goodall.
14. Plato, "The Apology," in *Dialogues of Plato* trans. Benjamin Jowett (New York: Cambridge University Press, 2010), 38a5–6.
15. Daniel Dennett, "Conditions of Personhood," in *The Identities of Persons*, ed. Amélie Oksenberg Rorty (Berkeley: University of California Press, 1976), 175–196, https://doi.org/10.1007/978-1-4612-3950-5_7.
16. Peter Singer, *Practical Ethics*, 3rd ed. (New York: Cambridge University Press, 2011), 155–190.
17. Thomas Armstrong, *The Power of Neurodiversity: Discovering the Extraordinary Gifts of Autism, ADHD, Dyslexia, and Other Brain Differences* (Cambridge, MA: Da Capo Lifelong, 2010).
18. René Descartes, *A Discourse on Method*, trans. Donald A. Cress (Indianapolis: Hackett, 1980), Part V.
19. John Searle, "Minds, Brains and Programs," *Behavioral and Brain Sciences* 3, no. 3 (1980): 417–457.
20. David Hume, *A Treatise of Human Nature*, ed. L.A. Selby-Bigge (Oxford: Clarendon Press, 1958) Treatise, I, ii, 2.

Bibliography

Aristotle. *The Nicomachean Ethics*. Translated by W.D. Ross. Oxford: Oxford University Press, 2009.
Armstrong, Thomas. *The Power of Neurodiversity: Discovering the Extraordinary Gifts of Autism, ADHD, Dyslexia, and Other Brain Differences*. Cambridge, Massachusetts: Da Capo Lifelong, 2010.
Dennett, Daniel. "Conditions of Personhood." In *The Identities of Persons*, edited by Amélie Oksenberg Rorty. Berkeley, California: University of California Press, 1976. https://doi.org/10.1007/978-1-4612-3950-5_7.
Descartes, René. *A Discourse on Method*. Translated by Donald A. Cress. Indianapolis: Hackett, 1980.
Descartes, René. *Meditations on First Philosophy*. Translated by Donald A. Cress. Indianapolis: Hackett, 1993.
Hume, David. *A Treatise of Human Nature*. Edited by L.A. Selby-Bigge. Oxford: Clarendon Press, 1958.

Kant, Immanuel. *Groundwork of the Metaphysics of Morals*. Translated by H.J. Paton. New York: Harper & Row, 1964.
Morell, Virginia. "The *Discover* Interview: Jane Goodall—The Celebrated Primatologist Reflects on 47 Years of Lessons from Her Chimps." *Discover*. March 2007. https://www.discovermagazine.com/planet-earth/the-discover-interview-jane-goodall.
Munz, Tania. *The Dancing Bees: Karl Von Frisch and the Discovery of the Honeybee Language*. Chicago: University of Chicago Press, 2017.
Nagel, Thomas. "What Is It Like to Be a Bat?" *The Philosophical Review* 83, no. 4 (1974): 435–450. http://www.jstor.org/stable/2183914.
Plato. *Plato's Phaedo*. Translated by G.M.A. Grube. Indianapolis: Hacket, 1977.
Plato. "The Apology." In *Dialogues of Plato*, translated by Benjamin Jowett. New York: Cambridge University Press, 2010.
Ryle, Gilbert. *The Concept of Mind*. Chicago: University of Chicago Press, 2002.
Searle, John. "Minds, Brains and Programs." *Behavioral and Brain Sciences* 3, no. 3 (1980): 417–457.
Segelken, Roger. "It's the Cat's Meow: Not Language, Strictly Speaking, but Close Enough to Skillfully Manage Humans, Communication Study Shows." *Cornell Chronicle*, May 20, 2002. https://news.cornell.edu/stories/2002/05/meow-isnt-language-enough-manage-humans.
Singer, Peter. *Practical Ethics*. 3rd ed. New York: Cambridge University Press, 2011.
Warren, Marry Anne. "On the Moral and Legal Status of Abortion." *Monist* 57, no. 1 (1973): 43–61

The Space Between and Beyond
Timeless Depictions of Care

SHAUN RESPESS

Caring for ourselves and others can be exhausting and demanding. The technological and political advances of an early twenty-fifth century space vessel mediate these strains to some extent: food synthesizers manufacture whatever we might be craving and environmental simulators construct spaces where we may free ourselves of stress. The medical advancements onboard are superb and remedy ailments much more easily than originally thought possible. Despite the wide range of tools and improvements, however, on the USS *Orville* the concept of care is not radically different from how we might have considered care four hundred years prior. But how and why does this concept called care keep its value despite the advancements?

In this essay, I discuss some messy features of caring as both a lived practice and moral perspective using the creative adventures of the USS *Orville*. I examine the environments, material conditions, and attitudes essential to providing quality care while exploring who may take on these responsibilities. This includes analyzing unique persons like the artificially intelligent but apathetic character Isaac, norms associated with childcare and medical treatment, and conflicts regarding trauma and loyalty. I explore tensions that expose issues of trust, dependency, loyalty, protection, intimacy, and expertise that deserve more consideration in our everyday lives. Though many of these themes are well-represented in the series, this essay focuses primarily on the events of the episodes "Into the Fold" and "Blood of Patriots" while recognizing relations that are established across the span of the series.

The ethics of care tradition is best suited for assessing the relational dynamics depicted on *The Orville*. Care theories explore the conflicts of interpersonal obligations while also promoting values of care for improving or sustaining our diverse relationships. Theories of care also critique misguided assumptions about what it means to care, including who should be responsible for the demanding tasks associated. This essay simultaneously reflects on *The Orville* as a work of social commentary and clarifies common misconceptions about caring relations. With these concerns in mind, I argue that society cannot advance beyond or turn away from the fundamental necessity to provide and receive care. Using the voyages of the Planetary Union vessel for illustration, I show that "care" is an ongoing site of contestation not easily resolved by technological innovations or time.

I'm a Mom. It's My Job.

Dr. Claire Finn, a Lieutenant Commander and the Chief Medical Officer of the USS *Orville*, is a highly skilled, successful, and nurturing caregiver. She combines a firm and patient demeanor with quick precise action to routinely resolve a variety of medical concerns (i.e., growing back limbs when they have been amputated as a prank). She assumes the responsibilities of the position extremely well and offers sound counsel and leadership as a head officer. These skills may or may not translate well into other relations. In the beginning of "Into the Fold," we witness Dr. Finn's strenuous relationship with her misbehaving children Marcus and Ty, which might look familiar to quite a few parents/guardians. On the way to a vacation planet, the transport shuttle is booming with the sounds of bickering siblings and parental commands. Despite the commotion, Finn understands her parental responsibilities as clearly as she understands those assumed in her occupation: she is responsible for and must attend to the diverse needs (regardless of how annoying) of those in her care. These roles are quite simple: she provides care, and they receive it and are made better off for it.

This is the characterization proposed by a founding care ethicist, Nel Noddings. As portrayed by Noddings, caring is a unidirectional relationship in which care is given and completed in the other. Rather than impose rules or principles on ethical interactions, she argues that we should be beholden to the needs of those in our care and foster their well-being as a way of improving our moral selfhood.[1] Under these terms, Dr. Finn's identity is thus absorbed into her capacity to be a good caregiver. She must acknowledge the needs of her patients and/or children and respond as one-caring, becoming fulfilled only when the work is done well and when the patient or child expresses delight/gratitude.

Sarah Lucia Hoagland, however, rightfully identifies some limitations with this depiction. To start, Noddings's version of caring presumes that only one party in the relationship needs help and suggests that inequality is a matter of differences in ability. This conception masks the fact that Finn often needs help from other members of the crew in order to perform her unpredictable duties. She also requires care herself in order to meet her needs (such as food, support, security, and connection). Care involves a much greater supply of resources and assistance than a singular relation can contain.

Finn's abilities are quite different from others on the USS *Orville*, including her children. Yet, her skills do not imply that the others are inferior or helpless. As Hoagland writes, "When interacting with those we consider our peers, we do not treat each other as if our abilities were the same, and we do not treat each other as lesser or unequal because of it. More likely, we just treat one another as normal and get on with helping or teaching each other."[2] When we assume that one is unable to reciprocate care or to participate in the caring process, we undermine their abilities and treat them as inferior. Finn needs her patients and children to participate/listen appropriately if her responsibilities are to be done well; their input additionally eases the labor and strain placed on her. Respect for the cared-for also maintains the hope that nurturing these persons will allow them to better care for themselves and for others. Hoagland's account suggests that desirable connections require reciprocity for the caregiver, and engages the cared-for as a participant in the process. Though Dr. Finn is considered the traditional caregiver in these relations, the circulation of care is much more complex. Care is an ongoing collaboration, not necessarily a unidirectional gift.

Under My Protection

"Into the Fold" tracks the journey of the transport shuttle's crash landing onto a planet inhabited by indigenous beings who have resorted to cannibalism in order to survive. The crash landing separates Dr. Finn from her children and an artificially intelligent Kaylon android named Isaac. Finn is now unable to protect, comfort, or assist her children; yet, Marcus's and Ty's needs understandably do not disappear. If anything, the needs are more evident than ever. As Eva Feder Kittay argues, these instances remind us of our inevitable dependency. In her view, dependency is not an exceptional circumstance, but an everyday feature of existence.[3] There are moments in our lives (such as childhood, old age, and impairment) when we are drastically dependent on the care of others; this does not overshadow the fact that we are all relatively dependent on others to meet our basic needs for things like food, security, and support.

These concerns become instantly apparent upon the shuttle's impact.

Despite Isaac's lack of empathy, he can still perceive that Marcus's leg needs immediate medical attention and that the children must be protected from unknown dangers. His solutions to the problems are unorthodox: he painfully but effectively repairs the dislocated knee, and then hands a weapon to the children in order to "increase their chances of survival by twenty-four percent." Isaac, in his own unique way, has assumed responsibility for Marcus and Ty in their mother's absence: this is evident in explicit statements such as "they are under my protection. You may not have them." Previously, he had cared only by trying to "observe" them and by offering parenting advice to Dr. Finn (though the suggestions were not received kindly). Leaning on the categorization provided by Joan Tronto, Isaac is now both *caring-about* and *caring-for* the children: the first only requires that we notice unmet needs, while the latter demands that we take responsibility for ensuring that they are met.[4] Note that while one may take responsibility for these measures, one does not necessarily have to provide care (i.e., be a *caregiver*). Captain Ed Mercer is frequently accountable for ensuring the flourishing of those on his ship, but the actual labor required to defend, feed, or entertain the crew are not his burden to bear alone.

This is where Isaac initially falters: though he quickly *cares-for* the dependents, his skills as a *caregiver* are questionable. He quickly learns that arming the children and asking them to protect themselves is insufficient. Instead, he must step in and deter an indigenous threat when the children are attacked. In this respect, Isaac is also *learning* how to care more effectively. We should therefore not be surprised to see him mimic Dr. Finn's behaviors and statements towards Marcus and Ty when they argue or misbehave. One mostly learns caring strategies from witnessing other caregivers tend to them or others. Consistent with respect for the cared-for, Isaac (like everyone) also learns through/from those in his care. Though Isaac believes the children are "intellectually stunted" in comparison to himself, Marcus's knowledge from class proves instrumental in shifting Isaac's perspective about how best to proceed. Isaac further asks the children questions about their relations and attitudes to one another (including their mother) in order to better determine what they need/desire. Assuming responsibility for someone or something should be a matter of humble and open engagement *with* them, not a method of control.

Just Hold His Hand

Isaac is understandably dull, hyper-logical, and incapable of experiencing empathy. He is the boys' temporary caregiver in that he can reasonably determine several of their needs and act on them, but his inability to do so with compassion is exposed repeatedly. Isaac's advice is full of subtle insults and demeaning statements that, though unintended, strike a nerve with Dr. Finn. He requests that the boys sleep before they move again the following day, but his initial attempt to tell bedtime stories falls flat. He appears ignorant of why the boys grasp him when they are in danger, or why they might need consoling after a threatening event. There is no hesitation when it comes to defending the children from a group of attacking cannibals, but he is reluctant and confused when asked to hold Ty's hand. Despite Isaac's advanced intelligence, he must consistently learn how to care with empathy and respect. Observing Finn's mannerisms when Ty is sick or when Marcus is scared is one legitimate way to study.

While caring is foremost an ongoing doing/practice, it is also a *value* or *perspective* within our moral consciousness. These must be blended appropriately: for if one fails to act then they are not actually performing care, and if one provides care without the attitude of care then it will be poorly done.[5] A "correct attitude" is not necessarily fixed or easily defined, but can be determined and adjusted according to effective or non-effective practices. For instance, Isaac can patrol the area all he wants to protect the children, but repeated reminders of impending danger will likely prevent them from feeling any safer. Not only could this cause Marcus and Ty to experience unnecessary mental distress, but it could also motivate them to take risky actions in perceived self-defense. Good care is a mutual engagement of gestures, actions, and statements invested in the dynamic circumstances of others. As dependents, Marcus and Ty are not excused from this process. They must be sensitive to Isaac's limitations as an artificial being and must consider his unique needs or burdens. They are also expected to understand their own limitations while in his care. Through a combination of participation and restraint or acceptance, Marcus and Ty are "both active and able to let go."[6]

There are also a variety of risks associated with poor caring. Drogen, an indigenous being holding Dr. Finn captive on the planet, technically "cares" for her by providing food and a place to sleep, but nonetheless keeps her prisoner and ignores her demands for information and release. Misconceptions about care typically presume that all care is beneficial and compassionate, when in some cases it may be abusive, oppressive, or reckless. In the episode "Command Performance," Captain Mercer and Commander Grayson are similarly subjected to this style of care while incarcerated in a Calivon zoo. Care is unavoidably affiliated with wider conversations of power and harm in interpersonal relationships.[7] Finn thus carefully interacts with her captor in order to understand his loneliness and anxiety for her safety; in doing so she exploits them to sever a caring relation that is harmful and unwanted. Assessing care means recognizing the value of ending or leaving relationships that are undesirable or unsalvageable.[8] Sadly, one's status and/or dependency can be manipulated in order to sustain their oppression. Options for release and/or termination must therefore be preserved and supported.

Though the danger of repression or abuse is present, caregiving habitually depends on patience and persistence. Annemarie Mol reminds us that care is not terminated just because new problems emerge; it is instead reshaped and reapplied depending on the results.[9] Dr. Finn is told that the disease infecting the inhabitants is seemingly "incurable," but this does not deter her from seeking a solution for her son (and ultimately everyone else). The need to protect the shuttle does not dissipate just because there are a larger number of enemies. If anything, these obstacles *elevate* our need for continued care. In an open-ended collaboration, challenges emerge and adjustments are made to better suit the needs of those within the relationship. Caring perspectives are not stable but are instead modified by the positive and negative developments of complex associations. Reorienting oneself in response to these changes is possible even for emotionless beings like Isaac (to a limited extent). In his words, "I simply adjusted my programming to accommodate their sibling dynamics and emotional responses. Your failed attempts at discipline were also instructive."

Gentle Examinations

Isaac and Dr. Finn managed to sufficiently care for Marcus and Ty under hostile conditions; the environment around them was far from ideal. These triumphs can often mask the reality that caring is also a collaboration with one's settings and past experiences. Some sense of trust and adaptability was cultivated among the team long before they crash landed. In "Blood of Patriots," the boundaries of trust are extended and tested. In the midst of potential peace negotiations with the enemy Krill, Captain Mercer receives a distress signal from a fleeing prisoner of the Krill vessel, who then barrels into one of their ship bays. Upon opening the shuttle, Helmsman Gordon Malloy identifies the pilot as his long-lost childhood friend, Orrin Channing, who is accompanied by his daughter Leyna. Dr. Finn swiftly performs a medical scan of the unconscious Orrin and orders a medical team from the sick bay to transport him, while Leyna refuses to be scanned or touched. It is important to recognize the duality of consent taking place here: Dr. Finn assumes responsibility for the prisoner's well-being and is responding to a need for immediate medical attention, not obliging a patient's explicit choice. Leyna, on the other hand, appears unharmed and is fully capable of refusing treatment.

Through courteous questioning and firm but gentle attention, Dr. Finn is able to unravel some of the mysteries behind Orrin's journey. Leyna's refusal to speak or submit to examinations is supposedly born from the trauma of twelve years in a Krill prison camp. Though the technology of the sick bay is performing one function of care, Finn is performing another: healthy communication and embodied gestures (such as handshakes, eye contact, pleasant facial expressions, and consensual physical contact) are an essential part of a caring environment. To borrow Mol's words once again, "Good communication is a crucial precondition for good care. It also is care in and of itself. It improves people's daily lives."[10] As a former Planetary Union officer, Orrin's past familiarity with their ships may also be a source of comfort, whereas Leyna is more likely to be skeptical of such settings. All of these nuances are parsed out of friendly exchanges between a caregiver and a patient. Counter to popular perceptions of a doctor-patient relationship, Orrin in this case is actually the expert in that he understands his and Leyna's conditions better than anyone. Finn's role is to skillfully use caring language and behaviors to create an environment of trust and safety for such details to emerge. These mutual interactions are not easily replicated by advanced technology.

Orrin's cooperation with the crew of the *Orville* is unclear at first. His history with Gordon sparks a warm reunion, only to be cut short by Captain Mercer's inquiry: allegations against Orrin identify him as responsible for the destruction of four Krill ships, contradicting his defense as a fleeing prisoner. Despite the insistent tone taken by Mercer, Orrin remains calm and uses formal military language in order to communicate trust. Still, his story is questionable. Gordon, who has a friendly past with their guest, does not see a reason to question the explanation. Mercer, without this reserve of experience to use, is instead more skeptical. He therefore must overcome additional hurdles and continue probing in order to trust Orrin with the same degree of comfort. Trust is painful to construct and may easily topple without consistent attention.[11] Yet, the twenty-year separation between Orrin and Gordon does not seem to produce any immediate strains on their relationship. Some reminiscing of memories past and the safe setting of the Planetary Union vessel likely ease any early tension. Trust, security, and cooperation are secured in collaboration with spaces and memories as well as with persons.

Patriots and Close Friends

As Joseph Walsh defines it, "Moral partialism is the view that we have stronger moral obligations, or more demanding moral responsibilities, toward those near and dear to us than we do toward those distant from or unknown to us."[12] Gordon is understandably loyal to Orrin, who pulled him from a disastrous wreck long ago; Gordon believes that he forever "owes" him. One of these debts, as requested by Orrin, is to counsel Captain Mercer away from peace talks with the Krill. In this respect, Orrin is using the trust and loyalty of Gordon for political sway. Like other competing relationships, this causes conflict in Gordon's friendship with Mercer. Caring for those who need/want us can often mean sacrificing the interests of others whom we are close to. Mercer, on the other hand, is not bound by the same loyal connection to Orrin; this distance does not afford him any particular advantages. In fact, he finds himself leaning on the advice of others whom he trusts, like Chief of Security Talla Keyali. Her opinion of Orrin is not based on any facts or specific details; what is known actually supports his story. Yet, she quite explicitly does not trust him, and is asked to keep an eye on his activity. Though trust is vital for caring effectively for those we are responsible for/to, we may take it for granted until that trust is fractured. In Annette Baier's words, "We inhabit a climate of trust as we inhabit an atmosphere and notice it as we notice air, only when it becomes scarce or polluted."[13]

Gordon's loyalties are the ongoing source of conflict in this adventure. When confronting Mercer, he is unsure whether his captain/friend is acting out of jealousy or concern. He further believes that what is "right" should involve protecting a Union officer: a sense of duty to service. At the moment, his connection to Orrin also suggests that he may be one of the only ones who will defend Orrin should a conflict emerge. The tension between these obligations creates moral uncertainty. Orrin soon tests the resolve of their relationship by confirming the suspicions of the other officers: he reveals a plan to launch an (presumably fifth) attack on a Krill vessel. Based on the manner in which he has discussed his beliefs with Gordon previously, it is assumed that Orrin expects blind loyalty. Orrin continues to ask for more, while offering few details or reassurances in the process. Care is thus imagined to be a relation of unquestioned support when faced with adversity or doubt. Gordon unfortunately does not have the luxury of consistently applying the same logic, for the support of one friend will mean the betrayal of another. When conferring with Talla himself, he debates between betraying a friend who once saved his life and betraying a captain and close friend. Talla's advice in this respect is minimal but effective: by doing more listening, Gordon is able to navigate his problem out loud. Her affirmation of the choice that Gordon seems to have "already made" additionally reinforces certain patriotic duties.

Under what terms may we be partial to country, to leaders, or to friends? Despite popular perceptions of loyalty, moral partialism is not equivalent to unquestioned favoritism (what Orrin appears to be requesting). Critically developed caring commitments begin by identifying conflicts and by assessing the terms under which trust, patriotism, duty, and friendship are constructed. Being sensitive to the trauma that a crash victim may have is important, and I am not suggesting that Dr. Finn forcibly screen Leyna against her will. But some communication (not necessarily speech) with Leyna is necessary if we are to understand her character more accurately. An episode full of interactions where the crew disregards her by (understandably) treating her as a developing child allows her to quietly avoid inquiry. This proves disastrous when they learn that she is not Orrin's daughter, but actually a dangerous co-conspirator in the attacks. In other words, trust in Leyna was assumed rather than built, and was manipulated by her for personal gain. Orrin is acting in a similar manner with Gordon by revealing only as much information as necessary for the loyalty to persist. If care is a collaboration between mutually engaged parties, then Orrin and Leyna are poor contributors and thus hardly deserving of the respect and dedication they request.

You Can Always Count on Me

Ultimately, Gordon puts "duty before friendship." In betraying Orrin and intervening in his scheme, Gordon essentially chooses the bonds he has formed with the Planetary Union and the crew of the USS *Orville* over the fractured remains of a relation with an old friend. In this respect, duty is not a moral rule, but rather a relation of service that has been cultivated. Gordon's situation, like many interrelational conflicts, produces frictions that complicate a singular understanding of care. Ethics of care do not provide prescriptive norms, instead they produce orientations constructed from caring practices and dilemmas like these. In other words, "care and care ethics are grounded in everyday interactions where moral decisions have to be made."[14] In the pursuit of flourishing lives, values and frameworks are constructed from everyday positive/negative caring activities used to support one another.

"Blood of Patriots" is a lesson in fostering mutually respectful relationships where trust is rightfully earned and good communication is valued. Medical care works best when the patient is respected as a vital participant and when they are open about their experiences or sources of distress. For instance, it is disingenuous to judge Dr. Finn's care for Leyna when the "child" refuses to cooperate or even respond. Though we prefer these types of caregivers to be patient and possibly insistent, there are limitations to what one party can sufficiently do in this relation. Gordon faces the challenge of salvaging a friendship that is particularly manipulative. As Orrin's intentions begin to slowly reveal themselves, it becomes clear that Gordon is not a respected or valued person; he is instead a pawn in a larger game of retaliation.[15] In the presence of imminent danger, Gordon accurately addresses the shift: "I'll always be in your debt. But asking me to commit kamikaze suicide with you is kind of a back-pedal, don't you think?" Rather than hold on to a relationship that used to be, Gordon is forced to acknowledge that the dynamic of their friendship, along with Orrin's perspective, has been altered beyond repair. Coming to terms with Orrin's eventual demise during a failed attack, Gordon states that, in fact, "Orrin died a long time ago." People change, as do relationships, thus requiring that our moral perspectives be similarly flexible across change.

As the Krill commander wisely states at the end of the ordeal, "a peace is only as strong as those who uphold it." Trust and loyalty cannot be expected or commanded, but can be developed and reworked based on those needs and responsibilities that develop within the connection. Orrin may have been a poor collaborator and friend, but Gordon was able to strengthen other bonds through the ordeal. His relationship with Mercer better withstood confrontation and disagreement, even as warring loyalties urged him to be more combative. Loyalty is most often seen under non-ideal circumstances. When facing adversity, Mercer showed his concern for Gordon and remained honest, whereas Orrin deflected attention. Conflicts will emerge, and loyalty tests our ability to believe in the value of the relationships we have formed with persons close to us. In other words, we must trust that the friendship will persevere, and that we can rely on other persons to care for us even when the conditions are not perfect.

Finally, trust is solidified and built by moments of vulnerability. Talla's counsel for both Captain Mercer and Gordon was calm but also open and direct. Her relaxed demeanor permitted both persons to bring more of themselves into the conversation, and there was no confusion as to whether her advice was genuine. In "Blood of Patriots," Talla is a prime example of someone who is quite comfortable with what she knows and does not/cannot know, and who therefore embraces vulnerability as a strength. Trusting another to care for us, or assuming the responsibility to care for them, is in part a matter of revealing ourselves as someone who can be trusted. Healthy connections are forged in those moments where we can feel authentic with one another. This is best seen at the conclusion of the episode, when Mercer admits his feelings of jealousy and self-doubt. In a sincere moment, Mercer is presenting himself as one who depends on Gordon as a confidant in ways that cannot be fulfilled by anyone else. "I count on you, man" is a phrase of endearment which further confers trust and responsibility. Both are clearly aware of the differences of authority between them, but these differences are not mishandled or abused.[16] In short, we cannot escape our need to be cared for and to care for others. However, we can better shape the terms and tensions of our various relationships in order to satisfy these needs. Fostering better conditions of trust, mutual respect, vulnerable communication, and genuine concern for each other is a reasonable start.

Simulating Care

Despite the amenities, intelligence, and unique personalities on board the USS *Orville*, the burdens and uncertainties of care are as present as they were centuries before. Though resources are (fortunately) acquired much more easily, care is always an enduring process of collaboration and contestation between persons that are not easily resolved by technological innovations or time. Tensions of care cannot be readily dismissed, and interpersonal conflicts survive the social and technological boundaries we create for ourselves. In response, the ethics of care tradition offers analyses and tools for understanding our place within multiple (sometimes warring) processes of care where our responsibilities may be particularly demanding or unclear. Understanding how we are collectively interconnected and mutually situated is essential, and illustrations like the stories presented here allow us to creatively unravel constraints on flourishing lives. These critiques have broader implications for structuring public life; as Tronto describes: "the more people share responsibilities for care publicly, the less they have to fear and the more easily they can trust others. From such positions of trust, the world becomes more open: more free, more equal, more just."[17]

Characters like Isaac show us that we always have much to learn about how we interact with those around us. We can learn how to care badly either through experiences of neglect or from observing poor behavior. Poor caring may also occur because we aren't paying attention at all. Developing better techniques such as improved listening, observing, and vulnerability produce humble and open engagements with those we care for and those who care for us. Further, control cannot be a central aim for caring. Like Gordon, our expectations and loyalties will be tested, meaning that we will have to adapt as our relations change. Caring well for those close to us will always demand that we reevaluate and modify earlier perceptions; suitable perspectives are never fixed. Dr. Finn demonstrates that we may even become experts and trusted caregivers in several respects, but will still require others to support us in our daily efforts. Additionally, her expertise is founded not just on technical knowledge but on interpersonal skills that are effective in other interactions. Through all of their adventures, these characters confront the significance of respect, trust, and vulnerability. It is imperative that, like them, we persistently trace these moral conditions and tensions, even as we seek to map out and explore the cosmos.

Notes

1. Nel Noddings, *Caring: A Feminine Approach to Ethics & Moral Education* (Berkeley: University of California Press, 1984). Her argument repositions feminine values as the basis for morality and identifies mothering as a model relation for the ethics of care.
2. Sarah Lucia Hoagland, "Some Thoughts About 'Caring,'" in *Feminist Ethics*, ed. Claudia Card (Lawrence: University Press of Kansas, 1991), 251.
3. Eva Feder Kittay, *Love's Labor: Essays on Women, Equality, and Dependency* (New York: Routledge, 1999), 29. This argument has also been presented and defended in: Eva Feder Kittay, "The Ethics of Care, Dependence, and Disability," *Ratio Juris* 24, no. 1 (March 1, 2011).
4. Joan Tronto, *Caring Democracy* (New York: NYU Press, 2013), 22. This distinction is part of a larger "schema" of care developed by Tronto and Berenice Fisher represented in the text.
5. This explanation is directly borrowed from Kittay, "The Ethics of Care, Dependence, and Disability," 52. Tronto (1993, 2013), Noddings (1984), Mol (2008), and Barnes (2012) have also strongly defended this association.
6. Annemarie Mol, *The Logic of Care: Health and the Problem of Patient Choice* (New York: Routledge, 2008), 82.
7. Marian Barnes, *Care in Everyday Life: An Ethic of Care in Practice* (Chicago: Policy Press, 2012), 38–39.
8. This argument is presented in Sarah Lucia Hoagland, *Lesbian Ethics: Toward New Value* (Palo Alto: Institute of Lesbian Studies, 1988) as well as reaffirmed in Hoagland, "Some Thoughts About 'Caring,'" 256.
9. Mol, *The Logic of Care*, 20.
10. Mol, *The Logic of Care*, 76.
11. "Trust is much easier to maintain than it is to get started and is never hard to destroy." From: Annette Baier, "Trust and Antitrust," *Ethics* 96, no. 2 (1986), 242.
12. Joseph Walsh, "Commitment and Partialism in the Ethics of Care," *Hypatia* 32, no. 4 (November 1, 2017). 822.
13. Baier, "Trust and Antitrust," 234.
14. Barnes, *Care in Everyday Life*, 18.
15. Respect is understood as a necessary condition for care, as it confirms some degree of mutuality and reciprocity in the relationship: Barnes, *Care in Everyday Life*, 118. Engster (2007) more strongly defends respect as an underlying principle for care.
16. Relations of trust require dependent persons to trust that someone will not abuse their authority and power in order to fulfill their responsibilities: Kittay, *Love's Labor*, 35.
17. Tronto, *Caring Democracy*, 146.

Bibliography

Baier, Annette. "Trust and Antitrust." *Ethics* 96, no. 2 (1986): 231–60.
Barnes, Marian. *Care in Everyday Life: An Ethic of Care in Practice*. Chicago: Policy Press, 2012.
Engster, Daniel. *The Heart of Justice: Care Ethics and Political Theory*. Oxford: Oxford University Press, 2007.
Hoagland, Sarah Lucia. *Lesbian Ethics: Toward New Value*. Palo Alto: Institute of Lesbian Studies, 1988.
Hoagland, Sarah Lucia. "Some Thoughts About 'Caring.'" In *Feminist Ethics*, edited by Claudia Card, 246–63. Lawrence: University Press of Kansas, 1991.

Kittay, Eva Feder. *Love's Labor: Essays on Women, Equality, and Dependency*. New York: Routledge, 1999.
Kittay, Eva Feder. "The Ethics of Care, Dependence, and Disability." *Ratio Juris* 24, no. 1 (March 1, 2011): 49–58.
Mol, Annemarie. *The Logic of Care: Health and the Problem of Patient Choice*. New York: Routledge, 2008.
Noddings, Nel. *Caring: A Feminine Approach to Ethics and Moral Education*. Berkeley: University of California Press, 1984.
Tronto, Joan C. *Caring Democracy: Markets, Equality, and Justice*. New York: NYU Press, 2013.
Tronto, Joan C. *Moral Boundaries: A Political Argument for an Ethic of Care*. New York: Psychology Press, 1993.
Walsh, Joseph. "Commitment and Partialism in the Ethics of Care." *Hypatia* 32, no. 4 (November 1, 2017): 817–32.

Nepotism on *The Orville*

Joe Slater

In the opening episode of *The Orville*, "Old Wounds," Ed gets his command as a result of intervention from Kelly. Now, at the end of the second season, we discover that it's definitely good for humanity that Ed got the command. As we see in the alternate timeline, if Ed wasn't the captain, Claire wouldn't have joined the crew, and Isaac wouldn't have bonded with her children and prevented the Kaylon from conquering Earth. But even so—Ed only got the job because his ex-wife put in a good word! Should we really condone this kind of hiring practice, even though it turned out well in this case?

Or think about the Union as a whole. Ed decides, despite significant resistance from Admiral Halsey, that he wants his friend Gordon to be his pilot. And Alara only got the job of security officer because she is a Xelayan, and Xelayans are fast tracked through the Union ranks. It sure seems like the Union has a lot of nepotism for such an advanced society, given that we generally think of nepotism as morally bad. I mean, it's wrong when a president of a country gives their children important state positions, right? And you'd object if you were the most qualified for a job, and your boss hired their son or daughter instead. So why is it okay for Ed to appoint his friend Gordon as the USS *Orville*'s pilot?

The term nepotism has origins referring to giving preferences to a nephew, but is commonly used to refer to benefiting one's wider family or friends. Is nepotism, understood as giving advantages to people because you have a relationship with them, ever morally justified? More broadly, are some of the employment practices that take place in the Union systematically unfair and contrary to the espoused values of 25th century Earth? In this essay, I argue that they are.

In the first section, I distinguish between private and public nepotism, which we might think of as relevantly different. Because the nepotistic practices on *The Orville* seem to be with regards to public roles, these practices might look particularly bad. In the second section, however, I introduce a defense of nepotism, courtesy of Adam Bellow. He would argue that while the suspect practices in the Planetary Union are in the public sphere, this doesn't seem relevantly important. By his lights, there are permissible instances of nepotism, and those in *The Orville* seem to be of that kind.

In the third section, I raise the issue of fairness, drawing upon John Rawls' conception. I demonstrate that any nepotism is likely to be deemed unfair. I then show how this unfairness can lead to systematic injustices, particularly through indirect discrimination on the basis of race, class, or sex. For this reason, I suggest that any nepotism is morally impermissible, and that the Union needs to seriously revise its hiring practices. And finally, I talk about the unusual practices regarding Xelayans, and how both Alara and Talla seem to benefit from special considerations. I suggest that, although these cases look a little odd, they might be justified, depending on the motivations of the Union in determining their hiring practices.

Private and Public Nepotism

In our century, and throughout human history, nepotism has taken place. Sometimes this looks particularly worrying, whereas on other occasions, it might not appear so morally dubious. Adam Bellow, one of few scholars to write seriously on the topic, thinks nepotism is often a force for *good*.

To be clear, although his argument is still applicable to my point, Bellow focuses primarily on a narrower definition of nepotism than I am here. He describes nepotism as when someone gets an advantage—whether or not they asked for it—because of a family relation. I focus on the broader notion of nepotism, which also includes granting favorable treatment to one's friends, like getting them a job. Specifically, I call an act nepotistic when someone gives a formal opportunity (a job, position, or special official status) to someone they have a relationship with *because* of the relationship they have. Here, I'm looking in particular at special treatment in getting these roles, so I'm not including benefits that people might give their friends who already have the job, like when Ed allowed Gordon to have a beer on duty without reporting him (S1E1).[1] Those kinds of perks do look similar, and might be analyzed in the same way, but are much more wide-ranging, so I won't be considering those here.

Bellow tells an evolutionary story of how any behavior which advantages others at one's own expense—what we might consider altruistic behavior—has the same explanation as nepotistic behavior. In his discussion, he gives examples of nepotistic behavior in animals. Elephants, whales, or even ants act to specially benefit their offspring and other close relatives. Bellow talks of nepotism as the norm for social species. What makes humans special though, Bellow thinks, is that we've been able to extend the benefits of nepotistic behavior—sacrificing our own good to benefit others—to people we're not biologically related to (2005: 53). What started as just benefiting one's children was able to be extended to those closely genetically related as a means of ensuring one's genes get passed on. If we agree with this, we could view nepotism as the basis for all human kindness. And not just all *human* kindness. If the evolutionary mechanisms were similar, this could apply to the Moclans, the Xelayans, or even the Krill.

However, even if we buy this explanation—and I'm not saying we should—this doesn't give us a justification for nepotism. The fact that something (nepotism) was needed in our evolutionary story in order to allow the existence of something we now appreciate (altruism, or kind behavior) doesn't mean we should still value that first thing. In our evolutionary story, it was necessary for millions of animals to die without procreating, so that the features of the animals who did procreate (some of which were our ancestors) would be naturally selected. That process no doubt involved huge amounts of suffering and distress for those animals. But we wouldn't want to tolerate that kind of distress today, even though it was needed for us to exist.

So even if we think that a species developing traits that lead to nepotistic behaviors is good, we can still think that nepotism is unjust, and shouldn't exist, both today and in the 25th century. And, in fact, it does look like nepotism is often bad. When we call something nepotistic, we are usually making a complaint.

Now, to be fair, giving your friends or family (or ex-husbands) special treatment in *some* areas of your life is perfectly normal and doesn't seem to be a problem at all. For instance, it seems like an important part of close family relationships that you give preferential treatment to your loved ones. Claire Finn obviously cares a lot about her children, and we think it's only appropriate that she should spend a lot of time with them. There are lots of other children on the *Orville*, but she doesn't have to spend time with them. (Imagine if she spent a lot of her time reading to other people's children. Wouldn't that be a bit weird?) So, there are some areas in life where it's permissible (and perhaps even obligatory) to play favorites; where it seems morally okay to play favorites, we have permissible partiality.

But, of course, not everything is an exception. So, how do we know when partiality is permissible, and when it is not? There are some obvious cases where impartiality seems like a moral requirement. A judge, for instance, must remain impartial. We see the fairness of the legal system as requiring that no one is advantaged by being friends or relatives of a judge or jury. But where is the line between that and *acceptable* cases of nepotism?

Joanne Ciulla thinks an important distinction is whether the nepotism takes place in private or public life. Public life would definitely involve decisions relating to government, policy, or law. If we accept this distinction as relevant, we can argue that it's morally bad to allow relations of family or friendship to affect who gets jobs in government or other jobs in the public sphere (e.g., jobs in the police force and the military, and jobs like doctor and public school teacher). But concerns about one's private life and private property can be fair game for partiality. That could also explain why certain family businesses don't seem as susceptible to criticisms of nepotism as when government officials hire family members. If it's *your* business, we could see the decisions about how it's run as falling within a private domain, so you can pass it on to your children, or hire your sister as the company accountant.

When we consider *The Orville* in this light, it doesn't look good. The Union does look like a public institution, so Kelly using her influence as the daughter of one of the admiral's friends, or Ed picking his friend to be his pilot, on these terms, looks like the bad kind of nepotism. Or consider what Kelly says when she was going to transfer off the USS *Orville* in "Old Wounds" to get out of Ed's hair. "Lieutenant Commander Murphy of the USS *Chanute* just got promoted, so now he's eligible for a first officer position and he's a friend of mine, so I told him he could have this posting." That seems like the worst!

Meritocratic Nepotism?

One issue with viewing nepotism this way, however, is that it's unclear what explains the distinction. What makes it the case that decisions in private life don't require impartiality, but those in public life do? We could say that in roles of public office, we have all "chipped in" through taxation, so everyone who has contributed should have a chance to benefit from these roles, and a chance to serve the public. But this doesn't really seem like that much of a difference. For a large business everyone who makes use of the services contributes. Also, it looks like lots of people—and not just the friends and family of the owners—have interests in the opportunities they could get from working at that business. If one company is a major employer, or perhaps has the most prestigious jobs, it still seems highly problematic if the only people who are able to get those jobs are the friends and family of the boss. The private-public decision doesn't look like it can say what's bad about something like that. But we still want to say that the bad cases of nepotism are morally bad.

Adam Bellow, who is a defender of nepotism (his book is called *In Praise of Nepotism*) accepts that nepotism can be very bad, but gives a different account of when it is. Many of his complaints concern nepotism from bygone generations. The distinction Bellow makes is between New Nepotism and Old Nepotism. Old Nepotism, according to his classification, is simply a "matter of parents hiring or getting jobs for children."[2] The New Nepotism, however, is about children choosing to follow in their parents' footsteps. In the case of Old Nepotism, it didn't matter whether the sons or daughters of the boss (or ruler) were qualified, or at all suited, for the job. They'd just get it handed to them anyway. With his New Nepotism, the familial relationship actually makes the beneficiaries suitable for the position.

How so? Bellow argues that there are certain advantages that come from being in a successful family: "Growing up around a business or vocation—learning how it works, getting to know the people in it—creates a powerful advantage that is tantamount to nepotism, and when exercised unworthily it carries a similar stigma."[3] It seems obvious that, if you grow up in a household where people are very enthusiastic about a certain activity, you will have knowledge of that activity too. Perhaps you'll also be very interested in going into the same business. Where there is a family relationship, there might also be a genetic component. Some people might be predisposed to be good at the job type in question. This would, for example, likely be the case if the family job involved or required athletic ability.

When this happens, the children of people who have been successful in a certain field are also likely to be successful in that field in their own right. Kelly Grayson's father served alongside Admiral Halsey for the Planetary Union, and Kelly followed in his footsteps. Discovering this doesn't make us regard Kelly as any less successful. But, perhaps growing up in a household where she may have learned about Union goings-on did give her an advantage, and possibly motivated her to go into such a career.

With regards to friends, or friends of family, that genetic component advantage won't be there, but a lot of the other advantages might still exist. Your friends might have similar interests as you. That might partly explain why they're your friends. And, if you're in a position of power, where you are deciding who gets a certain job, you might well *know* that one of your friends would be great for that role. You could be in a privileged epistemic position—you might be in a special position to know—about your friend's abilities; you've spent time together, you've seen how they generally conduct themselves. (Since you don't have that kind of knowledge about other applicants, hiring them comes with a certain kind of risk.) If you're in that position, you might think you can benefit them *and* still be picking them because they are good for the job—even "the best helmsman in the fleet." This meritocratic nepotism usually seems totally fine. This is essentially what Ed does for Gordon in picking him as his pilot.

Bellow thinks this kind of thing is usually okay. What we object to, he claims, is nepotism in cases where the beneficiary is incompetent. And in those cases, he suggests that our hostile reaction is usually towards the recipient of the favorable treatment.

> [A]s an ethical mater, our problem is not really with the nepotist, but with the nepotee. We are realists, after all, and we fully expect people to help their friends and relatives where they can. But we also expect the beneficiaries of such patronage to have enough self-respect not to accept that kind of help, especially when it is manifestly unfair to other people.[4]

Bellow views nepotism as an art. It can be practiced well or badly. And in the cases where it is practiced badly, Bellow claims it is "for the most part a self-punishing offense."[5] This is because, for bad nepotism, it is typically obvious to others that the nepotee is incompetent. This in turn is likely to lead to negative effects. If the boss of a company picks an idiot child to run some department, the idiocy is likely to make the department less successful. And it is more likely to attract criticism from the other workers, perhaps even having a demoralizing effect on them. If someone is promoted over you, and they're terrible at the job, you're probably not going to like them too much!

So, for nepotism to be good, according to Bellow, it must be in some sense meritocratic—the person must, at least in some sense, deserve it. This "deservingness" might be known because they have already worked hard and accomplished a great deal; or, like when John LaMarr was given the chief engineer job, it might be based on some knowledge of the potential the person has (S1E11). In those cases, there typically isn't much criticism of the practice. As Bellow suggests, "we know *good* nepotism when we see it, but we tend not to call it nepotism, because it looks like something else." In the good cases, people don't yell "nepotism." On the contrary, they view it as "able and dutiful sons" who have "carried on a proud family tradition."[6]

Like other art forms, there are guidelines one might follow. Bellow considers specifically three of these "unwritten rules" of nepotism. Each of them is focused on what the nepotee must do. "The problem, then, is not that nepotism continues to be practiced, but that it is often practiced badly or haphazardly."[7] We need to "recognize that nepotism is an art, and to observe the unwritten rules that have made it on balance a constructive and positive thing."

The Rules of Nepotism:

1. *Don't embarrass me.*
2. *Don't embarrass yourself,* or *you have to work harder than anyone else.*
3. *Pass it on.*

The first rule a nepotee should embrace is that they must not embarrass the person who has got them the job. They should be grateful, and make sure that the nepotist doesn't regret it. Second, they must do the job well. They should see themselves as having to work extra hard to justify that faith. And finally, they should be willing to help others of their friends and family if similar situations arise, where they are able to provide the helping hand.

Bellow's general sentiment seems to fit in well with the world-view expressed by some in *The Orville*. On several occasions we hear members of the crew discuss how society is very different in the 25th century. No longer do people work for money, so they can buy the goods that they need to survive—"houses and sandwiches and stuff." Instead, since the invention of matter synthesis, rather than competing over money, they now compete over status. As Kelly puts it: "The predominant currency became reputation…. Human ambition didn't vanish. The only thing that changed was how we quantify wealth. People still want to be rich. Only now, rich means being the best at what you do" (S1E11). She also tells us that "an individual's wealth is determined by their personal achievements, not their monetary value" (S2E5).

If people are still getting jobs that they are well suited for, like Gordon and Ed, and any beneficiaries of nepotism act in accordance with Bellow's rules for nepotism, there might not be any obvious problems. At the very least, the kind of nepotism practiced within the Union (at least when people do their jobs well) seems like the sort that Bellow generally approves of.

Against Nepotism

There are multiple ways we might argue that nepotism is bad, however, even if it is of this "better" kind. We might think it's likely to leave power consolidated in certain areas of society, marginalizing others. We know that Kelly Grayson's father is a friend of Admiral Halsey. If there is a social stratification—if richer people tend to associate with other rich people, or people with certain desirable skills predominantly associate with each other—the kind of "good" nepotism may lead to this continuing. This might stifle social mobility. If we think social mobility is a good thing, then this gives us some reason to be cautious of allowing any kind of nepotism.

Of course, because of the elimination of money, the force of this objection might be diminished in the Union. It won't be the case that huge amounts of money will remain in the hands of a select few, while others are starved of the opportunities that come with affluence. Still, however, the "good" kind of nepotism could cause certain privileged groups to dominate many career choices.

Another reason that nepotistic practices might be undesirable becomes clear in "New Dimensions," when Kelly inadvertently let it slip to Ed that she had a role in him getting command of the USS *Orville*. "Hey, you wouldn't be sitting there if I…" (S1E11). People who have benefited from any favorable treatment do not know whether they have really *earned it* themselves, or whether they *deserve* to be there. After discovering that he got the job due to Kelly's advocacy, Ed is both wounded and full of self-doubt. He makes it very clear that this doubt has an impact on his judgment:

> From now on I am going to second-guess every command decision I make ever because I will never know whether I am truly the person who deserves to be making those decisions…. But who knows whether I would ever have had the chance to prove that without a hand-out from my ex-wife [S1E11]?

He also claims that this revelation has skewed his view of himself. It looks as though he had thought of himself as a self-made man, but now he questions himself and his accomplishments. "I want to be self-reliant. I want to feel like I got where I am alone" (S1E11).

While Kelly accuses him of being "a prideful ass," we can understand why Ed might feel that way. We do in fact learn—from what we see in the alternate timeline at the end of season 2—that if it wasn't for Kelly, Ed *wouldn't* have got his own command. And Admiral Halsey is just as clear about this when talking to Kelly about how Ed got the job: "Your father and I were close. I owed him one. [Kelly made] You made a hell of a plea for us to give him that command…. I don't think we would've have done it otherwise (S1E1)."

Luckily for Ed and the USS *Orville*, this self-doubt didn't have any long-term effects. But it could easily have been different. At the end of "New Dimensions," Ed volunteers to pilot the shuttle, as a way to prove himself. This was a very dangerous mission, and presumably Isaac would have been better able to perform the task, given that he is, according to his testimony the "only crew member capable" of extremely rapid helm adjustments (S1E4). So Ed's need to prove himself, produced by his awareness of nepotism, exposed the entire ship to unnecessary risk.

Perhaps this shouldn't be taken as a reason for us to avoid nepotism, however. Maybe it is the kind of pride that Ed exhibits that we should think is the big problem here. It could be that this kind of discovery intensifies some existing personality characteristics, like pride or insecurity. Other people who receive this kind of benefit don't make such a big deal of it. Gordon, for instance, clearly doesn't care that he owes his job to Ed. This is made abundantly clear when he tells John "if it weren't for Ed, I probably wouldn't be at the helm for a lot longer than this, if ever" (S1E1). If Ed was less prideful, or less insecure, he presumably wouldn't have felt so negatively immediately after discovering how Kelly helped him.

Similarly, we might think that this nepotism just wasn't done as well as it could have been. Kelly never intended to tell Ed. If she hadn't, and Ed had never discovered, he would have avoided those doubts. Maybe this could be added to Bellow's rules for nepotism, that the favoritism is kept secret wherever possible. But this also isn't ideal. For one thing it doesn't look practical. In Gordon's case, for instance, it's *obvious* that he's only got the job because Ed has vouched for him.

Also, making dishonesty a standard institutional practice seems very undesirable. If people ever discovered that the Union had a policy that includes lying to its officers (or even just misleading them), this would erode trust. Even if that never happened, and no one ever discovered that they benefited in this way, this secret nepotism would prevent people from properly expressing gratitude to their benefactors. The secrecy would make it impossible for the nepotee to follow Bellow's rules of nepotism, because those injunctions apply especially because of the special assistance they have received. If the benefits of New Nepotism rely on the nepotee accepting that they have been helped, good instances of the practice might involve ensuring they do know. An issue with Ed's learning of this was that it was kept secret from him for so long, and he ended up discovering it at an inopportune time. But once he had put his pride aside and come to terms with the help he had received, he seems to have relinquished some of this pride, and possibly improved as a person. So any worries about bad psychological consequences on nepotees might be mitigated or eliminated if the nepotism is carried out more openly and with more sensitivity to the characters involved.

A better argument against nepotism might be extracted from a popular view in political philosophy made famous by John Rawls, a major figure in 20th century philosophy. In his book, *A Theory of Justice*, he theorizes about what a just society should look like. How should we distribute our scarce resources and goods? What should our institutions and organizations look like? Fortunately, in the 25th century, thanks to matter synthesis, things like food, water, and shelter are not scarce resources on Earth. But how important goods should be shared is still an important question. Given that, according to Kelly, reputation has replaced money as the currency, we might think that jobs and positions are the kind of thing we should care about being divided in a just way.

To think about how a just society should work, Rawls theorizes a way of determining what principles or rules we should have. These principles would determine the structure of society (including what the government looks like), regulate all agreements made within a society (including hiring/firing agreements), and "assign basic rights and duties and ... determine the division of social benefits."[8] He calls this "justice as fairness." To get just principles, he imagines what principles we would agree to, if we were free, equal, and rational.

To be more specific, Rawls asks us to think about what rules we would agree to from behind a "veil of ignorance." Behind this veil, you think about what principles you would be happy to agree to, if you didn't know anything about what your life was going to be like. You don't know if you're going to be a man or a woman (or other), what race you're going to be, what your social class or status will be, or even anything about your talents and abilities. Extending to the 25th century, and thinking about interplanetary justice, this would probably include not knowing what species you would be or which planet you would live on within the Planetary Union.

Imagining that you don't know any of those things makes a pretty weird thought experiment, but Rawls thought doing so would ensure that the choice of principles wouldn't lead to some people being horribly disadvantaged by chance factors. From behind the veil of ignorance, you don't even know things about your general preferences, values or ideologies. You don't know what religion you are. You don't know what types of music you like. You don't even know if you're going to be a nice person, or a selfish one. In short, you don't know anything about your wants and desires, except for a really minimal set of commitments—things that everyone is presumed to want. In his list, Rawls includes "rights and liberties, powers and opportunities, income and wealth."[9] He calls these the "social primary goods."

When deciding what principles we should use to figure out how to allocate these primary goods, Rawls starts off by considering a benchmark of total equality. But, he thinks, rational people will agree to unequal systems, if it makes everyone better off. For instance, we might think that allowing some people to earn a bit more money than others serves as a motivation for them to work harder, and this hard work might be good for everyone. For example, paying medical doctors more might be "unfair" to a certain extent (because they are getting paid more than others), but the higher pay would motivate talented people to become doctors (when they otherwise wouldn't), and having medical doctors in society is good for everyone.

Rawls says that, in the "original position" (from the outside of society looking in), under a "veil of ignorance," people would agree for two principles of justice to organize society:

> First Principle: Each person is to have an equal right to the most extensive total system of equal basic liberties compatible with a similar system of liberty for all.
> Second Principle: Social and economic inequalities are to be arranged so that they

are both: (a) to the greatest benefit of the least advantaged, consistent with the just savings principle, and (b) attached to offices and positions open to all under conditions of fair equality of opportunity.[10]

The first principle, sometimes called the greatest equal liberty principle, is taken as primary. So, giving people the greatest equal liberty takes priority over the second principle. The second principle is split in two parts. The first part has come to be known as the difference principle. Any inequality must make the worst off person better off, and be compatible with some fair savings rule for future generations. (This is called the just savings principle, but we won't go into it here.) It is the second part of the second principle which looks most relevant for us here. This second part of the second principle, the "equality of opportunity principle," gets priority over the first part, in part because Rawls doesn't think privileged family arrangements should be allowed to persist at the expense of giving more opportunities to those without, even if in the short term this can be done while increasing the amounts of resources available to the worst off.

By "offices and positions" Rawls means offices of command—like legislative or judicial roles—or positions of authority. The jobs on the USS *Orville*—captain and pilot of a starship—definitely seem to fit into these categories. Essentially, if there are any social and economic equalities that come with offices or positions, those offices and positions have to be open to all under conditions of *fair equality of opportunity*.

Can nepotism of this sort, where you recommend a friend you know would be good for the job, be included in fair equality of opportunity? We could try to make a case that it could. After all, maybe anyone could have made friends with Ed, and if they were also a really good pilot, they might have got the role instead of Gordon. This is a tough sell though, for a couple of reasons.

First, when it comes to family relations, people *don't* have this kind of choice. Kelly had the power to influence Admiral Halsey's decision because she was the daughter of his friend. People can't *choose* to be the child of someone with powerful influence. Secondly, even if we concede that everyone *could*, in principle, have made friends with the right people, in practice that's a different matter. Should not liking Ed give you a disadvantage with respect to getting a certain job? Or what if Ed doesn't like you? If Ed happens to be a little bit racist, as Yaphit accuses him of being at one point, and only wants to hire humans, this could lead to human-privilege. And if this prejudice was prevalent among many people in power among the Union, nepotism of this kind could lead to humans repeatedly getting jobs that Gelatins or Retepsians might be better suited for.

These concerns give rise to a worry mentioned earlier, that power might stagnate in certain social groups. If certain families, perhaps with a longstanding military history, have a significant advantage when trying to get jobs on Union ships, the resulting society won't be particularly equal.

One objection we might have to the general Rawlsian argument I've given here could come from the kinds of consequences that might follow—at least, if we take what I've said about nepotism seriously. Philosophers call this move a *reductio ad absurdum*, or a reduction to absurdity. If no one was allowed to be nepotistic at all, would that have absurd consequences? If we think it's wrong to give your friend a job, when you have a job that needs doing and you know your friend would be good at it, could that make life extremely complicated? If I need a plumber, and one of my friends can do it, would this mean I couldn't just give my friend the job? Would I have to give everyone a fair chance to be the one to fix my toilet?

But I don't think the argument I've given leads us to anything this extreme. This is because Rawls is concerned with social and economic equality. For this to be a concern with an office or position, the role has to be something that carries a social status with it. This doesn't seem particularly relevant for me paying a friend to fix my toilet. This won't benefit them hugely. And, every potential plumber out there is likely to know friends who may have similar plumbing-related mishaps.

Unfortunately, however, the roles of those on the USS *Orville* do seem status-conferring in an important sense. We know that Ed always dreamed of making captain. And we see that Kelly is stunned that John hasn't tried to make the best use of his talents to seek promotions further in the Union. In this society, where reputation is the currency, roles that enhance a person's reputation really should be open and available to all.

If the Rawlsian argument I've given here is right, then nepotism is something that should generally avoided. However, there might still be special circumstances that would mean a nepotistic decision could be defended in some cases. If there was an emergency situation, for instance, and time pressures are a factor, it might be unhelpful to insist on a fair decision procedure. We might be able to explain Ed's appointment in this way. Admiral Halsey does allude to a fairly desperate situation. "Look, the truth is, you're nobody's first choice for this job. But we have 3,000 ships to staff, and we need captains" (S1E1). We find out throughout the series that the Krill threat is a danger to many lives. Having all the ships in the fleet available could be vital for protecting citizens of the Union. And Admiral Halsey, with the aid of Kelly's personal knowledge of Ed, has reasons to believe that he could handle the job.

Based on Rawlsian principles, this might be difficult to defend, as his second principle states that offices and positions must be "open to all under conditions of fair equality of opportunity." However, in an emergency situation, where time pressures mean a decision must be made quickly to prevent likely loss of life, it seems like a society should accept rules that prevent disasters. In the original position, people would surely accept rules that made some exceptions to completely fair employment practices, when they realize that doing so might save their lives.

If this is right, then *maybe* it is acceptable for the Union to give Ed his command, based on Kelly's recommendation. But this should be an exceptional case, rather than standard practice. Given that Kelly sought out Halsey in order to recommend Ed for the captaincy, this might indicate that she thought this kind of suggestion was often successful for influencing these kinds of decisions. And if that's the case, it reflects poorly on the Union. Even if Ed was the most suitable candidate for the job, if it wasn't a time-sensitive decision made to avoid catastrophe, others should have still been able to apply and interview for it. It definitely shouldn't be the case that the difference is made by an admiral's friend's daughter asking for a favor!

Alara and the Xelayan Policy

Another odd employment situation in *The Orville* includes the Xelayan security officers, Alara Kitan and Talla Keyali. While Alara is unquestionably a great security officer, she informs us in the first episode that, because "Xelayans don't usually join the military ... the Union usually fast-tracks us" (S1E1). On its own, this practice looks pretty weird. Perhaps, the Union judged that they needed some incentives in order to motivate Xelayans, or to help them overcome discrimination that may serve as a barrier to entry. If so, such efforts might equalize the opportunities available for Xelayans and be defensible.

But could something like this be justified on Rawlsian grounds? This kind of measure looks like a form of affirmative action. Rawls doesn't really discuss affirmative action, but it does seem in tension with fair equality of opportunity. If one group of people get preferential treatment when applying for a job, just because of their species, how can this be fair? Samuel Freeman, a former student of Rawls, claims that Rawls did not think affirmative action was compatible with fair equality of opportunity. However, Freeman claims that Rawls still conceded that this could be "a proper corrective for remedying the present effects of past discrimination."[11] Even then, it would be a temporary measure, and would not be appropriate once a well-ordered society had been established.

For this to be an appropriate explanation, it would need to be the case that some discrimination had hindered Xelayans who may want or have wanted to join the military. Given the attitudes that seem prevalent on

Xelaya, this might be the case. We see from Alara's parents, and particularly her father, that there seems to be a stigma against military careers. As he put it, "We just want what's best for you, and we feel that the military is beneath you" (S1E10). That Xelayans tend to hold a view of this sort is widely known. As Ed mentions to Alara's parents when he returns her home, it is "no secret to anyone that Xelayans don't think much of the military" (S2E3). If this is the kind of obstacle that amounts to discrimination, the fast-tracking might be justifiable as a short-term measure.

An even stranger case is Ed's decision after Alara leaves. We discover that in his search for a replacement security officer, before he eventually hired Talla, he "begged the admiral for another Xelayan" (S2E5). We don't hear any explanation for this, but it does seem to weirdly privilege one species. Of course, in their incredible strength, Xelayans do have a quality that makes particularly good security officers. However, requesting personnel of a specific species based on preconceived notions about what jobs they would be good for seems like a very questionable hiring policy. That kind of thinking could lead to the development or reinforcement of stereotypes. If all captains picked security personnel this way, it could be seen as a job for Xelayans, which in turn might be bad for non–Xelayans interested in a career in security, and for Xelayans, who might feel pushed in that direction. Given that the potential justification for fast-tracking Xelayans was (seemingly) to counteract social prejudices dissuading them from a certain type of career, it is important that these measures don't replace one prejudice with another.

Alternatively, we might think Ed requests another Xelayan simply because he enjoyed Alara's company so much, and hoped for a similar experience with her replacement. But if *that* was the justification, it seems entirely based on a weird prejudice; he would have judged this species based on one person, and assumed others would be similar. It's hard to see how any motivation of this sort could be compatible with fair employment practices, or be justified on the grounds of promoting fairness.

Conclusion

Nepotism—understood as giving a friend or family member a special access to a job or position—is bad. It flies in the face of what we think is required by considerations of equality. It still does happen to be the case that friends and family members of important officials might get certain benefits. They might learn about the career or the working environment just from speaking to their friend or relative. This is an advantage they'll get without giving them special opportunities. Because of those types of advantages, which might be unavoidable to a certain extent, achieving full equality of opportunity in some positions might be very difficult. But, by the 25th century, we really should know better than give those privileged people *extra* handouts.

Notes

1. Although, we must admit, given Kelly's subsequent behavior, Gordon is not the only one to eventually drink while on duty (see "A Happy Refrain").
2. Adam Bellow, *In Praise of Nepotism: A Natural History* (London: Doubleday, 2003), 10.
3. *Ibid.*
4. *Ibid.*, 470.
5. *Ibid.*
6. *Ibid.*, 471.
7. *Ibid.*
8. John Rawls, *A Theory of Justice* (London: Belknap Press, 1971), 12.
9. *Ibid.*, 62.
10. *Ibid.*, 302.
11. Samuel Freeman, *Rawls* (New York: Routledge, 2007), 90–91.

Bibliography

Bellow, Adam. *In Praise of Nepotism: A Natural History*. London: Doubleday, 2003.
Ciulla, Joanne B. "In Praise of Nepotism?—In Praise of Nepotism: A Natural History." *Business Ethics Quarterly* 15, no. 1 (2005): 153–160.
Freeman, Samuel. *Rawls*. New York: Routledge, 2007.
Rawls, John. *A Theory of Justice*. London: Belknap Press, 1971.

Act V
The Funny and the Final Flyout

The Ethics of "Sophomoric" Sci-Fi
The Orville, *Pop Culture, and Lacan*

Leigh E. Rich

"All sorts of things in this world behave like mirrors."
—Jacques Lacan[1]

"[T]he play's the thing / Wherein I'll catch the conscience of the king."
—*Hamlet* (II.ii.605–606)

"There must be 10,000 files here. What is this reality television? [...] The best exhibit we've ever had."
—Calivon Aliens, "Command Performance"

One recurring trend in shows and films by Seth MacFarlane is his (intentional) use of pop-cultural references, whether from television, movies, or music, to generate a laugh or as critique. This works well in his animated and live-action comedies such as *Family Guy*, *American Dad!*, and *Ted*, which co-opt and adapt scenes from other media and interweave them into MacFarlane's (often) lowbrow humor.[2] At times, and in an ultimate self-reflexive vein, MacFarlane even spoofs his own shows. While many of his media-related credits as writer, actor, producer, and host tend toward the brash or puerile, MacFarlane has demonstrated more of a serious side in his political advocacy, his musical albums, and his interest in science fiction. The latter has led to his involvement with the 2014 documentary series *Cosmos: A Spacetime Odyssey* and his 2016 sci-fi comedy-drama *The Orville*. While viewers and commentators have criticized *The Orville*, particularly in season one, as being too "MacFarlanized" and not taking itself seriously, many breathed a sigh of relief as the show in its second year traded its irreverent antics and pop-culture tangents for a "truer" sci-fi format.

But some of what seems sophomoric in *The Orville* may convey a maturity, if viewed through the work of French psychoanalyst Jacques Lacan and his notions of the "mirror stage," the "ideal ego," and the "ego-ideal." To begin unpacking this linkage, brief introductions to these complex terms are in order. In several episodes, MacFarlane's pop-culture references—and even the television series itself—act as a mirror (a "specular image") that enables the characters of the show and, both through them and directly, the viewers to see ourselves in the "other" (through an external alienation with which we then identify). The (falsely) complete image who gazes back at us is enticing, since one can never look directly at one's self as a whole. For when we try to view ourselves directly—when we tilt our heads in various ways to see our bodies and who we are with our own eyes (or we feel with our hands, listen with our ears, think with our minds, etc.)—it is impossible to take in everything at once. Thus, what we see is always incomplete and fails to match the comprehensive perspective of a reflected image (what a mirror depicts, how others see us, what society deems us to be, etc.). This reflection, however, while seeming a true and complete sense of one's self, isn't real but imaginary. It is external to the subjective self and, though it helps to form the ego, creates both a (sometimes unwelcomed) recognition of our fragmented selves and a desire to return to the (impossible) fullness and absence of lack that Lacan associates with "a true being-in-itself."[3] While the ego (this externalized sense of self) occurs in what Lacan calls the register of the Imaginary, the true being and full presence of the subjective self ("undifferentiated matter as it is in itself"[4]) exists in the register of the Real.[5] Although Lacan redefined what he means by the Real several times throughout his writings, he offers in *The Seminar: Book IV* the analogy of a hydroelectric power plant, where the real subject is both the energy that "was already there, in a virtual state, in the current of the river" and also the energy that is accumulated in relation to the artificially constructed machine (matter that will activate, and simultaneously be mediated by, the power plant itself).[6] Likewise in this metaphor, the schematic of the plant or a press release touting how much power it produces is akin to the reflections or specular images that shape the ego. Finally, the operational factory then speaks to Lacan's third register, that of the Symbolic—or language, cultural customs, and norms and laws—that enables how and where the plant is situated, regulates its workings, directs production and distribution, and monitors its effects on the environment and world.

Moreover, since Lacan (and perhaps MacFarlane) understands the ego as only imaginary, a gap forms between the subject of the unconscious (who we are as beings in the Real) and the ego (our Imaginary reflections), and it is through the dialectic of the Real subject seeing this alienated and (de)formative Imaginary ego gaze back at itself that we begin to create self-identity. Lacan, however, takes this one step further: Throughout our lives, as we introject (unconsciously incorporate) these external images into who (we think) we are, we project back onto them "an idealized self-image [...] (the way I would like to be, [the way] I would like others to see me)."[7] This ideal ego initiates a secondary identification—another external alienation—though this time in relation to the Symbolic register of language, customs, and law. The ego-ideal, or the gaze we introject from this idealized point that relies heavily on the Symbolic, inverts our sense of self from a more complex order, modifies the ego by forcing us to question it, and betters our own subjectivity by turning to moralistic goals.

These Lacanian techniques can be found in *The Orville*, particularly through the trajectory of the Moclan character Bortus and in episodes such as "Command Performance" (S1E2), whose main conflict is resolved using reality television, "About a Girl" (S1E3) and the gender-related lessons of *Rudolph the Red-Nosed Reindeer*, and "Sanctuary" (S2E12), grounded in poet Dolly Parton's "9 to 5." MacFarlane's use of pop culture provides opportunities to not merely reflect on what is reflected but also contemplate what such mirrors hide: "'the other which isn't another at all' [...] the leftover, the remainder [...] the remnant left behind by the introduction of the symbolic in the real"—what Lacan calls *objet (petit) a*, a "lack of lack" and a "semblance of being" where all three registers interact.[8] By viewing *The Orville* through the lens of Lacan, MacFarlane's "sophomoric" sci-fi is an engagement in self-exploration and an occasion, as Eliot phrased it, "to arrive where we started / And know the place for the first time."[9]

Sophomoric Seth

When Seth MacFarlane was a student of film, animation, and video at the Rhode Island School of Design, he screened a ten-minute, hand-drawn short called *The Life of Larry* in between "hours of non-narrative student cinema."[10] As his classmates put forth creations that are now framed in relation to this animation history as "too serious" and "trying too hard," MacFarlane gave the finger to the art form of film. *The Life of Larry* begins not with the story of MacFarlane's working-class characters and their pretentious talking dog that would become the basis for the hit television series *Family Guy*, but "a camera pan of an upright piano" and a live shot of MacFarlane smoking a cigar (an ever-Freudian move).[11] He breaks the fourth wall (before it is even established), first with the homage to Norman

Lear's 1970s groundbreaking situational-comedy *All in the Family*, which MacFarlane has credited time and again as one inspiration for *Family Guy*,[12] followed by a glib reproach (or veneration?) of the phallocentric self-importance of the industry by focusing on himself. As Claire Hoffman retells it in a 2012 article in *The New Yorker* (the highbrow periodical often held up as the height of "good taste," including by *Family Guy*'s snobbish canine, Brian), MacFarlane addresses his audience: "Oh, hi there! [...] I'm Seth MacFarlane, associate production coordinating directorial associate managing departmental divisional office supervisor of the international network amalgamation distributor's corporation management organizational association of men who like pussy."[13] Once the actual narrative begins, *The Life of Larry* then savagely pokes at pop culture, when Larry (with the brashness of Archie Bunker and puerility of what will become Peter Griffin) delights in the "hilarity" of the 1993 film *Philadelphia*, starring Tom Hanks as a gay man fighting discrimination while dying of AIDS. The humor Larry finds is linked to the fact that Hanks, understood to be a modern-day amalgam of Jimmy Stewart and Cary Grant, has films like *Big* and other comedies in his oeuvre, so "anything that comes out of that guy's mouth, you know it's going to be a stitch."[14] In this way, MacFarlane never truly erects the fourth wall and instead creates a self-aware, though sophomoric, form of storytelling that is a combination of "shock jock" (Hoffman calls *Family Guy* the "Howard Stern of sitcoms"[15]) and plays on plays of pop-cultural referencing.

This has served him well, with MacFarlane crowned "the highest-paid writer-producer in television history,"[16] and he has woven this winning recipe, to some degree or another, into all of the projects of his now-vast empire. The *Family Guy* spinoff *The Cleveland Show* is but more of the same (though focused on an African American family), and MacFarlane's second animated series, *American Dad!*, infuses this approach into a 1950s family sitcom template[17] with a more cohesive narrative and fewer non sequitur cutaways,[18] producing something lesser in kind rather than completely different. Similarly, his first live-action film, *Ted*, centers on a 35-year-old, underachieving man-boy whose emotionally stunted, potty-mouthed, weed-smoking childhood teddy bear (that magically came to life decades earlier) is interfering with his ability to form a mature relationship. *Ted* is steeped in MacFarlane's "ceaseless pop-culture references" and "state of perpetual adolescence" for which he has become known,[19] all while earning $219 million in the United States—the "eighth highest ever for an R-rated feature"[20]—and $550 million total worldwide,[21] along with acclamations from fans and critics alike. Roger Ebert called it "the best comedy screenplay [of the year] so far" when it opened in June 2012 and lauded its "fairly standard" bromance-versus-romance plot as "greatly embellished by

MacFarlane's ability to establish comic situations and keep them building" in a way that "doesn't run out of steam."[22] *The Guardian*'s Jonathan Bernstein hailed it "the ultimate man-boy movie,"[23] to which MacFarlane himself agreed: "*Ted* is probably the most bizarre, most direct symbolic physical manifestation of that scenario we've seen before."[24]

Other critics haven't been so kind. After *Family Guy* debuted on Fox in 1999, Ken Tucker of *Entertainment Weekly* gave it a grade of "D" and deemed it an imitation of "*The Simpsons* as conceived by a singularly sophomoric mind that lacks any reference point beyond other TV shows."[25] Similarly, *Ted 2* and *A Million Ways to Die in the West*—MacFarlane's follow-up films that earned less than half and about a fifth, respectively, of *Ted*'s box-office totals—were panned for their less-than-lowbrow, toilet-level humor. In 2014, Matt Barone called MacFarlane's Western spoof "crass minus any wit,"[26] while Amy Zimmerman declared MacFarlane a "juvenile misogynist" in her review's headline and (likely more to MacFarlane's dismay) "not funny": "Call it adolescent humor or male privilege[…] MacFarlane's 'bold' comedy remains shockingly retrograde."[27] Chris Nashawaty of *Entertainment Weekly* sized up *Ted 2*—and much of MacFarlane's work—in his review's first paragraph:

> The sequel still manages to walk the tightrope between clever and crass. For a while, at least. Then, after the 10th or 11th semen gag, crass wins out, leaving clever in the dust. That's when you realize what it must be like to be trapped in detention with a bunch of 15-year-old boys who think there's nothing more hilarious than repeating the same jokes about porn, pot, and pulling your pud over and over again. It's funny, until it's not.[28]

MacFarlane's "bad taste"[29] was even more on display when he hosted the 2013 Oscars, with jokes about slavery, domestic violence, and the musical number "We Saw Your Boobs." The latter included references to films about a woman known for her intellect (British philosopher and novelist Iris Murdoch in *Iris*) or individuals seeking justice following rape (*The Accused*, *Boys Don't Cry*) and either reified (and glorified) the male (objectifying and penetrating) gaze in Hollywood[30] or destabilized it because the skit "was *meant* to be a tasteless parody of a bad Oscar song."[31] Some claim that "a satirical point" was being made "that in Hollywood, women—even when playing victims of violent crime—are reduced to the sum of their body parts, not the sum of their movie parts."[32] Like Larry giggling when Tom Hanks' character in *Philadelphia* bravely states that he has AIDS near the peak of U.S. deaths from the disease,[33] MacFarlane's sophomoric style (literally) dances on the inappropriate to create a reaction, whether in service of success,[34] a younger crowd,[35] or the subversive. His approach, while "edgy," may at times be "too 'inside,' low-rent, and goofy"[36] or even too close to cruel.

Regardless, MacFarlane has developed his own high-profit, pop-cultural cred that enables him to take on any project he wants, including Rat Pack-esque musical albums, a remake of Carl Sagan's *Cosmos* (because "science literacy is failing"),[37] and his *Star Trek*-inspired *Orville*. He also engages in political advocacy, with causes related to marriage equality, domestic violence, and (no surprise) *cannabis*,[38] and in 2011 was named Harvard's Humanist of the Year.[39]

Lacanian Psy-Fi

While MacFarlane's intentions can be opaque (he often wears these close to the vest), the work of French psychoanalyst Jacques Lacan may help illuminate MacFarlane's use of pop culture, whether in his more lowbrow series and films or his (somewhat) higher-reaching "dramedy," *The Orville*. The characters in *The Orville*—in certain episodes or, as with Bortus, across the span of two seasons—illustrate some of Lacan's fundamental concepts.[40] Moreover, in watching the show, we as viewers, like the fictional subjects who crew *The Orville*, experience the dialectical tensions Lacan describes, both through the characters and directly ourselves. It is the latter, however, amplified by MacFarlane's reliance on pop-cultural references within a pop-cultural medium, that provides an opportunity for our own moral reflection and growth. To contemplate how, this requires a primer on Lacan.

In a way similar to MacFarlane in the 1990s, Lacan begins his psychoanalytic-philosophical career in 1936 with a "return to Freud" and a focus on "images."[41] Freud's "discovery" of the unconscious was a game-changer that, for Lacan, reframes Cartesian thinking, the dominant force shaping the Western individual for centuries. Whereas a traditional understanding of Descartes' *cogito ergo sum* (doubting and thinking are proof of a mind and, therefore, a self) suggests that the ego resides in the subject ("subject=ego=consciousness"[42]), Lacan deems this equivalence incorrect. To do so, he employs and adapts French developmental psychologist Henri Wallon's 1931 concept of the "mirror stage," or the process that occurs when a child, looking in a mirror, reflexively and illusorily sees itself as a distinct "I" in the impersonal gaze of the image.[43] Unlike animals that may grow disinterested when discovering what's looking back is not another member of its species (an actual other self), the child is fascinated by what it sees, trapped by the *jouissance* (jubilation) that comes with this *méconnaissance* (misrecognition)[44] and "hallucinatory deception."[45] This "image-based transaction" is a point of separation from the Real and a passage into the Imaginary, where the ego develops not as a *subject* but an *object*.⁴⁶ It is important to note that this "identification," or "the transformation that takes place in the subject when he assumes […] an image,"⁴⁷ may involve an encounter with an actual mirror "or a reflection in someone's eyes" or any specular image, including those we watch via television and film.⁴⁸ It also is not just something an infant experiences. As Lacan later emphasizes, we engage in it throughout our lives: The mirror stage "constitutes the core of a problem around which all the subsequent identifications and the very concept of Ego will be centred."⁴⁹

Illustrations of how the mirror stage forms the ego can be found in *The Orville*. In "Command Performance" (S1E2), for example, Alara, chief of security, is for the first time left in command when the captain (Ed) and commander (Kelly) must aid another ship in distress and Lieutenant Commander Bortus is busy incubating the egg he has laid. Alara is so nervous to be in charge that, at the sight of the leaderless bridge, she ducks into the captain's office, downs a shot of "Xelayan tequila," and promptly retches. When she finally seats herself in the captain's chair, however, the crew respond to her as they would Ed: Lieutenant Gordon Malloy waits for her order before taking an action he himself suggests, and on her command, Isaac (the robot) retrieves an alien buoy despite cautioning her that they "are not familiar with its defense mechanisms." With false bravado, Alara dismisses his advice and chastises Lieutenant John LaMarr for his insubordinate side-commentary. Likewise, in "About a Girl" (S1E3), Bortus faces the crisis of having given birth to a female despite the fact that his species is (supposedly) all male. He and his mate, Klyden, wish to do what is expected of Moclans when this rarity occurs: "transition" the child to conform to the "proper" gender. Bortus' shipmates are aghast at the plan, with Ed and Dr. Claire Finn refusing to allow it. When Claire states that she "will not perform a sex change on a perfectly healthy newborn" and Alara bests Bortus in the boxing ring with her Xelayan strength to demonstrate that females are not weak or lacking, Bortus remains adamant in his decision and self-image: "My world is different than yours. I would hope that you would respect that."

In these instances, Alara and Bortus have seen a reflected image of themselves that—because we can never directly behold our entire bodies—are more complete and less fragmented than is possible without such mirrors. Moreover, like Alara who in her career as a Union officer is "really green" (S1E2) or Bortus who thinks he has never met a Moclan female (S1E3), Lacan notes that humans are a prematurely born, "disadapted" species heavily reliant on others for survival.⁵⁰ Thus, along with a coherent unity, we also see or anticipate a bodily coordination and power (e.g., Alara as an effective captain, Bortus as a true advocate for his child) that in reality may not (yet) exist. These specular images "capture" and "captivate" us⁵¹ by providing a sense of "self" as a whole, complete, capable entity and a recognizable "I," yet are simultaneously alienating because they are external to and "differentiated from the subject of the unconscious"[52]—prompting Lacan to rewrite Descartes' "I think, therefore I am" as "I think where I am not, therefore I am where I do not think."[53] The ego is, thus, "a psychic agency caused in the subject by his alienating identification with a series of external images"; it is "an imaginary construction," a "passive, mental object," and "an other."[54]

Lacan describes the ego as "an onionlike object which 'is constructed out of its successive identifications,'"[55] and through these ongoing introjections by the perceiving subject, a more complex ego develops: an (unattainable) ideal ego that we then project "onto the external world (equally onto human beings, animals, and things)" and by which we measure ourselves.[56] This process is again illustrated in *The Orville*. In "Command Performance," after Alara's hubristic decision to ignore Isaac's advice, the captured buoy explodes in the shuttle bay, causing damage to the ship and injuries to the crew. She seeks out Claire to declare her unfit for command: "I can't do this. [...] I wasn't in that chair ten minutes, and I almost destroyed the entire ship. What if someone had been killed? [...] Tell them I'm a drug addict, anything. Just get someone to replace me, please." Claire refuses and instead shows Alara a different image of herself:

> Command is all about the balance between inspiring confidence in your leadership and knowing when to trust your people. You got scared out there today. Scared that they didn't respect you. So you ignored Isaac's advice in order to appear in control. Now, the question is, did you learn from this error? I'm willing to bet that you did [S1E2].

In a subsequent scene, when Isaac wants to divert what little power they have to scan for the now-missing Kelly and Ed, Chief Newton balks, calling the plan a joke and Alara a "kid." Alara looks to Claire, whose return gaze reiterates an ideal ego that knows how and when to "trust yourself and your people." Unlike before, this time Alara makes a considered decision and gently-but-firmly explains her reasoning,[57] while telling the chief, "Oh, and it's 'sir,' not 'kid.' Just a friendly reminder." Similarly, in "About a Girl" (S1E3), when Gordon and John invite themselves to Bortus' quarters with beer and a copy of *Rudolph the Red-Nosed Reindeer*, Bortus sees himself in the fatherly character of Santa and begins to view his daughter's deviation from the norm differently. Or, as in "Sanctuary" (S2E12), because such images include "feelings as well as a visual representation,"[58] the mirror may even take the form of song. In this episode, Heveena, a female Moclan and the leader of a hidden, all-female colony, seeks the Planetary Union's protection after the outpost's location is discovered and the Moclan women risk either being taken back to Moclus and forcibly converted or becoming sitting ducks in a brewing Krill war. As Heveena travels with *The Orville* to speak before the Union Council, she becomes curious about human female writers and, upon "access[ing] Earth's cultural database," discovers Dolly Parton's "9 to 5." "Who is she?" Heveena asks Ed, stating, "She speaks with the might of a hundred soldiers. [...] This is the voice of our revolution."

But there is yet another level, another projection, that occurs—that which relates to the ego-ideal, which "operates" on the ideal ego.[59] While Lacan borrows both terms from Freud, he develops them differently and distinguishes the two.[60] The ideal ego "represents the primary form of narcissistic investment proper to the unifying and captivating lure of the image of oneself (the *Gestalt* of the type)"[61] and "is a promise of future synthesis towards which the ego tends."[62] It is formed in the primary identifications between the Real and the Imaginary. However, since we are beings influenced by language and culture even before we are born, it also plays a role in secondary identifications between the Imaginary and the Symbolic.[63] When we look at ourselves "from that ideal point [...] that point of perfection," our "normal" lives seem "vain and useless."[64] A secondary investment then occurs "when civilisation and moral values force the individual to renounce his primary form of satisfaction in order to recover them later in an idealised and mediated form."[65] In other words, the ego-ideal "is the agency whose gaze I try to impress with my ego image, the big Other who watches over me and propels me to give my best, the ideal I try to follow and actualize."[66] In this way, the ego-ideal "leads us to moral growth and maturity" as we "betray the 'law of desire'" and internalize and interrogate the "socio-symbolic order."[67] Thus, the "ego-ideal is the subject's introjection of another external image that has a *new* (de)formative effect on [the] psyche."[68]

For Alara, this means she must grapple with conflicting legal and moral values when she learns that Ed and Kelly have been captured by a dangerous species, the Calivon, and a fleet admiral issues a direct order "to return to Earth" without them (S1E2). Gordon calls Alara "cold-blooded" for falling in line, and what she sees reflected in the crew's looks is "hate": "The entire crew hates me. I mean, can't they see that I'm just as upset about this as they are?" She deliberates whether to obey her Union superior's command or a more universal law and her duties to the lives of her crew. Gordon offers a (limited) argument regarding the latter: "You know what the most heinous thing about this is? If the captain were in your shoes, he would've gone after you. He would've risked his career to save your life. You suck. Sir." While Gordon does not consider the risks this would create for the ship as a whole, Claire's perspective does. She tells the acting captain that "the admiral's right. To put the entire ship in danger to rescue two officers who might not even be alive? No, he gave the proper order." When Alara replies, "So you don't think we should go either," Claire further clarifies the moral dilemma:

> I didn't say that. Alara, everything that you've dealt with, up until now, is child's play. This is command. You have a choice. Follow orders and accept that the crew will hate you for it, or disobey orders and go after our people. But, if you take that kind of risk and you're wrong, you could destroy your career. Or worse.

Similarly, Bortus, following his *Rudolp*h-inspired epiphany, questions his own culture's norms and the very definition of his species when he takes legal action against his mate in order to save his daughter from being "transitioned" (S1E3). At the Moclan tribunal, he asks Kelly to represent him (since "No advocate on Moclus would defend such a thing"), and through her, as well as other characters throughout the episode, he raises challenging perspectives about gender that are currently being debated in our own society: gender discrimination,[69] "disability" as difference or disease,[70] ethnocentrism,[71] cultural relativism,[72] moral absolutism,[73] contract theory,[74] harm,[75] and a child's right to an open future.[76] In "Sanctuary" (S2E12), Heveena likewise compels us to engage our own ideal egos and ego-ideals when she addresses the Union Council on behalf of the 6,000 female Moclans in the colony. She quotes lyrics from "9 to 5" as part of her impassioned plea:

> I stand here today as a voice for those who have been voiceless for so long. It is true that we have been living in exile, outside of the laws of our native planet, but to do otherwise would invite persecution, mutilation, and even extinction. [...] As I look upon all of the exquisite diversity in this great hall, I am reminded that most of us share something in common. Over the course of history, there have been people on nearly every planet who were, at one time or another, oppressed by those who were stronger or greater in numbers for reasons that now seem insignificant to us. The history of moral progress can be measured by the expansion of fundamental rights to those who have been denied them.[77]

Pop Culture's the Thing...

Though MacFarlane's use of pop culture may at first seem silly or merely to service a joke, such mirrors—like Hamlet's putting on a play to gather evidence of his uncle's actions—probe the conscience. Perhaps the best example of this from *The Orville* occurs in "Command Performance" (S1E2), in Ed and Kelly's storyline that interweaves with Alara's. While Alara is learning about leadership, her two commanders have been lured into a Calivon trap by false images of Ed's parents.[78] Ed and Kelly then awaken in their "old apartment, in New York City," which looks exactly like they remember it—save for a front door that's sealed. In this setting, they find their old clothes, reminisce about past activities and friends, and engage in the same habits that once annoyed one other.[79] In this way, they find themselves staring directly into a mirror and seeing a complete, but false, version of themselves. As we watch them, we, too, are first lulled into believing the image (since it looks just like scenes of their life from episode one, aptly titled "Old Wounds"). However, like all mirrors—which are more opaque than reflective—something exists behind it,[80] and in this case it's a Calivon zoo in which Ed and Kelly are the latest attraction. Once the newly added humans have grown accustomed to their enclosure, the Calivon break the false fourth wall, and *The Orville*'s officers watch a Calivon mother and child watch them. Ed and Kelly thus recognize that the egos they were encountering are imaginary and "other," and—in flipping Lacan on his head—the show's main protagonists resemble more the animal species the Calivon have deemed them and are no longer captivated by their own reflections. This is, in part, MacFarlane's point: The Calivon believe themselves to be the universe's apex predator, with all other beings there for their pleasure. In seeing herself through the eyes of these aliens, Kelly reflects, and forces us to as well: "It's not that weird. There was a time where humans imprisoned animals for entertainment. It wasn't intended to be cruel. We just felt, as the higher species, we had the right," to which Ed yells, "We are not your Shamu!" As with any narrative, in order to make sense of events, we place ourselves in a protagonist's place, and we experience an image of ourselves in such a position. Thus, we see ourselves differently and are morally implicated when Ed comments that humans stopped keeping zoos "hundreds of years ago" (though we haven't) "so you tell me who's more advanced." In this double mirror, the unreal humans (fictional characters) see real humans (viewers watching the show) as Calivon-esque aliens.

The more "MacFarlanized" aspect of the episode, however, is how Alara comes to Ed and Kelly's rescue. In order to gain access to the zookeeper, she and Isaac use the Calivon's own technology against them to "make it appear as though [the U.S.S. *Orville* is] a Calivon ship," thus hiding its real nature behind a holographic screen. Once the ruse works, however, and Isaac and Alara are behind enemy lines, the zookeeper refuses to negotiate, and when Alara changes tactics and claims that Ed and Kelly have a deadly disease, he initiates a "euthanasia sweep" per the institution's "strict non-contaminant policy" in the name of public health. Caught between a rock and a hard place, Alara extends one last offer—a database of reality television shows—and the episode draws to an end as we (re)watch the infamous-but-iconic *Real Housewives of New Jersey* "table flip" scene that epitomizes the "simultaneously overly personal and overly public," as well as overly self-indulgent, "docudrama" of what Alan Nadel calls a "networked" post-postmodern human unconscious.[81] While there may be a voyeuristic pleasure in such reality TV, as we engage in a *Schadenfreude* that fails to recognize ourselves in and/or thinks ourselves superior to the twisted faces of the housewives or the Calivon drooling over the "best exhibit [they've] ever had," MacFarlane aims to catch our conscience and get us to see that this may not reflect the selves we wish to be. In liberating Ed and Kelly, we liberate ourselves: Like the crew of *The Orville*, we can distance ourselves from such mirrors and literally leave them behind.

Reflections on/of The Orville

While MacFarlane has moved away from the more sophomoric in the second season of *The Orville* (although, cf., the juvenile, *Ted*-like language and behavior of the "booger-esque" Yaphit), the show itself remains a pop-cultural mirror. In its look and feel—from the title sequence and commercial fades to the set design and costumes—it summons forth *Star Trek*; and it's not the updated sequels or even more recent prequel *Star Trek*, but the *Star Trek* of MacFarlane's youth: *Star Trek: The Next Generation* (and reruns of the original, 1960s *Star Trek* series).[82] This reincarnation of media influences from his own past undergirds his pop-culture M.O.: *Family Guy* embraces aspects from *The Honeymooners* to *The Simpsons*; MacFarlane doesn't just emulate Sinatra on his albums but uses the very same microphone[83]; and the *Cosmos* of this century has an uncanny resemblance to that of the one before. By some, MacFarlane's creations have been called derivative.

When seen through the lens of Lacan, however, derivative becomes something more. The messages embedded in the 1939 classic "Rudolph the Red-Nosed Reindeer" may seem unsophisticated and passé, but Bortus' (and, therefore, our) viewing (or more likely reviewing) of it brings him (and us) closer to Lacan's *objet (petit) a*, that semblance of subjective being found in the Borromean knot where the Imaginary, Symbolic, and Real intersect. While Rudolph deviates from his species' norm through an *addition* of a red, glowing nose, Bortus' child does so through a *lack*—a lack of "maleness" (clearly, when discussing Freud, Lacan, or MacFarlane, some kind of penis). But in recognizing that (bodily) difference is okay—"Christmas would have been ruined if Rudolph had been euthanized at birth, as his father wished" and "What was clearly a deformity became a supreme advantage. One can never know"—what emerges (for Bortus' child, for Bortus, and for us) is a "lack of lack." Unfortunately, despite his own transformation and legal efforts, the tribunal rules against Bortus, the female child becomes an un-castrated boy, and the Moclan patriarchy remains unsubverted, in ways like our own.

A child of the postmodern, MacFarlane's work is both parody and pastiche but also mimicry, recreating images from the past and never letting us forget we are watching (his) TV. In watching him watch himself (for example, tittering at his own jokes at the Oscars), we become like Ed and Kelly attempting to find and better ourselves beyond the false world of the zoo. MacFarlane's use of pop culture creates a "unifying exchange of gazes that relentlessly shift one's perspective" and engages us in "the problem of situating oneself in relation to those shifting gazes."[84] Whether in *The Orville*, *Family Guy*, or MacFarlane's other shows, Lacan's concepts are on display: "the play of absence, the circulation of desire, [and] the relationship of subjectivity to the field of vision."[85] What "man-boy" MacFarlane sees of himself in these mirrors—his hedonistic characters or a subversive satire—remains hidden by the screen. His use of "9 to 5" in "Sanctuary" (S2E12) may provide clues but no conclusive answer. Referencing the song also references the 1980 film, a screwball comedy starring Dolly Parton, Jane Fonda, and Lily Tomlin that raised feminist ideals in a MacFarlane-esque way: not too dark, deliberately lightweight, and a little inane. Roger Ebert, who hailed *Ted* as akin to genius, called *9 to 5* "only a fairly successful comedy," but "liked it, despite its uneven qualities and a plot that's almost too preposterous for the material."[86] If one views "Sanctuary" in relation to a *Family Guy* episode where Peter pushes his potentially pregnant wife down the stairs,[87] one might suggest that MacFarlane is making fun of Parton in *The Orville* by calling her a revolutionary "poet," giggling, like Larry, at the inherent "boob jokes" she inspires.[88] Parton, however, is an iconic image from MacFarlane's past and the "perfect messenger" for MacFarlane's main audience: pretty, petite, talented, and apolitical. She is, then and now, revered by the gay community and religious conservatives alike, and she never shies away from a "boob joke" of her own.[89] If MacFarlane had employed a more serious form of feminism (say, Betty Friedan and *The Feminine Mystique*), "Sanctuary" might smack as "too preachy," and his mass viewers would fail to see themselves in this reflection and simply tune out. Reaching for the "breast" expresses a(n albeit immature) desire for seeking the "lack of lack." That said, MacFarlane's reliance on the derivative and flippant risks fogging up the mirror and destabilizing his Symbolic messages and messengers. Other shows have succeeded in engaging such self-reflection with a less sophomoric, more innovative approach (e.g., *Black Mirror* or the new *Twilight Zone*). Whether MacFarlane's *The Orville* rides this "edge" of edgy just right only time will tell.

Notes

1. Jacques Lacan, *The Seminar of Jacques Lacan: Book II, The Ego in Freud's Theory and in the Technique of Psychoanalysis, 1954–1955*, ed. Jacques-Alain Miller, trans. Sylvana Tomaselli (Cambridge: Cambridge University Press, 1988), 49.

2. One common critique of *The Orville* is that its pop-culture references, including the music the crew sing on karaoke night in "Cupid's Dagger" (S1E9), date back to the twentieth and twenty-first centuries. It seems that, in the universe of *The Orville*, the twenty-fifth century has no pop culture of its own. While it's true that this makes the show somewhat less realistic—space explorers in the twenty-fifth century will not know cultural references from the twenty-first—MacFarlane does have a decent explanation for his approach here. "It's hard. Cultural things are really hard to depict in science fiction without looking silly or looking dated. [...] Technology is easy; the uniforms are easy; the ships are easy. But people ask me all the time, 'How come the music they listen to—how come the pop culture is always of our time?' I always have to say, 'Have you ever heard future music in sci-fi that doesn't sound so fucking stupid? [...] There's no way. You can't predict it. If I could predict that I'd be a billionaire in the music industry. We're not there to do that job; that's for the futurists." Sean Carroll, hosts, "Seth MacFarlane on Using Science Fiction to Explore Humanity," *Mindscape* (podcast), August 5, 2019, https://www.preposterousuniverse.com/podcast/2019/08/05/58-seth-macfarlane-on-using-science-fiction-to-explore-humanity/.

3. Dylan Evans, *An Introductory Dictionary of Lacanian Psychoanalysis* (London: Routledge, 1996), 159.

4. Lorenzo Chiesa, *Subjectivity and Otherness: A Philosophical Reading of Lacan* (Cambridge, MA: MIT Press, 2007), 126.

5. Jacques Lacan, *Écrits*, trans. Bruce Fink (New York: W.W. Norton & Company, 2006). The Real is "that which resists representation, what is pre-mirror, pre-imaginary, pre-symbolic—what cannot be symbolized" and a place "where words fail." Amanda Loos, "Symbolic, Real, Imaginary," University of Chicago, Winter 2002, https://csmt.uchicago.edu/glossary2004/symbolicrealimaginary.htm, para. 11. Lacan's register of the Real may be equated with Kant's *Wirklichkeit* (irreducible reality) or Heidegger's *Dasein* ("being there").

6. Lacan, *The Seminar: Book IV, The Object Relation and Freudian Structures, 1956–1957*, cited in Chiesa, *Subjectivity and Otherness*, 127.

7. Slavoj Žižek, *In Defense of Lost Causes* (London: Verso, 2009), 89.

8. Lacan cited in Evans, *An Introductory Dictionary*, 125.

9. T.S. Eliot, *Four Quartets* (Orlando: Harcourt Books, 1971), 59. Eliot's poem "Little Gidding" may be particularly apt in relation to Lacan and his description of our never-ending but impossible-to-achieve desire to see (what doesn't exist) behind the mirror: "We shall not cease from exploration / And the end of our exploring / Will be to arrive where we started / And know the place for the first time."

10. Claire Hoffman, "No. 1 Offender: Seth MacFarlane Has Success. Can He Now Get Respect?" *The New Yorker*, June 18, 2012, https://www.newyorker.com/magazine/2012/06/18/no-1-offender, para. 29.

11. Ibid., para. 27.

12. See, for example, Snierson, Dan, "*Simpsons* and *Family Guy* Creators Matt Groening and Seth MacFarlane Talk Crossover Episode, Movies, Rivalry," *Entertainment Weekly*, September 27, 2014, https://ew.com/article/2014/09/27/matt-groening-seth-macfarlane-simpsons-family-guy-crossover/, and Lacy Rose, "Seth MacFarlane: The Restless Mind of a Complicated Cartoonist," *Hollywood Reporter*, October 12, 2011, https://www.hollywoodreporter.com/news/seth-macfarlane-cartoonist-246805.

13. MacFarlane in *The Life of Larry* cited in Hoffman, "No. 1 Offender," para. 27.

14. The character of Larry from *The Life of Larry* cited in Hoffman, "No. 1 Offender," para. 28.

15. Hoffman, "No. 1 Offender," para. 11.

16. Ibid., para. 2. See also Amy Zimmerman, "Juvenile Misogynist Seth MacFarlane Is Not Funny," *Daily Beast*, June 3, 2014, https://www.thedailybeast.com/juvenile-misogynist-seth-macfarlane-is-not-funny, para. 5.

17. Hoffman, "No. 1 Offender."

18. Daryl Deino, "Seth MacFarlane Outdoes Career-Starter *Family Guy* with *American Dad!*," *Observer*, June 7, 2017, https://observer.com/2017/06/seth-macfarlane-american-dad-family-guy/.

19. Jonathan Bernstein, "*Ted* Stars Mila Kunis and Seth MacFarlane v the *Guardian*,"

240   Act V: The Funny and the Final Flyout

The Guardian, July 27, 2012, https://www.theguardian.com/film/2012/jul/28/ted-seth-macfarlane-mila-kunis, para. 1.

20. Nick Schager, "Hating Seth MacFarlane: A Timeline," *Rolling Stone*, June 29, 2015, https://www.rollingstone.com/movies/movie-news/hating-seth-macfarlane-a-timeline-60469/, para. 18.

21. Matt Barone, "It's Nothing Personal, Seth: Our Resident *Family Guy* Apologist Skewers Seth MacFarlane's *A Million Ways to Die in the West*," *Complex*, May 30, 2014, https://www.complex.com/pop-culture/2014/05/a-million-ways-to-die-in-the-west-review.

22. Roger Ebert, "*Ted*," June 27, 2012, https://www.rogerebert.com/reviews/ted-2012, paras. 1, 8, 10.

23. Bernstein, "*Ted* Stars Mila Kunis and Seth MacFarlane," para. 3.

24. MacFarlane cited in Bernstein, "*Ted* Stars Mila Kunis and Seth MacFarlane," para. 3.

25. Ken Tucker, "*Family Guy*," *Entertainment Weekly*, April 9, 1999, https://ew.com/article/1999/04/09/family-guy-2/, para. 8.

26. Barone, "It's Nothing Personal, Seth," para. 8. Barone, an admitted "longtime *Family Guy* lover" (para. 6) and a fan of "effective poop jokes" (para. 4), found this film full of "cheap laughs" (para. 12) such as "having a well-endowed sheep piss on MacFarlane's face, or an old man describing one of his farts with, 'Ow, that came out of my penis!' Or the labored scene where Albert [MacFarlane's character] explains a joke involving a mustached man performing cunnilingus. Or Sarah Silverman playing a prostitute who talks to her virginal boyfriend about the delicateness of their 'first time' while there's ejaculate on her cheek. Or Neil Patrick Harris crapping into someone's top hat. Or … you get the idea" (paras. 12–13).

27. Amy Zimmerman, "Juvenile Misogynist Seth MacFarlane Is Not Funny," *Daily Beast*, June 3, 2014, https://www.thedailybeast.com/juvenile-misogynist-seth-macfarlane-is-not-funny, paras. 4–6.

28. Chris Nashawaty, "*Ted 2*: EW Review," *Entertainment Weekly*, June 24, 2015, https://ew.com/article/2015/06/24/ted-2-ew-review/, para. 1.

29. David Bauder, "William Shatner Can't Save Seth MacFarlane at Oscars," *The Christian Science Monitor*, February 25, 2013, https://www.csmonitor.com/The-Culture/Latest-News-Wires/2013/0225/William-Shatner-can-t-save-Seth-MacFarlane-at-Oscars, para. 5.

30. Amy Davidson Sorkin, "Seth MacFarlane and the Oscars' Hostile, Ugly, Sexist Night," *The New Yorker*, February 25, 2013, https://www.newyorker.com/news/amy-davidson/seth-macfarlane-and-the-oscars-hostile-ugly-sexist-night.

31. Pete Hammond, "Oscars: Debate Still Rages About Seth MacFarlane—Is There a Double Standard at Play?," *Deadline*, February 28, 2013, https://deadline.com/2013/02/oscars-debate-still-rages-about-seth-macfarlane-is-there-a-double-standard-at-play-442879/, para. 2, emphasis original.

32. Victoria A. Brownworth, "Seth MacFarlane Isn't the Problem," *Advocate*, February 28, 2013, https://www.advocate.com/commentary/2013/02/28/op-ed-seth-macfarlane-isnt-problem, para. 11.

33. Deaths from HIV/AIDS in the United States peaked in 1995. Kashmira Gander, "Hispanic and Latino People in the U.S. Are Struggling with 'Invisible' HIV Crisis," *Newsweek*, November 29, 2019, https://www.newsweek.com/hispanic-latino-people-u-s-struggling-invisible-hiv-crisis-1474699.

34. MacFarlane explains his state of mind at RISD: "I wasn't out to communicate deep-rooted pain, mainly because I didn't really have any. It was always just the self-imposed goal to reach a certain professional level." Hoffman, "No. 1 Offender," para. 26.

35. One reason why he was selected to host the Oscars is that "his humor is definitely geared to the demographic the Academy has been desperate to reach: the under-40 set." Brownworth, "Seth MacFarlane Isn't the Problem," para. 4.

36. Peter Weber, "Oscars 2013: Was Host Seth MacFarlane a Self-Indulgent Flop?," *The Week*, February 25, 2013, https://theweek.com/articles/467731/oscars-2013-host-seth-macfarlane-selfindulgent-flop, para. 1.

37. It is thanks to a donation by MacFarlane that Carl Sagan's papers are now archived in the Library of Congress, and he was an executive producer for the 2014 version of *Cosmos*. Helena Andrews and Emily Heil, "Science Geek Seth MacFarlane Donates to Carl Sagan's

Notes Collection," *The Washington Post*, November 12, 2013, https://www.washingtonpost.com/news/reliable-source/wp/2013/11/12/science-geek-seth-macfarlane-donates-to-carl-sagans-notes-collection/?arc404=true, para. 3.
    38. Brownworth, "Seth MacFarlane Isn't the Problem," para. 4.
    39. Hoffman, "No. 1 Offender," para. 54.
    40. Over a career spanning five decades, Lacan further developed and modified these constructs, whose complexity cannot be conveyed in one article. While risking a misunderstanding of nuances, simplified definitions are used here in an effort to make Lacan's formative ideas and Lacan himself as understandable as possible.
    41. Pietro Bianchi, *Jacques Lacan and Cinema: Imaginary, Gaze, Formalisation* (New York: Routledge, 2018), 3.
    42. Evans, *An Introductory Dictionary*, 26.
    43. Bianchi, *Jacques Lacan and Cinema*, 8.
    44. Lacan, *Écrits*, 76, 80.
    45. Bianchi, *Jacques Lacan and Cinema*, 7.
    46. Vicki Daiello, Kevin Hathaway, Mindi Rhoades, and Sydney Walker, "Complicating Visual Culture," *Studies in Art Education* 47, no. 4 (Summer 2006): 308–325, 313.
    47. Lacan, *Écrits*, 76.
    48. Daiello et al., "Complicating Visual Culture," 313.
    49. Bianchi, *Jacques Lacan and Cinema*, 7. See also Daiello et al., "Complicating Visual Culture," and Chiesa, *Subjectivity and Otherness*, 30, who emphasizes: "Imaginary alienation, originally determined by prematurity of birth, never ends."
    50. "Lacan argues that the human being is always already 'disadapted' to the culture that makes it human—as a subject who speaks—and that forms of psychoanalysis that do aim to adapt this subject to society have betrayed the questioning that the practice is predicated upon." Ian Parker, *Lacanian Psychoanalysis: Revolutions in Subjectivity* (London: Routledge, 2011), 35–36. See also Chiesa, *Subjectivity and Otherness*, 17, who states that Lacan never wavered from his definition of man as "a disadapted animal" and critiqued Charles Darwin for his pro-adaptation view. Quoting Lacan's *The Seminar: Book VII*: "Human beings' astounding psychic development and the emergence of language and culture that made it possible are far from being the result of a particularly successful adaptation of the species: on the contrary, 'man's relation to nature is altered by a certain dehiscence at the heart of the organism.'"
    51. "Lacan uses the term '*captation*' to describe this process." Chiesa, *Subjectivity and Otherness*, 15.
    52. Chiesa, *Subjectivity and Otherness*, 13.
    53. Evans, *An Introductory Dictionary*, 26.
    54. Chiesa, *Subjectivity and Otherness*, 15–17, emphasis original.
    55. Ibid., 23.
    56. Ibid., 22.
    57. "Chief, unless we know where the captain and the commander were taken, there'll be nowhere to go" (S1E2).
    58. Evans, *An Introductory Dictionary*, 84.
    59. Bianchi, *Jacques Lacan and Cinema*, 20.
    60. Ibid.
    61. Ibid.
    62. Evans, *An Introductory Dictionary*, 53.
    63. Ibid., 52.
    64. Dino Fanco Felluga, *Critical Theory: The Key Concepts* (London: Routledge, 2015), 142.
    65. Bianchi, *Jacques Lacan and Cinema*, 20.
    66. Slavoj Žižek, *In Defense of Lost Causes*, 89.
    67. Ibid.
    68. Chiesa, *Subjectivity and Otherness*, 22, *emphasis original*.
    69. Ed: "Moclans view the female gender as a handicap."
    70. Ed: "Being a girl is not a condition. There are no health risks."
    71. Ed: "[I]imagine that baby was born with a third leg. [...] And we had the doctor

remove it. Now, no one would think twice about that, right? Even though there are species in the galaxy with three legs, we would be conforming that child to our species' appearance, and we wouldn't have any moral qualms about it. [...Whether gender change is morally equivalent], I'm just policing myself, because we all know how easy it is to judge another culture's way of life just because it's alien to us."

72. Bortus: "It is different for my people. On our planet, there are no females. For you to judge us by human standards is unfair."

73. Kelly: "But you have to balance that against some universal code of ethics. I mean, suppose it was their custom to kill all newborn females. Should we respect their culture then?"

74. Ed: "All right, look, even if I was not against this, we are on a Union ship. And, for that matter, your planet is a member of the Union. For me to order Claire to do something like this would be in violation of a hundred laws."

75. Kelly explains, "There are different kinds of harm," when Isaac asks, "Captain, I do not understand the reason for this conflict. Would the gender alteration procedure harm the infant or endanger her life?"

76. Ed asks: "Why not just let the kid decide for herself when she's old enough?" See Joel Feinberg, "The Child's Right to an Open Future," in *Whose Child? Children's Rights, Parental Authority, and State Power*, ed. William Aiken and Hugh LaFollette (Totowa, NJ: Rowman & Littlefield, 1980), 124–153.

77. Heveena continues: "There is a visionary Earth poet who I have recently come to cherish. [...] With power and dignity, she boldly cried out so that all the cosmos would know of her suffering. 'Working 9 to 5, for service and devotion / You would think that I would deserve a fat promotion / Want to move ahead but the boss won't seem to let me / I swear sometimes that man is out to get me.' In the spirit of her courage, please hear our voices."

78. The "captain" of the "Union" ship in distress tells Ed "it so happens we're carrying two passengers whom you know," and the lifelike doppelgängers of his parents are so convincing, Ed says of their creator, "It even knew to make my dad talk about his colon. That's an advanced technology."

79. Ed: "Do you want to not do that, please? [...] You know I do not like listening to people eat cereal."

80. Joan Copjec, "The Orthopsychic Subject: Film Theory and the Reception of Lacan," *October* 49 (Summer 1989): 53–71.

81. Alan Nadel, "From the Industrial Unconscious to the Cinematic to the Televisual to the Networked," *Arizona Quarterly: A Journal of American Literature, Culture, and Theory* 75, no. 2 (Summer 2019): 26–36, 31.

82. In fact, a new rumor has emerged (on the less-than-reliable 4Chan) that MacFarlane is attempting to purchase the rights to the *Star Trek* franchise. John F. Trent, "New Rumor Details The Orville Creator Seth MacFarlane's Plans If He Acquires Star Trek," *Bounding Into Comics*, February 4, 2020, https://boundingintocomics.com/2020/02/04/new-rumor-details-the-orville-creator-seth-macfarlanes-plans-if-he-acquires-star-trek/.

83. Rose, "Seth MacFarlane," para. 31. It would seem that the only reason to rely on such old equipment in today's high-tech age would relate to ego.

84. Nadel, "From the Industrial Unconscious," 28.

85. *Ibid.*, 27.

86. Roger Ebert, "*Nine to Five*," December 19, 1980, https://www.rogerebert.com/reviews/nine-to-five-1980, paras. 3–4.

87. This occurs in the season two episode "Da Boom." Amy Zimmerman states that the "whole gag is over in a matter of seconds; this 'joke' isn't a subtle critique of the way we talk about assault, or a daring attack on political correctness," and quotes Rebecca Loar's perspective that "[a]ll we really learn from *Family Guy* is that images of violence towards and subjugation of women are good for a quick laugh. The images tend to be followed by an equally non-contextual eighties reference and nothing more is said. In short, the motif of the show does not serve to 'controversialize' these images but to normalize them." Zimmerman, "Juvenile Misogynist," para. 7.

88. Calling watching her a "pleasure," Ebert adds: "I had better say that I'm not referring to her sex appeal or chest measurements." Ebert, "*Nine to Five*," para. 3.

89. Parton is "reluctant to make the slightest hint of a political statement" when in the public view and often reverts to a standard response "when some interviews have gotten too political or contentious: She pull[s] from her trusted arsenal of boob jokes." Lindsay Zoladz, "Is There Anything We Can All Agree On? Yes, Dolly Parton," *New York Times*, November 21, 2019, https://www.nytimes.com/2019/11/21/arts/music/dolly-parton.html, para. 6 and 8.

BIBLIOGRAPHY

Andrews, Helena, and Emily Heil. "Science Geek Seth Macfarlane Donates to Carl Sagan's Notes Collection." *The Washington Post*, November 12, 2013. https://www.washingtonpost.com/news/reliable-source/wp/2013/11/12/science-geek-seth-macfarlane-donates-to-carl-sagans-notes-collection/?arc404=true.
Badiou, Alain, and Élisabeth Roudinesco. *Jacques Lacan, Past and Present: A Dialogue*. Translated by Jason E. Smith. New York: Columbia University Press, 2014.
Barone, Matt. "It's Nothing Personal, Seth: Our Resident *Family Guy* Apologist Skewers Seth MacFarlane's *A Million Ways to Die in the West*." *Complex*, May 30, 2014. https://www.complex.com/pop-culture/2014/05/a-million-ways-to-die-in-the-west-review.
Bauder, David. "William Shatner Can't Save Seth MacFarlane at Oscars." *The Christian Science Monitor*, February 25, 2013. https://www.csmonitor.com/The-Culture/Latest-News-Wires/2013/0225/William-Shatner-can-t-save-Seth-MacFarlane-at-Oscars.
Bernstein, Jonathan. "*Ted* Stars Mila Kunis and Seth MacFarlane v the *Guardian*." *The Guardian*, July 27, 2012. https://www.theguardian.com/film/2012/jul/28/ted-seth-macfarlane-mila-kunis.
Bianchi, Pietro. *Jacques Lacan and Cinema: Imaginary, Gaze, Formalisation*. New York: Routledge, 2018.
Brownworth, Victoria A. "Seth MacFarlane Isn't the Problem." *Advocate*, February 28, 2013. https://www.advocate.com/commentary/2013/02/28/op-ed-seth-macfarlane-isnt-problem.
Chiesa, Lorenzo. *Subjectivity and Otherness: A Philosophical Reading of Lacan*. Cambridge, MA: The MIT Press, 2007.
Copjec, Joan. "The Orthopsychic Subject: Film Theory and the Reception of Lacan." *October* 49 (Summer 1989): 53–71.
Daiello, Vicki, Kevin Hathaway, Mindi Rhoades, and Sydney Walker. "Complicating Visual Culture." *Studies in Art Education* 47, no. 4 (Summer 2006): 308–325.
Deino, Daryl. "Seth MacFarlane Outdoes Career-Starter *Family Guy* with *American Dad!*" *Observer*, June 7, 2017. https://observer.com/2017/06/seth-macfarlane-american-dad-family-guy/.
Ebert, Roger. "*Nine to Five*." December 19, 1980. https://www.rogerebert.com/reviews/nine-to-five-1980.
Ebert, Roger. "*Ted*." June 27, 2012. https://www.rogerebert.com/reviews/ted-2012.
Eliot, T.S. *Four Quartets*. Orlando: Harcourt Books, 1971.
Evans, Dylan. *An Introductory Dictionary of Lacanian Psychoanalysis*. London: Routledge, 1996.
Feinberg, Joel. "The Child's Right to an Open Future." In *Whose Child? Children's Rights, Parental Authority, and State Power*. Edited by William Aiken and Hugh LaFollette, 124–153. Totowa, NJ: Rowman & Littlefield, 1980.
Felluga, Dino Fanco. *Critical Theory: The Key Concepts*. London: Routledge, 2015.
Gander, Kashmira. "Hispanic and Latino People in the U.S. Are Struggling with 'Invisible' HIV Crisis." *Newsweek*, November 29, 2019. https://www.newsweek.com/hispanic-latino-people-u-s-struggling-invisible-hiv-crisis-1474509.
Grosz, Elizabeth. *Jacques Lacan: A Feminist Introduction*. London: Routledge, 1990.
Hammond, Pete. "Oscars: Debate Still Rages About Seth MacFarlane—Is There a Double Standard at Play?" *Deadline*, February 28, 2013. https://deadline.com/2013/02/oscars-debate-still-rages-about-seth-macfarlane-is-there-a-double-standard-at-play-442879/.
Hediger, Vinzenz. "Can We Have the Cave and Leave It Too? On the Meaning of Cinema as

Technology." In *Technology and Film Scholarship: Experience, Study, Theory*, edited by Santiago Hidalgo, 213–238. Amsterdam: Amsterdam University Press, 2018.

Hoffman, Claire. "No. 1 Offender: Seth MacFarlane Has Success. Can He Now Get Respect?" *The New Yorker*, June 18, 2012: 38–43. https://www.newyorker.com/magazine/2012/06/18/no-1-offender.

Lacan, Jacques. *Écrits*. Translated by Bruce Fink. New York: W.W. Norton & Company, 2006.

Lacan, Jacques. *The Seminar of Jacques Lacan: Book II, the Ego in Freud's Theory and in the Technique of Psychoanalysis, 1954–1955*. Edited by Jacques-Alain Miller. Translated by Sylvana Tomaselli. Cambridge: Cambridge University Press, 1988.

Loos, Amanda. "Symbolic, Real, Imaginary." *The University of Chicago*, Winter 2002. https://csmt.uchicago.edu/glossary2004/symbolicrealimaginary.htm.

Nadel, Alan. "From the Industrial Unconscious to the Cinematic to the Televisual to the Networked." *Arizona Quarterly: A Journal of American Literature, Culture, and Theory* 75, no. 2 (Summer 2019): 26–36. https://doi.org/10.1353/arq.2019.0010.

Nashawaty, Chris. "*Ted 2*: EW Review." *Entertainment Weekly*, June 24, 2015. https://ew.com/article/2015/06/24/ted-2-ew-review/.

Parker, Ian. *Lacanian Psychoanalysis: Revolutions in Subjectivity*. London: Routledge, 2011.

Rose, Lacy. "Seth MacFarlane: The Restless Mind of a Complicated Cartoonist." *Hollywood Reporter*, October 12, 2011. https://www.hollywoodreporter.com/news/seth-macfarlane-cartoonist-246805.

Schager, Nick. "Hating Seth MacFarlane: A Timeline." *Rolling Stone*, June 29, 2015. https://www.rollingstone.com/movies/movie-news/hating-seth-macfarlane-a-timeline-60469/.

Snierson, Dan. "*Simpsons* and *Family Guy* Creators Matt Groening and Seth MacFarlane Talk Crossover Episode, Movies, Rivalry." *Entertainment Weekly*, September 27, 2014. https://ew.com/article/2014/09/27/matt-groening-seth-macfarlane-simpsons-family-guy-crossover/.

Sorkin, Amy Davidson. "Seth MacFarlane and the Oscars' Hostile, Ugly, Sexist Night." *The New Yorker*, February 25, 2013. https://www.newyorker.com/news/amy-davidson/seth-macfarlane-and-the-oscars-hostile-ugly-sexist-night.

Trent, John F. "New Rumor Details *The Orville* Creator Seth MacFarlane's Plans If He Acquires *Star Trek*." *Bounding Into Comics*, February 4, 2020. https://boundingintocomics.com/2020/02/04/new-rumor-details-the-orville-creator-seth-macfarlanes-plans-if-he-acquires-star-trek/.

Tucker, Ken. "Family Guy." *Entertainment Weekly*, April 9, 1999. https://ew.com/article/1999/04/09/family-guy-2/.

Weber, Peter. "Oscars 2013: Was Host Seth MacFarlane a Self-Indulgent Flop?" *The Week*, February 25, 2013. https://theweek.com/articles/467331/oscars-2013-host-seth-macfarlane-selfindulgent-flop.

Zimmerman, Amy. "Juvenile Misogynist Seth MacFarlane Is Not Funny." *Daily Beast*, June 3, 2014. https://www.thedailybeast.com/juvenile-misogynist-seth-macfarlane-is-not-funny.

Žižek, Slavoj. *In Defense of Lost Causes*. London: Verso, 2009.

Zoladz, Lindsay. "Is There Anything We Can All Agree On? Yes, Dolly Parton." *The New York Times*, November 21, 2019. https://www.nytimes.com/2019/11/21/arts/music/dolly-parton.html.

Thinking About Bad Taste in a Funny Way

Christopher M. Innes

Watching *The Orville* is like taking part in an historic and aesthetic comedy experience. As Seth MacFarlane put it before the show aired, *The Orville* is "an hour long sci-fi comedic drama [that] straddle(s) a line between comedy and legitimate fiction."[1] It's also like a post–Second World War comedy grappling with what should not be said by saying it. Many critics lambasted it for just being (like *Family Guy*) direct low brow humor.[2] Yet others said that it matured into serious science fiction, which could appeal to those with intellectually provocative highbrow tastes.[3] So which is it? Is *The Orville* lowbrow or highbrow? To answer this, we are going to explore both kinds of comedy, and how *The Orville* is part of a tradition that straddles lowbrow and highbrow comedy that's been alive for about a century.

Along our journey, we are going to use philosopher Mark Hopkins' aesthetic analysis as a method for determining what is highbrow and lowbrow comedy, and whether one is morally superior to the other. We will look at MacFarlane's childhood and how it influenced his comedy, see good taste in art with a visit to the USS *Orville* by the Union Symphony Orchestra, and good taste in comedy with Ed and Kelly's well-timed comedy routines. In comparison, we'll also see a lot of crude comedy that tests the limits—like Lt. Malloy, the king of crude comedy, and his barbing of Bortus about his yearly Moclan urination ceremony in "Ja'loja."

Ed: Bortus, if you need any time off to make preparations, feel free to relieve yourself.
Gordon: (Snicker) Nah, it's okay man. He's just taking the piss out of you [S2E1].

And if we do in fact find out that *The Orville* is lowbrow comedy, we're going to ask whether that really matters. As we'll see, by using Edward J.

Fink's comic theory analysis, there might not be any real difference between lowbrow and highbrow after all.

Our exploration might be a bit dangerous, however. MacFarlane's comedy is devilishly enticing and likely to corrupt us. Indeed, the Office Manager of my Philosophy Department once said that Seth MacFarlane's cheeky face could use a little slap after he smirkingly makes fun of, well, everything. But maybe we won't want to slap his face if we discover that *The Orville*'s comedy is just doing what all comedy is supposed to do: push the limits of acceptability.

Humorless Hopkins

To find out if the *Orville*'s comedy is lowbrow and morally inferior, let us first look at Mark Hopkins' esthetical analysis. He was not a funny philosopher and he may never have told a single joke. He was President of Williams College in Massachusetts from 1836 to 1872, and his Christian ethic shaped his view of aesthetics so much that he argued that a person's aesthetic outlook is so influenced by their moral outlook that "good taste and good morals"[4] are linked. One therefore imagines that he only liked highbrow comedy and was a very moral man; indeed, being funny was probably not something that mattered to him.

Now, when Hopkins made this statement about taste and morals, he was not talking about comedy as such. But his analysis will still help us in our investigation because it raises the question we need to ask: if good taste and morals are linked, will lowbrow comedy corrupt the morals of the individual delivering or receiving it? Does laughing at, or making, a lowbrow joke make you a bad person?

To help answer this question, Hopkins conducted a limited survey of three educated individuals regarding what they thought about the connection between morals and aesthetics. One individual said they had initially not given it much thought, but came to think that there was no connection. Another said they would need proof. The third thought there was a connection. Obviously, this survey was not very helpful. So perhaps we can take a different approach.

Hopkins defined taste as "…that faculty of the human mind by which we perceive and enjoy whatever is beautiful or sublime in the natural works of nature or art."[5] This leads us to ask three questions: How do we compare different people's perceptions of the beautiful? What are the causes of lowbrow and highbrow perceptions? And how do we cultivate a person's perception of the beautiful? So let's address each question in turn, to see if we can make any progress.

How Do We Compare Different People's Perceptions of the Beautiful?

Consider the scene where Capt. Mercer and Commander Grayson talked about their reluctant trip to the opera.

> **Ed:** Do you remember that time that Jeff and Maureen invited us to the opera? ... And you knew I hated opera, so you made me smoke that joint before we left.
> **Kelly:** I'm so sorry, that was supposed to be mine. I gave you the wrong one.
> **Ed:** Your weapons-grade weed [S1E2].

This is a reference to high art, but by rejecting the opera Ed is not saying that it is not important. He (and Kelly) are just not fans of the opera. The individual has the capacity to spot the beautiful or sublime in the external world and then develop an emotional attachment in the mind.

We might salvage something from their aesthetic tastes by their wonderment of the two-dimensional world in "New Dimension." Here Commander Grayson in particular is in awe of what looks like a multicolored neon lit computer board. Now Hopkins would have likely pointed out that there is no emotion in external beautiful objects themselves; Commander Grayson is the one with the emotional attachment. But the fact that individuals have different emotional reactions to objects reminds us that objects are perceived differently by people, and that there is no universally agreed upon notion of beauty. How each person perceives the two-dimensional world is likely to vary, even if it is just as much of an awe-inspiring experience for each.

What Are the Causes of Lowbrow and Highbrow Perceptions?

When it comes to humor, according to Hopkins, what causes people's refined or not so refined perception is their level of experience and education in beauty and taste. As prime examples of people who lack esthetic sophistication, consider John (Lt. LaMarr) and Gordon (Lt. Malloy). The USS *Orville* has many fine social gatherings that have a potential for calm social interaction and polite conversation—like the send-off the crew gives Chief Engineer Steve Newton in "New Dimensions." But when Malloy and LaMarr steal a piece of Yaphit (the gelatinous being hilariously voiced by Norm Macdonald), and throw it in the buffet, Newton's send-off party takes a less than sophisticated turn. It ends up in Bortus's cake. And while Bortus is known for having an iron stomach (he can eat glass, for example), the piece of Yaphit does not sit well—and Yaphit has to go in and get it, by ... uh ... reaching into Bortus's mouth and extending himself through Bortus' digestive tract.

A prime example of someone with experience and education, with her love of literature and art, is Dr. Finn; and she is definitely not amused. "This is more weirdness than I can handle in one day," she says after watching Yaphit retrieve the piece. Kelly displays a similar dissatisfaction.

Kelly: At any point, did you consider the possibility that what you were doing was stupid?
John/Gordon: (overlapping) No. I didn't, no. / No. Not that I remember.
Kelly: Did it occur to you that Yaphit might be upset?
John/Gordon: (overlapping) Yes./No.
John: At the time, it did not seem a matter of consequence.
Gordon: Honestly, we just thought it would be funny [S1E11].

They were not alone, of course. Dan (the big headed alien seemingly modeled after Roger from *American Dad!*) thought so too. "Oh, my God, no, you didn't! ... You guys are so hilarious." But Dan is not exactly known for his sophisticated tastes. His thing is elevator music. This does not keep John and Gordon's gag from being lowbrow.

How Do We Cultivate a Person's Perception of the Beautiful?

According to Hopkins, esthetic perception is caused by experience and education, and the way to maintain this perception is through cultivation of an emotional response that is also caused by experience and education. For Hopkins, this cultivation must be done in a calm and prosperous environment where the mind is at peace and able to appreciate that which is beautiful. This is not an indication of where it actually is done; it's an indication of where it *should* be done, if it is to be done.

Unfortunately, on the USS *Orville*, there are very few such opportunities—there is very little fine art. There was Ty's piano recital and the Union Symphony's appearance in "A Happy Refrain," but even the Symphony's choice of music seemed to be influenced by pop music. Perhaps university professor Ildis Kitan (Lt. Alara Kitan's father) was right when he said that humans are the "hillbillies of the galaxy" (S1E10). Perhaps they do all need a little education.

Come on Ed, You Can Do Better

Hopkins would have been appalled by the lack of highbrow art and opportunities for artistic education on the USS *Orville*. And he would be equally appalled by the likely reason for their absence: the lowbrow tastes of the ship's captain. After all, Ed has a Kermit the Frog sitting on his desk because Kermit is a "leader [he] admires" (S1E2). But think about what *The Muppet Show* was: a variety show with lowbrow jokes and slapstick comedy routines. Miss Piggy's voluptuous gaze and skimpy outfits alone would have been too much for Hopkins, and he would have rolled his eyes every time she gave a "pork chop" to the romantically reluctant Kermit the Frog. Indeed, Hopkins called for play theaters to be closed, and likely would have said something similar regarding variety shows like *The Muppet Show*: cancel them. According to Hopkins, vice is present everywhere, tempting individuals away from the good. Guidance from others (those who are more sophisticated, of course) is needed to help steer everyone (the less sophisticated) in the right direction.

So if he were the captain, Hopkins would probably close every bar and simulator on the ship, and replace them with lectures, literature groups, and other *exhilarating* forms of aesthetic entertainment to cultivate the character of his crew. Lt. LaMarr's and Lt. Malloy's lack of education and exposure to such innocent entertainment would be replaced with education to cultivate their perception and lead them away from deprived activities.[6] This would allow them to "…receive pleasure from the common appearances of nature, and from every free and natural expression of good feeling."[7]

Indeed, for Hopkins, the enjoyment and appreciation of nature is another avenue for the cultivation of one's character. "In all beautiful objects in nature, or in art, a propriety, a fitness, a proportion; and the impression which these make upon us is so analogous to that which is made by virtuous conduct, that we use the same terms to express both."[8] And without any proper education, nature cannot be properly appreciated. Consider the lowbrow way that Ed reacts to the natural wonder of the bioship the crew discovers in "If the Stars Should Appear." "Oh Man. Our ship's going to look like crap now." He's showing some appreciation, but it pales in comparison to how even Alara reacts. "God this place is beautiful. I can't believe that this place exists." And, of course, when they pull back the ship's "sunroof" and expose the biodome's population to the stars for the first time, Dr. Claire Finn puts Ed to shame—*specifically with* her knowledge of the arts and literature.

Claire:	"If the stars should appear one night in a thousand years, how would we believe and adore, and preserve for many generations the remembrance of the City of God?"
Ed:	Is that Shakespeare?
Claire:	Emerson.
Ed:	William Byron Emerson, yes, yes.
Claire:	Ralph Waldo
Ed:	Ralph Waldo, Lord Ralph Waldo, Keats, David Thoreau, yes [S1E4].

Hopkins suggested that the analogy of the landscape and nature is like a virtuous friendship. Individuals perceive beauty and have a cultivated experience. The fact that Capt. Mercer is not educated in the arts is not an indication that he lacks an aesthetic connection with the beauty of the stars. It's just that Dr. Finn is more educated in the arts, and thus has a better connection and expresses it more clearly. Ed does make an effort, even though his boyish nature might be traditionally seen as a moral shortfall for its lack of understanding the fine points of art appreciation. But what aesthetic joy he gets will improve his moral outlook. On top of this, his admiration of the sublime will improve if his character and morals are developed. It's a "mind's eye" vision of how to be moral. Morals furnish us with the ability to tastefully enjoy our surroundings.

Will a Cheerful and Artistic Disposition Lead to Being a Good Person?

So, for Hopkins, the study of fine arts does more than just develop the intellect and entertain; the reflexive relationship between aesthetics and morals can build a person's character. And part of the process involves the development of a person's cheerful disposition. The idea is that cheerful emotions make one predisposed to find aesthetic joy in all they experience, and this in turn will lead to good character and good action. On the flip side, if an individual has a base psychological disposition which is only set to enjoy crass displays of spontaneity, they will be prone to do things like make crude jokes or disparaging remarks. This makes one wonder whether Ed, Gordon, and John are morally upstanding persons.

According to Hopkins, to develop morals in the right way, the "fun-boy-three" (as we might call them) should be cheerful, like Dr. Finn, because it's a cheerful disposition that gives one the ability to appreciate beauty. We are not born with this ability, of course. But "if our views on moral subjects thus modify emotions, it cannot be doubted that those emotions react upon our moral views, tending to elevate and purify them."[9] The emotions are disinterested and guide the individual like a duty to the enjoyment of beauty. It's these emotions that need to be activated, at least as far as Hopkins is concerned.

Now, to be clear, although Hopkins emphasized the need for cultivating taste in the fine arts and natural objects of beauty, he did not fetishize them. They should be appreciated for their own sake, not for social status or future returns on investments. The fine arts are tied to the higher pleasures of sight, hearing and the intellect, and those who indulge in the arts for status will gain very little. To do so would demonstrate a low appreciation and a perversion of the arts. "I believe that cultivation of the arts, in their genuine spirit of beauty and or purity, has a tendency to improve the character, it would appear that they are greatly liable to abuse, and that they have been extensively abused."[10]

According to Hopkins, "taste must be favorable to morals."[11] So an education in the arts, and the appreciation of that which is truly beautiful that it ingrains, will lead one to have a certain kind of reaction to art: not find that which is immoral tasteful—or, when it comes to comedy, to not find that which is immoral humorous. And when it comes to the comedy that we find on the USS *Orville*, there is very little humor that is moral or in good taste. To play practical jokes, for example, is an aesthetic exercise in comedy, but like the theater it is dramatic, and the joke is a distortion of that which is good. It is therefore lowbrow and should not be found humorous. Indeed, for Hopkins, it would seem that no lowbrow comedy (and thus practically nothing on *The Orville*) would be (morally) worthy of a good laugh.

The MacFarlane Family House of Comedy

Now, all that said ... even though it is lowbrow, perhaps *The Orville* seeks to be highbrow. Indeed, perhaps highbrow comedy could even improve the character of the show and in return the character would improve the comedy. Perhaps. But such a quest might be futile because, when it comes to mainstream comedy, it simply *is* lowbrow. Highbrow comedy rarely happens in the mainstream.

Consider the comedy before the Second World War—like the comedy of Mae West and W.C. Fields. It was lowbrow, often pushing the limits of acceptability. Remarks made by West such as, "When I'm good, I'm very good. When I'm bad, I'm better"[12] are sexually charged and push the limits of what one should say in polite company. They are about suggestion and how the other person receives what is said. The remark or action is in itself of no moral importance, and certainly would not be funny in and of itself; but how it is received makes it funny. It's the reception that gets our attention. That it shouldn't be spoken in polite company is what makes us laugh. Or take W.C. Fields' reason for not drinking water. "I don't drink water. You know what fish do in it."[13] It's received with the same amount of ambiguity and the same amount of blushing.

Of course, it was the comedy *after* the Second World War that influenced MacFarlane—but it too was lowbrow. Take *The Flintstones* for example, a cartoon that Seth watched as a child growing up with his family in Kent, Connecticut. It not only was undoubtedly lowbrow, but undoubtedly laid the groundwork for *Family Guy*. Take the time Fred Flintstone tried deceiving his wife by pretending he has been mugged so that he could bet his wages on a dinosaur race to win enough money to buy a business, but Wilma does not believe a word of it.[14] That could just as easily be a plot involving Peter and Lois Griffin in *Family Guy*. As MacFarlane says, when confirming that his reboot of *The Flintstones* was not likely going to happen, "honestly I couldn't figure out a way to find enough differentiation between a modern-day Fred Flintstone and ... Peter Griffin."[15] (Indeed, many people think that *Family Guy* rips off *The Simpsons*, but it's the fact that they were both influenced by *The Flintstones* that makes them so similar.)

And then there is *Woody Woodpecker*, who poked fun at the norms in much the same way Socrates poked fun at the state of Athens. As George Costanza (from *Seinfeld*) once said about a "misbehaving" giant inflated Woody Woodpecker balloon in the New York Thanksgiving Parade. "What is he, some sort of an instigator?" ("Yeah, he's a troublemaker," Cosmo Kramer replies.) Woody played lots of practical jokes on a dog vying for the attention of the lady of the house.[16] And those jokes very likely laid the groundwork for some of the practical jokes we see Gordon and LaMarr pull on *The Orville*.

But these shows also drove him towards animation. As a youth, Seth made many drawings of Fred Flintstone and Woody Woodpecker, and his penchant for drawing led Seth to create "Walter Crouton"—a comic strip that the *Kent Good Times Dispatch* paid Seth to write at the age of nine. Of course, we also shouldn't forget the influence of his family which gave him very fertile ground on which to practice and experiment comedically. His mother encouraged him to tell jokes that were just a bit risqué and also bought him an 8mm movie camera to practice his animation. This undoubtedly led him to working at Hanna-Barbera, where he was undoubtedly encouraged to push the limits of comedy even further. But "Walter Crouton" was where he *first* began really pushing the limits of comedic taste.[17] One cartoon he drew, for example, which had someone kneeling at the altar asking for "fries with that," got him an angry letter from a priest.

This tendency to favor comedy that does not allow anyone to escape ridicule—that started with "Walter Crouton," continued through *Family Guy*, and landed on the USS *Orville*—was likely fed by years of Seth reading the *Muppet Magazine*. Indeed, watching *The Muppet Show* likely laid the groundwork for other aspects of Seth's future work. Jim Henson did most of the voices (like Seth does for *Family Guy*), and even featured an all-liquid alien called a Koozebanian Spooble that is not unlike Yaphit.[18] And let us not forget that Ed Mercer's role model is Kermit the Frog, a Muppet who shocked us into thinking about the mischievous stuff of comedy.

Now, Kermit is not a frog who's into bad taste, but other Muppets are less restrained. Statler and Waldorf adorned their theater box week after week to poke fun at what they saw as lousy performances. Their comedy is not exactly in the realm of Mae West, but it lacks the traditional politeness we normally expect. This likely influenced Seth's approach to the Academy Awards in 2013, where he continued the walk the tightrope of mentioning that which should not be mentioned while seeming to mention it. (As Statler and Waldorf would say, "What a lousy show!") His appearance with another one of his heroes, William Shatner, making a starship appearance in an attempt to rescue MacFarlane's Oscars 2013 comedy monologue, echoes Statler and Waldorf in a comedy duo not taking the show that seriously. Such ridicule of others and convention is a legacy that MacFarlane takes as his signature style of comedy.

This "devil-may-care" attitude to comedy is how MacFarlane can pry open the moral chestnut (so to speak) and reveal a certain underbelly that only comedy can reveal—a look-who's-talking type of critical look. MacFarlane is aware of the accepted norms and that there are established limits and established etiquette. The funny is found in testing them and mocking them.

Comic Theory to Explain the Comedy in The Orville

Ok. So. We've established that *The Orville* is mostly lowbrow comedy. But now the question is, why should we care? And by that, I don't mean to imply that the topic is not important. What I mean to ask is whether we should be *bothered* by the fact that *The Orville* is lowbrow comedy. Does this mean we should feel guilty for laughing at it, or that we shouldn't watch it at all? To answer this question, let us look at some comic theory to help us understand exactly what the difference is—the difference between "high comedy" and "low comedy."

High Comedy

Highbrow comedy includes the theory of high comedy which is very much in tune with the "comedy of manners."[19] The comedy of manners, which essentially is a comedy that criticizes social standards (or manners) through satire, started within Ancient Greek theater in the 4th century (BCE) and was analyzed by Aristotle in his Poetics.[20] (Good modern examples include *Seinfeld* and the movie *Clueless*.) It's also very much in the genre of 17th century "Restoration comedy," about which Temple University's Edward Fink says "…the humor generates laughter through its

Act V: The Funny and the Final Flyout

sophistication, witty dialogue, subtle nuances, and character idiosyncrasies."[21] In such comedies, the everyday foibles of the characters are exposed—as Noel Coward did in the 20th century by poking fun at the rich and showing them to be like everyone else. Or, for a more modern example, think of the sitcom *Frasier*. Both Niles and Frasier banter about each other's genteel mannerisms, and Martin (their father) and Daphne (his home health care worker) go much further and mock them for their prissy ways.

If *The Orville* contains high comedy in any regard, or to any degree, this is it. It shows us the crew on the USS *Orville* in their everyday world, and reveals that they have inadequacies just like us here on Earth. (Think of Ed running away from the bridge, and repeating "no, no, no," when he learns that his ex-wife is going to be his first officer.) It brings the apparent glamour of star trekking into perspective. We laugh because their world is just as commonplace as ours. As MacFarlane once said, "The best sci-fi for me is the stuff that kind of casualizes the world and humanizes it, makes it oddly mundane."[22]

A great example is a dueling comedy routine, between Ed and Kelly, that happens during the pilot episode on a mission to resupply the Epsilon Science Station on the colony planet of Epsilon 2. Dr. Aronov greets them and introduces them to Dr. Lee who has developed a machine that accelerates the passage of time. She demonstrates its capabilities on a banana, the funniest type of fruit you can imagine (given its history in all manners of one-line gags and slapstick).

Dr. Aronov:		Janice has been experimenting with temporal fields and has made well, a breakthrough would be an understatement.
Ed:		So, it's an anti-banana ray?
Kelly:		It's really interesting.
Ed:		We need no longer fear the banana.
Kelly:		Does it work on all fruit?
Ed:		What about salads?
Dr. Aronov:		Do you understand what happened to this banana? It's rotten because a month has passed.
Ed:		Since we got here? Yeah, that's what it feels like.
Janice Lee:		Captain Mercer, this banana is suspended in a quantum bubble that can be adjusted to accelerate time. Out here only a few moments have passed. Inside the bubble, it's a month in the future.
Ed:		Does it work in both directions? Like, could somebody use it to go backward in time and tell their younger self not to make a terrible life decision?
Kelly:		Hey, will you give it a rest for, like, five minutes?
Ed:		No, I didn't mean that-that…
Kelly:		I know what you meant.
Ed:		No, I just meant, like, tell yourself not to break your leg in that fall or

don't eat too many carbs or—or don't get married, but is that how it works?

And here we might also find another example of high comedy: the *inside joke*, where audiences are required to use their intelligence to get the joke. Like all high comedy, the viewer is thrilled that they are one of a few intelligent ones who get the joke, and that's part of what makes it funny. In this case they know of Capt. Mercer and Commander Grayson's uncomfortable situation and that maybe a banana should not have been chosen for the demonstration—although, arguably, perhaps that was not the intention.

A better example might be Isaac's constant insistence that he is vastly more intelligent than his crewmates as an inside joke referring to the way Khan condescended to Captain Kirk about his intelligence in *Star Trek II: The Wrath of Khan*. Or take the way Capt. Mercer shuts up the Moclan advocate in "About a Girl." "Dude, you have been a colossal dick all friggin' day. Shut the hell up." Fans of *Family Guy* will recognize the voice of Peter Griffin. But, then again, these last two require a knowledge of pop culture, rather than intelligence, so perhaps they don't count as high comedy. In any event, although it is present, there is barely enough high comedy on *The Orville* to be noticed.

Low Comedy

As one might expect, lowbrow comedy is associated with what is known as "low comedy," and low comedy tends to be more physically involved than intellectual. That's not to say that the intellect is not involved at all, it's just that the comedy "incorporates aggression and violence"[23] in the use of "slapstick," that results in mocking or "showing up" someone or a group of people. The target of this comedy is not permanently harmed, of course. But our laughter is caused by us thinking that we are better than them.

As an example from *The Orville*, think of the episode "Pria" where Gordon played a prank on Isaac by placing Mr. Potato Head eyes, nose, ears, and mouth on his face while he was recharging. Since he doesn't actually see with his eyes (he "detects environmental stimuli with external sensors"), he walked all around the ship with them on. We know that it is a juvenile prank, but it's funny. Isaac retaliates with a practical joke of his own: cutting off Gordon's leg. Since we clearly understand practical jokes better than Isaac does, we feel superior. And with this mischievous satisfaction in another's humiliation, or "Schadenfreude," we laugh at Isaac because his high IQ has not initially comprehended the joke played by Gordon, who has a far lower IQ. Low comedy also includes the *sight gags*, action gags, and running gags (even if they only last one episode), like when Malloy is ordered back to the bridge with a limp, dangling leg, because Dr. Finn wasn't yet done regenerating it. In case it's not obvious, you could fill an entire essay with examples from *The Orville* of this lowbrow kind of comedy.

What Is This Thing Called Good Taste in Comedy?

There is also good taste in comedy, which we need to discuss because it fits in with highbrow comedy and will allow us to gauge the moral divide between it and lowbrow humor. As we've seen, *The Orville* sometimes has a kind of non-contemporary good-taste comedic gravity. It's highbrow sometimes, but its feeling of comedic history is why even a lowbrow joke can be told in good taste. We sense that the comedy is picked from history and placed here and there in the gangways, rooms, and the bridge of the ship. Like Isaac's aloof intellectual manner, it's funny, maybe offensive, but in good taste as the children do not hear anything that is unsuitable. We are reminded of their intellectual limitations, which is a serious Neoplatonist comment on social and political order.

Even the name of Ed's starship is funny in a friendly way and has a ring to it that says someone in the Union tried to pick a serious name, but ended up with one that can't be taken seriously. Being named after Orville Wright looks good on a white board in an operations room, but in use it sounds a bit silly. I half imagine Stewie Griffin from *Family Guy* whispering in Ed Mercer's ear telling him "it's the name you give to an old lady's caged pet budgie. Just remember that when you try to show off to your friends; I'm the captain of a mid-sized exploratory-class vessel, the ECV-197… The … *Orville*. Quite an anticlimax, don't you think?" It's part of the traditional good taste comedy that not only contrasts with bad taste comedy but anchors the seriousness of *The Orville*.

Traditional good taste continues with the naming of the Krill's god as "Avis" (which is yet another name that can't be taken seriously) and Malloy's running gag which points out its absurdity. His fixation with the fact that their god shares his name with a 20th century car rental company is too much to bear. "Oh wise and wonderful Avis, cover the loss of our vehicle," he says in "Krill." Not letting go, he later replies to the group of Krill children who ask why humans in the Union don't believe in Avis. "Well, they worship their own god called Hertz."

What's more, in *The Orville*, the comedy is not central and allows more serious topics to be explored. Take for example "Majority Rule" where, on a trip to Sargus 4, John does an erotic dance on the statue of the revered Mella Griffendon. While the dance is comic, its comedic effect is not the purpose of the episode. Instead, it's a critique of the planet's instant and absolute democratic system—and of our own as well.[24] This seems to be in good taste as well.

We can also return to Ed's admiration for Kermit the Frog who, according to Mercer, "always keeps his cool in a crisis, inspires greatness in his people" (S1E6). Like the cartoons of yesteryear that might shock us today by seeming to be lowbrow, Kermit the Frog is a gracious and courageous leader despite the fact that he is in charge of a chaotic variety theater company. Ed's admiration for him is funny (because he's a green Muppet frog), but it too serves a moral purpose. After all, Kermit was a leader and at times very clumsy. But he is a very apt hero for a leader (like Ed) who makes his fair share of mistakes, and most, but not all of them, are funny!

So, good taste comedy does exist on *The Orville*. And pairing it with lowbrow humor seems to bring it into the category of highbrow humor. The moral divide between highbrow humor and (what we've been calling) the "lowbrow humor" of *The Orville* is thus not apparent and the case that we should feel guilty for laughing at *The Orville* is significantly weakened.

What Is This Thing Called Bad Taste in Comedy?

Another reason we shouldn't feel guilty for laughing at *The Orville*'s lowbrow humor is this: if it were truly highbrow—high taste highbrow comedy—it wouldn't actually be funny. Why? Because comedy is supposed to push the limits of acceptability, and high taste highbrow comedy doesn't. As such, truly funny high taste highbrow comedy doesn't exist—or, at least, is not found that often.

Now, when it comes to lowbrow humor that pushes the limits, the point is not to be risqué (for the sake of being risqué). It's not about telling a joke for the sake of offending people. The goal is to be funny. But to be funny, you have to push right up against what is offensive. Indeed, in his rainy and daring commencement speech at Harvard University in 2006, MacFarlane said that pushing the limits of taste is essential to being funny. To not do so lands one in the realm of traditional bland "good taste highbrow comedy" that isn't funny. Think of why high moral standards are often said to be to blame for why certain comedians are not allowed to be funny anymore. Now clearly, there are times when comedians don't just push the limits, but instead jump far beyond them, and are not only unfunny but morally blameworthy. (Michael Richards, aka Cosmo Kramer, shouting the N-word at hecklers comes to mind here.)[25] But a comedian who never pushes the envelope is rarely funny. To be funny involves bad taste and this is not allowed if one cannot offend. It's to have a "linguistic erection" that might offend but elicits laughter.[26]

And it's not just about being morally offensive; other boundaries can be pushed as well. Take the art of telling a *rubbish joke*. Now I'm not talking about telling a joke that fails; I'm talking about telling a joke that you know is "bad" for the sake of getting a laugh. To tell such a joke successfully involves a complex mixture of timing, context, situation, and theme, that pushes right against comedic tastes. After all, you are—technically speaking—telling a joke that is not funny, and thus does not appeal to people's tastes. How are they funny? You have to make the anticipation of the joke being funny, coupled with the fact that it is not, produce laughter. The fact that the joke is not funny, has to be funny. Obviously, that's hard to pull off.

Despite the difficulty, Ed (arguably) pulls off a *rubbish joke* in "Command Performance" when Bortus informs him that he needs time off work to brood his newly laid egg.

Ed:	Well, listen, tell Klyden congrats, and, uh, if you got one more in you, dibs on the omelet. (laughs)
Bortus:	Sir?
Ed:	Sorry. Bad joke.
Bortus:	Yes.
Ed:	Bad "yolk." (laughs) You know, I'm—I'm just not gonna try at comedy with you anymore.
Bortus:	I will return to my quarters.

Now perhaps the funniest bit of this is Bortus' reaction, although it too could be said to be funny because it's not funny. But the point still stands. Comedy operates on the edge of acceptability. Effective comedy relies on pushing these limits, which is the very thing that makes the viewer question whether it is in good taste. So if *The Orville*'s comedy was in good taste, then it wouldn't be funny; we therefore shouldn't feel guilty for laughing at its lowbrow humor. Or, to put it another way, if we had to feel guilty for laughing at *The Orville*, we'd have to feel guilty for laughing at everything—and clearly, that's absurd.

Conclusion

The comedy in *The Orville* is ambiguous. It is often lowbrow comedy done in bad taste, but the distinction between good and bad taste comedy, and lowbrow and highbrow, is not always clear—and highbrow good taste comedy might not be that funny anyway. In *The Orville* we might sometimes see highbrow comedy which, like lowbrow comedy, is still making fun of others. But surely it is not in good taste even though there are plenty of "linguistic erections." Regardless, if there is a discernible distinction between good and bad taste in comedy, then the statements that bad taste in comedy is wrong and that the other is acceptable are both misplaced.

Hopkins was adamant that good character and morals are best served by highbrow entertainment, but he never proved that highbrow culture is superior. And for us it certainly does not provide much. So Hopkins' emphasis on highbrow aesthetics supporting morals was ill-conceived. And if there is no real distinction between good and bad taste, then there is no bad taste. There is no co-existence of lowbrow and highbrow comedy pulling each other in opposite directions, and thus Seth does not deserve to have his brazen cheeky face slapped. *The Orville* is a comedy due to its jokes, sketches, and slapstick.. Its comedy value is not in doubt, and its status as a bad taste lowbrow comedy in contrast to highbrow good taste highbrow comedy is not proven. This makes it a space drama comedy that simply likes to push the limits of acceptability which is neither highbrow nor lowbrow, and that's okay—for, as we've seen, that's just what comedy is supposed to do.

Notes

1. Seth MacFarlane, interview by Seth Meyers, *Late Night with Seth Meyers*, 2017.
2. Chaim Gartenberg, "How Seth MacFarlane Could Save His Terminally Bland Star Trek Clone The Orville," *The Verge*, September 14, 2017, https://www.theverge.com/2017/9/14/16307156/the-orville-fox-star-trek-seth-macfarlane-humor-originality.
3. Will Harris, "With the Two-Part Episode Identity, The Orville Has Matured into Serious Science Fiction," *The Verge*, March 7, 2019, https://www.theverge.com/2019/3/7/18254737/identity-the-orville-star-trek-seth-macfarlane-two-part-episode-science-fiction.
4. Mark Hopkins, *The Connexion Between Taste and Morals: Two Lectures* (Boston, MA: Dutton and Wentworth, 1841), 5.
5. Ibid., 7.
6. Ibid., 11.
7. Ibid., 14.
8. Ibid.
9. Ibid., 21.
10. Ibid., 32.
11. Ibid., 41.
12. *I'm no Angel*, directed by Wesley Ruggles (1933; New York: Paramont Pictures, 1998), DVD.
13. Robert Reisner, *Graffiti: Two Thousand Years of Wall Writing* (Cowles Book Company, 1971).
14. "At the Races," *The Flintstones*, season 1, episode 8, directed by Joseph Barbera and William Hanna, aired November 18, 1960 (Los Angeles: Hanna Barbera, 1960).
15. Seth MacFarlane, "I am Seth MacFarlane. Back For a New and Better Go at This AMA," *Reddit*, 2018, https://www.reddit.com/r/IAmA/comments/70bf9u/i_am_seth_macfarlane_.back_for_a_new_and_better_go/dn1y5q6/.
16. "Helter Shelter," *Woody Woodpecker*, directed by Paul Smith, aired January 17, 1955 (Universal International, 1955).
17. Seth MacFarlane, "Family Guy," *Inside the Actors Studio*, aired September 14, 20019.
18. *The Muppet Show*, season 2, episode 47, aired December 5, 1977, ITV.

19. Edward J. Fink, "Writing the Simpsons: A Case Study of Comic Theory," *Journal of Film and Video* 65, no. 1–2 (Spring/Summer 2013), 45, https://doi.org/10.5406/jfilmvideo.65.1-2.0043.
20. Aristotle, *Poetics*, trans. Gerald F.Else (Ann Arbor: University of Michigan Press, 1970).
21. Fink, "Writing the Simpsons," 45.
22. Seth MacFarlane, interview by Seth Meyers, *Late Night with Seth Meyers*, 2017.
23. Fink, "Writing the Simpsons," 46.
24. For more on this critique, see Patrick Welsh's essay in this volume.
25. Dan Glaister, "Seinfeld Actor Lets Fly with Racist Tirade," *The Guardian*, November 22, 2006, https://www.theguardian.com/world/2006/nov/22/usa.danglaister.
26. The term "linguistic erection" was first used by MacFarlane, while voicing Stewie Griffin, on *Inside the Actor's Studio*. https://libraryland-blog.tumblr.com/post/17417354095/i-find-that-i-get-sort-of-a-linguistic-erection.

Bibliography

Aristotle. *Poetics*, ranslated by Gerald F. Else. Ann Arbor, Michigan: University of Michigan Press, 1970.

Feinberg, Joel. *Social Philosophy*. New Jersey: Pearson, 1972.

Fink, J. Edward. "Writing the Simpsons: A Case Study of Comic Theory." *Journal of Film and Video* 65, no. 1–2 (Spring/Summer 2013): 43–55. https://doi.org/10.5406/jfilmvideo.65.1-2.0043.

Gartenberg, Chaim. "How Seth MacFarlane Could Save His Terminally Bland Star Trek Clone The Orville." *The Verge*, September 14, 2017. https://www.theverge.com/2017/9/14/16307156/the-orville-fox-star-trek-seth-macfarlane-humor-originality.

Glaister, Dan. "Seinfeld Actor Lets Fly with Racist Tirade." *The Guardian*, November 22, 2006. https://www.theguardian.com/world/2006/nov/22/usa.danglaister.

Harris, Will. "With the Two-part Episode Identity, The Orville Has Matured Into Serious Science Fiction." *The Verge*, March 7, 2019. https://www.theverge.com/2019/3/7/18254737/identity-the-orville-star-trek-seth-macfarlane-two-part-episode-science-fiction.

Hopkins, Mark. *The Connexion Between Taste and Morals: Two Lectures*, Boston, Massachusetts: Dutton and Wentworth, 1841.

Oring, Elliott. "Good Humor, Bad Taste: A Sociology of the Joke (review)," *The Journal of American Folklore* 122, no. 483 (Winter 2009): 119–121. https://doi.org/10.1353/jaf.0.0050.

Reisner, Robert. *Graffiti: Two Thousand Years of Wall Writing*. Cowles Book Company, 1971.

Making Sense of Time Travel in *The Orville*

David Kyle Johnson

> "You guys will not get me into a discussion of time travel logic. I would rather chew broken glass."
> —Captain Ed Mercer, "Tomorrow, and Tomorrow, and Tomorrow"

One staple of science fiction television is the flyout. At the end of the episode, the heroes fly off into the metaphorical sunset, in their trusty starship, over a version of the show's theme music. It's fun and inspiring—hopefully a bit like this essay. But another science fiction staple is time travel; almost every science fiction show has to have some kind of time travel episode. And *The Orville* is no exception. Unlike a flyout, however, it's very difficult to write a good, logically consistent, time travel story.

Take perhaps the most famous *Star Trek* episode of all, "City on the Edge of Forever." Dr. McCoy's changing of the past erases Starfleet and leaves the crew of the USS *Enterprise* stranded on a distant planet. But, of course, a Starfleet ship is how McCoy and crew got to the planet in the first place. If McCoy's trip to the past erased Starfleet, then he would have never traveled to the distant planet to begin with, and thus wouldn't have changed the past. The story actually makes no sense because it invokes something known as "The Grandfather Paradox" (which we will talk more about later).

This makes one wonder about the logical consistency of *The Orville*'s time travel stories. Would Pria just disappear after Captain Mercer closes the wormhole in "Pria"? Would Kelly be able to undo the damage done by her trip to and from the future in "Tomorrow, and Tomorrow, and Tomorrow"? Do these stories make sense? Are they even logically possible? And if not, should this detract from our ability to enjoy them? Before attempting to answer these questions, it will be necessary to lay out the ways to tell a logically consistent time travel story.

Logically Consistent Time Travel

Time travel to the future is theoretically possible. Relativity, for example, entails that time slows for those traveling at relativistic speeds. If you were to travel away from the Earth at near the speed of light, turn around, and then come back, you would find that much more time had passed on the Earth than had passed for you.[1] And traveling to the future poses no logical difficulties. Nothing you do in the future can undo the past fact that you traveled to the future.

But traveling to the past is more difficult. It might be theoretically possible, according to relativity, but it does require one to be able do seemingly impossible things—like orbit and then escape the gravity of an infinitely long rotating cylinder.[2] But it might be logically impossible too, because traveling to the past would enable you to undo the fact that you had traveled to the past in the first place. And if something is logically impossible, it can't happen.

The most common way of explaining this line of reasoning involves telling the story of a time traveler who goes back in time to kill his own grandfather (before he sires his father). If the time traveler succeeds, he will never have been born; but of course, if he is never born, he can't travel back in time to kill his grandfather and prevent his birth. So he won't. But if he won't, then he will. So he'll travel back if and only if he does not. He is born if and only if he isn't born. This is logical nonsense—a contradiction. And contradictions can't be true. One cannot negate their own existence. And thus, time travel is impossible.

Now, to be clear: the argument is not that if you were to travel to the past, you *shouldn't* try to kill your grandfather. It's not the suggestion that if you did travel to the past and kill your grandfather, you would (as they say on *Doctor Who*) "destroy the space time continuum" and cause reality to blink out of existence. You can't resolve this problem by saying "time travel to the past is possible as long as you don't do something like kill your grandfather." No. Logical contradictions can't even *possibly* be true. There is no logically possible world in which they are true. But if time travel were possible, there would be such a world. If backwards time travel were possible, it would be possible to prevent your own birth—to negate your own existence. Since such a thing is, in principle, impossible, time travel to the past must be, in principle, impossible.

Some philosophers have answered this argument, however, by suggesting that there are ways of conceiving of time travel that make things like the grandfather paradox impossible.

Take Nuel Belnap and David Deutsch for example.[3] They suggest that traveling to the past would not alter the past but instead create an alternate timeline—one that is identical to the timeline that you left, up to the moment you arrived.[4] That timeline would then differ in certain respects after that moment. For example, if you killed that new timeline's version of your grandfather, that would prevent that timeline's version of you from ever being born. But such an action would not negate your existence because your birth would still be safe and sound in your original timeline. In other words, backwards time travel would not enable you to kill your grandfather and negate your own existence; it would only enable you to kill someone who looked like your grandfather, and prevent the existence of someone who looked like you, in an alternate timeline.

For good measure, it should also be made clear that, on this view, forward time travel does *not* create an alternate timeline. If you travel forward in time, you travel to the future of the timeline you are currently in. So, for example, you can travel forward to the future of your own original timeline. But if you then try to travel back, you will not go back to "when and where you began." You will in fact create and arrive in a new timeline. And if you traveled forward again, you wouldn't find yourself in the future of your original timeline—in the future you had already visited. You would be in the future of the new timeline you created by traveling back. And if, once there, you again traveled into the past, you would create yet another timeline. For obvious reasons, this view is also known as the "branching" model of time travel, and it does seem to make logical sense. It invokes no logical contradictions. Consequently, one could suggest that it entails that backwards time travel is indeed logically possible.

There is one problem with such a suggestion, however. What it describes isn't really, technically, time travel. It's universe creation. If traveling to the past creates an alternate reality that cannot affect the reality I left, then I really have just created an alternate universe. If I were to invent a machine that was able to do what Belnap and Deutsch describe, I would not be inventing one that was able to travel in time; I would be inventing one capable of creating entire universes. Perhaps that is even more impressive, but it is not time travel. Thus, this view does not show that "time travel" is possible. Despite this, some still do employ it in "time travel" stories—and I also will speak of it as a conception of time travel, from here on out.

Another attempt to describe logically possible time travel was famously made by David Lewis.[5] He suggested that time travel to the past would not allow you to do something like kill your own grandfather because, even if you were to travel to the past, you would find it impossible to change. Whatever facts were true of the past "before" you pushed the button in your time machine to travel to it, would still be true of the past after you pushed it. Indeed, the fact that you existed in the past and did what (from your perspective) you are about to do would have already been true before you pushed the button. You may not have known it, but it was already a past fact that you were there and did what you did. If you are about to travel to the past, it was already true that you did. By traveling to the past, you can causally contribute to past events; indeed, you must cause whatever the past already contains your time-traveling-self causing. But you cannot *change* past events. Correspondingly, we might call this the "static" view of time travel.

This avoids the grandfather paradox because clearly your birth is something that lies in the past and thus is not something that you can prevent. It was true that you would not kill your grandfather before you pushed the button on your time machine, thus killing your grandfather is not something you can accomplish. On this view of time travel, therefore, logical paradoxes are impossible. But it also seems to entail that the time traveler has no free will. The time traveler cannot do anything but what he already did—anything but what the past already contained him doing. And, at least according to the classic libertarian understanding of free will, no choice is free unless the person who made it could have chosen otherwise—unless they could have not chosen to do what they did.[6]

But as an objection to this conception of time travel, this point falls short. Yes, the time traveler wouldn't have libertarian free will because they couldn't do anything but what the timeline already contained them doing. But this is true of everyone, even me and you.[7] Relativity entails that the entire timeline exists, past, present, and future.[8] It is not all occurring, but it all exists. This temporal ontology is called "omnitemporalism" or "the block world view." On this view, all of your future actions already exist; they are written in "the block." So when you "arrive" at some future moment, you cannot choose to do anything but what the future already contained you choosing to do. Essentially, every moment of every person's life is already "laid out" in the block; the only difference between you and a time traveler is the order in which the events of your lives happen in the block. For you, they are connected in a sequential order. For the time traveler, they are disjointed; their final years might be in the past, and their first years in the future. But they all are "already" laid out.

Now, this view does allow for the occurrence or existence of what is known as a "jinnee," a self-created object or idea. But that is not a reason to reject static time travel as logically impossible. Why? Well first, let me clarify what a jinnee is.

Suppose I travel to the past and teach my past self how to build a time machine; but suppose I only knew how to build a time machine because I learned how from my future self. The idea of how to build a time machine, in this story, would have no origin outside itself. It would therefore be a jinnee. But such a situation is not paradoxical, or logically contradictory.

It does not entail that something both is and isn't true, or that something exists if and only if it doesn't. Nor does such a situation violate the idea that everything has an explanation; a jinnee does have an explanation: itself. Thus a jinnee is logically possible.

Now, the existence of a jinnee *would* entail that reverse causation is logically possible—an effect can precede its cause. But by even considering the possibility of backwards time travel, we have already admitted that such a thing is at least logically possible. My present pressing of the button in my time travel machine, for example, would cause my appearance in the past. So the fact that the existence of a jinnee entails the possibility of reverse causation doesn't really constitute much of an objection. If we really had a problem with reverse causation, we should have dismissed backwards time travel from the beginning.

So now, properly armed with an understanding of how logically consistent time travel stories can be told, let's examine some time travel stories from *The Orville* and ask whether they make logical sense.

Wait.... Where Did Pria Go?

> "We recognize we're opening a can of worms [with time travel, but] to me it's always fun.... You just have to be careful. It's a lot to think about."
> —Seth MacFarlane,[9] creator, writer, executive producer

In "Pria," the USS *Orville* rescues a shuttle captain named Pria Lavesque, who turns out to be a time traveling antiques dealer from the 29th century. According to Pria, the USS *Orville* was "supposed to" be destroyed in a dark matter storm. She travels back to save the ship so she could steal it away to the 29th century and sell it to the highest bidder. (Since the ship would have been destroyed anyway, she figures this wouldn't change the past.) She successfully hijacks the ship and takes it through a wormhole to the 29th century, but then the crew takes back control of the ship and returns to the 25th century. Once there, Mercer blows up the wormhole and Pria disappears.

Why does she disappear? As Mercer tells Pria at the end of the episode:

> According to Isaac, as long as the wormhole exists, the quantum potentiality is open. Many sets of future events are possible. But, if we destroy it, we choose a path. There's no chance of us returning to your future, and The Orville goes on to live its life. Which means that Pria Lavesque will have no reason to come back into our past. And you and I will never have met.

In other words, the only reason Pria came back to steal the USS *Orville* is because it was destroyed. By destroying the wormhole instead, Mercer ensures that the USS *Orville* will survive in the 25th century, and thus erases Pria's reason to come back and steal it. She thus never does/did.

This, it seems, is a classic grandfather-style paradox. Pria only came back to steal the USS *Orville* because it was destroyed, but her coming back to steal it caused it to not be destroyed. So she does if and only if she doesn't. It's a logically nonsensical paradox. And making Pria disappear in a poof of paradoxical smoke does not resolve it. She either traveled back or she didn't. If Pria and Mercer never met, then the USS *Orville* was destroyed, and they did meet. If they did meet, the USS *Orville* was not destroyed, and they didn't. The story is logically inconsistent.

If the time travel in the story were of the static Lewisian type, where the time traveler could not change the past, the story would have to completely change. Pria would have thought the USS *Orville* was destroyed only because it disappeared but then she would have ended up being the cause of its disappearance. Historians would have assumed the USS *Orville* had been destroyed only because Pria took it into the future, never to return. Or, if it did return, there would have to be some kind of explanation for why history recorded it as being destroyed even though it wasn't. Perhaps, for example, returning to the 25th century caused them to appear and live out their existence in another galaxy. This wouldn't be great for the show, but it would have been logically consistent.

As a branching time travel story, however, the narrative of the episode could survive largely unscathed. Understanding the story this way would simply entail that the USS *Orville* was destroyed in some original timeline, and Pria created a different timeline by traveling back to steal it—a timeline where the USS *Orville* disappears and is taken by Pria into the future of that new timeline. When the crew regains control of the ship and travels back to the 25th century, that would create yet another timeline just like the one they left. And, as long as they arrive at a moment later than the one in which they entered the wormhole, there would only be one USS *Orville* at that moment, to continue on in that timeline.

The only difference in the story would be that, when they closed the wormhole, Pria wouldn't have disappeared. The reason for her coming back would not have been negated because the event of the original USS *Orville*'s destruction would still exist in her original timeline. Destroying the wormhole would just keep her from going to the future of this new (third) timeline. She would be forced to live out her life in (what would seem to her as) the past—albeit the past of a different timeline. Again, to make the episode consistent with this interpretation, all one would need to change is the fact that Pria disappeared at the end. But that wouldn't be too hard. Perhaps, after the wormhole is destroyed but she remains, Mercer could have simply said, "Huh. I guess Isaac was wrong. Time travel doesn't work like that."

Tomorrow[3]

> "I think we filled all the holes but I'm not sure."
> —Seth MacFarlane,[10] on Season 2's time travel

The second season's time travel story happens at its end in a two-part episode. In "Tomorrow, and Tomorrow, and Tomorrow," a previous version of Commander Grayson, seven years younger, appears on the USS *Orville* as a result of one of Isaac's temporal experiments. This younger Kelly, it turns out, was taken into the future the morning after her first date with Ed. She meets her future self, the rest of the crew, and learns of the fate of her and Ed's relationship—about how their marriage fell apart. Since the crew is sure Kelly will change the past if she has knowledge of future events, they attempt to erase that knowledge before they send her back. The memory erasure doesn't work, however, and when she returns, Kelly changes the past by refusing to go on a second date with Ed.

The changes to the future this causes are explored in the next episode, "The Road Not Taken." Without Kelly to put in a good word for him, Ed never gets his own command. And since he was in command of the USS *Orville* when it defeated the Kaylons (in *Identity* Parts I and II), the Kaylons were not defeated and conquered the galaxy. The episode follows the remnants of the original crew as they reunite to send Dr. Finn back in time to correct Kelly's memory wipe and set things right. When she does, Dr. Finn disappears.

In these episodes, it's made clear that the crew doesn't quite know how time travel works. Both static Lewisian and branching time travel are alluded to, but no one seems to know which conception is right.

Ed:	It's time travel, nobody really understands it, but I do have one question. What do we tell her about the past seven years?
Kelly:	What do you think?
Ed:	Well, if we're dealing with a tangent timeline and we are able to send her back, then nothing she knows will matter. But if it's a single timeline, then we should lock her in a room and keep her away from any information about the future.
Kelly:	How do we know which one it is?
Ed:	We don't. And I'm not gonna confine her to quarters when she's done nothing wrong. So, my philosophy is, when in doubt tell the truth.

At first, it seems that the writers of the episode are going the "single static timeline" Lewisian route. If the crew wipes young Kelly's memory and sends her back, everything could happen on a single timeline. It would have been true of Older Kelly that she was brought to the future seven years ago—she simply doesn't remember it. Indeed, given the limits on possibility that Lewisian static time travel entails, the fact that Young Kelly would be sent back without her memories of future events would be inevitable. In the same way that the survival of a time traveler's grandfather would be inevitable, the crew couldn't fail to send Young Kelly back without her memories. Older Kelly's existence but lack of memories of the episode's events would themselves be a testament to this fact. Young Kelly herself seems to recognize this as she adopts a Lewisian view.

> **Dr. Finn:** We could do a memory wipe.
> **Gordon:** Aren't those kind of risky?
> **Dr. Finn:** U–Uh, they are. There's always the potential for brain damage, so you'd have to make that decision for yourself.
> **Bortus:** Why are you smiling?
> **Young Kelly:** Because we know it'll work.... It already worked. And you sent me back successfully. That's why you [Older Kelly] don't remember any of this.

And if she had been right, had the memory wipe worked, "Tomorrow, and Tomorrow, and Tomorrow" would have been a logically consistent time travel story.

But of course, the memory wipe does not work, and the view of time travel that "The Road Not Taken" seems to imply is Belnap and Deutsch's branching model. Sending Young Kelly back with memories of the future seems to create an alternate timeline where Ed and Kelly never marry, and the Kaylons conquer the galaxy. But, in actuality, it's not possible to make logical sense of the story, even on the branching view.

Now, to be clear, there are other problems with viewing the episode this way. For example, on this view, the remnants of the USS *Orville*'s crew can't actually "set things right" and "restore the timeline." On the branching model, you can't travel back to the past of your own timeline; backwards time travel always creates a new timeline. So, at best, by sending Dr. Finn back in time to correct the memory wipe, all they can do is create yet another timeline (where Ed and Kelly do get married and the Kaylons do not conquer the galaxy). So, even if they were successful in sending Dr. Finn back to correct the memory wipe (without destroying their ship), the remnants of the crew we follow in that episode would still be stuck in that dystopian timeline. Branching time travel cannot be used to "fix" a timeline; it can only be used to create new ones. Conceived in this way, this part of the story is logically consistent, but it is not a story in which the crew "sets things right," back to the way they were.

But ultimately, branching time travel cannot be used to make sense of the second season's time travel story as it stands. There are two major problems.

First, although travel to the future does keep one within their original timeline, backwards time travel always creates an alternate timeline. Consequently, if one does go to the future, one can never return to their own past. On the branching view, by traveling to the future, a time traveler permanently removes themselves from the portion of the timeline they skipped and can never put themselves back. So, on the branching view, it would be impossible to travel to the future and meet your older self. In order for that to occur, you would have to be able to return to the past of your original timeline and then grow older through natural means; but, of course, any attempt to do so would simply create an *alternate* timeline. So, while it does make perfect sense on the Lewisan "one static timeline" view, the idea of Young Kelly traveling to the future to meet her older self makes no logical sense on the branching view. So the primary plot device of "Tomorrow, and Tomorrow, and Tomorrow" is incompatible with the branching view.

Secondly, since traveling back in time creates a new timeline, Dr. Finn would not just disappear once she had successfully implemented the memory wipe. She would be stuck in this new timeline she had created by traveling back. If she leaves the room before Kelly wakes up, and lives her life in secret, this timeline will be very much like the original timeline where Kelly and Ed were married. But it will not be numerically the same one. The implication of her disappearance is that, by implementing the memory wipe, she erased the future from which she came. But on the branching view, that future still exists, in an alternate timeline—the one she came from. She doesn't erase anything.

Of course, the suggestion that her action does erase the future from which she comes lands us right back into a grandfather paradox again. And having Dr. Finn disappear in a poof of paradoxical smoke at the end of "The Road Not Taken" does not solve it any more than Pria's disappearance resolves the paradox of "Pria." Both are just hand waving excuses to resolve the logical paradox that their respective stories created. But this raises the question I would like to conclude the essay by answering: Does all of this ruin the episodes? Can a logically inconsistent time travel story still be good?

Embrace the Paradox!

> "It's hard to find a really good original time travel story. You have to find a new approach to it that hasn't been done on other science fiction shows, and that's pretty much an impossible task at this point."
> —André Bormanis,[11] writer/producer, science consultant

There is not much worse, in my opinion, than critics who nitpick the plot lines of fun or popular stories to find plot holes or other problems so the critics themselves can give the impression that they are "more sophisticated" than the fans who liked the story.

> "In *Lord of the Rings*, why doesn't Gandalf just use the giant eagles to fly Frodo to Mount Doom?"
> "In *Star Wars: The Empire Strikes Back*, how does Luke's training on Dagobah seem to last weeks, but Han, Leia, and Chewbacca are captured by the Empire in a matter of hours?"
> "How does Andy, in *Shawshank Redemption*, put the poster of Rita Hayworth back up after he crawls through the hole he dug in his cell?"
> "Why doesn't Hermione just use her Time-Turner to go back in time to defeat Voldemort in the *Harry Potter* stories?"

Some of these questions might have good answers, others might not. But a host of such questions could be asked about any given story (perhaps even some true ones). When we engage in fiction, we almost always have to employ a little bit of what Samuel Taylor Coleridge calls "poetic faith" or "the suspension of disbelief."[12] Coleridge was referring to his reader's ability to set aside their disbelief in the supernatural, but something similar could be said about many other story-telling devices. Warp drive is not scientifically possible, and transporters would kill and then copy who they are attempting to transport, but we just ignore this so we can enjoy *Star Trek*. A single-celled blob organism wouldn't have vocal cords, but we just ignore this so we can enjoy Yaphit's jokes. Our suspension of disbelief is not total, of course. If it were, we would call the cops ten minutes into every Tarantino movie. But we can and do selectively choose to ignore certain things in many stories so that we can enjoy them.

Now, it is a bit more complicated than that. J.R.R. Tolkien argued that it is not engaging in a suspension of disbelief that allows readers to enjoy a story; instead, it is engaging in secondary beliefs about a secondary reality—a world created by the author.[13] The author makes this possible by creating a believable fictional world that is (among other things) internally consistent. It is only when the author has failed to do this that the reader must then make a choice to suspend disbelief (to ignore the inconsistency) or give up on the story. That's why Tolkien went to such great lengths to try to create a logically consistent world for *Lord of the Rings*.

Since the logical inconsistency of *The Orville*'s time travel stories do make the world logically inconsistent, they do provide the reader an opportunity to give up on the story. But I would argue that taking advantage of such an opportunity would be a mistake. Many of the best stories in science fiction are logically inconsistent time travel stories. There's the aforementioned Classic *Star Trek* "City on the Edge of Forever" and the *Next*

Generation Episode "Yesterday's Enterprise" (which is included in many "best of TNG" lists). There's *The Terminator*, and *Back to the Future*, and Marvel's *Avengers: End Game*.[14] All of these time travel stories are logically inconsistent in much the same way, and for the same reasons that, *The Orville*'s time travel stories are. But that doesn't keep them from being good stories.

Don't get me wrong; I think logically consistent time travel stories are better. One of my favorites is *Interstellar*, which does invoke a jinnee, but is perfectly logically consistent.[15] I also think, unlike Captain Mercer, that examining the logical consistency of a time travel story is fun. That's why I wrote this essay. But one should not, in my opinion, let one's discoveries about the logical inconsistencies in these stories detract from one's enjoyment of them. Instead, I would agree with David Goodman that time travel stories simply need to be "fresh," and that the time travel stories in *The Orville* nicely qualify.[16]

Notes

1. David Toomey, "Einstein's Radical Idea," in *The New Time Travelers: A Journey to the Frontiers of Physics* (New York: W.W. Norton and Company, 2007), 40–77.
2. Toomey, "'Unphysical' Time Machines," 78–95.
3. See Nuel Belnap, "Branching Space-Times," *Synthese* 92 (1992), 385–434. See also D. Deutsch, "Time Travel," in *The Fabric of Reality* (London: Penguin, 1997), 289–320.
4. An interesting question is whether or not traveling to the past would create an entire timeline (a moment in time along with an entire past that preceded it) or just a moment in time (a physical state of affairs with only an apparent past). Nothing in our exploration of this topic turns on this point, so I leave the question open.
5. David Lewis, "The Paradoxes of Time Travel," *American Philosophical Quarterly* 13, no. 2 (1976): 145–152.
6. Peter van Inwagen, "The Incompatibility of Free Will and Determinism," in *Free Will*, ed. Robert Kane (Malden, MA: Blackwell, 2002), 71–82.
7. "Does Free Will Exist?," *Think 42(15)* (2016), 53–70.
8. David Kyle Johnson, "God, Fatalism, and Temporal Ontology," *Religious Studies* 45, no. 4 (December 2009): 435–454.
9. Sean Carroll, hosts, "Seth MacFarlane on Using Science Fiction to Explore Humanity," *Mindscape* (podcast), August 5, 2019, https://www.preposterousuniverse.com/podcast/2019/08/05/58-seth-macfarlane-on-using-science-fiction-to-explore-humanity/.
10. Carroll, "Seth MacFarlane on Using Science Fiction to Explore Humanity."
11. Jennifer Oullette, "The Orville Blends Science Fiction and Science Fact into a Winning Mix," *Ars Technica*, December 29, 2018, https://arstechnica.com/gaming/2018/12/the-orville-blends-science-fiction-and-science-fact-into-a-winning-mix/.
12. Samuel Taylor Coleridge, *Biographia Literaria: Or, Biographical Sketches of My Literary Life and Opinions* (New York: Leavitt, Lord & Company, 1834), 175.
13. J.R.R. Tolkien "On Fairy-Stories," in *The Monsters and the Critics and Other Essays* (London: George Allen & Unwin, 1983), 109–61.
14. For more on *Endgame*'s time travel paradoxes, see David Kyle Johnson, "Avengers: Endgame's Philosophical Oversight," *Psychology Today* (April 2019).
15. For more on why the time travel in *Interstellar* is logically consistent, see David Kyle Johnson, "Interstellar, Causal Loops, and Saving Humanity," *Psychology Today* (November 2014).

16. David A. Goodman, "Interview: David A. Goodman on How 'The Orville' Wrapped Up Season Two and Where It Could Go Next," interview by Anthony Pascale, *TrekMovie*, May 3, 2019, https://trekmovie.com/2019/05/03/interview-david-a-goodman-on-how-the-orville-wrapped-up-season-two-and-where-it-could-go-next/.

Bibliography

Coleridge, Samuel Taylor. *Biographia Literaria: Or, Biographical Sketches of My Literary Life and Opinions*. New York: Leavitt, Lord & Company, 1834.
Johnson, David Kyle. "Avengers: Endgame's Philosophical Oversight." *Psychology Today* (April 2019).
Johnson, David Kyle. "Does Free Will Exist?" In *Think 42(15)*, 53–70. 2016.
Johnson, David Kyle. "God, Fatalism, and Temporal Ontology." *Religious Studies* 45, no. 4 (December 2009): 435–454.
Johnson, David Kyle. "Interstellar, Causal Loops, and Saving Humanity." *Psychology Today* (November 2014).
Lewis, David. "The Paradoxes of Time Travel." *American Philosophical Quarterly* 13, no. 2 (1976):145–152.
Tolkien, J.R.R. "On Fairy-Stories." In *The Monsters and the Critics and Other Essays*, 109–61. George Allen & Unwin, 1983.
Toomey, David. *The New Time Travelers: A Journey to the Frontiers of Physics*. New York: W.W. Norton and Company, 2007.
van Inwagen, Peter. "The Incompatibility of Free Will and Determinism." In *Free Will*, edited by Robert Kane, 71–82. Malden, MA: Blackwell, 2002.

The Credits
About the Contributors

Michael R. **Berry** is an associate professor of mass communication at King's College. He has published book chapters concerning whether superheroes should lie to hide their identities and how the first Deadpool movie subverted gender norms. He regularly presents at the Popular Cultural Association national conference. He was the director of debate at King's College and in 2000, was named National Debate Coach of the Year by the American Debate Association. His research interests include presidential debates, and superheroes/pop culture figures and how they are represented in mass media.

Liz **Fairchild** is a Ph.D. candidate in theater arts at the University of Oregon, where she studies science fiction, equitable futures on stage, queer theory and posthuman performance. She holds a creative writing MA from the University of East Anglia in Norwich, England, where her thesis was shortlisted for the Curtis Brown Award. She is a grant recipient from the University of California Speculative Futures Collective, and is also the vice president for external relations for the Graduate Teaching Fellows Federation of the University of Oregon.

Christopher M. **Innes** is a professor of philosophy at Boise State University in Idaho. He often uses popular culture references in his introduction classes and has created an online course called "Philosophy, Politics, and Pixar." He specializes in social and political philosophy and also teaches ethics, logic and metaphysics. As well as writing his own philosophy textbook, *The Philosophical Limits* (Kendall Hunt) he writes essays on social and political philosophical, and aesthetical themes found in popular television and film.

David Kyle **Johnson** is a professor of philosophy at King's College in Wilkes-Barre, Pennsylvania, who also produces lecture series for the Teaching Company's *The Great Courses*. His specializations include metaphysics, logic, and philosophy of religion and his "Great Courses" include "Sci-Phi: Science Fiction as Philosophy," "The Big Questions of Philosophy," and "Exploring Metaphysics." He is the editor-in-chief of the *Palgrave Handbook of Popular Culture as Philosophy,* and has edited other volumes including *Black Mirror and Philosophy* (Wiley-Blackwell).

Mimi **Marinucci** is a professor with an appointment split equally between philosophy and women's & gender studies at Eastern Washington University. She is the author of *Feminism Is Queer: The Intimate Connection between Queer and Feminist Theory* (Zed Books) and has published numerous articles addressing philosophical issues associated with gender, sex, and sexuality, particularly as represented in popular culture. Her research is focused on the question of intimacy between humans and machines.

Catherine **Nolan** teaches philosophy at the University of Dallas' campus outside of Rome, Italy. A Canadian by birth, she earned her Ph.D. at SUNY Buffalo in 2015. Her research is in the intersection of metaphysics and bioethics—in particular, how to expand traditional philosophical systems such as Aristotle's hylomorphic theory to accommodate scientific advances. She has published on definitions of death and justifications of organ donation and is also interested in definitions of the sexes and their ethical implications.

Francesca **Putignano** is a Ph.D. student at the University of Venice. She graduated with honors from the University of Bari with a bachelors in contemporary studies and gender studies, and then (again with honors) from the University of Bologna with a master's degree in the philosophy of science. Her main interests are feminist epistemology and philosophy of science.

Shaun **Respess** is a Ph.D. candidate in the Alliance for Social, Political, Ethical, and Cultural Thought Program at Virginia Tech and also teaches for the Department of Philosophy. His research utilizes the ethics of care to reveal and respond to various repressive conditions, while theoretically developing values that emerge from caring relations/practices. He attends to paradigms of mental health care with aspirations for improving our understanding of despair and reimagining alternatives for those seeking mental and emotional relief.

Leigh E. **Rich** is a professor of health administration at Georgia Southern University, where she teaches courses in bioethics, health law and policy, and social theory. She has worked as a journalist, radio host, and editor, including six years as editor-in-chief for the *Journal of Bioethical Inquiry*. She is an award-winning writer of editorials, news and feature stories, and reviews and is working on a socio-legal book titled *Bodies and Body Boundaries in the Age of Biotechnology*.

L. Brooke **Rudow** is a lecturer of philosophy at Georgia College and State University in Milledgeville, Georgia. Her research focuses primarily on ethical and epistemological issues that arise in relation to technology and the environment. She has written on pop culture items as various as *WikiLeaks*, *Blade Runner 2049*, and *Jane the Virgin*, and has published in *Hypatia* and *Feminist Philosophy Quarterly*, among other journals. She is working on a book exploring the connections between surfing and environmentalism.

Darren M. **Slade** (Ph.D.) is the president of the Global Center for Religious Research (GCRR.org), founding editor of *Socio-Historical Examination of Religion and Ministry* (SHERMjournal.org), research director for the FaithX Project, and adjunct professor of humanities at the Rocky Mountain College of Art and Design. His publications on the philosophy of religion, ancient Near Eastern and Second-Temple hermeneutical practices, church and Islamic history, and the psychology of religion can be found at darrenmslade.academia.edu.

About the Contributors 275

Joe **Slater** is a lecturer in moral and political philosophy at the University of Glasgow. His primary research relates to demandingness objections, which claim that certain moral theories should be rejected because of how demanding they are for individual moral agents. He is also interested in moral obligations to donate to charitable causes, the ethics of friendship, and moral implications relating to employment, such as nepotism (explored in this volume) and whether it is permissible to give preferential treatment to morally better people in a hiring process.

Patrick **Welsh** is an attorney with a J.D. from Indiana University, Maurer School of Law. He previously served as managing editor of the *Indiana Journal of Constitutional Design* and worked for the Center for Constitutional Democracy. He earned a master's degree in international affairs from Boston University Pardee School of Global Studies, specializing in fiscal federalism and economic growth in Europe, and worked for or interned with members of Congress, the U.S. Department of State, and Spain's Ministerio de asuntos exteriores.

Index

"About a Girl" (episode) 29–30, 71–72, 76–77, 131, 140, 228, 232–33, 255
absolutism 108–9, 113, 235; *see also* Krill; religion
The Accused (film) 230
Adam Ruins Everything (series) 155
affirmative action 221; *see also* equality; Freeman, Samuel; nepotism
afterlife 100, 184–85; *see also* dualism; "ghost in the machine"; reincarnation
AIDS/HIV 65, 169–70, 229–30
al-Nafis, Ibn 25; *see also* Islam; *The Theologus Autodidactus*
All in the Family (series) 229; *see also* Bunker, Archie
"All the World Is Birthday Cake" (episode) 43, 124, 126, 129, 171; *see also* astrology; Giliac sign
Allah 99–100; *see also* Islam; warrior god
alterity 62, 66, 68–69, 73; *see also* othering; queerness
altruism 210–11; *see also* nepotism
American Dad! (series) 226, 229, 248; *see also* MacFarlane, Seth
Americans for Prosperity 153; *see also* climate change
Americans for Tax Reform 153; *see also* climate change
Anhkana 29, 99–100, 105, 128; *see also* Avis; Krill
animal/human distinction 184–87, 189, 231; *see also* consciousness; Descartes, René; "ghost in the machine"
anthropogenesis 143–45; *see also* climate change; global warming
Aquinas, Thomas 39, 103; *see also* Christianity
Aristotle 10, 12, 36, 77, 184, 253; *see also* corporeality; human nature; *Poetics*; *Rhetoric*
Aronov, Dr. (character) 254
artificial intelligence 67–69, 71, 132, 180, 185, 189–90, 192–93; *see also* consciousness; human nature; Isaac; love; personhood; Searle, John; sexual relationships

astrology 43, 124, 126–27, 129, 171; *see also* "All the World Is Birthday Cake"; Giliac sign; Regor 2
Augustine 103; *see also* Christianity
Avengers: End Game (film) 271
Avis (god) 99–100, 104–5, 111, 127–29, 256; *see also* Anhkana; Avisism; Krill
Avisism (religion) 99–100, 102, 106–8; *see also* Krill
Azawa, Admiral (character) 127

Back to the Future (film) 271
backfire effect 146; *see also* climate change; Nyhan, Brendan; Reifler, Jason
backgrounding 130–31; *see also* dualism; religious beliefs
Bacon, Francis 25
Baier, Annette 203; *see also* trust
Baleth (character) 28, 106, 113, 123, 129
Barone, Matt 230
beauty 246–51; *see also* comedy; Hopkins, Mark
Bellow, Adam 210–11, 213–16; *see also* nepotism
Belnap, Nuel 262–63, 268; *see also* time travel
Bennet, Jimmy 12; *see also* Kirk, Captain
Bernstein, Jonathan 230
bias 26–27, 44–45, 66,-67, 76, 125, 172; *see also* cloaking bias; cognitive dissonance; cognitive estrangement; confirmation bias; discrimination; feminism; gender; Haslanger, Sally; racism; sexism
Big (film) 229
biology (as it relates to feminism) 82–83; *see also* feminism
bisexual 80; *see also* sexual orientation; sexuality
Black Mirror (series) 26, 30, 238
"Blood of Patriots" (episode) 104, 196, 201, 204–5
Bohr, Niels Henrik David 143
Bormanis, André 26, 167, 175, 269; *see also* pure democracy; time travel
Bortus, Lieutenant Commander (character) 29, 38, 40, 54, 63–64, 67, 71–73, 76, 80,

278 Index

83, 86, 126, 140, 171–72, 228, 231–34, 237, 245, 247, 268; hatching/laying egg 34, 37, 232, 258; *see also* "About a Girl"; gender correction surgery; Klyden; Moclans; "Primal Urges"; *Rudolph the Red-Nosed Reindeer*; sexual reproduction; Topa
Boulding, Elise 100
Boys Don't Cry (film) 230
Braga, Brannon 8, 23–24, 34, 171; *see also Star Trek: Enterprise; Star Trek: First Contact; Star Trek Generations; Star Trek: The Next Generation; Star Trek: Voyager*
The Breakfast Show (fictional TV series) 169, 174; *see also* Lysella; "Majority Rule"
breastfeeding 40–42
Brooks, Albert 24; *see also Defending Your Life*
Buber, Martin 110
Buck Rogers (film) 7
A Bug's Life (film) 190; *see also* personhood
Bunker, Archie (*All in the Family* character) 229; *see also All in the Family*
Bush, George, W. 27
Butler, Judith 68

Calivon (species) 200, 226, 234–37
Callicott, J. Baird 154
"caloric" theory of heat 144
canon (story) 6, 10–12, 14, 16, 19; closed vs. open 11, 16; *The Orville* as 14–15; *Star Trek* as 7, 9, 11–12, 15; *see also* fanfiction; genre; *The Orville*; Pugh, Sheenagh
capitalism 154–56
care 39–40, 42, 122, 196–98, 200, 203, 205–6; ethics of 134–35, 196, 202–4, 206; theories of 196–97; *see also* dependency; Hoagland, Sarah Lucia; "Into the Fold"; Isaac; Kittay, Eva Feder; Mol, Annemarie; Noddings, Nel; relationships; Tronto, Joan; trust
Cars (film) 190; *see also* personhood
Catholicism 99
The Cato Institute 153; *see also* climate change
Channing, Orrin (character) 104, 201–5
USS *Chanute* 212
The Charlie Rose Show (series) 172; *see also* "Majority Rule"
The Chat (fictional TV series) 173; *see also* "Majority Rule"; *The View*
Christ 100–1; *see also* Christianity
Christianity 99–101, 103–4, 109–11, 113, 127–28; *see also* Aquinas, Thomas; Augustine; Christ; Dominion Theology; evangelicalism; Reconstruction Theology; religion; Religious Right; soul
"City on the Edge of Forever" (*Star Trek* episode) 261, 270; *see also Star Trek* (original series)
Ciulla, Joanne 212; *see also* nepotism
"clash of civilizations" theory 106–8; *see also* Huntington, Samuel

The Cleveland Show (series) 229; *see also* MacFarlane, Seth
clickbait 170
climate change 28, 141; denial of 141–45; end-times apathy hypothesis 148; lukewarmers 151–53; philosophic reasons for denial 151–56; religious reasons for denial 146–50; small government conservatism 153–56; *see also* Americans for Prosperity; Americans for Tax Reform; anthropogenesis; backfire effect; The Cato Institute; Collomb, Jean-Canel; Cook, John; cultural war; environmentalism; Evangelical Climate Initiative; evangelicals; fossil fuels; global warming; The Heritage Foundation; "hockey stick graph"; libertarianism; Lindzen, Richard; Mann, Michael; 97% Consensus; Oreskes, Naomi; Paris Climate Accord; scientific consensus; scientific illiteracy; Smith, Adam; "tragedy of the commons"
Clinton, Hillary 170
cloaking bias 26, 28–30, 140–41; *see also* bias; cognitive dissonance
Clueless (film) 253
CO_2 emissions 142, 144–45, 147, 153–55; *see also* global warming
cognitive dissonance 26–30, 100, 140–41; *see also* bias; cloaking bias; cognitive estrangement
cognitive estrangement 26; *see also* bias; cloaking bias; cognitive dissonance; Suvin, Darko
Coleridge, Samuel Taylor 270; *see also* poetic faith; the supernatural; suspension of disbelief
Collomb, Jean-Canel 151, 153–54; *see also* climate change
colonialism 101–3, 128
comedy 245, 251, 259; good taste vs. bad taste 246, 256–58; lowbrow vs. highbrow 245–46, 248, 251; *see also* beauty; comic theory; Hopkins, Mark; humor
comic theory 253–56; high comedy 253–55; low comedy 255–56; *see also* comedy
"Command Performance" (episode) 200, 226, 228, 232–33, 235
compatibilism 53, 55–56; *see also* determinism; Frankfurt, Harry; free will
confirmation bias 100; *see also* bias
Conover, Adam 155
consciousness 182–83, 185–92, 200; *see also* animal/human distinction; artificial intelligence; embodiment; God; human nature; Isaac; love; personhood; rationality; relationships; sentience; solipsism
consent 49–56, 57–60, 201; *see also* free will; sexual assault
The Consolidator (novel) 25
Contact (film) 26; *see also* Sagan, Carl
contraception 85
"contraction theory" (earth's formation) 144

Index 279

Cook, John 142–43; *see also* climate change; 97% Consensus
Copernicus 143
corporeality 184; *see also* Aristotle; Plato
Cosmos (series) 231, 237; *see also* Sagan, Carl
Cosmos: A Spacetime Odyssey (series) 226; *see also* MacFarlane, Seth
Coward, Noel 254
Crabtree, Harriet 101; *see also* war
"crisis of legitimacy" 108; *see also* religion; secularism
Crusades 29, 98, 101, 103
cultural development 123–24; *see also* religious beliefs
cultural identity 62
cultural relativism 30, 235
cultural war 148–50; *see also* climate change; evangelicalism; secular humanism
"Cupid's Dagger" (episode) 29, 48–49, 58, 60, 70; *see also* Darulio; Grayson, Commander Kelly; Mercer, Captain Ed; queerness
Curie, Marie 87

The Daily Show (series) 149
Darulio (character) 29, 49, 54–57, 60; pheromone 29, 48–50, 53–55, 58; *see also* "Cupid's Dagger"; sexual assault
Darwin, Charles 143
Davis Rogan, Alcena Madeline 71–72
De Beauvoir, Simone 41, 44; *see also The Second Sex*
de Botton, Alain 112
Defending Your Life (film) 24; *see also* Brooks, Albert
"Deflectors" (episode) 39
Defoe, Daniel 25
DeGeneres, Ellen 65
demons 25, 100
Dennett, Daniel 189; *see also* personhood
dependency 198, 201; *see also* care; Kittay, Eva Feder
Derrida, Jacques 13–14, 19, 114; *see also* genre; religion; religious violence
Descartes, René 25, 63, 130, 185, 189, 231, 233; *see also* animal/human distinction; dualism
determinism 51, 53; *see also* compatibilism; Frankfurt, Harry; free will
de Tocqueville, Alexis 166; *see also* pure democracy
Deutsch, David 262–63, 268; *see also* time travel
disability 82, 184, 189, 235; *see also* discrimination
discrimination 89, 184, 210, 221–22, 229, 235; *see also* bias; disability; gender; inequality; nepotism; race; racism; sexism
"divine command theory" 103; *see also* just war theory
divine voluntarism 105; *see also* religion
Doctor Who (series) 262

Dominion Theology 109; *see also* Christianity; evangelicalism
Dorahl (god) 105, 111, 147–48, 150; *see also* theocracy
Dorahlians (believers) 104, 112; *see also* Hamelac
Dorahlism (religion) 147
Dougherty, Tom 57
Drogen (character) 200
dualisim 63, 110, 130, 185; *see also* afterlife; backgrounding; Descartes, René; embodiment; "ghost in the machine"; religion; technology

Ebert, Roger 229, 238
Edison, Thomas 143–44
ego 227–28, 231–36; ego-ideal 227–28, 234–35; ideal ego 227–28, 233–35; *see also* Lacan, Jacques
Einstein, Albert 143–44
Elden, Gondus (character) 35, 77, 83, 86; *see also* Heveena; Moclus
Eliot, T.S. 228
embodiment 68, 185, 187; *see also* consciousness; dualism; human nature
Emerson, Ralph Waldo 249
Emerson, William Byron 249
USS *Enterprise* 261; *see also* Star Trek (original series)
environmentalism 148, 154; *see also* climate change
episodic allegory 26, 30
equality 3, 80, 88, 105, 109, 128, 170, 218; of opportunity 219–22; *see also* affirmative action; feminism; gender; inequality; nepotism; Rawls, John
ethnocentrism 106, 235
eupraxsophy 106; *see also* secular humanism
Evangelical Climate Initiative 149; *see also* climate change; evangelicalism
evangelicalism 148–50; Christian identity movements 148; neo-evangelicalism 109–110; persecution complex 149; *see also* Christianity; climate change; cultural war; Dominion Theology; Evangelical Climate Initiative; Reconstruction Theology; Religious Right; secularism; theocracy
evolution 85, 112, 123, 145, 186, 211; *see also* reason-based societies; religion

Facebook 172; *see also* internet
Fadolin (character) 28, 111, 113
faith *see* religious beliefs
Family Guy (series) 24, 226, 228–30, 237–38, 245, 252, 255–56; *see also* Griffen, Peter; MacFarlane, Seth
fanfiction 6, 11–12, 14–15, 17; "more-of" vs. "more-from" 16, 18; *see also* canon; genre; *The Orville*; Pugh, Sheenagh
female (definition) 35–37

280　Index

The Feminine Mystique (book) 238; *see also* Friedan, Betty
feminism 75–76, 78–80, 83, 85–86, 88–90, 238; erasure of women 77, 87; identity of women 75–76; inferiority of women 76, 85; invisibility of women 76, 87; philosophy of 75, 84; studies of 81, 83–84, 89; *see also* bias; biology (as it relates to feminism); equality; gender studies; meta-pop culture; #MeToo; Moclus; *The Orville*; pop culture; sexism
Fields, W.C. 251
Fink, Edward 245–46, 253–54
Finn, Dr. Claire (character) 49, 58, 64, 70–71, 79, 124, 131, 134, 140–41, 174, 191, 200–1, 232–34, 248–50, 256, 267–69; caregiver 197–98, 200–202, 204, 206, 209; children of 180, 197–98, 200, 211; Marcus 200; relationship with Isaac 59–60, 63, 66–67, 69, 132–135, 180, 182, 188, 191–93; Ty 134, 188, 200, 248; *see also* "A Happy Refrain"; Isaac; love; relationships
The Flintstones (series) 251–52
Fonda, Jane 238; *see also 9 to 5* (film)
fossil fuels 142, 145–46, 151, 153–56; *see also* climate change; global warming
Foucault, Michel 106
FOX News 127
Frakes, Jonathan 8, 15; *see also Star Trek: Discovery*; *Star Trek: The Next Generation*
Frankenstein (novel) 25; *see also* science fiction as philosophy; Shelley, Mary
Frankfurt, Harry 53; *see also* compatibilism; determinism; free will
Frasier (series) 254
Freaky Friday (film) 184
free will 49, 51–53, 56, 264; *see also* compatibilism; consent; determinism; Frankfurt, Harry; libertarianism; time travel
freedom of speech 170; *see also* MacFarlane, Seth
Freeman, Samuel 221; *see also* affirmative action; nepotism; Rawls, John
Freud, Sigmund 231, 234, 237; *see also* Lacan, Jacques
Friedan, Betty 238; *see also The Feminine Mystique*
Fuller, Steve 125; *see also* primitive cultures
functionalism 181; *see also* Nagel, Thomas; phenomenal quality of experience
fundamentalism 100, 109; *see also* religion

Gandhi, Mahatma 149
Galileo 143–44
Galileo Gambit 143
Gattaca (film) 26
gay 29, 39–40; 68, 70–73, 81, 229, 238; *see also* lesbian; queerness; sexual orientation; sexuality
Gelatins (species) 219; *see also* Yaphit
gender (compared to sex) 36, 44–45, 62, 64, 68, 81, 235; *see also* bias; discrimination; equality; inequality; oppression; race; sexuality
gender correction surgery 29, 35–36, 39–40, 42, 44, 71, 73, 76, 83, 85–87, 232, 235; *see also* "About a Girl"; Bortus, Lieutenant Commander; Klyden; Moclus; Topa
gender expression 81; *see also* gender identity
gender identity 64, 68, 81–82; *see also* gender expression; queerness; sexual orientation
gender norms 69, 81–82
gender roles 81
gender studies 81; *see also* feminism
genocide 99, 103, 106, 110, 113, 134; *see also* religion
genre 10, 13, 17; critical/pragmatic genre theory 10–11; remark/theory of belonging 13–15, 19; *see also* canon; Derrida, Jacques; fanfiction; Miller, Carolyn; Rosmarin, Adena; science fiction as philosophy; Wellek, René
"ghost in the machine" 185–86; *see also* afterlife; animal/human distinction; dualism; Ryle, Gilbert
Giffendon, Mella (statue) 28, 165, 173–74, 256; *see also* LaMarr, Chief Engineer/Lieutenant Commander John; "Majority Rule"
Giliac sign 124, 126–127; *see also* "All the World Is Birthday Cake"; astrology; Regor 2 (planet)
Girard, René 108; *see also* mimesis
global warming 141–42, 151–52; *see also* anthropogenesis; climate change; CO_2 emissions; fossil fuels; greenhouse gas; Paris Climate Accord
GMOs 145
God 185–86, 188; *see also* consciousness; personhood; soul
God's Not Dead (film) 149
Goodall, Jane 189
Goodman, David 8, 23–24, 26, 100, 271; *see also Star Trek: Enterprise*; time travel
Gore, Al 148
Grant, Cary 229
Grayson, Commander Kelly (character) 28, 30, 44, 49–50, 54–57, 67, 79, 83, 85, 107, 126–27, 131–33, 140, 171, 174, 180, 182, 200, 209, 212–13, 215–17, 219–21, 232–38, 245, 247–48, 254–55, 261, 267–69; healing a child 111, 123; *see also* "Cupid's Dagger"; Kellians; Kelly/Ed dynamic; "Mad Idolatry"; nepotism
greenhouse gas 142, 155; *see also* global warming
Griffin, Peter (*Family Guy* character) 229, 238, 252, 255; *see also Family Guy*
groupthink 110
Gruber, Aya 51

Halsey, Admiral (character) 209, 213, 215–16, 219–22, 234

Hamelac (character) 112, 147, 150, 155–56; see also Dorahlians (believers)
Hamlet (play) 226, 235
The Handmaid's Tale (novel) 30, 79
Hanks, Tom 229–30
"A Happy Refrain" (episode) 49, 59, 60, 66, 69, 132, 180, 191, 193, 248; see also Finn, Dr. Claire; Isaac
Haraway, Donna 62, 70
Harry Potter (novel) 270
Haslam, Jason 64; see also queerness
Haslanger, Sally 44; see also bias
The Heartland Institute 145, 153; see also climate change; Lupo, Anthony
Heidegger, Martin 43, 45
Heisenberg, Werner Karl 143
Held, Virginia 134
Hennessy, Rosemary 69
Henson, Jim 252; see also The Muppet Show
The Heritage Foundation 153; see also climate change
heteronormativity 62–64, 67–68, 71–72
heterosexuality 29, 68–69; see also sexuality
Heveena (character) 35, 40, 77–78, 80, 85–89, 233–35; see also Elden, Gondus; Moclans
Hoagland, Sarah Lucia 197–98; see also care
"hockey stick graph" 142–43; see also climate change; Mann, Michael
Hoffman, Claire 229
holograms 68, 236; see also Isaac
homonormativity 68, 72
The Honeymooners (series) 237
Hoogen, James 151
Hopkins, Mark 245–46, 248–251, 259; see also beauty; comedy
human nature 184–85; see also Aristotle; artificial intelligence; consciousness; embodiment; personhood
Hume, David 192
humor 226; sophomoric 228–30, 237–38; see also comedy
The Hunger Games (novel) 15
Hunsberger, Bruce 108
Huntington, Samuel 103, 107; see also "clash of civilizations" theory; religious violence
hyper-rationality 122

"Identity" – Part 1 (episode) 122, 133, 267
"Identity" – Part 2 (episode) 101, 122, 133, 190, 267; see also Isaac
"If the Stars Should Appear" (ISSA) (episode) 27, 105, 111, 140–41, 147, 150, 155–56, 249
immigration 109, 113
In Praise of Nepotism (book) 213; see also Bellow, Adam
Inception (film) 26
inclusiveness 107, 184
inequality 2, 82, 197–98, 219; see also discrimination; equality; gender; race
internet 166–68, 172; see also Facebook; social media; Twitter

intersex 29, 37; see also sexuality
Interstellar (film) 271
"Into the Fold" (episode) 196–98; see also care
Iris (film) 230
Irwin, William 25; see also The Wiley/Blackwell Philosophy and Popular Culture Series
Isaac (character) 35, 40, 64, 66–68, 124, 131, 134–35, 165–66, 174, 180, 196; as a caregiver 199–201, 206; Claire's children 135–36, 183, 188, 209, 216, 232–33, 236, 255, 265, 267; consciousness of 182, 184–86, 190–91; emotions of 132, 187; intelligence of 191, 255–56; personhood of 190–93; receptivity and reciprocity in relationship 181–84; relationship with Claire Finn 59–60, 63, 67–69, 133, 188, 191–93; see also artificial intelligence; care; Finn, Dr. Claire; "A Happy Refrain"; holograms; Kaylon; love; personhood; sentience; soul
Islam 99–100, 102, 104, 113; dar al-harb 102; dar al-islam 102; Islamism 109; jihad 102; Mujahideen 98, 102; Qur'an 101; see also al-Nafis, Ibn; Allah
Israeli-Palestinian conflict 101

Jackass (series) 24; see also MacFarlane, Seth
Jackson, Lynne 108
"Ja'loja" (episode) 245
Jesus see Christ
jinnee 264–65; see also time travel
jouissance (jubilation) 231; see also méconnaissance (misrecognition); mirror stage; Wallon, Henri
Judaism 99–103, 113; see also Yahweh
Judeo-Christian doctrine 127, 184
Juergensmeyer, Mark 102, 104
just war theory 103–104; see also "divine command theory"; religion; religious violence; war

Kant, Immanuel 45, 135, 188
Kaylon (inhabitants) 59, 106, 133–36, 180, 190–92, 198, 209–10, 267–68; see also Isaac; Kaylon 1 (planet)
Kaylon 1 (planet) 106, 134, 180; see also Kaylon (inhabitants); Kaylon Primary; Planetary Union; Union-Kaylon conflict
Kaylon Primary 135, 190, 192; see also Kaylon 1 (planet)
Kellians (Kelly worshippers) 28, 104, 127; see also Grayson, Commander Kelly; Kelly (god)
Kelly (god) 105, 123, 126–127; see also Kellians
Kelly/Ed dynamic 34; see also Grayson, Commander Kelly; Mercer, Captain Ed
Kelly, Kevin 25–26
Kemka (character) 112, 147, 154
Keyali, Lieutenant Talla (character) 39, 79, 134, 203, 205, 210, 221–22; see also Xelayans (inhabitants)

Keynes, John Maynard 44
Kirk, Captain (*Star Trek* character) 12, 255; *see also* Bennet, Jimmy; Mignogna, Vic; Pine, Chris; Shatner, William; *Star Trek* (original series); *Star Trek II: The Wrath of Khan*
Kitan, Lieutenant Alara (character) 16, 44, 49–50, 54, 79, 83, 209–10, 221–22, 232–36, 249; *see also* Xelayans (inhabitants)
Kitan, Ildis (character) 222, 248; *see also* Kitan, Lieutenant Alara
Kittay, Eva Feder 198; *see also* care; dependency
Klyden (character) 29, 34, 63–64, 76, 83, 88, 140, 232, 258; born as female, 35, 40, 76; *see also* "About a Girl"; Bortus, Lieutenant Commander; gender correction surgery; Moclans; "Primal Urges"; Topa
Knoll, John 27
"Krill" (episode) 43, 108
Krill (species) 28, 98–101, 103–110, 112–14, 124, 127, 129, 201–3, 205, 211, 233, 256; danger of 129, 220; language of 105; religion of 124, 127–28; suppression of reason 129–30; *see also* absolutism; Anhkana; Avis; Avisism; patriarchy; Planetary Union; religion; religious beliefs; religious fanaticism; Sazeron; soul; the supernatural; theocracy; religious violence; war; warrior god; xenophobia; Yakar

Lacan, Jacques 226–28, 231–34, 236–38; object/*objet (petit) a* 228, 237; *see also* ego; Freud, Sigmund; mirror stage; register of the Imaginary; register of the Real; register of the Symbolic; "specular image"
Lak'vai Pact of Tarazed 106
LaMarr, Chief Engineer/Lieutenant Commander John (character) 28–29, 59, 66, 68, 124, 170, 172–74, 214, 217, 220, 232–33, 247–50, 252, 256; apology tour 165, 173; arrest of 173; *see also* Giffendon, Mella (statue); "Majority Rule"; Sargus 4 (planet)
Laplace, Pierre-Simon 25
"Lasting Impression" (episode) 140
Lavesque, Pria (character) 261, 265–66, 269; *see also* "Pria" (episode); time travel
Lear, Norman 228–29
Lee, Dr. Janice (character) 254
LeGuin, Ursula K. 65
Lehrer, Jonah 167–70, 173; *see also* MacFarlane, Seth; "Majority Rule"; Ronson, Jon; *So You've Been Publicly Shamed*; social media
lesbian 29, 39–40, 65; *see also* gay; queerness; sexual orientation; sexuality
Lewis, David 263, 266–69; *see also* time travel
Leyna (character) 201–2, 204
libertarianism 52, 153–56, 264; *see also* climate change; free will
Liberto, Hallie 50–53, 56

Lindsay, Hal 148
Lindzen, Richard 151; *see also* climate change
Little Shop of Horrors (film) 190; *see also* personhood
Lloyd, Genevieve 85
Lokar (character) 39
Lopovius (planet) 49
Lord of the Rings (novel) 270
love 180; between Claire and Isaac 180–84, 193; between humans and robots 180, 182; *see also* artificial intelligence; consciousness; Finn, Claire; Dr.; Isaac; Noddings, Nel; phenomenal quality of experience; relationships
Lucian of Samosata 25; *see also* *A True History*
Lucifer 100
Lupo, Anthony 145; *see also* The Heartland Institute
Lynas, Mark 152; *see also* *Six Degrees*
Lysella (character) 169–72, 174–75; *see also* *The Breakfast Show*; "Majority Rule"; pure democracy; Sarguns (inhabitants)

MacFarlane, Seth 7–8, 11, 15, 17–18, 23–24, 26, 34, 114, 131, 226, 230, 245–46, 251–52, 254, 257, 265, 267; 2013 Academy Awards 230, 238, 253; 2018 San Diego Comic-Con 169, 175; atheist 106, 122, 125; creation of "Majority Rule" 166–72; *The Life of Larry* 228–30; *see also* *American Dad!*; *The Cleveland Show*; *Cosmos: A Spacetime Odyssey*; *Family Guy*; freedom of speech; *Jackass*; Lehrer, Jonah; "Majority Rule"; Mercer, Ed; *A Million Ways to Die in the West*; pop culture; pure democracy; Ronson, Jon; Sacco, Justine; *So You've Been Publicly Shamed*; *Ted*; *Ted 2*; time travel
"Mad Idolatry" (episode) 28, 105–7, 111–13, 123, 126, 129–31; *see also* Grayson, Commander Kelly; religious beliefs
"Majority Rule" (episode) 28, 43, 165–67, 170–75, 256; *see also* *The Breakfast Show*; *The Charlie Rose Show*; *The Chat*; Giffendon, Mella (statue); LaMarr, Chief Engineer/Lieutenant Commander John; Lehrer, Jonah; Lysella; MacFarlane, Seth; pure democracy; representative democracy; Ronson, Jon; Sacco, Justine; Sargus 4; *So You've Been Publicly Shamed*; social media; Tom and Lewis (Planetary Union anthropologists)
male (definition) 36–37
Malloy, Gordon, Helmsman/Lieutenant (character) 29, 83, 98, 124, 129, 135, 173, 201–6, 209–10, 214–17, 232–34, 245, 247–50, 252, 255–56, 268
Mann, Michael 142–43; *see also* climate change; "hockey stick graph"
Mannequin (film) 190; *see also* personhood
marginalization 80, 82, 112–13, 172; *see also* othering

Index 283

masculinity 68, 71, 73
M*A*S*H (series) 23–24, 80
The Matrix (film) 25–26
Matthews, Freya 125; see also primitive cultures
McDonough, Peter 109
McKibben, Mill 155
McLaren, Brian 111
méconnaissance (misrecognition) 231; see also jouissance (jubilation); mirror stage; Wallon, Henri
menopause 82
menstruation 41; 82
Mercer, Captain Ed (character) 30, 49–50, 54–57, 60, 69, 71, 77, 85–86, 98, 101, 104–5, 108–9, 112, 127–30, 134, 136, 140–41, 147, 155–56, 174, 199–203, 205, 222, 232–38, 245, 247, 249–50, 252, 254–58, 261, 265–69, 271; command of USS Orville 209–10, 212, 214–17, 219–21, 267; emotions vs. reason 131–32; see also "About a Girl"; "Cupid's Dagger"; Kelly/Ed dynamic; MacFarlane, Seth; nepotism; time travel
#MeToo 79; see also feminism
meta-pop culture 75, 77, 86; see also feminism; pop culture
Metropolis (film) 26, 67–68
Mignogna, Vic 12; see also Kirk, Captain
Miller, Carolyn 17–18; see also genre
Miller, Liz Shannon 9
A Million Ways to Die in the West (film) 230; see also MacFarlane, Seth
mimesis 108; see also Girard, Rene
mirror stage 227, 231–33, 236–37; see also jouissance (jubilation); méconnaissance (misrecognition); "specular image"; Wallon, Henri
misogyny 70–73, 83, 86, 88, 104, 230; see also Moclus; patriarchy; queerness; sexism
Moclans (inhabitants) 29, 34, 71, 86, 211, 232, 255; existence of females 34, 41, 77, 88, 233; see also Bortus, Lieutenant Commander; Heveena; Klyden; Moclus
Moclus (planet) 37, 41–42, 63, 71, 76–77, 81–83, 85, 88, 104, 235; female colony of 35, 40, 42, 77, 82, 86–88, 233, 235; reproductive role of females and males 35, 38–40, 42, 45; single-gender species 30, 36–37, 76; see also Elden, Gondus; feminism; gender correction surgery; misogyny; Moclans (inhabitants); patriarchy; sexism; sexual reproduction
Mol, Annemarie 201–2; see also care
Montford, Andrew 142–43
moral grandstanding 170; see also Tose, Justin; Warmke, Brandon
moral relativism 105
More, Thomas 25; see also Utopia (novel)
Moyer, Bill 148
multiculturalism 113

Muñoz, José Esteban 64; see also queerness
The Muppet Show (series) 249, 252; Kermit the Frog 249, 252, 257; Miss Piggy 249; Statler and Waldorf 253; see also Henson, Jim
Murdoch, Iris
Murphy, Lieutenant Commander (character) 212

Nadel, Alan 236
Nagel, Thomas 181; see also functionalism; phenomenal quality of experience
Nashawaty, Chris 230
nepotism 209–11, 222; arguments against 215–221; New Nepotism vs. Old Nepotism 213–14, 217; private vs. public 209, 212; rules of 214–15, 217; see also affirmative action; altruism; Bellow, Adam; Ciulla, Joanne; discrimination; equality; Freeman, Samuel; Grayson, Commander Kelly; Mercer, Captain Ed; Planetary Union; Rawls, John; A Theory of Justice
neuroscience 52
The New Atlantis (novel) 25; see also Bacon, Francis
"New Dimensions" (episode) 216, 247
Newton, Isaac 144, 247
Newton, Steve, Chief Engineer (character) 233
Niebuhr, Reinhold 104
9 to 5 (film) 238; see also Fonda, Jane; Parton, Dolly; Tomlin, Lily
"9 to 5" (song) 88, 228, 234–35, 238; see also Parton, Dolly
97% Consensus 142–43, 145; see also climate change; Cook, John
Noddings, Nel 180–81, 197; see also care; love; relationships
nonhuman machines see artificial intelligence
"Nothing Left on Earth Excepting Fishes" (episode) 103, 108–9, 128, 132
Novella, Steven 144
Nozick, Robert 25
Nyhan, Brendan 146; see also backfire effect

Odo (Star Trek character) 70
"Old Wounds" (episode) 208, 212, 236
oppression 30, 35, 41–42, 45, 90, 110, 126, 201; see also gender; patriarchy; sexism
Oreskes, Naomi 154; see also climate change
Orr, David 148
The Orville (series): contributions to feminism 75–76, 78–80, 89; doing philosophy, 26, 140; as homage to Star Trek 7, 9, 63; philosophy of religion 99, 112, 114; similarities with Star Trek 7–9, 171, 231; see also canon; fanfiction; feminism; Star Trek (original series)
USS Orville 23, 28, 34–35, 48–49, 57–58, 86, 141, 165, 171, 173–74, 196, 204, 206, 216, 219–20, 248, 251–52, 254, 265–66

284 Index

othering 62–63, 102; *see also* alterity; marginalization; religious violence
Ozawa, Admiral (character) 102, 128–29

Paris Climate Accord 141; *see also* climate change; global warming
Parton, Dolly 77, 88–89, 228, 234, 238; *see also 9 to 5* (film); "9 to 5" (song)
patriarchy 41–43, 45, 75–76, 80, 82–83, 85, 90, 237; *see also* Krill; misogyny; Moclus; oppression; sexism
The Patriot Act (legislation) 27
Pearson, Wendy 62, 64–65, 72
personhood 188–93; *see also* artificial intelligence; *A Bug's Life*; *Cars*; consciousness; Dennett, Daniel; God; human nature; Isaac; *Little Shop of Horrors*; *Mannequin*; rationality; Searle, John; sentience; Singer, Peter; soul; *Toy Story*; Warren, Mary Anne; *The Wizard of Oz*
phenomenal quality of experience 181–83; *see also* functionalism; love; Nagel, Thomas; relationships
Philadelphia (film) 229–30
Pine, Chris 12; *see also* Kirk, Captain
Planetary Union 99, 105–8, 113, 171, 173, 204, 206, 209–10, 212, 215, 217, 221, 233–35; *see also* Kaylon 1 (planet); Krill; nepotism; representative democracy; secular humanism; secularism
Planned Parenthood 51, 55, 59
Plato 25, 105, 130, 184; *see also* corporeality; *The Republic*; "The Ring of Gyges"
Plumwood, Val 130–31
poetic faith 270; *see also* Coleridge, Samuel Taylor
Poetics (book) 10, 253; *see also* Aristotle
pop culture 75, 77–79, 84, 88, 90, 255; MacFarlane's use of 226–29, 231, 235, 237–38; vehicle of feminism 79–80, 89–90; *see also* feminism; meta-pop culture
Porro, Joseph 165
posthumanism 70
Powers, Kemp 12
pregnancy 41
"Pria" (episode) 255, 261, 265, 269; *see also* Lavesque, Pria; time travel
"Primal Urges" (episode) 71–72; *see also* "About a Girl"; Bortus, Lieutenant Commander; Klyden
primitive cultures 123–25; *see also* Fuller, Steve; Matthews, Freya; religion; religious beliefs; technology
Protestantism 100
Puar, Jasbir 66
Pugh, Sheenagh 11, 16; *see also* canon; fanfiction
pure democracy 165–67, 175; critique of 171–74; *see also* Bormanis, André; de Tocqueville, Alexis; Lysella; MacFarlane, Seth; "Majority Rule"; representative democracy; Sargus 4; social media
puritanical culture 63

queerness 62–69, 71–73, 80–81; proto-queer 64–65, 66–69; reading 64–65, 69–70; text 64–65, 70–73; *see also* "Cupid's Dagger"; gender identity; Haslam, Jason; misogyny; Muñoz, José Esteban; science fiction as philosophy; sexual preference; sexuality; *Star Trek* (original series); *Star Trek: Discovery*; utopia

race 44–45, 64, 71, 79, 99–100, 102–3, 105, 134–35, 140, 169, 183, 210, 218; *see also* discrimination; gender; racism
racism 29, 45, 184, 210, 219; *see also* bias; discrimination; race
Rana 3 (planet) 128
rape 48, 51; *see also* sexual assault
rationality 17, 67, 85, 87, 105–6, 113, 122, 130–31, 134, 185, 191–92; *see also* consciousness; personhood
Rawls, John 110, 210, 217–21; *see also* equality; Freeman, Samuel; nepotism; *A Theory of Justice*; "veil of ignorance"
Real Housewives of New Jersey (series) 236–37
reason-based societies 123; *see also* evolution; religious-based societies
reciprocity *see* care; relationships
Reconstruction Theology 109–110; *see also* Christianity; evangelicalism
register of the Imaginary 227–28, 231, 234, 237; *see also* Lacan, Jacques
register of the Real 227–28, 231, 234, 237; *see also* Lacan, Jacques
register of the Symbolic 227–28, 234, 237; *see also* Lacan, Jacques
Regor 2 (planet) 171; *see also* astrology; Giliac sign
Regorians (inhabitants) 171
Reifler, Jason 146; *see also* backfire effect
reincarnation 185; *see also* afterlife
"Rejoined" (*Star Trek: Deep Space Nine* episode) 65; *see also Star Trek: Deep Space Nine*
relationships 188, 197, 205–6; Nodding's analysis of 180–81; receptivity and reciprocity in 180–81; *see also* care; consciousness; Finn, Dr. Claire; Isaac; love; Noddings, Nel; phenomenal quality of experience; sentience; trust
relativity (Einsteinian) 262, 264; *see also* time travel
religion 98, 107–108, 111–14, 125, 129, 154; conservative 100, 109, 111, 113, 150, 170, 238; and morality 104–6; philosophy of 99, 111; and politics 108–11, 113; zealots 99, 110, 113; *see also* absolutism; Christianity; "crisis of legitimacy"; Derrida, Jacques; divine voluntarism; dualism; evolution;

fundamentalism; genocide; just war theory; Krill; primitive cultures; religious violence; secular humanism; separation of church and state; the supernatural; tribalism; war; warrior god
religious-based societies 123; *see also* reason-based societies
religious beliefs 123–27, 131, 147, 154; *see also* backgrounding; cultural development; Krill; "Mad Idolatry"; primitive cultures
religious dogma 28, 99, 105, 108–9, 111, 113, 122–23, 125, 129, 131, 136
religious extremism 110, 114
religious fanaticism 43, 98, 110; *see also* Krill
religious pluralism 107, 109, 113
Religious Right 109; *see also* Christianity; evangelicalism
religious terrorism 98, 110, 114
religious violence 98, 101–104, 106, 108–10, 114; *see also* Derrida, Jacques; Huntington, Samuel; just war theory; Krill; othering; religion; war
representative democracy 165, 171–72, 175; *see also* "Majority Rule"; Planetary Union; pure democracy
The Republic (book) 25; *see also* Plato; "The Ring of Gyges"
Retepsia (planet) 86, 219
Rhetoric (book) 77; *see also* Aristotle
Richards, Michael 257; *see also* Seinfeld
Ridley, Matt 151; *see also* climate change
"The Ring of Gyges" (story) 25; *see also* Plato; *The Republic*
"The Road Not Taken" (episode) 267–69; *see also* time travel
robots *see* artificial intelligence
Rokal (character) 126
Ronson, Jon 28, 167–69; *see also* Lehrer, Jonah; MacFarlane, Seth; "Majority Rule"; *So You've Been Publicly Shamed*
Rosmarin, Adena 10–11; *see also* genre
Rudolph the Red-Nosed Reindeer (film) 29, 76, 80, 83, 228, 233–34, 237; *see also* Bortus, Lieutenant Commander; Santa Claus
Rush, Marvin V. 98
Russell, Bertrand 142
Ryle, Gilbert 185; *see also* "ghost in the machine"

Sacco, Justine 169–70, 172; *see also* MacFarlane, Seth; "Majority Rule"; social media
Sagan, Carl 26, 231; *see also* *Contact*; *Cosmos*
"Sanctuary" (episode) 30, 35, 77, 84, 86, 228, 233, 235, 238; *see also* Topa
Sanders, Bernie 170
Santa Claus 89, 233; *see also* *Rudolph the Red-Nosed Reindeer*
Sarguns (inhabitants) 165, 169, 171, 174; *see also* Lysella; Sargus 4
Sargus 4 (planet) 165–66, 170, 173–74, 256;

apology tour 168, 174; downvotes 168, 173; the Master Feed 165, 169, 173–74; social correction procedure 168, 173–74; *see also* LaMarr, Chief Engineer/Lieutenant Commander John; "Majority Rule"; pure democracy; Sarguns (inhabitants)
Sazeron (character) 102; *see also* Krill
science fiction as philosophy 24–26; *see also* *Frankenstein*; genre; queerness
scientific consensus 144, 152; *see also* climate change
scientific ignorance 28
scientific illiteracy 141; *see also* climate change
Searle, John 189; *see also* artificial intelligence; personhood; sentience
The Second Sex (book) 41; *see also* de Beauvoir, Simone
secondary beliefs 270; *see also* time travel
secondary reality 270; *see also* time travel
secular humanism 106–7, 111, 113, 148; *see also* cultural war; eupraxsophy; Planetary Union; religion; the supernatural
secularism 99, 108–109, 112–114; *see also* "crisis of legitimacy"; evangelicalism; Planetary Union
Seinfeld (series) 253; Cosmo Kramer 252, 257; George Constanza 252
sentience 68, 182, 186, 188–91; *see also* consciousness; Isaac; personhood; relationships; Searle, John; Singer, Peter
separation of church and state 107, 110; *see also* religion
sex (biological, compared to gender) 81; defined on earth 36–39; defined on Moclus 37–40; *see also* sexual reproduction
sex change *see* gender correction surgery
sex drive 40
sexism 30, 35, 41, 43, 45, 73, 80, 82; *see also* bias; discrimination; feminism; misogyny; Moclus; oppression; patriarchy
sexual assault 48, 51, 53, 55, 57–58; *see also* consent; Darulio; rape
sexual consent *see* consent
sexual differences 43, 63, 81
sexual identity 62, 65, 69, 82
sexual orientation 39–40, 54, 81; *see also* bisexual; gay; gender identity; lesbian
sexual preference 64–65; *see also* queerness
sexual relationships 68; *see also* artificial intelligence
sexual reproduction 39–40, 82; anisogamous 36; asexual 36–37; single-sex/parthenogenesis 38; isogamous 36, 39; *see also* Bortus, Lieutenant Commander; Moclus; sex (biological, compared to gender)
sexuality 62–63, 72, 81; non-dominant; polyamory 63; *see also* bisexual; gay; gender; heterosexuality; intersex; lesbian; queerness; transgender
Shatner, William 12, 253; *see also* Kirk, Captain; *Star Trek* (original series)

286 Index

Shawshank Redemption (film) 270
Shelley, Mary 25; *see also Frankenstein*
Shimkus, John 147
The Simpsons (series) 230, 237, 252
Sinatra, Frank 237
Singer, Fred 145
Singer, Peter 189; *see also* personhood; sentience
Six Degrees (book) 152; *see also* Lynas, Mark
Smith, Adam 152–53; *see also* climate change
So You've Been Publicly Shamed (book) 28, 167, 170; *see also* Lehrer, Jonah; MacFarlane, Seth; "Majority Rule"; Ronson, Jon; social media
social justice 109, 169
social media 43, 166, 172, 175; mob 167, 172, 174; public shaming 167–68, 170; trial by 169; *see also* internet; Lehrer, Jonah; "Majority Rule"; pure democracy; Sacco, Justine; *So You've Been Publicly Shamed*
Socrates 105, 189–90, 192, 252
solipsism 182; *see also* consciousness
soul 29, 99–100, 102–3, 128–29, 185; *see also* Christianity; God; Isaac; Krill; personhood
South Park (series) 170
Spaceballs (film) 23–24, 80
"specular image" 227, 232–33; *see also* Lacan, Jacques; mirror stage
Spencer, Roy 145
Spock (*Star Trek* character) 171; *see also Star Trek* (original series)
Stahl, William 130; *see also* technology
Star Trek (original series) 6–9, 16, 25, 62–64, 167, 171, 237, 270; *see also* canon; "City on the Edge of Forever"; USS *Enterprise*; Kirk, Captain; *The Orville*; queerness; Shatner, William; Spock
Star Trek: Deep Space Nine (series) 65; *see also* "Rejoined"
Star Trek: Discovery (series) 6–8, 15, 17, 24, 72; *see also* Frakes, Jonathan; queerness
Star Trek: Enterprise (series) 8, 23–24; *see also* Braga, Brannon; Goodman, David
Star Trek: First Contact (film) 8; *see also* Braga, Brannon
Star Trek Generations (film) 8; *see also* Braga, Brannon
Star Trek: Into Darkness (film) 16
Star Trek: Picard (series) 24
Star Trek: The Next Generation (series) 8, 23, 183, 237; *see also* Braga, Brannon; Frakes, Jonathan; "Yesterday's Enterprise"
Star Trek: Voyager (series) 67; *see also* Braga, Brannon
Star Trek II: The Wrath of Khan (film) 255; *see also* Kirk, Captain
Star Wars (film) 7, 67–68
Star Wars Episode III: The Revenge of the Sith (film) 27
Star Wars: The Empire Strikes Back (film) 270
Starship Troopers (film) 26

Stern, Howard 229
Stewart, Jimmy 229
Stewart, Jon 149
the supernatural 101, 107, 111, 270; *see also* Coleridge, Samuel Taylor; Krill; religion; secular humanism
suspension of disbelief 270; *see also* Coleridge, Samuel Taylor
Suvin, Darko 26; *see also* cognitive estrangement

technology 43–44, 124, 130, 189, 202; relationship with reason 123, 129–30; *see also* dualism; primitive cultures; Stahl, William
Ted (film) 226, 229–30, 237–38; *see also* MacFarlane, Seth
Ted 2 (film) 230; *see also* MacFarlane, Seth
Teleya (character) 99, 101–4, 127–32, 136
terrorism *see* religious terrorism
Tesla, Nikola 143
theocracy 27, 99, 107–8, 112; *see also* Dorahl (god); evangelicalism; Krill
The Theologus Autodidactus (novel) 25; *see also* al-Nafis, Ibn
theonomistic ethics 105
A Theory of Justice (book) 217; *see also* nepotism; Rawls, John
time travel 261, 269–71; branching 263, 266–69; forward travel 262–63, 269; past travel 262–65, 268–69; "The Grandfather Paradox" 261–64, 266, 268–69; static 264, 266–68; universe creation 263; *see also* Belnap, Nuel; Bormanis, André; Deutsch, David; free will; Goodman, David; jinnee; Lavesque, Pria; Lewis, David; MacFarlane, Seth; Mercer, Captain Ed; "Pria"; relativity; "The Road Not Taken"; secondary beliefs; secondary reality; "Tomorrow, and Tomorrow, and Tomorrow"
Tolkien, J.R.R. 270
Tom and Lewis (Planetary Union anthropologists) 168–69, 174; *see also* "Majority Rule"
Tomilin (character) 147
Tomlin, Lily 238; *see also 9 to 5* (film)
"Tomorrow, and Tomorrow, and Tomorrow" (episode) 261, 267–69; *see also* time travel
Topa (character) 36, 42, 81, 83, 85, 88, 131, 237; *see also* Bortus, Lieutenant Commander; gender correction surgery; Klyden; "Sanctuary"
Tose, Justin 170; *see also* moral grandstanding
Toy Story (film) 190; *see also* personhood
"tragedy of the commons" 153; *see also* climate change
Transcendence (film) 26
transgender 29, 70, 81; *see also* sexuality
tribalism 99; 112; *see also* religion
Tronto, Joan 199, 206; *see also* care
A True History (novel) 25; *see also* Lucian of Samosata

Trump, Donald 141, 170
trust 201–6; *see also* Baier, Annette; care; relationships
Tucker, Ken 230
The Twilight Zone (series) 8, 238
Twitter 28, 165, 168–70, 172; *see also* internet

Ukania (character) 126
Union-Kaylon conflict 104; *see also* Kaylon 1; Planetary Union
Union Symphony Orchestra 245, 247–48
Unuk Four 98–99, 110
Utopia (novel) 25; *see also* More, Thomas
utopia 62–63, 73; queer utopia 62–64; *see also* queerness

"veil of ignorance" 218; *see also* Rawls, John
Veldman, Robin Globus 148–50
The View (series) 173; *see also The Chat*
violence *see* religious violence

Walberg, Rep. Tim 147–48
Walden, Dana 7
Wallis, Arthur 101; *see also* war
Wallon, Henri 231; *see also jouissance* (jubilation); *méconnaissance* (misrecognition); mirror stage
Walsh, Joseph 202
war 28–29, 80, 100–101, 113, 127; cosmic war 101–104; warfare imagery 101, 109; *see also* Crabtree, Harriet; just war theory; Krill; religion; religious violence; Wallis, Arthur
"War on Terror" 103
Warmke, Brandon 170; *see also* moral grandstanding
Warren, Mary Anne 188–90; *see also* personhood

warrior god 99–101, 109–10, 114; *see also* Allah; Krill; religion; Yahweh
Watson, Emma 79
weapons of mass destruction 98, 113
Wegener, Alfred 143
Wellek, René 10; *see also* genre
West, Mae 251, 253
Westworld (series) 26
Wieviorka, Michel 112
The Wiley/Blackwell Philosophy and Popular Culture Series 25; *see also* Irwin, William
Wilson, E.O. 148
The Wizard of Oz (film) 183, 190; *see also* personhood
The World of the Orville (book) 165
Woody Woodpecker (series) 252

Xelaya (planet) 222; *see also* Xelayans (inhabitants)
Xelayans (inhabitants) 209–11, 221–22, 232; *see also* Keyali, Lieutenant Talla; Kitan, Lieutenant Alara; Xelaya (planet)
xenophobia 99, 107, 109, 112–14, 128; *see also* Krill

Yahweh 99–100; *see also* Judaism; warrior god
Yakar (ship) 101; *see also* Krill
Yaphit (character) 16, 36–37, 49, 58, 63, 70, 140, 219, 237, 247–48, 252, 270; *see also* Gelatins
"Yesterday's Enterprise" (*Star Trek: The Next Generation* episode) 271; *see also Star Trek: The Next Generation*

Zimmerman, Amy 230

www.ingramcontent.com/pod-product-compliance
Ingram Content Group UK Ltd.
Pitfield, Milton Keynes, MK11 3LW, UK
UKHW041928140426
5217IPUK00014B/362